EMPIRE OF TEA

EMPIRE OF TEA

THE ASIAN LEAF THAT CONQUERED THE WORLD

MARKMAN ELLIS, RICHARD COULTON,
MATTHEW MAUGER

REAKTION BOOKS

For Ceri, Becky, Chelle

Published by
REAKTION BOOKS LTD
Unit 32, Waterside
44–48 Wharf Road
London N1 7UX, UK
www.reaktionbooks.co.uk

First published 2015

Copyright © Markman Ellis, Richard Coulton, Matthew Mauger 2015

First paperback edition published 2018
Transferred to digital printing 2021

Printed and bound in the USA by Universtiy of Chicago Press

A catalogue record for this book is available from the British Library

ISBN 978 1 78023 898 2

Contents

'A Sort of Tea from China', *c.* 1700, a material survival of Britain's encounter with tea in the late seventeenth century. The specimen was acquired by James Cuninghame, a physician and ship's surgeon who visited Amoy (Xiamen) in 1698–9 and Chusan (Zhoushan) in 1700–1703. Remarkably, some of the hand-rolled leaves retain vestiges of their original green hue.

Introduction

We encounter 'Vegetable Substance 857' on a visit to the Darwin Centre at the Natural History Museum in London. It occupies a boxboard container about six inches long, lined with white card, covered in black fabric. Through the glass lid, we can just make out an ounce or two of dried leaves: on opening the box their curled forms and brittle textures, mottled with hues of green and brown, emit the faint ghost of an odour. Half-buried in this tiny heap are two scraps of paper inscribed in dark-brown ink by an eighteenth-century hand. One explains that this vegetable substance is 'A sort of tea from China', the other provides its classifying number, 857. What we are viewing is instantly familiar – yet it is a source of wonder. Here, within the temperature-controlled airlock of the Special Collections Room, is a sample of tea prepared for market in China around 1698. Intended for immediate consumption, it nonetheless survives into the twenty-first century, a passage of over 300 years. As such, Vegetable Substance 857 is a unique physical remnant of a commerce that has shaped the patterns and practices of global modernity.

The collection of Vegetable Substances to which this tea belongs were compiled over many decades by the Irish physician and natural historian Sir Hans Sloane (1660–1753). From a total of 12,523 boxes, around two-thirds are extant. Beginning with specimens he gathered on Jamaica in the 1680s, Sloane eventually collated plant life from across the known world. His method was to store items of botanical interest such as seeds and fruits, as well as vegetable products in which he perceived potential utility for trade or medicine. The Vegetable Substances, spectacular in their range, were nonetheless just one component of Sloane's trove of antiquities, books and natural rarities – all bequeathed to the public as the inaugurating repository of the British Museum (and later the British Library and Natural History Museum). Today, the Vegetable Substances share a section of the Darwin Centre's eighth floor with Sloane's vast herbarium, also known as a *hortus siccus* or 'dried garden'. Its samples of flowers and leaves were dispatched from Europe, Africa, Asia and the Americas before being mounted and pressed in London into leather-bound folios (each of which now claims its own Perspex-enclosed shelf). Within these volumes, curator Charlie Jarvis locates cuttings from the tea shrub *Camellia sinensis*, taken variously in China and Japan around the turn of the eighteenth century. Reading the Vegetable Substances and Sloane Herbarium together, we begin to understand Sloane's intellectual desire to assemble, systematize and understand the whole of nature. The presence of centuries-old tea gradually becomes less surprising, more enlightening.

For many decades, Sloane's Vegetable Substances were scattered miscellaneously in drawers and cabinets across museum backrooms, but recent work by Jarvis and researcher Victoria Pickering means that the contents can now be readily searched and retrieved. This enables us to situate item 857 in historical context. The smaller, numeric label in our box cross-refers with an original manuscript catalogue, which advises that this 'sort of tea' came 'from Mr Cunningham'. Further investigation among Sloane's correspondence and scientific papers at the British Library confirms that this is James Cuninghame (d. 1709), a Scottish ship's surgeon who twice travelled to China. It is not clear whether this tea is the produce of the hill country of Fujian, acquired when Cuninghame joined a private trading voyage to Amoy (Xiamen) in 1698, or the local manufacture of Chusan (Zhoushan), where Cuninghame accompanied an abortive East India Company settlement in 1700 and found wild tea trees growing amid other evergreens. But we do know that Cuninghame, the first Briton to examine Chinese plants in their native habitat, was a keen and attentive natural historian who was fascinated (like Sloane) by their characteristics and uses. Tea, he recognized, remained sufficiently unusual to appeal to his friends at home in London: it was both an object of curiosity for students of medicine and botany, and of immense interest to men of trade and lovers of exotic novelty. In this way, Cuninghame reminds us that Britain's incipient relationship with China was not simply about the commercial transmission of commodities, but formed a conduit for intellectual and cultural exchange. Early importers of tea to Britain, among whom Cuninghame sailed, brought with them precious knowledge of the beverage's origins and consumption in the orient.

The hot infusion of the oxidized and prepared leaves of *Camellia sinensis* was an extraordinary innovation when discovered by British drinkers in the seventeenth century. There was no language to describe its flavour, and few directions about how to consume it. Encountering tea for the first time was a creative and experimental process of curiosity and habituation. Grasping for analogies, a physician described tea as being 'somewhat like Hay mixt with a little Aromatick smell, 'tis of a green Colour, and tastes Sweet with a little Bitter'.[1] It was also remarkably expensive: up to 60 shillings per pound for the best quality, ten times the cost of the finest coffee.[2] Initially restricted to urban elites, the demand for tea and the number of its regular drinkers increased in Britain through the eighteenth century. In the nineteenth century, tea became closely associated with the British way of life, transcending distinctions of social class, national geography and cultural background: as early as the 1820s, commentators instinctively identified the British as 'a tea-drinking nation'.[3]

Tea became a defining symbol of British identity in a period when it all came from China and Japan: it was not until 1839 that the first 'Empire' tea from Assam found its way to the London markets. So although the history of Britain's obsession with tea is often associated in the popular imagination with the nineteenth-century plantations of colonial India and the dramatic races between tea clippers, these aspects of its story were the effect – rather than the cause – of the widespread demand for tea. Moreover it was Britain's appetite for this Asian leaf that led to its international adoption among its former colonies, becoming by one measure the world's most popular beverage after water. One crucial inference of the 'Empire of Tea' that this book narrates is therefore the trajectory of the British Empire. Indeed, tea was peculiarly central within the complex international currents of cash, commodities, people and ideas that drove British imperialism in the eighteenth century: as the bedrock of a highly lucrative trade with China, as a symbol of the mother country's arbitrary disposition in North America, as the mainstay of agricultural colonization across South Asia, and as a partner of Caribbean sugar (the other non-native foodstuff with which it transformed patterns of British consumption) in so many humble cups. Through tea, Britain announced and experienced the strangeness of global connectedness, and the gratification of an emerging imperial confidence that flowed reciprocally between the state and the wider populace.

Tea's remarkable ascendance relied upon the capacities of British individuals and institutions to comprehend and deploy its exotic otherness – its botanical characteristics, its physiological effects, its social purposes, its cultural meanings. Yet this book is reluctant to understand tea merely as an inert material commodity in these processes, for it actively transforms those subjected to its influence. Victorian Britain was an 'empire of tea', but it was also a territory that had been conquered by tea during the preceding 150 years. Our title *Empire of Tea* embraces this suggestive and deliberate counter-history to examine and explain how tea – originally alien to Europe – inserted itself within Britain's social and economic life.

An illustrated handbill (or 'trade card') from the early 1790s implies that such an understanding was not remote from eighteenth-century imaginations. The image visualizes the striking new sign that John Hodgson had concocted for his 'Tea Warehouse', a shop on the corner of a newly built terrace on Tottenham Court Road in the fashionable West End of London. A strange, segmented insect crawls across an undulating landscape. The hills over which it moves are featureless, with the single exception of a cylindrical many-storeyed building which rises on the horizon: a Chinese pagoda. The creature – head reared, antennae twitching – has at first glance seven wings, but these appendages are unlike those borne by any European flying insect. On closer inspection, five transpire not to resemble wings so much as leaves, with prominent veins and gently serrated edges. For this – according to the banner displayed above – is a 'Living Leaf', reported by European explorers in the East Indies since the early eighteenth century (though more familiar to us now as a 'leaf insect' or 'walking leaf' of the family Phylliidae). Below the insect, within a cartouche, is the name and address of Hodgson's business: patrons are guaranteed that they may purchase here 'the purest genuine unadulterated Teas'. Behind this scroll, which is partially rolled up as if offering its viewers privileged access to an inner sanctum, four wooden chests can be glimpsed, stamped with Chinese lettering.

In the many newspaper advertisements he placed in the period 1787–96, Hodgson flamboyantly described his shop's redefinition of its street location: this is the 'Living Leaf corner' of Tottenham Court Road and Bedford Street. Hodgson was exploiting the marketing opportunities such an image offered for selling his tea as a 'living leaf', inviting potential customers to interpret the drawing as an animated version of the tea plant itself. The image, perhaps deliberately, provokes an habitual human aversion to insects, an unsettling response augmented by the creature's alert posture. Tea – the advertisement imagines playfully – is a sentient being, setting out on a long journey from the Chinese landscape in which it is has been nurtured to colonize the homes and tastes of a land far away. The chests at the bottom of the image acknowledge how tea was brought to market, for it was local grocers such as Hodgson's Warehouse, rather than the great European mercantile companies, that were at the vanguard of its advance. Distributed from businesses such as these, tea quietly infused itself within the nation's habits.

In English, the word 'tea' denotes at least five separate significations: the shrub, the leaf from that shrub, the dried commodity produced from that leaf, the infusion of that commodity, and the event for partaking that infusion. The first stages are agricultural: planting tea bushes in the soil, cultivating the plant, harvesting the tea leaves after they flush. Fresh tea then undergoes a multi-step manufacture in workshops and factories to create a form suitable for consumption. The leaves are crushed and encouraged to oxidize, an enzymatic operation arrested by the careful application of heat (a form of dry-frying called panning or 'tatching'), before being further readied for market by curling, twisting and rolling. The tea production

The Living Leaf – Hodgson's Warehouse, Corner of Bedford Street, Tottenham Court Road, London, The Purest Genuine Unadulterated Teas, c. 1792, etched trade card. An exotic 'leaf insect' crawls across an undulating landscape, over which a Chinese pagoda presides. Its wings playfully suggest the appearance of fresh tea leaves, a suggestion emphasized by the leafy foliage resting on the trade card's cartouche. The name and address of John Hodgson's tea business are printed on a scroll that has been partially rolled up to reveal a number of tea chests, stamped with Chinese lettering.

narrative then enters its commercial phase: the dried leaves are packed, shipped and sold at wholesale auctions before being graded and blended, repackaged and finally retailed to consumers. Sloane's specimens in the Natural History Museum evidence three seventeenth-century forms of tea: the shrub, the leaf and the commodity.

The preparation of the commodity into tea's fourth stage, an infusion as a hot beverage, enmeshes it within a complex and changing web of cultural attitudes. Tea in eighteenth-century Britain was an exotic novelty: an unknown quantity that divided sentiment. Its delicate aroma, multi-dimensional flavour landscape and gently insidious addictiveness spurred writers to describe it in a series of soubriquets that were by turns soothing and alarming. To some, tea was the civilizing juice, the gentle herb, the lovely liquor, the sovereign drink, the nectar of sobriety, the drink of chastity, the sweet restorer, the celestial dew, a wondrous panacea. To others, it was nothing but a bitter draught, scandal broth, a universal poison, the fatal stream; in his satire on 'polite conversation', Jonathan Swift described a cup of weak 'Bohea tea' as 'no more than Water bewitcht'.[4] In its fifth stage, as a form of social interaction, tea has always been a highly mediated event, its rituals repeatedly reimagined in art and literature. This was as true in the eighteenth century as it is now. In *The Female Spectator* (1744–6), the satirist Eliza Haywood joked that the first thing a genteel wife did upon waking was 'to ring the bell for her maid, and ask if the tea-kettle boils'. When the tea arrived, she sat down to her table, 'with all her equipage about her, and sips, and pauses, and then sips again, while the maid attends assiduous to replenish, as often as called for, the drained vehicle of that precious liquor'.[5] In the twentieth century, tea drinking spawned a whole host of comforting idiomatic phrases: 'tea and sympathy' (kindness shown to someone who is upset), 'a nice cup of tea and a sit down' (a tea break when things are tough), 'shall I be mother?' (the offer to pour tea by someone, not mother), 'more tea, vicar?' (a falsely polite expression to overcome social impropriety). These phrases continue to evolve: since 2005, Wikipedia's editing culture has used the coded expression 'a nice cup of tea and a sit down' (abbreviated to wp:tea) variously to pay a compliment and to enforce polite behaviour. From the seventeenth century to the present day, tea in Britain has created and recreated a series of scripts for its consumption, which define appropriate activities and conduct by imagining and directing verbal and social performance.

Anthropologists use the concept of 'foodways' to capture how different ethnic groups develop shared habits of food consumption that respond to local social and economic conditions. *Empire of Tea* accounts for tea's British foodways by looking beyond the beverage itself to its effects and significance, tangible and intangible, within wider national (and international) culture. As the mass-produced agricultural commodity of a distant

Margaret Thatcher (left), Prime Minister of the UK between 1979 and 1990, visits the home of Maureen and James Patterson in Harold Hill, London, on 11 August 1980. A kitchen-table tea is deployed to collapse the social distance between stateswoman and her suburban supporters (and instead to emphasize their shared values and identity), although it is noticeable that the best crockery has been reserved for Mrs Thatcher.

land, tea helped make Britons modern, globalized citizens. As a vital element of domestic life, tea has long been at the heart of home and community, often (although not always) in harmony with the feminizing forces of politeness and civility. As the habitual drink of the nation, reaching across all echelons of society, tea has long been said to connect the palace with the cottage: all share in its comforting rituals. Each cup of tea prepared and drank in Britain symbolically rehearses these myths of identity. Such a realization was not lost on the stage managers of Prime Minister Margaret Thatcher's visit to the home of Maureen and James Patterson on 11 August 1980 to celebrate the couple's purchase of their former council house under Right to Buy legislation. The photographic record depicts this kitchen-table tea as an event that can dissolve the awkwardness of power and distance into an everyday sociable encounter – although on closer inspection it implies the failure as much as the success of such a strategy. Exploring such paradox and complexity is the focus and purpose of this book: the story of an Asian cash crop, a necessary luxury, utterly free of nutritional value, shipped halfway around the world, saturating a mass market, inescapably foreign, indispensably British.

ONE

EARLY EUROPEAN ENCOUNTERS WITH TEA

Before tea could establish a global empire, it required a local power base. Over the course of centuries, it had established its influence across East Asia, above all in its native China and the neighbouring islands of Japan. Here tea was afforded a privileged significance within religious and political rituals, and granted a pervasive power to facilitate temperate sociability. It was also widely eulogized as a universal medicine. So when tea first came to the attention of Europeans during the sixteenth and seventeenth centuries – via encounters and exchanges on a distant continent – these early interlopers were exposed to its ancient and elaborate foodways. Accounts by Jesuit missionaries and Dutch merchants, oscillating between bewilderment at and acceptance of the widespread daily ritual of taking tea, indicate that such travellers regularly assimilated tea's range of meanings and purposes within the routines of their own lives. It was as much an effect of their distant reports as of the tiny quantities of dried leaves which first made the journey west that tea increasingly came into focus – above all in Great Britain – as one of the most desirable, accessible and (ultimately) affordable products of the East Indies. The sense of awe with which China was regarded during the seventeenth century (its wealth beyond measure, its intricate bureaucracy regulating an expansive territory, its documented history coeval with biblical records, its enviable cultural achievements) further enhanced conditions for tea's favourable reception in Britain.[1] During little more than half a century – in a world where the sea-routes to Asia were long and hazardous, and Sino–European trade was politically and practically convoluted – tea stole upon the palates of Britons, insinuating itself within their diets. The triumph of this traditional Asian decoction resulted from tea's emerging capacity to function as a very modern, global and globalizing commodity, yet one around which older inferences of exotic, social and pharmacological power continued to resonate.

Haunting, Strange and Lasting

Tea has been consumed in China more or less since time immemorial. The eighth-century sage Lu Yu teaches in his *Chajing* (Classic of Tea, 760 CE) that 'tea, used as a drink, was first discovered by the Emperor Shen Nung' (Shennong), a legendary ruler of China whose reign is customarily dated to 2737–2698 BCE.[2] One commonly recounted tale concerning this invention of Shennong – whose name means 'Divine Husbandman' – is that in an experiment to assess the pharmaceutical properties of Chinese flora, he systematically observed the effects upon his own body of 100 herbs. Seventy-two were found to be poisonous; one of the remaining 28, tea, counteracted all of these toxic substances and was acknowledged as a panacea.[3] Chinese lore has therefore long praised the curative virtues of the leaf (although it is important to note that the literature which documents the medical trials undertaken by Shennong significantly post-dates the era of the Three Sovereigns and Five Emperors during which he is said to have ruled). The earliest reference to tea as a processed foodstuff with a marketable value and an unequivocal function as an everyday drink is itself over 2,000 years old. In the satirical 'Contract for a Slave' by Wang Bao, a poet and humorist in the court of Emperor Xuan (91–49 BCE, reigned from 74 BCE), an innumerable list of duties required from an irascible household servant includes the purchase of tea at Wuyang market (now Xinjin, near Chengdu) and the domestic preparation of the hot infusion.[4]

The *Chajing* is the most highly regarded of all early Chinese writings on tea.[5] Even Samuel Ball, via whose selective mediation the text first reached a British public in the mid-nineteenth century, grudgingly acknowledged its author to be a 'learned personage'.[6] Alert to the distinctions between the best terrains for its cultivation, the finest waters in which to steep its leaves and the most aesthetically pleasing ceramics for its display and consumption, Lu Yu's text is drenched in cultural practices that the writer presents (and surely experienced) as long gestated and deeply entrenched. 'Tea has been traditionally taken so extensively that it is immersed in our customs and flourishes in the present Dynasty both North and South'; indeed 'it is the common drink of every household.'[7] Unsurprising as this observation appears today, one must not discount the distance of some 1,250 years between then and now. What emerges from the early sections of Lu Yu's work is that the most coveted teas of Tang dynasty China were processed not as dried individual leaves, but rather as moulded blocks of compressed foliage. One of Lu Yu's favoured methods as a writer is to construct systematic lists that anatomize the prerequisite tools for tea lovers: his register of fifteen utensils for high-quality tea production includes a mortar and pestle for pounding steamed tea leaves, an iron shaper (round or square) for moulding them into cakes, an awl for drilling holes, and bamboo strips on which the blocks were to be strung and hung in a drying chamber before they were ready to use.[8] When it comes to the objects comprising the equipage for preparing tea to drink, the list is even more elaborate (although of the 24, one is a storage cabinet for the other implements). The moulded tea was to be roasted over a brazier, ground in a wooden crusher, cooled in a paper bag, sieved through gauze in a bamboo frame, measured into a tea bowl and infused with water that has reached (but has not lingered at) a rolling boil.[9] Further instructions direct the reader how to wash the apparatus and dispose of the dregs after the tea has been taken.

The ritual of 'tea' is demarcated therefore as a high-status event requiring technical, aesthetic and social expertise. Lu Yu's precepts for tea drinking are no less exacting. 'The really superior taster will judge tea in all its characteristics and comment upon both the good and the bad', he insists; 'its goodness is a decision for the mouth to make.'[10] This connoisseurship is multi-sensory, incorporating the physical textures of the equipage, the sound of the water bubbling on the stove, the aromas of the beverage, the visual appearance of the tea in its bowl. Of particular value was the froth generated as the boiling water was ladled onto the leaves. Later accounts in the Song era would recommend the use of a whisk to augment this fine foam, a practice ritualized in the convening of *doucha* or tea contests, and more famously in the Japanese ceremony of *chanoyu* ('boiled water for tea').[11] For Lu Yu, however, restraint was the key: lightly frothed tea should be sipped delicately to maximize the appreciation of flavour, while – excepting cases of extreme thirst – multiple servings are to be

Lobed bowl (Yue ware), *c.* 10th century, pale grey stoneware with celadon glaze. This tapered tea-bowl with a pentafoil rim, just over 12 cm in diameter at the top, has been fired using the grey-green celadon glaze typical of Yue ware from Zheijiang in eastern China. The great Chinese tea sage Lu Yu recommended the aesthetic qualities of such dishes in his *Chajing* (Classic of Tea, 760 CE).

discouraged (tea bowls of this period were typically broad, shallow, inverted cones, 12 to 15 centimetres in diameter at the top, but tapering sharply to leave a modest liquid capacity). The first cup is the best, Lu Yu implies, with a 'haunting flavour, strange and lasting': 'tea does not lend itself to extravagance'.[12] This temperate and refined mode of appreciation is judged in sharp contrast to the execrable plebeian consumption of recipes that supplement tea leaves with 'such items as onion, ginger, jujube fruit, orange peel, dogwood berries or peppermint', and produce concoctions worth 'no more than the swill of gutters and ditches'.[13]

Lu Yu's explication of the skilful crafting of compressed leaf cakes and the deliberate rituals for preparing and consuming tea exemplify key contexts for understanding tea's significance in Chinese society around the turn of the second millennium. Tea was popularized in part because its various physiological effects – stimulating wakefulness, ensuring sobriety – found congruence with aspects of Buddhist spirituality. Moreover, the *Chajing*'s deep fascination with the present materiality of tea and its accoutrements harmonizes with the Zen insistence on seeking transcendent truth in the here and now (tea's Buddhist adherents were also vital for its export to and popularization within Japan).[14] Tea simultaneously attracted social prestige: the most sought after cake teas – the finest of which were coated with camphor wax and stamped with intricate decorative insignia – achieved high commercial prices, with the very best requisitioned by the Emperor and his retinue as 'tribute'.[15] Nonetheless, despite tea's personal fascination for rulers such as the late Song gourmand and aesthete Huizong (1082–1135, ruled 1100–1126), the state's fundamental interest in the commodity lay elsewhere. Over the centuries, successive Chinese governments exploited the people's taste for tea, initially by imposing a 10 per cent levy on its trade (under the Tang emperor Dezong), and later essentially nationalizing the tea industry via a combination of 'tea rents' (a property tax on plantations) and a controlled market (within which officials bought at mandatorily low prices from farmers, and then sold to wholesale merchants at mark-ups in excess of 200 per cent).[16] Such arrangements even became crucial for imperial defence policy: throughout the Southern Song, Yuan and Ming dynasties, whole plantations of tea grown in Sichuan were requisitioned to resource trade with neighbouring Tibetans, whose trained pedigree horses were repeatedly in demand for Chinese cavalries.[17]

While Lu Yu's scholarly and gastronomic preoccupation was with compressed teas, he acknowledges in passing that 'the beverage that the people take may be from coarse, loose, powdered or cake tea'.[18] What comprises these apparently more vulgar versions is not made explicit. However, the availability of alternative modes of preparation to the 'cake tea' of the elite is also evident from near-contemporary verses by the Tang poet Liu Yuxi (772–842), which relish the scent-filled kitchens where tea leaves are

A Tea Plantation in China with Women Picking and Sifting Tea Leaves, c. 1800, gouache with oxidization. Images of traditional tea cultivation and manufacture in China were popular in Britain during the late eighteenth and early nineteenth centuries. This example comes from a series of nine paintings, and depicts women hand-plucking fresh leaves from tea shrubs. In the buildings to the right, other workers sort the leaves into their various grades and sizes prior to firing.

pan-fired (the denaturing heat treatment that arrests oxidation and preserves verdure is the critical first step in the manufacture of loose-leaf green tea).[19] Moreover, by the time of the Mongol-led Yuan dynasty (1271–1368), loose-leaf teas had come to dominate the Chinese market. The first emperor (Hongwu) of the succeeding Ming Dynasty (1368–1644) demanded tribute in this form – rather than cake teas – after 1391.[20]

Throughout this period, the method for producing leaf teas was explored, improved and perfected. Tea masters scrutinized the modifications of flavour and appearance (of both the leaves and their infusion) made available through implementing variations in the choice of *terroir*, time of harvest, duration of stir-frying, manner of hand-rolling and means of drying (such as by sunning or in a heated chamber). Often associated with the technical expertise of tea-enamoured monks, one of the most significant innovations was that of communities ensconced amid the Wuyi mountains of Fujian Province. It was discovered that by exposing freshly picked leaves to the sun and wind rather than firing immediately after picking, the resultant withering and oxidation alters the colour and flavour of the tea. This 'fermentation' renders the leaf darker and bitterer – yet less astringent – than its green sibling. Now known as *wu lung* ('oolong' or 'dark dragon'), such tea may have been manufactured in Wuyi monasteries since the thirteenth century; although only later do contemporary documents testify unequivocally to its existence, let alone acknowledge the possibility of its acceptance within the traditional canon of fine teas.[21]

By the time that European merchants and missionaries began arriving concertedly in East Asia during the final century of the Ming dynasty, tea cultivation, consumption and connoisseurship were rooted deeply within the substrata of Chinese commerce and culture. Long feted as a cure-all for bodily and spiritual ailments, tea was focal within both religious and political ceremony. As an object of elite appreciation and mass diet, its production and distribution comprised a variegated market ranging from highly prized first flushes (such as *Yinzhen Baihao*, or 'Silver Tip Pekoe') and meticulously sunned Wuyis (like the legendary monkey-picked *Dahongpao*, or 'Big Red Robe'), to cheap undifferentiated low grades of green and oolong. The medical, ritual, social and commercial significations that had accrued to the spectrum of Chinese tea practices were integral to the ways in which its first European drinkers tasted and perceived the beverage.

The Best Sort of Chaw

Tea first reached Europe via whispers. Perhaps first noticed by travellers to Japan in the mid-sixteenth century as a strange predilection for drinking 'hot water', the earliest definitive reference surfaced in the second volume of *Navigationi et viaggi* (Voyages and Travels) by the powerful Venetian merchant-scholar Giovanni Battista Ramusio (1485–1557).[22] Ramusio was a member of the city-state's governing Council of Ten from 1533. In the 'Espositione' that prefaces his book's anthology of medieval texts on China by Marco Polo and Hayton of Corycus, Ramusio recounts a conversation with Hajji Mohamed (or 'Chaggi Memet'), a trader from Chilan in Persia (Gilan in modern-day Iran). Their principal topic of interest is the export market in Asian rhubarb – a vegetable which had long since been brought along the so-called Silk Road into the Middle East and Europe. However, Mohamed also confides in Ramusio that 'throughout the country of Cathay they make use of another plant, or rather its leaves, which the people call *Chiai Catai*'. This mysterious herb, Mohamed continues, can be used dried or fresh in order to produce an infusion that is drunk 'as hot as can be tolerated', and which promotes relief from a litany of ailments affecting the head and stomach. So highly valued is it that the Chinese travel nowhere without a ready supply, and they would willingly exchange 'a sack of rhubarb for an ounce of *Chiai Catai*'. Indeed, according to

Mohamed's reports of Chinese opinion, if only Persians and Europeans had tasted it 'their merchants without doubt would no longer want to buy *Revend Cini* (as rhubarb is called there)'.[23] The prescience of these words is startling.

By the time that Ramusio and Mohamed were trading tales in Venice, Portuguese navigators had already made incursions into East Asia, establishing a presence in strategic ports across the region. Although relations with the Ming authorities were uneasy and even violent during the first half of the sixteenth century, by the late 1550s the visitors had won significant concessions (not least in return for naval assistance in repulsing coastal pirates). They included permission to rent and administer – under certain restrictions – the territory of Macau at the mouth of the Pearl River (Zhu Jiang) which leads to Canton (Guangzhou). Among the first settlers were Christian priests whose roles typically oscillated between ministry to the immigrant community, missionary work among local peoples, and (as educated Europeans who were strangely free from either commercial or military demands) detailed study of the history, nature and culture of the lands in which they now found themselves.

The Dominican friar Gaspar da Cruz (1520–1570) spent almost twenty years of his life moving between factories in India, Malaysia and China, including a period on Lampacau, an island to the east of Macau and the precursor of its Portuguese colony. After he had returned to Lisbon in the mid-1560s, da Cruz wrote a 'Treatise on the Things of China' (*Tratado das cousas da China*), which makes evident his regular encounters with tea as both a social and a remedial commonplace in Chinese culture.[24] As his earliest English translator Samuel Purchas (that great compiler of travel writers) rendered it, da Cruz recounts that 'Whatsoeuer person or persons come to any mans house of qualitie, hee hath a custome to offer him in a fine basket one Porcelane [cup] . . . with a kinde of drinke which they call *Cha*, which is somewhat bitter, red, and medicinall.' Da Cruz's observation concerning tea's red ('vermelha') colour implies that his exposure was to an oolong.[25] That the account draws on the writer's personal experience is particularly emphasized: 'with this [*Cha*] they welcome commonly all manner of persons that they doe respect, be they strangers or be they not; to me they offered it many times.'[26]

Da Cruz was just one of many European migrants who embedded themselves in Chinese society. The Italian Jesuit missionary Matteo Ricci (1552–1610) spent the last 28 years of his life in China, moving permanently in 1601 to Peking (Beijing) at the invitation of the Wanli Emperor (1563–1620, reigned from 1572), although the two never met. The Imperial Court was impressed not so much with Ricci's theological prowess as with his scientific acumen: his capacity to predict celestial eclipses was signally admired as natural philosophical expertise that outstripped the

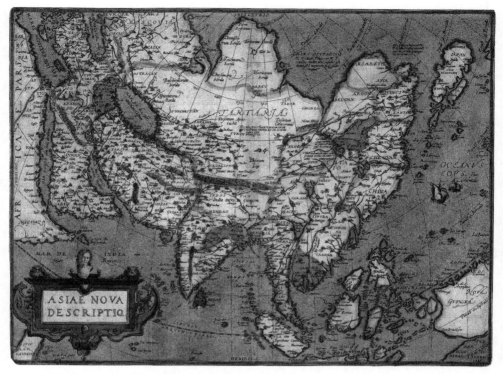

Abraham Ortelius, 'Asia Novae Descriptio.', in *Theatrum orbis terrarum; or, The Theatre of the Whole World* (London, 1606). The Flemish cartographer Abraham Ortelius is credited with producing the first modern atlas of the world (*Theatrum orbis terrarum*), published in multiple editions from 1570 onwards. This plate (from an early seventeenth-century London edition) depicts the continent of Asia as the earliest merchants and seamen of the East India Company understood it. The known coast of China runs no further north than 'Quinsai' (Huangzhou); although Japan is visible, there is no sign of the Korean peninsula.

best Chinese astrologers.[27] Like da Cruz, Ricci records the widespread tea habits of those he lived among, and its centrality within rituals of domestic hospitality: 'Here they gather its leaves in the springtime and place them in a shady place to dry, and from the dried leaves they brew a drink which they use at meals and which is served to friends when they come to visit. On such occasions it is served continually as long as they remain together engaged in conversation.' His brief account of its processing again (like da Cruz) suggests his familiarity was with a semi-fermented variety; although it may be that he was unfamiliar with the stir-frying and rolling that preceded the final drying 'in a shady place' (it is even plausible that he is describing a simple, folk manufacture of tea that merely required picking and dehydrating the leaves). While Ricci was wrong in his etymologically driven speculation that tea's use in China was not of prehistoric memory ('no ideography in their old books designates this particular drink and their writing characters are all ancient'), he does identify its shared nomenclature in Japan as 'Cia', and distinguishes the Chinese method of steeping dried leaves in hot water from the Japanese preparation of tea from a pulverized powder.[28]

It was in fact almost certainly from Japan that tea was first procured and transported to Europe. Indeed, the earliest reference to tea in an English text is from a chapter 'Of the Iland of Japan' in *Iohn Huighen van Linschoten: His Discours of Voyages into the Easte & West Indies* (1598). This is a translation of one of a series of texts by the Dutch merchant and adventurer Jan Huyghen van Linschoten (1563–1611), who sought to emulate and exploit Portuguese navigational and cultural knowledge about remote lands and seas. Concerning the dietary and social habits of the Japanese, van Linschoten observes that 'after their meat they use a certain drinke, which is a pot with hote water ... made with the powder of a certaine hearbe called *Chaa*, which is much estéemed, and is well accounted of among them'. Likening it to the Turkish 'manner of drinking of their *Chaona* [coffee]', van Linschoten marvels that in Japan 'the gentlemen make it themselves, and when they will entertaine any of their friends, they give him some of that warme water to drinke'. Even stranger than the fact that preparing tea is held to be a genteel rather than a servile function is the value that the Japanese place upon the tea equipage: 'the earthen cups which they drinke it in, they estéeme as much of them, as we doe of Diamants, Rubies and other precious stones, and they are not esteemed for their newnes[s] but their oldnes[s], and for that they were made by a good workman'.[29] This sense of astonishment – combining cultural condescension and discombobulation – was frequently experienced by Europeans in Japan. The Jesuit Alessandro Valignano accepted that while he would not give 'two farthings' for an old earthenware caddy bought by the feudal lord *Daimyo* Otomo Sorin for 'fourteen thousand ducats', this was primarily because he lacked the discernment of local connoisseurs better able to 'understand in what consists [the] value [of these *cha* vessels] and how they are different from the others'.[30]

Van Linschoten's endeavours (both practical and textual) were instrumental in opening routes between Holland and Japan, successfully facilitating the pragmatics of political and commercial exchange, as well as overcoming the challenges of oceanic geography. After the Dutch East-India Company (Vereenigde Oost-Indische Compagnie or voc) was founded in 1602, the establishment of a Japanese factory was one of its earliest priorities. Indeed it may have been that on the *Roode Leeuw met Pijlen* (Red Lion with Arrows), which had docked alongside *De Griffioen* (The Griffin) in 1609 at Hirado – an island port to the northwest of Nagasaki and an intended colony of the voc – that the first cargo of tea was carried to Europe, when the ship returned to Amsterdam on 20 July 1610. Five years later and also on Hirado, Richard Wickham documented the earliest known British tea habit. A disgruntled factor to an incipient project of the English East India Company (which was disastrously attempting to play catch-up with its Dutch rivals), Wickham wrote plaintively on 27 June 1615 to his friend William Eaton in metropolitan Meaco (Kyoto), pleading to be sent a luxury that was presumably unavailable in his coastal fishing resort. 'I pray you buy for me a pot of the best sort of chaw', he implored, before also requesting two bows with arrows, and 'some half a dozen' square gilt boxes 'for to put in tobacco'.[31]

That Excellent China Drink

By the second decade of the seventeenth century – and possibly some years earlier than that – European travellers to East Asia did not just perceive tea as an exotic social ritual or local remedy, but were incorporating it within their own diets and lifestyles. Even if the commodity was yet to catch on back home (silk and spices remained very much the focus of trade), the experimental consumption of tea by friars and factotums instigated its private dispatch to favoured friends, relatives and patrons in Amsterdam, Paris and Lisbon. There is little doubt that the first quantities to ship westwards were minuscule, intended simply to amuse as a curiosity. By 1637, however, the Heren XVII (Gentlemen Seventeen), board of directors to the Dutch East-India Company, perceived enough European interest to write to Anthony van Diemen, their governor-general in Batavia (Jakarta), that 'as the tea begins to come into use with some people, we expect some jars of Chinese as well as Japanese tea with all ships'.[32] Less than fifteen years later, tea was being commercially imported in modest batches, and began to find its way into the shops of elite retailers in Paris and London as well as Holland.[33]

Almost as soon as this European tea market had been established, complaints about Dutch mercantile practices began to circulate. The foremost voice was that of Alexandre de Rhodes (1591–1660), a French Jesuit priest who had spent the 1630s in Macau, sandwiched between periods in Vietnam (whence he was ultimately exiled and effectively compelled to return via Rome to Paris). Two publications from the early 1650s narrate – first in summary (1653), then at greater length (1654) – de Rhodes's experiences in China and other 'Kingdoms of the Orient'. Keen to communicate to his compatriots the potential advantages of both learning from and trading with the Chinese people, de Rhodes wrote enthusiastically about tea, 'which is beginning to be known in France through the agency of the Dutch'. Unfortunately, de Rhodes laments, the quality of these imports was poor ('usually it is of the kind that is old and ruined') and the price high ('they sell it in Paris for thirty francs per pound; the same that they bought in [China] for just eight or ten sols'). Meanwhile, the unmerited profit (de Rhodes implies a mark-up of around 6,000 per cent) flowed back to the Low Countries. 'Les Holandois', de Rhodes opines, shame the inertia of 'our good Frenchmen, [who] allow Foreigners to enrich themselves through commerce with the East Indies, whence they could reap the most extravagant riches in the world, if they had the courage of enterprise which matched that of their neighbours'.[34] This Gallic suspicion of Dutch commercial ethics – born, one suspects, from a combination of economic envy and religious tension – persisted into the following decade, when the French scholar Melchisédech Thévenot (1620–1692) reported a rumour about voc merchants that persisted long thereafter:

> In order to obtain Chinese tea for themselves, the Dutch have taught themselves to dry sage leaves, then to roll them, and to prepare them after the fashion in which one would prepare tea, and they carry these [leaves] to the Chinese as an extraordinary rarity; this [method of] commerce has been so successful, that for one pound of sage leaves they are now given in that country four times as much tea, which they sell here most dearly.[35]

Despite his somewhat jaundiced cynicism about Dutch profiteering, de Rhodes valuably elucidates the early tea encounters of Europeans living in China. Throughout that region of the world, he observes, 'the use of Tea is so commonplace that those who don't take it three times each day, are the most moderate'. Indeed, many 'take it ten or twelve times, or one might better say at all times'. As well as describing its manufacture (the leaves are picked, oven-dried and then sealed in pewter vessels), de Rhodes offers directions for selecting processed tea. 'To know whether the Tea is good, you must observe whether it is really green, bitter, and dry so that it crumbles in your fingers.' He also details the Chinese manner of preparing tea: 'they bring water to the boil in a really clean vessel, and when it is bubbling strongly they take it from the stove, and put this leaf in it, the quantity relative to that of the water; that is to say an *écu*'s weight of Tea, for a good glass of water' (de Rhodes presumably has in mind the weight of a *Louis* or *écu d'or*, 6.75 grams of gold, equivalent to around two teaspoonfuls of tea). Moreover, tea's intertwined physiological and religious benefits are evident from de Rhodes's own experience. 'Personally when I have had a migraine, by taking Tea, I have felt greatly relieved, such that it has seemed to me as if I have taken away my entire headache with my hand', he attests; for 'the main strength of Tea is in abating the gross vapours that rise to the head' (although he also recommends it for afflictions of the stomach and kidneys). This very 'strength' ('la principale force') explains tea's great power to subdue sleepiness, a professional benefit for a Jesuit priest: 'I myself have experimented quite often when I was obliged to listen all night to the Confessions of my good Christians, who would regularly arrive' at such times.[36] In accommodating himself to local preparations and perceptions of tea, de Rhodes assimilated long-standing Chinese attitudes towards the drink's medical and spiritual efficacy. The meditative simplicity of Japanese tea practices was similarly Christianized by European priests – some of whom established a ceremonial *chanoyu* or tea-room in their own quarters – and their local converts.[37] Tea, in other words, had become an agent not just of commercial mediation, but of intercultural transformation.

French qualms about Dutch merchants were founded of course upon jealous suspicion more than ethical concern, for throughout the East Indies the VOC was engineering remarkable wealth for its shareholders. Tactics of aggression – financial, diplomatic, military – were fundamental to its success; yet China was proving relatively impervious to Holland's riches, charm and power. The VOC had been frustrated by the Portuguese stranglehold on Sino–European relations, and by the limited access to Chinese commodities that it had achieved at Canton (not just because of Catholic-Iberian interests in nearby Macau, but also due to the complex bureaucratic and personal tensions structuring commerce and governance in Qing China following the Manchu conquest of the Ming Dynasty in 1644). As a consequence, the VOC decided to appeal directly to the Shunzhi Emperor in Peking. In the mid-1650s two ambassadors, Peter de Goyer and Jacob de Keyzer, undertook an arduous overland journey from Canton to Peking, accompanied by a small retinue of assistants and servants, transporting what bribes or 'tribute' they had been afforded, and depending utterly on contracted translators to ensure their progress. De Goyer and de Keyzer were eventually granted an audience with the Emperor on 3 September 1656, but the concessions that they won were rather limited: a dispensation to bring a ship crewed by no more than 100 men to trade at Canton every eight years, and even this under the proviso that twenty of the visitors accompanied the conveyance of an acceptable tribute to the Imperial Court. Undermined by its own apparent stinginess, some fickle translation and the counter-intriguing of influential Jesuit missionaries such as Johann Adam Schall von Bell (1592–1666), the VOC was forced to dispatch further embassies during subsequent decades – as well as to supply naval assistance in the Chinese state's efforts to overcome the Ming loyalist Zheng Chenggong (known in English as 'Koxinga') – before any significant privileges were bestowed.[38]

The glorious failure of the first Dutch embassy was documented painstakingly by the ambassadors' steward Johan Nieuhof (1618–1672), his text incidentally detailing the function and place of tea within the highest echelons of Chinese society.[39] In his lavishly illustrated folio, Nieuhof recounts how from Canton to Peking ambassadorial audiences with mandarins and viceroys were routinely initiated with elaborate servings of the beverage.[40] Even in the presence of Shunzhi himself, pomp and majesty were ritually integrated with the purposely public consumption of the hot infusion:

> The Emperour . . . sat about thirty paces from the Embassadours, his Throne so glitter'd with Gold and Precious Stones, that the Eyes of all that drew near dazzled: The Embassadours themselves discerned nothing of him but a little of his Face; next and on his side sat the Vice-Roys, Princes of the Blood, and all other great Officers of the Court, all likewise drinking *Thea* in Wooden Dishes, and that in great abundance.[41]

In the Imperial Court, as elsewhere within Nieuhof's itinerary, this 'Thea' is prepared after the 'Tartar' fashion of the ascendant Manchu: 'they infuse half a handful of the Herb *The* or *Cha* in fair water, which afterwards they boyl till a third part be consumed, to which they adde warm Milk about a fourth part, with a little Salt, and then drink it hot as they can well endure'.[42] The sense of ethnic differentiation that is enacted through tea practice is inflected by Nieuhof's revelation that this milky recipe of the northern conquerors 'is not so well approved' by southern peoples. Anticipating by some three and a half centuries the tea purist's denigration of *chai latte*, their apparently more traditional habit was to do no more (when 'this Liquor proves bitter to the taste') than to 'mingle a little Sugar with it'.[43] Nonetheless, that tea was unquestionably integral to the social and political rituals of both Manchu and Han dignitaries is acknowledged not only in the performance of feasts and audiences, but also in the itemizing of '*Two Toel of Thea*' (about 80 grams, or 3 ounces) in each ambassador's daily allowance of provisions while in Peking.[44] A decade or so later, this sense of tea's ritual political significance was exported to the Restoration court of Charles II when the English East India Company chose tea as an appropriate gift for the king (see chapter Two).

The VOC might have had to invest a little more time, talk and silver before its access to Chinese markets was enhanced, but Dutch-shipped tea was already reaching the more fashionable residents of Protectorate London. On 23 September 1658 the businessman Thomas Garway (d. 1692?) advertised in the news periodical *Mercurius Politicus* that the 'Excellent, and by all Physitians approved, *China* Drink, called by the *Chineans, Tcha*, by other Nations *Tay alias Tee*, is sold at the *Sultaness-head*, a *Cophee-house* in *Sweetings* Rents by the Royal Exchange, *London*' (Garway later claimed to have retailed tea 'in Leaf and Drink' since 1657).[45] Within a few years Garway was operating a second tea outlet 'at the signe of the *China-man*' in Charing Cross, with the intention of attracting 'all Persons of

Eminency and Quality, Gentlemen, and others residing in or neer the Court, *Westminster*, and Parts adjacent'.[46]

Garway's notice articulates a neologism that was to gain currency in English more effectively than the '*Chaa*' of van Linschoten's translator or the 'chaw' of Richard Wickham (even if echoes and resurrections of this other term still persist). Within a couple of lines of newsprint, Garway offers four alternative labels for his highly prized new commodity, among which the only obviously 'English' option is '*China* Drink'. '*Tcha*' or *ch'a* is the name of the most prominent Mandarin character for tea (as used by Lu Yu), transliterated by Hajji Mohamed as '*Chiai*' and by Gaspar da Cruz as 'Cha'. It is however – as Garway notes – no longer used by 'other Nations'.[47] 'Tay' meanwhile is how de Rhodes had referred to the plant and its product in 1653 (the first appearance of the word in English came in an early reference to the *Divers Voyages*); and it is likely that on his return to Europe he had fixed upon this in preference to the Cantonese *ch'a* to which he would have been exposed in Macau.[48] Indeed fairly early in its trade with Asian nations the VOC adopted *te* or '*thee*' from the Amoy (Xiamen) dialect favoured both in that port and on Formosa (Taiwan), as well as by Malay merchants in Indonesia. A letter of 1629 from the Batavia factory to the Heren XVII bemoans the fact that 'neither Japanese *cha* nor Chinese tea ['thee'] can be obtained', indicating that a distinction was now drawn between the powdered and loose-leaf forms associated with different national origins.[49] In English, moreover, two competing pronunciations – 'tay' from the French (de Rhodes's introduction was soon Gallicized as *thé*) and 'tee' derived from the Dutch – both appear to have obtained for some decades around the hybrid formulation 'tea', the spelling that was preferred by Garway himself by 1670. In this ambivalent linguistic guise, tea began its quest to discover a distinctively British cultural form.

The long history of tea in East Asia (particularly China) that preceded European maritime expansion in the sixteenth and seventeenth centuries evidences a wide range of uses and significations. Tea acquired instrumental value as a vegetable product and cash crop; as a ubiquitous feature of daily diet; as a focus for social, religious and political rituals; as a medicine ascribed far-reaching properties. When tea's virtues and attractions began to percolate within Europe – first in rumours, then in small-scale canisters, eventually as a wholesale luxury commodity – the beverage was supped not in a cultural vacuum but rather in the contexts of its supposed connotations for distant Chinese and Japanese societies, as they were reinterpreted within the local precincts of Venice and Paris, Amsterdam and London. As such, tea was not merely an object of exchange and consumption, but a colonizer of tastes and a transformer of its drinkers. Tea required its new devotees – necessarily Eurocentric in their perspectives and perceptions – to experience and internalize the exotic strangeness of unimaginably

'The Royall Banquet' in Peking, from Ogilby's 1669 translation of Johan Nieuhof's *Embassy to China* (1665). This illustration depicts tea's ceremonial importance in the political theatre of Qing China. At point 'F' in the foreground is the serving area 'Where the Tee and other drink is fild-out and carried to the Table'. Chinese dignitaries sit in state towards the rear, with Dutch ambassadors and their retinue on the left.

A. The Vice King sitting alone at a Table.
B. The Iegu or the person next to the King.
C. The Hollands Ambassadours with their chief followers or traine.
D. The rest of said traine.
E. Divers Tartarian, and Cheang Lords.
F. Where the Tee and other drink is fild-out and carried to the Table.
G. Divers Tartarian and Cheang Servants.

The Royall BANQVET.

klyck
T

A. De Onder Koninck sittende alleen
    aen een Taefel.

B. De Isju of tweede persoon naest hem

C. De Hollantse Ambassadeurs met de voornaenste van haer.

D. De rest van haer gevolgh

E. Verscheyden Tartariss en Chineese Heeren.

F. Daer de Tee en andere Dranck vort
    geschoncken en op gedraegen.

G. Verscheyden Tartars en Chineese Dienaers.

distant civilizations. They did so both directly, by ingesting the infusion of an Asian leaf, and indirectly, by encountering intellectual and social meanings that had accrued elsewhere. Portuguese priests, Dutch merchants and (eventually) London retailers all contributed to the tentative, almost unconscious first stirrings of tea's empire in the western hemisphere.

TWO

Establishing the Taste for Tea in Britain

When tea first made itself known in Britain in the mid-seventeenth century, it did so in the context of a great hunger for exotic novelties. This desire was especially prominent among the upper echelons of society, and was common to the Protestant countries of northern Europe – Britain and the Netherlands in particular. Tea from China, coffee from Arabia and chocolate from Mexico came into public notice in Britain virtually simultaneously in the 1650s. Though distinct in origin and flavour, they shared four qualities: they were served hot, had a bitter flavour that was ameliorated with sugar, were made with rare and expensive botanical ingredients and had intriguing psychoactive properties. This taste for exotic hot drinks grew – among those who could find and afford them – in competition with the customary alcoholic drinks of British culture, including domestic beer, cider and mead, and imported wine and spirits.

The British encounter with tea began in different ways among three distinct groups of people: virtuosi, merchants and maids of honour. Each of these groups brought their own understanding of tea and left their own impression on the cultures of its consumption. The first group, the virtuosi, comprised various men of science, natural philosophers and doctors of medicine who took an interest in tea in the context of the new global pharmacopeia from Asia and the Americas, and recognized in it some distinct physiological effects with potential therapeutic benefits. The second group, perhaps the least alert to tea's special properties, were the merchants and men of commerce who approached tea as an exotic commodity whose sale in Britain might be profitable should demand be encouraged in the proper way. The final group was the elite female court culture surrounding the queen, Catherine of Braganza, wife of the restored king, Charles ii, for whom tea was an exotic and expensive luxury whose consumption was conspicuously about display and spectacle, both of tea and its paraphernalia. For all three groups, the primary avenue through which tea became known was their European contacts, especially the Dutch and Portuguese, although towards the end of the century the English East India Company became increasingly important.

Men of Science and Men of Commerce

The first Englishmen to take notice of tea in London in the 1650s were men of science, or 'virtuosi', as they called themselves. The staunchly Protestant governments of the Republic and Protectorate were not hostile to natural philosophy, and encouraged groups of learned men to continue Bacon's project of the New Science, committed to reason and empiricism. One influential group was assembled around Samuel Hartlib (c. 1600–1662), a self-confessed 'intelligencer' who saw his primary role as collecting information and disseminating it to appropriate recipients. In the mid-1650s, among many other projects, he worked on a 'Discourse on Drinks', which would collate and evaluate knowledge of the medicinal properties and commercial potential of drinks of all kinds: from staples such as cider, wine and beer to the new exotics like tea and coffee. Although Hartlib had been cognizant of coffee since at least 1654, when his friend John Beale noted the Turkish 'cuphye-house' in St Michael's Alley in London, Hartlib did not mention tea until 1657, when he read the praise of it by the Dutch physician Nicolaes Dirx (1593–1674), known as Tulp or Tulpius, in the treatise *Observationes medicæ*, a collection of medical case notes published in Amsterdam in 1652.[1] Hartlib and his circle transcribed and summarized Tulp's account of tea for his *Ephemerides*, or diary archive. In the entry for May 1657 Hartlib noted that

> Tulpius writes mightily in the commendation of herba The or Te the herbe which is used as an Universal Medicin in China et Jappan curing fumes indigestions stone and gout. It is bought from thence to Amsterdam but very deare one lb. for 6 lb. sterling. But Sir Charles Herbert undertakes to procure it for 10 shillings at Amsterdam. My Lord Newport uses it with great succes. Mr. Waller (who study's his health as much as any man) a great taker or user of it. It tastes a little bitterish.[2]

The expense of the commodity was astonishing: £6 for a pound of tea is equivalent, in purchasing power, to more than £847 today.[3] Hartlib's summary observed that users personally sourced their supplies from Amsterdam at great expense, noting among them Sir Charles Herbert, who had lived in the Netherlands for several years in the 1640s, Mountjoy Blount, first Earl of Newport (1597–1666), and the poet Edmund Waller. These men considered tea as physic, or medicine, as was confirmed by its 'bitterish' taste. Beale suggested to Hartlib that tea would be 'a curious ornament to your

Pieter van Roestraten, *Teapot, Ginger Jar and Slave Candlestick, c.* 1695, oil on canvas. Painted in London, this *pronkstilleven* ('showy' still-life) is designed to display, in conspicuous detail, exotic and luxurious commodities. A silver-coloured ginger jar forms the backdrop to a range of objects: a lacquer tea caddy and a Chinese blue-and-white tea set, including a teapot and stand, a lidded bowl filled with cane sugar, a silver-gilt teaspoon and a tea bowl with saucer. The silver-gilt English candlestick, which has a base in the form of a kneeling slave, recalls the origins of the cane sugar in Caribbean slave plantations.

discourse of drinks, of which I see you are excellently stored. But I pray you thinke not of such costly ware for my triall. For, I thanke God, I have noe minde to it, nor neede of it.'[4] In Beale's view, therefore, tea was literally too expensive for experiments. Nonetheless, Hartlib was fortunate in December 1657 when his son-in-law Frederick Clodius informed him that an anonymous wealthy donor in Islington 'hath sent for 8 lb. of herba Thee' from Amsterdam, 'having a friend a Merchant there'.[5] By then, of course, Hartlib could have himself encountered tea in London coffee-houses. Thomas Garway, who first advertised tea's sale in a London newspaper in September 1658, confirmed in a later broadside advertisement that it was he who 'about the yeer 1657 . . . first publiquely sold the said *Tay* in Leaf and Drink' in England.[6]

Dutch scholarship about tea was nearly as valuable to Hartlib as supplies of the leaf itself. Tea drinkers required instruction on how to prepare the beverage to make use of their luxury import, but they also needed instruction about what it meant. Tea required mediation and interpolation. Information about tea, whether Dutch in origin or translated from Chinese, was in this sense a valuable commodity. Tulp's description of 'Herba Theé' in 1652 claimed to be based on information from informants in China, presumably from among the Jesuit mission and through the conduit of the VOC in Batavia.[7] Tulp defended the wholesomeness of tea and recommended it for a variety of complaints:

> Not only does it enliven the body, but it also wards off painful stones, from which, they say, no one here suffers. Indeed, it counters headache, cold, inflammation of the eyes, drooping or disturbing of the spirits, weakness of the stomach, intestinal dysentery, lassitude, and sleep, which it so evidently checks. Sipping this decoction, one may sometimes spend entire nights working, without any troubling effects, and without being otherwise overcome by the need for sleep.

He also notes that while the Japanese prepare tea as a powder beaten into hot water, the Chinese make an infusion using the whole leaves. 'The decoction thus heated, it is customary to raise a toast to invited guests with it, and to whatever honour attends their coming.' Tulp's description notices the important role tea has in high-status socializing and gift giving in China and also the range of luxury equipment associated with its preparation and consumption, such as the 'curious service of tripods, pouring vessels, cups, spoons, and other refined culinary instruments, which are valued at several thousand pieces of gold'.[8] Tulp's account of tea was celebrated in further Dutch scholarship, including that of Willem Pies (known as Piso) in 1658 and the 'tea doctor' Cornelis Bontekoe in 1678. All of this research was closely examined by English natural philosophers. These Dutch physicians established for tea a range of medically advantageous properties that justified its peculiar flavour, rarity and great expense. As Pies argued,

> The decoction so made is of bitter taste, and is sipped warm. The Chinese regard tea as a sacred drink; with it they welcome strangers, and with it they take leave of their guests; nor do they think

they have fulfilled the laws of hospitality without giving it. They esteem it in the same degree as the Mahommedans do their caveah [coffee].[9]

Pies notes that despite tea's odd taste and temperature, it had a high status among the Chinese, just like coffee among the Muslims.

The peculiar strangeness and foreign origin of tea and the other hot drinks seemed emblematic to some of turbulent times. These drinks represented a departure for English consumers in that they were consumed hot and tasted bitter – and in addition, they were expensive, imported from across the globe and extensively mediated by esoteric medical tracts. A satirist in 1659 demanded

> Whether the learned Colledge of Physicians, if they be not too full of practise, should not do a good act to meet, and examine, Whether Coffee, Sherbet, that came from *Turky*, Chocolate much used by the Jews, Brosa by the Muscovites, *Ta* and *Tee*, and such other new-fangled drinks, will agree with the Constitutions of our *English* bodies.[10]

What the satirist observed here was a strange correlation between the strong, bitter flavours of these hot drinks and the political and religious conflicts of the end of the English Commonwealth and the restoration of monarchy. These drinks were stimulants, but their consumption did not lead to inebriation or other forms of rowdiness, as did alcohol. So although the psychoactive effect of tea and coffee on drinkers was conspicuous, the forms of behaviour associated with them were broadly congruent with the programmes of moral reform and regulation promoted by Protestant sects in the period.[11] Encouraged by the medical fraternity, not actively opposed by the religious and civil authorities, tea and coffee were open to exploitation by merchants and the state.

Within a few years of Garway's first advertisement of tea in 1658, there was some relish among consumers for these 'new fangled', 'bitterish' drinks, especially as they were so hard to come by. Samuel Pepys records in his diary his first encounter with the drink in 1660. He was at a meeting in the Navy Office with Sir Richard Ford, a wealthy Spanish merchant, who 'talked like a man of great reason and experience. And afterwards did send for a Cupp of Tee (a China drink of which I never had drank before) and went away.'[12] But while he drank coffee regularly in early 1660s, several times a week, Pepys did not drink tea often or with much enthusiasm. In December 1665, he wrote that at the house of a Mr Pierce 'he and his wife made me drink some tea'.[13] In June 1667, he noted his wife's 'making of tea', but only because she was advised to do so on medical advice – it was, he reflected, 'a drink which Mr Pelling, the Potticary [apothecary], tells her is good for her cold and defluxions'.[14] The poet Edmund Waller, listed by Hartlib among the tea takers in 1657, was documented by the natural philosopher Sir Kenelm Digby as observing that English tea drinkers 'let the hot water remain too long soaking upon the Tea, which makes it extract into itself the earthy parts of the herb. The water is to remain upon it, no longer then whiles you can say the *Miserere* Psalm very leisurely.' The length of Psalm 51 was a common unit for the measure of time in recipes, delineating a period of about two and a half to three minutes. Waller concluded: 'Thus you have only the spiritual parts of the Tea, which is much more active, penetrative and friendly to nature.'[15]

London newspaper advertisements of the 1660s reveal that coffee-houses undertook both the sale of dry tea, a grocer's commodity, and the prepared hot beverage. Prices were high. The coffee man William Elford, of the Great Coffee-house at the sign of Morat the Great in Exchange Alley, advertised in the newspaper *Mercurius Publicus* on 19 March 1663 that he sold tea priced at six to 60 shillings a pound 'according to its goodness' – still remarkably costly (60 shillings was £3 sterling). In Elford's schema all tea was merely 'tea', without differentiation between kinds.[16] By way of comparison, at the same time he offered coffee at between one and six shillings a pound depending on the quality of the beans. This means that tea was six to ten times more expensive than coffee, which, even allowing for the different manner of preparation, suggests that it was an outrageously expensive luxury.

Aware of the expense of tea, and the more general curiosity about exotic oriental goods among the elite, the English East India Company began to take an interest in the product. In 1664 the Company's Court of Directors selected tea as an appropriate gift for their friends in the royal court. In July 1664, when a Company ship returned from Bantam in Java, the directors expected that it would be carrying exotic rarities – strange birds or animals – fit for the king's curiosity. When the ship arrived in port, they were disappointed, as there were few suitable curiosities of natural history. On 22 August 1664 the governor of the Court of Directors noted that 'the Factors' had failed to supply the Company 'of such things as they writ for to have presented his Majestie with'. Instead, so that the king 'might not find himself wholly neglected by ye Company, he was of opin-ion if ye Court think fitt, That a silver Case of Oile of Cinnamon . . . and some good Thea be provided for that, and which he hopes may be accept-able.' The Court of Directors, having 'approved very well thereof' these gifts of tea and cinnamon oil, had them despatched to the king.[17] In mak-ing this gift, the Company assumed that tea would be recognized as a luxury worthy of its recipients and an exotic commodity representative of the supplier. In doing so, they perhaps unwittingly replicated the role of tea in the China trade, where the ritual gifting of tea was important for state and court occasions.

The East India Company in this period had no direct trading contact with China, and was often forced to rely on imports of tea from Holland. In 1666, it imported 22 pounds and 12 ounces of tea, for which they paid £56 17s 6d on the Amsterdam market. The Company occasionally found a secondary trade in tea from Chinese junks calling at their trading post at Bantam (Bantem) on the Sunda Strait in Java (subsequently lost to the Dutch in 1682). In 1669 the East India Company received 143 pounds of tea, and in 1670 a further 79 pounds came via this route.[18] Throughout the late seventeenth century, the East India Company's main focus for its trade with Asia was luxury textiles, especially silks and velvets, although it was also keen on spices and rare metals. Tea played a very small role. A voyage between the Company's factory at Bombay and Amoy in 1687 was rare for having 'positively ordered on the Company's Account' a significant quantity of tea.[19] In 1689, another Company ship, the *Princess*, traded with Amoy: when its goods were sold in London, the Court of Directors complained

> Trade hath been much overlaid of late, and must be declined for a while to recover its reputation. Lacq'd ware of Tonqueen & China are great drugs, & so is Tea, except it be superfine, & comes in pots, tubs or chests that give it no ill scent of the oyl or any other matter. The Custom upon Thea here [in England] is above five shillings per. Pound, whereas a mean sort of Thea will not sell for above two shillings or two shillings sixpence.[20]

Tea was too expensive for an active trade in England, where the purchase cost could not be recovered, especially while cheaper imports were available from Holland. As a result, tea, like porcelain and lacquer wares, was what contemporaries called a 'drug upon the market': a commodity in great supply for which there was so little demand that it had become unsaleable. Imports of tea by the East India Company from China, by whatever route, remained small and sporadic throughout the 1690s.

Maids of Honour

In England, demand for tea was consolidated in the upper echelons of society, stimulated by interest shown in the royal court and by wealthy merchants and medical authorities. The very high retail price buttressed tea's elite connections. Two stories are often told about how this came about: both are probably apocryphal or garbled. The first concerns the queen and her maids of honour; the second, the wives of two courtiers. Both stories reinforce the association of tea with women and the social life of elite court circles in the seventeenth century. The problem with these anecdotes is that there is no evidence that either is true. Both were first related long after the events they describe, the result of historical confusion and fantasy. Nonetheless, it is also fair to say that tea socializing was notably popular among women at the royal court, and in other aristocratic circles, in the late seventeenth century.

On 14 May 1662, the restored king Charles II married Catherine of Braganza (properly Catarina Henriqueta de Bragança, 1638–1705), a Portuguese princess who became queen consort of England, Scotland and Ireland. The alliance had been made for diplomatic reasons, and the queen remained an unhappy second to the king's beautiful mistresses. Catherine brought with her a very large marriage portion, both in cash and territory, including the strategic trading posts of Tangiers and Bombay, and the right of free trade with Portuguese colonies in Brazil and the East Indies (including the Portuguese factory at Macau). In royal hagiography Queen Catherine is supposed to have established a patronage for oriental taste in furnishings, and drinking tea for pleasure – but it was only in the mid-nineteenth century that the royal historian Agnes Strickland (1796–1874) first proposed that Catherine introduced tea to England, although she offered no evidence to support the claim.[21]

The second apocryphal story concerns the wives of two statesmen at the court of Charles II. According to this anecdote, tea was introduced to England in 1666 by Henry Bennet, first Earl of Arlington (1618–1685) and secretary of state, and Thomas Butler, sixth Earl of Ossory (1634–1680), when they returned to London from a diplomatic mission to The Hague. In Holland, this story suggests, they had purchased a parcel of tea, which their wives used convivially to leverage their social position in court circles on their return. Lady Arlington and Lady Ossory were the Dutch sisters Elizabeth (1633–1718) and Emilia (1635–1688), daughters of Lodewyck van Nassau, heer van Beverweerd (1602–1665), the illegitimate son of Prince Maurice of Orange and cousin to William of Orange. The story suggests that the novelty of tea-drinking parties eased the Dutch women's rise in society.[22] The germ of this story was first related in 1756 by the philanthropist Jonas Hanway in an essay he wrote about the pernicious effects of tea drinking. There is no reason to suppose it is true, especially as Arlington and Ossory did not make a diplomatic mission to Holland in 1666 (although they did in 1674). In 1756, Samuel Johnson, in his review of Hanway's book, observed that the claim that they introduced tea drinking into England was clearly untrue, for, as he said, tea had been taxed since 1660. Johnson's objection, of course, applies equally to Strickland's claim about the queen.[23]

Both of these accounts have been repeated as if true by many historians of tea in the past century. Why? Perhaps the answer is that these pretty stories establish an aristocratic and royal context for the taste for tea drinking. Tea companies and their marketing departments enjoy such associations – far more than they do tea's real associations with republican intelligencers from Bohemia (Hartlib) or pedantic Dutch doctors (Tulp). These anecdotes of elite individuals enacting historical events are also simple narratives – rather than complicated analyses – of demand, addiction and exploitation. But while both of these stories are in themselves inaccurate, they do point to the important association of tea with elite female circles in England in the 1680s and 1690s. Queen Catherine did evince a taste for tea renowned enough for poets to eulogize. The courtier Edmund Waller published posthumously in 1690 a poem entitled 'Of Tea, Commended by Her Majesty'. Its date of composition is not known, although circumstantial evidence has led the most recent scholarship to suggest that it was written in the early 1680s.[24] The poem, occasioned by the celebrations of her birthday (25 November), is a panegyric to Catherine through praise for her taste in tea:

> Venus her myrtle, Phoebus has his Bays;
> Tea both excels, which she vouchsafes to praise.
> The best of Queens, and best of Herbs we owe
> To that bold Nation, which the way did shew
> To the fair Region, where the Sun does rise;
> Whose rich Productions we so justly prize.
> The Muses Friend, Tea, does our fancy aid;
> Repress those Vapours, which the head invade:
> And keeps that Palace of The Soul serene,
> Fit on her Birth-day to salute the Queen.

Birthday odes are necessarily sycophantic. Here Waller celebrates the Queen through her poetic association with tea and the trade with the East Indies. The poet links explorers from Portugal – that 'bold Nation' – with the new eastward trade routes opened to China, 'the fair Region, where the Sun does rise', which have encouraged the trade in luxuries, those 'rich Productions we so justly prize'. Among these, Waller identifies tea as the pre-eminent prize of these voyages, as the 'Muses Friend' both by association and physiological effect. Tea, Waller concludes, aids the poet's 'fancy' or imagination, and encourages tranquillity and calm by keeping 'that Palace of The Soul serene'.[25] Waller himself had been an enthusiast since the 1650s, when he was noted by Hartlib as 'a great taker or user of' tea.[26]

By the 1680s, tea drinking had become an established aspect of elite and aristocratic social and domestic life in England. Evidence for the dimensions of this new habit of tea drinking can be found in the records of William Russell, fifth Earl and first Duke of Bedford, whose household at Woburn

Abbey left a considerable archive, including account books, letter books and bills, that allow a detailed account of their consumer expenditure. This family, who had begun making domestic purchases of coffee since 1670, discovered tea in 1685. Tea was such an expensive luxury, however, that its purchase could not be left to the steward like most of the family's grocery consumables, including coffee. Instead tea purchases were specially entrusted to a Mr Dawson, an upper servant of the family known as the 'receiver-general', or his wife, Eliza. Their purchases, from Mr Richards in London, were made on behalf of a particular family member, each of whom also purchased his or her own teaset. As this suggests, tea drinking was like no other aspect of their consumer habits. Despite coming to it late, the family soon spent more on tea than coffee. In 1685 the family spent in total £10 on tea, the price of which was 23–5 shillings a pound; in 1687, when total expenditure reached nearly £15, the price paid was usually 25 shillings per pound, but with some as high as three guineas a pound (£3 3s.). This was an extremely expensive commodity. The tea sets ordered by each member of the family were also very expensive: in 1685, Lady Margaret Russell, for her first consignment of tea, was given a tea set by her father's steward that cost £1 14s.: in 1688 she added another set of six dishes for 24 shillings, a silver tea salver for five shillings, and two years later a teapot for £2 3s. The price of tea, its spectacular equipage and its esoteric sourcing indicated the high social prestige accorded the beverage.[27]

Locke's Mistress Tea

John Locke (1632–1704), one of the most influential English moral and political philosophers, discovered tea in the 1680s through encounters with all three innovating groups: medical men, merchants and maids of honour. Locke had encountered 'theá' in Oxford in 1682, but his taste for it began after his arrival in Holland in 1683, to which he had been forced into exile in fear of Stuart persecution.[28] In the period in which Locke was resident in Holland, tea was more generally available than in England, and was consumed in greater quantities, though remaining an expensive luxury. The VOC had access to regular supplies, both through a trade conducted by Chinese merchants in Batavia, and through the yearly Dutch voyage to Japan.[29] Locke, who had studied medicine while at Oxford, was curious about tea's sanative or healthful properties – and when he arrived in Amsterdam in December 1683, he had unwittingly walked into a full-scale medical controversy about tea.

The most furious proponent in the tea fight was Cornelis Dekker, known as Bontekoe, author of a widely read treatise on tea, *Tractat van het excellenste kruyd thee* (1678), the full title for which can be translated as *Treatise about the Most Excellent Herb Tea: Showing What the Right Use*

Attributed to John Nost the Elder, *John Locke*, c. 1700, lead portrait bust on stone base. In exile in Holland in the 1680s, the English philosopher John Locke (1632–1704) became an enthusiast both of green tea and of the sociable practices of tea consumption that he encountered in Dutch intellectual circles. When he returned to London in 1689 in the retinue of Queen Mary, he continued his tea-drinking habit, expending considerable sums to source superior kinds of green tea.

of it is, and its Valuable Qualities in Times of Health and Sickness.[30] In it, Bontekoe attempted to describe the numerous ways that tea might have beneficial therapeutic effects, located within advice about how to lead a good and healthy life. In Bontekoe's physiology, a proper circulation of the blood was the key to maintaining good health. The most significant way to maintain the blood in a healthy state was through diet: and tea, he argued, was beneficial by maintaining the blood in a warm and thin condition.[31] Tea, he claimed, had thereby cured his body of the gravel (kidney stones). In addition, his treatise offered chapters describing how tea was efficacious in healing illness in the mouth and throat, stomach, bowels, blood, brain, eyes and ears, chest, bowels and belly, kidneys and bladder. It also had the effect of 'banishing sleep without any harm to health'. Bontekoe did not claim that tea was a panacea, but rather that it worked these effects through chemical processes that corrected the circulation of the blood. Rather than drink it strong and bitter, like most physic or medicine, Bontekoe argued that tea should be consumed in a dilute form. In this way, tea drinkers could usefully drink many cups without ill effect, 'as much tea as he pleases, provided he does not forget to regulate his sleep', prescribing 'eight or ten cups twice a day'. Nonetheless, for all his enthusiasm for tea, Bontekoe knew comparatively little about it: the treatise considers tea as one commodity, not divided into different classifications or preparations. To the tea doctor, all tea was green tea: 'The colour of the grains of tea should always be greenish-blue and should have the gloss of a newly dried herb; the more it approaches red the less valuable the tea is.'[32]

Bontekoe's treatise was reprinted twice (in 1679 and 1685), and gained him sufficient notice to be appointed physician to Friedrich Wilhelm, Elector of Brandenburg, the ruler of Prussia. In England, the treatise attracted the attention of Robert Hooke, secretary of the Royal Society, who sent '*Bontecoes* book *of tea*' in June 1685 to a Dutch merchant resident in London, Francis Lodwick, to translate (that translation is now lost).[33] Bontekoe also attracted followers in the medical profession, including a young Dutchman named Steven Blankaart, who published a treatise developed from Bontekoe's writings and titled the *Use and Abuse of Tea* in 1686.[34] But Bontekoe was a difficult and disputatious man whose forthright expression of his views saw him ejected from some medical circles. He was attacked especially by Pieter Bernagie (1656–1699), a versatile physician

CORNELIUS BONTEKOE
*Medicina Doctor, Electoris Brandeburgici à Consiliis Ejusdemque
Archiater, ac Professor Francofurti ad Oderam, etc. etc.*

Adriaen Haelwegh, *Cornelis Bontekoe*, c. 1680, printed engraving. Known as the 'Tea-doctor', Cornelis Bontekoe (1640–1685) published a controversial treatise on tea drinking in Amsterdam in 1678, advocating tea consumption as a beneficial therapy for a wide variety of symptoms and diseases. Bontekoe argued that tea should be consumed in a dilute form, and prescribed as many as eight to ten cups, twice a day.

and anatomist who had also found success as a playwright. Bernagie did not attack tea drinking in itself, but rather the excesses of Bontekoe's enthusiasm for it, and suggested that Bontekoe was in the pay of certain directors of the voc who stood to profit from the trade. The second edition of Bontekoe's *Theetractat*, which contained further analysis of coffee and chocolate, replied in furious fashion to Bernagie. In the 'Apology of the Author against his Slanderers', Bontekoe belittled Bernagie as a 'ground-beetle' whose head [was] full of air, his heart full of envy, his tongue full of gall and his pen full of lies'.[35] When Locke sought refuge in Holland in the winter of 1683–4, he became a friend of Bernagie, and would have encountered talk of the tea scandal, however unedifying. But he was also persuaded that tea, and the practice of drinking it, was valuable both as a therapeutic and a social practice.

In Amsterdam Locke fell in with a sociable group of medical men who entertained each other, as he said, with 'tea and the like' – the first time he had regularly socialized over tea.[36] With these men, Locke formed a private medical research club known as a *collegie*, a word in Dutch denoting a group of friends who met together regularly to discuss and study a common interest.[37] Locke greatly valued his *collegie*, in which he 'found such delightful, such subtle, such profitable and solid converse'.[38] This group of eight included some distinguished doctors: the chief medical officer of the Admiralty in Amsterdam, Dr Pieter Guenellon; a successful physician, Dr Egbert Veen; Bernagie himself, Bontekoe's opponent in the tea controversy; and several laymen interested in medical matters, such as the Protestant clergyman Dr Philip van Limborch and the English scholar Matthew Slade. All except Locke were Remonstrants, followers of a form of Dutch Protestantism established by Arminius, who rejected Calvinistic dogmas about predestination and were to be very influential on Locke's ideas about religious toleration. In discussions with these men, and through further visits to medical schools and anatomy demonstrations, Locke proposed devoting his exile to medical study – although he actually spent it writing his major philosophical treatises. Locke was nonetheless absorbed by the debate in pharmacological writings about tropical plants and their benefits. One such was cinchona, the natural source of quinine, whose preparation in 'Jesuits Bark' delivered almost miraculous cures for malaria and fever.[39] Locke's curiosity about exotic botany led him in 1684 to visit the Leiden Physic Garden, which he found 'well stored with plants especially from the East Indies', where he had a discussion with Paul Hermann (1640–1695), a professor of botany at Leiden, about the properties of cinnamon he had observed in Ceylon.[40] Exotic botany had much promise for modern medicine, Locke learned.

Locke's discovery of a fondness for, and curiosity about, tea in Holland complemented his long-felt distrust of coffee and the sociable world of

Jan Josef Horemans, *The New Song*, 1740–60, oil on panel. An interior scene of noisy Dutch tea socializing, in which a group of men and women sit around a table listening to a young woman playing the harpsichord. On the tea-table are Chinese blue-and-white porcelain teacups, a Yixing teapot, and a brass urn. A plate or saucer has been broken on the floor, suggesting that such sociable pleasures are fleeting. Note the kettle and brazier in the left foreground. A commotion in the background proposes that less polite forms of social interaction are never far away.

the coffee-house in England. The coffee-house was the most characteristic form of sociability in late seventeenth-century London: there, men assembled around the common table to drink coffee, read news and satires, and debate with each other on matters of importance, from politics to religion, from gossip to philosophy. Locke enjoyed none of this. He thought his own 'temper' unsociable, 'always shie of a crowd and strangers'.[41] In Holland in 1684, he wrote in his own defence that

> Coffee houses, it is well known, I loved and frequented little in England, lesse here. I speake much within compasse when I say I have not been in a coffee house as many times as I have been months here, haveing noe great delight either in the conversation or the liquor.[42]

In the 1690s, after he had returned to London, he continued to distrust coffee-houses and their distinctively public forms of social encounter.

They who know my way of liveing [know] that when I am in town I doe not goe once in three months to a coffee house and never to seek company but to finde some one with whom I have particular businesse.[43]

Instead, Locke preferred his study and his private life: in Holland, he said, 'my time was most spent alone, at home by my fires side, where I confesse I writ a good deale'.[44] The private and intimate arena of tea drinking, with a few men and women gathered around the tea-table in the salon or garden of a private house, limited to the members of his *collegie*, provided Locke with the sociable encounters he valued. Tea drinking was central to this.

Locke's friendship with the clergyman Philip van Limborch found expression through their mutual delight in fine tea. Locke asked van Limborch to help him find and purchase high-quality teas, both in Holland in the 1680s and later as an intermediary from England in the 1690s. Their correspondence in 1685 and 1686 discusses the difficulties and expense of their plans for the purchase of tea, as gifts and for their own consumption, Locke lamenting his 'tiresome importunity'.[45] Van Limborch, a noted connoisseur of tea, also composed an extraordinary poem in praise of tea, a copy of which he sent to Locke. This tea poem was a Virgilian *cento*: a humorous exercise of scholarship in which the poet created a new poem out of a patchwork of quotations from the classical Roman poets. Van Limborch restricted himself to Virgil, composing his own motley poem by careful quotations of half-lines of Virgil's verse. The formal joke redoubled an additional difficulty: as tea was unknown to Virgil, van Limborch's *cento* worked by repeatedly working a pun on tea and Te (in Latin 'thee' or 'you', the second-person singular pronoun). When Locke received Limborch's 'Cento Virgilianus de Te' he made his own copy, now in the Bodleian Library.[46] But he also promised to keep it private: 'Your Mistress Tea, sung by Virgil, I am keeping by me with due caution and attention to modesty.' Only Locke's English friend John Freke, a lawyer and fellow exile, being 'very desirous of being granted her favours', was allowed to see the verses.[47] The poem itself praised tea as a beautiful exotic visitor much favoured by the gods.

Locke's notebooks record his research about tea in Holland, especially its properties and preparation. The key aspect of Bontekoe's preparation of tea was dilution: unlike the robust coffee, tea was delicate and watery. Bontekoe advised:

Put a little [tea] in a tea-pot (either of tin, red earth or Delfs Porceleyn) which has been cleaned by rinsing it out with a little hot water, then pour water on and immediately put the lid on the pot; leave the pot a little while or put it in a bowl of hot water to draw, till the water has colour and taste; then pour a little of this

extract or tincture, through the spout into a china cup, or in as
many cups as there are drinkers and fill them up with water to
the brim; then everybody takes a cup and without fearing the
heat or scalding, he drinks the tea, blowing on it two or three
times, always carefully sipping off the top part and going on like
this till the cup is empty and only the grounds remain.[48]

Other natural philosophers whom Locke encountered were more
experimental with their tea. Locke noted in his manuscript journal (now
in the British Library) on Thursday, 16 March 1684, of a method for the
improvement of tea that he learned from Dr Caspar Sibelius in Leiden:

Take a crust of bread and burn to a black cinder. Take straight
from the fire and while still hot take about 1 drachm with 1 or
2 grains of ambergris. Place the still hot powder into the bottom
of a jar and on top of it 1 fluid ounce of Thea leaves. Keep thus
till required; in this way its pleasing smell and taste will be mingled
with the infusion.[49]

Adding charred bread and ambergris (the waxy substance produced by
sperm whales that was used by perfumers for its pronounced animalic musk)
would produce a strongly flavoured brew. A month later, on 14 April, Locke
met a Mr Bremen at Sibelius's house, a man who had lived for eight years
among the 'Japaners'. His preparation specified that:

He beat the yolkes of eggs with sugar candie in a basin and then
powderd in it the hot infusion of Thee always stirring of it. When
it was well mixed makeroons were broken and sopd in it and rose
water added. This was a very pleasante drinke or rather caudle.
The preparation was about 3 eggs to ½ a pint of the liquer.[50]

Through reports from the voc factory in Nagasaki, the Dutch had a good
understanding of the Japanese ceremonial tea preparation: Blankaart, for
example, noted its differences from Chinese tea service. But although Japanese
tea does involve whisking finely ground tea powder, this rather fanciful
'caudle', normally a hot spiced wine and gruel mixture usually given to sick
people, seems to have borrowed elements from other preparations such as
chocolate or sabayon (a warm egg custard dessert).[51] Locke's curiosity about
tea's sanative properties encouraged his adoption of the habit of drinking it.

When Locke returned to England in February 1689 in the retinue of
Queen Mary after the Revolution of 1688, he found English tea culture
was not nearly so sophisticated. Locke's letters to his *collegie* friends still in
Holland recorded his efforts to organize private shipments of good-quality

tea, which now served as part of his own convivial networking in Britain. In his pursuit of tea, Locke was prepared to spend very large sums to acquire distinctive varieties. Locke involved his friend van Limborch in an elaborate scheme to import a parcel of fine tea – 'a whole or half-pound of the best tea' – in the diplomatic bag of the Earl of Pembroke so as to avoid high import taxes. 'I should like the best tea, even if it should cost forty gulden a pound.' Locke's unusual extravagance suggests that tea had for him an important social purpose.

> I know you are a most experienced buyer of this herb, just as you have been its most eloquent panegyrist. You see how freely I make use of your services; nothing would please me more than to be able to do as much for you, nor can you doubt my willing-ness; only try me![52]

Van Limborch's reply, written ten days later, explains the relish with which he had fulfilled his task and his regret that he has missed Pembroke's return.

> I set out forthwith in search of a superior kind of tea, if such could be found anywhere, and in my own opinion I was quite successful, for I am thoroughly pleased with both its bouquet and its flavour. There is another kind of tea, greatly relished by many people, which is commonly called the Imperial, with larger and looser leaves; but I gathered that you did not want that sort, as it is on sale in London at Mrs. Ferguson's shop. I drank some of the new kind at the same time as some Imperial, to see which I preferred; and in fact it seemed better to me both in bouquet and flavour. There is also a considerable difference between the prices of the two; a pound of the Imperial is valued at 48 of our gulden, but this other kind at only 28. The box costs 1 gulden 8 stivers.[53]

After the tea arrived in London some weeks later, Locke wrote to van Limborch that 'I have received the tea and the books which you took such trouble to procure and send to me, for which I give you my best thanks.'[54] The correspondents distinguished between kinds of tea, one of which, Imperial, is noted for 'larger and looser leaves', and they were knowledge-able about what was available in London tea shops, such as that of Mrs Ferguson. Although nothing is known about this tea merchant, newspaper advertisements in the 1690s suggest that fashionable spa towns had shops and teahouses run by women, aimed at a mixed clientele of gentlemen and ladies. In 1689, Mary's Tea-house and Mrs Mainwaring's Tea-house were advertising their presence in Tunbridge Wells for example.[55] Over the

Jean-Étienne Liotard, *Still-life: Tea Set*, c. 1781–3, oil on canvas mounted on board. Tea, interrupted: Liotard's delicate still-life depicts a Chinese *famille rose* porcelain tea-set upon a painted lacquer or tinware tray, prepared with six cups and saucers (each with its matching silver teaspoon), a teapot, sugar bowl with tongs, water jug, lidded canister of tea leaves, plate of bread and butter and slops bowl, into which a used cup and saucer have been unceremoniously dumped. A teaspoon standing in a cup half-full with cold tea reveals the pale brown hue of bohea (oolong) consumed without milk.

following decade, Locke received further gifts of tea from his Dutch friends. In 1690, he was sent a 'box of Tea' from Amsterdam by his *collegie* friend Dr Guenellon, a gift in return for a copy of Locke's *Essay concerning Human Understanding* (1689): and again in 1697, he received some 'excellent Imperial tea' from Monsieur Cost (Pierre Coste?) by way of the merchant Monsieur Cowls.[56]

Locke did not choose to publish on tea, its therapeutic properties or the sociability of the tea-table. The one mention of tea in his printed work is in *Of the Conduct of the Understanding* (published posthumously in 1706). He offers a case study of a woman who has night-time visions after 'drinking a large dose of dilute tea (as she was ordered by a physician) going to bed',[57] demonstrating that Locke was aware of the beverage's psychoactive properties. From his medical associations, he understood that tea had powerful medicinal qualities, affecting mood and behaviour, even if he was reluctant to follow Bontekoe's more extreme propositions. From his correspondence, it is also clear that Locke recognized that tea was available in a wide variety of forms, some of which were more refined and rarer, and so more expensive than others, and that this expensive tea could produce highly esteemed taste experiences. Locke developed a deep interest in China in the 1690s, compiling 45 closely written pages of notes about Chinese religion and philosophy from his library of travel writing and memoirs, including the Jesuits Matteo Ricci and Louis Le Comte.[58] But his connoisseurship of tea did not develop further. His taste for tea occurred largely outside any discursive system that might contain it, either in natural philosophy or Chinese scholarship. Although he could purchase from Mrs Ferguson tea in different kinds whose flavour profiles admitted of distinct impressions, Locke did not have any sophisticated or informed language to describe it. Knowledge lagged behind the taste for tea in elite culture.

Locke's discovery of the virtues of tea drinking in Holland in the 1680s was in this way typical of his countrymen. In the late 1680s, the debate among Dutch medical writers, especially the inflated claims made by Bontekoe for its virtues, made some headway in London. A summary of tea's excellencies made by Blankaart in 1686, and thereafter published as a broadside in Dutch,[59] was translated and circulated in manuscript in scientific circles in London. One transcription entitled 'The Qualities and Operations of the Herb Called Tea or Chee' found its way to Robert Hooke at the Royal Society. It was made by Thomas Povey (1614–1705), a former merchant, colonial administrator and fellow of the Royal Society. Povey was a gentleman of fashion as much as science: when John Evelyn dined with him in 1676, he described him as a 'nice contriver of all Elegancies, & exceedingly formall'.[60] Povey's house in Lincoln's Inn Fields was much admired for some unusually convincing *trompe l'oeil* perspective paintings, a splendid wine cellar and neat stables lined with pretty Dutch tiles. Povey's manuscript promised much about tea:

1. It purifyes the Bloud of that which is grosse and Heavy.
2. It Vanquisheth heavy Dreames.
3. It Easeth the brain of heavy Damps.
4. Easeth and cureth giddinesse and Paines in the Heade.
5. Prevents the Dropsie.
6. Drieth Moist humours in the Head.
7. Consumes Rawnesse.
8. Opens Obstructions.
9. Cleares the Sight.
10. Clenseth and Purifieth adults humours and a hot Liver.
11. Purifieth defects of the Bladder and Kiddneys.
12. Vanquisheth Superfluous Sleep.
13. Drives away dissines [dizziness], makes one Nimble and Valient.
14. Encourageth the heart and Drives away feare.
15. Drives away all Paines of the Collick which proceed from Wind.

16. Strengthens the Inward parts and Prevents Consumptions.
17. Strengthens the Memory.
18. Sharpens the Will and Quickens the Understanding.
19. Purgeth Safely the Gaul.
20. Strengthens the use of due benevolence.[61]

Povey's list of tea's twenty qualities – slightly abridged from Blankaart's 25 – claims to be derived from a Chinese source, yet was also influenced by Dutch medical thinking. Nonetheless, in its conjuncture here between China, Holland and England, Povey's little manuscript encapsulates the history of knowledge about tea in the late seventeenth century.

By the end of the 1690s, tea was still a luxury so expensive as to be unavailable to the great mass of people, and was restricted to a wealthy elite. John Ovington remarked in 1699 that 'the Drinking of it has of late obtain'd here so universally, as to be affected both by the *Scholar* and the *Tradesman*, to become both a private *Regale* at *Court*, and to be made use of in places of *publick Entertainment*.'[62] As Ovington suggests, tea appealed to different social interests, each of whom offered distinct interpretations of its properties and virtues: medical, gendered, foreign (Dutch) and exotic

Tea canister, Staffordshire, England, 1760–70, salt-glazed stoneware, painted in enamel colours. Bohea was one of three kinds of tea generally available on the British market at the beginning of the eighteenth century, alongside two forms of green tea, singlo and imperial. Originally a Wuyi oolong, the preparation of bohea tea allowed it to oxidize after being picked, a process encouraged by rolling, giving the leaves a black colour that imparted to the tea prepared from it a brownish-red tint.

(Chinese). Despite these interpretations, both drinkers and sellers of tea were overwhelmingly ignorant about the tea they were drinking in terms of its origin, manufacture and quality. Nascent European discourses on tea nonetheless created or encouraged a demand for the product that during the first decades of the eighteenth century would establish tea as a commodity with much broader appeal to the market. The conditions for meeting this demand were commercial and geopolitical, tied especially to the ambitions of the East India Company in gaining regular access to Chinese markets in Canton.

CANTON.

Johannes Vinckboons, attr., *View of Canton in China, c.* 1662, oil on canvas. Ships of the Dutch East-India Company at anchor before the Chinese city of Canton. The details of the city itself are indistinct behind the long defensive wall, though the buildings which appear at the shoreline may represent the warehouses servicing European trade (foreshadowing the later factories). The scene itself lacks important topographical detail. In practice, the shallow waters of the Pearl River estuary precluded the passage of these deep-keeled oceangoing vessels.

THREE

The Tea Trade with China

On 19 August 1704, Thomas Flint – in command of the *Stretham*, already eighteen months out of London – placed his ship, its crew and its valuable 'treasure' in the hands of a 'China pilot', weighed anchor at the Portuguese settlement of Macau and began the perilous journey up the braided estuary of the Pearl River to the Chinese city of Canton. The pilot was equipped with the local knowledge necessary to guide the frigate through the narrow channels that led to the safe anchorage at Whampoa Island. Using his experience of the tidal flows, the prevailing winds and the ever-shifting contours of the river bed, the pilot would guide the ship over two treacherous sandbars whose exact position and height altered with each season.[1] But even with this expertise, progress was slow, methodical and achieved only with the greatest care, the ship dropping anchor a full five days after entering the mouth of the river. A late seven-teenth-century painting attributed to Johannes Vinckboons captures something of the uncertainty and vulnerability that Flint and his officers must have felt as they surveyed the landscape within which they were to spend the next four months. In front of the ramshackle warehouses servicing the European trade, two Dutch merchant ships appear atypically fragile, exposed, out of place. The immense brooding city of Canton itself is barely glimpsed behind the long defensive wall that reaches across the canvas, while on the hillside beyond a pagoda surveys the visiting ships that are effectively imprisoned in this small stretch of deep water.

The officers and crew of the *Stretham* – numbering around 70 in total – were, we might imagine, relieved to have reached this natural harbour. Their outward voyage had been prolonged by problems associated with the changing seasons, maritime discipline, piracy and enemy action, and unsettled further by the death of its commander, and they may initially have expected to have been on their way back to England by now. But although their sojourn in China was to last nearly four months, there would be little or no opportunity for the seamen to savour the pleasures of dry land.[2]

This was a privilege allowed by the Chinese authorities only to a specific group of passengers, who were employed not by the ship's private owners but by the distant Court of Directors of the East India Company. These 'supracargos' (literally 'over the cargo', though the term was soon corrupted to 'supercargo') were to oversee the procurement of the various goods which the ship was to carry back to London. The *Stretham* carried three super-cargoes – Christopher Brewster (as chief), William Daniel and Matthew Gibbon.[3] They would spend most of the next four months at a rented 'factory' outside the walls of Canton, a large warehouse with associated office and living space.

The *Stretham*'s four-year journey (1703–7) occurs at a pivotal phase in the emergence of the Sino–British tea trade. First, the *Stretham* was a part of the first fleet of ships dispatched by the rebuilt and rebranded 'United East India Company' that was to enjoy a monopoly on the British tea trade until the 1830s. Second, the *Stretham* sailed at the beginning of the wholesale concentration of the China trade at Canton, in preference to the ports of Amoy and Chusan. Third, the *Stretham*'s voyage occurred at the moment when a regular direct tea trade between China and Britain was first established; indeed, it sailed in the company of a ship that was ordered to obtain a tea cargo of unprecedented size. There is a further reason why the voyage of this particular ship offers a compelling account of the long-distance high-risk voyages that enabled the early eighteenth-century China trade: the *Stretham* also carried as a passenger Charles Lockyer (d. 1752) – later chief accountant to the South Sea Company – who was to publish in 1711 the first detailed survey of a British East Indies trading voyage, *An Account of the Trade in India: Containing Rules for Good Government in Trade, Price Courants, and Tables: with Descriptions of Fort St. George, Acheen, Malacca, Condore, Canton . . ., their Inhabitants, Customs, Religion, Government, Animals, Fruits, &c.*[4] As the long title indicates, his book is an occasionally unwieldy hybrid, acting variously as a memoir, a merchant's manual and a travel narrative. Nonetheless, it contains a unique record of the China trade at Canton in the first decade of the eighteenth century, and includes a rare snapshot of the way in which the exciting new Asian commodity – tea – was being bought and sold by the British. Taken together with archival materials now in the India Office Records maintained at the British Library, the *Stretham*'s story – and those of the ships in whose company it sailed – can be recovered in detail.

The Managers of the United Trade

Tea's elevation from occasional supplementary cargo to primary object of trading voyages could not have been foreseen in the late seventeenth century. It was not the principal object of the Company's trade, nor were the Company's directors initially persuaded by its overtures. By the time of the *Stretham*'s voyage, the East India Company – incorporated on 31 December 1600 as the 'Governor and Company of Merchants of London Trading with the East Indies' – had for over a century enjoyed a monopoly on British trade with the part of the world that was imagined, with breath-taking imprecision, as the 'East Indies'. This region was defined throughout the Company's existence as the land east of the Cape of Good Hope (where the Atlantic and Indian oceans meet at the southernmost point of Africa), and west of the Straits of Magellan (a sea passage south of the South American mainland, used by shipping to cross from the Pacific to the Atlantic oceans).[5] Civil War and Restoration had done little to disturb the configuration of this monopoly. Oliver Cromwell's initial instinct had been to throw the trade open; but ultimately the Company was granted a new charter in October 1657, and Charles II confirmed the approbation of the restored Stuarts in April 1661.[6] The Company's business had then flourished for over twenty years, a growth occasioned in part by the astute development of its traffic in fabrics and in part by what historians have identified as a general surge in world trade in this period.[7]

The fall of the Stuart dynasty in 1688 emboldened those who sought a share in the profits of the East India trade. In return for a £2 million loan to the government, a deeply indebted William III allowed a group of wealthy merchants to associate in June 1698 as the 'English Company Trading to the East Indies'.[8] This was not a decision driven by the success of arguments concerning the benefits of free trade.[9] The initial – endlessly deferred – intention had been for the original East India Company (popularly designated 'the Old Company') to be wound up, and for this 'New Company' to enjoy its own monopoly. This uneasy commercial situation occasioned con-siderable domestic concern: the flood of East India goods shipped by two separate companies produced gluts in supply and further threatened a local textile industry struggling to compete with cheap foreign imports. As early as 1700 negotiations were taking place to merge the two companies, and an Instrument of Union was agreed in April 1702. This agreement set up a third East India Company – 'the United Company of Merchants of England Trading to the East Indies' – and granted the two existing businesses seven years to wind up their affairs.[10]

The rivalry between the Old and the New Companies may have been brief; but the intense competition between them was to change funda-mentally the direction, purpose and execution of Britain's China trade generally, and its tea trade in particular. Perhaps because of the difficulties encountered in establishing the necessary trading infrastructures (and gaining access to Old Company entrepôts further west), New Company innovation impacted commerce with China most extensively. Sino–European mercantile practices were, after all, far less entrenched. The Old Company's China business had been tentative, hesitant and (on occasion) disastrous, and it had typically sent just one ship every two or three years. Trade with China represented, on average, less than 4 per cent of imports from Asia throughout the 1680s, rising to just over 7 per cent in the period 1690–96.[11] The more certain profits associated with the established factories on the Indian coast had made the Company less adventurous, and it had little reason to risk large capital investment in seas beyond its sphere of influence. By contrast, the directors of the New Company were eager to find untapped markets, and resolved in June 1700 to 'drive the Trade to the utmost'.[12] In the period of less than five years that it functioned as an independent trading operation, the New Company dispatched seventeen ships to China, compared with ten sent by its older rival. The increased dispatch rate of even the Old Company demonstrates the extent to which the China trade had been galvanized by this short-lived competitive marketplace.[13] Imports from China during the decade following the creation of the New Company (1697–1706) rose to almost 14 per cent of the combined Asia imports of the three companies.

An innovative approach is evident in other practical aspects of the China trade. Whereas the Old Company continued to favour Amoy, the New Company appears to have been keen to develop alternative commercial trading posts. It sent only five of its seventeen China ships to Amoy: eight were directed to Chusan and four to the relatively untested Canton. Moreover – and of the greatest significance for this book – the statistics suggest that it was at this moment of corporate uncertainty and commercial experimentation that tea finally found merchants willing to be persuaded by its gentle, insistent tactics; within a century it would come to monopolize the affairs of the United Company. According to the authoritative figures established by K. N. Chaudhuri, over 200,000 pounds of tea were imported from China in the five-year period 1700–1704. Though dwarfed by the quantities imported in later decades, this must nevertheless have been reckoned a vast amount given that – by Chaudhuri's computation – less than 150,000 pounds had been shipped in total prior to 1700.[14] The surviving records for ships' individual cargoes indicate that the companies were trying to outpace each other in terms of their investment in tea.

Tea, Fine, a Good Quantity, All Well Packed

Tea's conquest of British taste began quietly. The dried leaves rode on the success of the more lucrative trade in wrought fabrics, in their many and diverse varieties. Though tea occasionally made its way to England in the second half of the seventeenth century, this was often via the Company's trading posts elsewhere in the East Indies, rather than by direct trade with China. Tea's early success was consolidated in the late 1680s, when it first appeared in the 'List of Investments' required of vessels heading to China. The supercargoes of the *London* and the *Worcester*, sailing from Bombay to Amoy, were told to procure a very large quantity – nearly 20,000 pounds – in May 1687, with specific instructions to 'lett yᵉ Tea you buy be Extraordinary good and fresh, being for England'.[15] Though there is no record of whether this quantity was forthcoming, moderate quantities of tea brought into London by the *Modena* and the *Rochester*, returning from Bombay in 1689 and 1690, presumably derived from this cargo.[16] In January 1694, the supercargoes of the *Dorothy* were required to obtain wrought fabrics, china ware, lacquer ware and live birds, but they were also told to procure an unspecified amount of the new commodity:

> Tea fine, a good Quantity, all well pack't in Tutenague as closd as can be, and then wrapt round in the leaves of the Country, and then put into Tubs[.] Be sure you buy the newst Tea can be got and the best . . . Bring no tea in small Pots, in sweet wood Chests, nor in any Pots 'till well assured that they are cleared from all Scents, especially from yᵉ smells of yᵉ so[l]dering oyle.[17]

The *Dorothy* was thus the first English ship to set out from London with a specific instruction to buy tea in China. 'Tutenague' – known popularly as 'Chinese copper' – was much prized for its strength and malleability. It could be hammered into a thin foil, within which a fragile cargo like tea could be protected from the damp and salt associated with the voyage back to England, and offered some protection from the strong smells with which it could easily be tainted. A 'tub' was a type of open barrel, as wide as it was tall. It was often reckoned to carry regular amounts of the various cargoes which it might store. As such, the term was used in the early eighteenth century as an approximate measure of weight varying according to commodity: in the case of tea, a quantity of 60 pounds. The Company's Commerce Journal for 30 June 1697 notes that the ship did indeed carry a 'good quantity': 119 'tubs and chests' of tea amounting to some 8,922 pounds, realizing total sales of just over £8,000.[18]

In 1696, the supercargoes of the *Amity* were given further strictures about the importance accorded the freshness of the tea to be carried: 'be sure that it be of the very best sort, and the newest can be got, always remembering in this and all other Commodityes that the worst payes as much in freight as the best.' They were asked to procure 80 tubs of tea (about 4,800 pounds). The Company directed that the tubs should be 'laid uppermost in the ship, and as often as may be . . . carried on the Deck'.[19] The *Amity* never reached China; but just a year later, the *Trumball* and the *Nassau* (carrying as an 'assistant' Christopher Brewster, later Chief Supercargo on the *Stretham*) were despatched to purchase tea, between them bringing back to London over 50,000 pounds.[20] The East India Company's directors' increasing knowledge about this intriguing new commodity is reflected in the instructions given to the supercargoes of the *Fleet*, sent to Amoy in 1698, who were not only asked to procure 'three hundred Tubs of the finest Newest Tea can be got' but were also ordered specifically to 'let ten of the Tubs be Bohee Tea good'.[21] They ultimately brought back nearly twice this quantity, 1,100 pounds, an amount nevertheless dwarfed by 23,000 pounds of 'Singloe'.[22] Even more tellingly, the supercargoes of the *Northumberland*, bound for Canton in 1700, were advised that tea 'does very much obtaine in reputation among persons of all qualities'.[23]

By 1702, when the rivalry between the two East India Companies had galvanized the China trade, tea was coming onto the London market in quantities hitherto unimagined, and featured more prominently in many China trade itineraries. The supercargoes of the *Fleet* and the *Union* were that year advised that:

> Tea is a Commodity of that Generall use here and so nicely to be managed in its package to preserve its flavour and virtue, that you cannot be too carefull therein. It being a very considerable article in the profits or loss of the Investment[,] wherefore be sure buy of the freshest and best sorts . . . We have found of late the Chest Tea has prov'd better than that in Tubs occasiond as some think from the quantity pack'd up in a Chest, which holds more than a Tubb . . . Keep the Tea in the Coolest places of the Ship . . . [and] open the Hatches in fair Weather to give it air as often as you have opportunity.[24]

The required investments detail relative quantities of 'singlo' (the standard-grade green tea), 'bing' (or elsewhere 'imperial', a finer grade green tea) and 'bohee' (referring to darker, semi-oxidized leaves). These terms became – from around the time of the *Stretham*'s voyage – a part of the conventional nomenclature of the tea trade. The practical expertise and vocabulary necessary for a trade in the leaves of the tea shrub were clearly in place before the first decade of the eighteenth century had ended, established via a quickly growing rate of importation which had (on the one hand)

Marginal notes (left side, fragmentary):

m Mr Price's death
pra Cargo
, and Mr

Invoice of
d to your ~
Copy of our
s you will
n the ~

agement of
mounto ~
y be most
keeping a
enough to
t would be
hat freight

for taking
nd from
to apply ~
and inviting
tructions ~
with the ~
it run your
of all the
aide and ~

are and ~
We would ~
your expe
antage ~
een of each
lly y richest
our to furnish

to observe y
provided
here not ~
ments appro
wisment to
or sorts which

you

Inner margin notes:

and will turn to most accot

Provide no Goods of English pattern

Buy 300 Pt odd fashion silks or Gold or silver stuff

Fill up y Pallating with China Ware stowed by needfull props.

Enlarge in China Ware to stiffen your ship and fill up

Increase the Tea to 100 Tubs

how to pack up & preserve it

Buy 4 or 5 Tons of Raw silk if cheap

Fill up with Lacker'd boards

Body text (17th-century hand, best reading):

you shall find to been a much greater value then expected Our Principall aim
in giving you this Liberty being to give a scope to your fancy in providing such
Goods as may turn us to best Account not knowing how Markets there may
vary before your Arrivall /

We would have you in your whole Investment to provide such sorts of silk
whose works may be according to the fancy of the Country, and as much diffe-
ring as possible from our English Patterns, and then it is not much matter
of what work they are /

As soon as you can with Convenience, We would have you search all or as
many of the shops in Amoy as possible, and buy up here and there 5, or 6 or
more peices of any sorts of Gold or Silver stuff or other silks of any odd or old
fashion, so they be fresh and strong, that you never saw before or never were
sent to England, 300 peices in the whole, the cheapest you can gett /

We would have you in the first Place to take care, that the ships pallating
be filled up as tight as possible with course usefull China Ware instead
of Ballast and so secured by Timbers and needfull props, as to be out of danger of being broken by the setling of the weighty Goods above, and the ships
labouring at Sea /

We are sensible, that what we have hitherto ordered is not sufficient to
compleat your ships Tonnage, And it is not for our advantage to have any va-
cant room, when freights and Demorage are at such excessive rates and therefore
if you should not be able to procure all the sorts of Kintlage Goods mentiond in
the said List or that you have not enough to stiffen your ship and make her sail
worthy, in such case you may enlarge in China Ware, but be sure it be of the finest
best painted and usefullest sorts possible /

You may also encrease the number of your Tubs of Tea to 100, so as you
take care it be well packed up in Tutenague as close as possible, and then wrapt up
in the leaves of the Country, and put into good Tubs so close as to preserve it from
all sorts of scents, which it is very subject to imbibe to the rendering it of very
little value by the time it comes here, and to be sure let it be of the very best sort
and the newest can be gott, allwayes remembring in this and all other Commodities
that the worst payes as much freight as the best, and here we must remind you, y
you doe by no means put up any Tea in Chests made of Camphire wood, neither
suffer any Camphire or Camphire wood, or any other such like strong scents to
come within the ship, lest you spoil all the Tea, that is near them, and for the
like reason, let no Tea be put in any sweet wood Chest or in small Potts nor in
any Potts or tutenague, till well assured the smell of the soldering Oyle or any
other scents are perfectly removed /

You may enlarge your raw silk to 4 or 5 Tons, if you find it so cheap as to
turn to a good Account here, but take great care it be well stowed in the ship
for otherwise being a bulky Commodity the very freight will eat out again part
of the expected profit /

What Tonnage shall yet remain to be compleated you may partly supply w[th]
some more boards, lacquered Boards on both sides fitt for Skreens and Pannells to
be done by the best Artists, and of the finest Lacker & works procurable, or else

being

Printed caption at bottom:

'Instructions for Mr Charles Price, Supra Cargo of the Ship Amity bound for Amoy in China, and Mr John Hillar his Assistant', 1696, manuscript. Taken from the East India Company's 'Despatches to the East' letter books, which contain fair copies of the formal instructions accompanying each trading voyage. These instructions, directed to the supercargoes of the ship *Amity*, detail the required investments in 'the very finest and best sorts of China Goods'. The Company's directors specify in detail the manner in which the various tea varieties are to be conveyed to London. The supercargoes are reminded that 'in this and all other Commodityes that the Worst payes as much freight as the best.'

acknowledged and (on the other) occasioned the growing domestic curiosity for this exotic commodity. The trade's growth had already acquired an irresistible momentum, and the mercantile foundations had been laid for the still little-imagined burgeoning of the British taste for tea (not to mention tea's taste for Britain) across the first half of the eighteenth century.

Make All Imaginable Haste

The principal maritime technology on which the British tea trade was to depend for the next 150 years was the 'East Indiaman', a term used in the period for any ship owned or chartered by the European East India companies. The heaviest of these vessels, built in the early nineteenth century and often weighing over 1,000 tons, would be some of the largest wooden sailing ships ever built. The *Stretham* was a more modest 350-ton frigate built on the Thames in 1700, and was typical of the ships plying the East India trade around the turn of the eighteenth century.[25] A frigate was a three-masted vessel built primarily for speed and agility. It commonly carried a deck of 30 to 40 cannon – the *Stretham* itself had 28 – an armament maintained on East India trading voyages as a defence against piracy and the actions of Britain's wartime enemies.

In February 1703, the *Stretham* – carrying over £10,000 of the Company's 'treasure' (probably in silver Spanish dollars) for its investments in the East Indies – had moved down the Thames to the Downs, a semi-sheltered roadstead in the southern part of the North Sea.[26] The ship's captain, Roger Myers, was an experienced officer who had commanded the *Stretham* on its first voyage with the Company, to Bengal, in 1700.[27] By the time the convoy of East India ships and their naval escorts had assembled (this being a time of war with France), another month had passed. China trading missions normally departed in January, so as the *Stretham* made its way through the English Channel in the last week of March 1703 – its supercargoes bearing orders to 'make all imaginable haste to Amoy for fear of losing your Passage' – it was already dangerously late in the season. As with all ships bound for the East Indies, the voyage began with a zigzag across the Atlantic: ocean currents dictated that the fastest passage to the Cape of Good Hope was achieved by striking out in a southwesterly direction across the mid-Atlantic, until islands off the coast of Brazil were sighted. From here, ships could take advantage of southeasterly currents to the Cape of Good Hope.[28] The *Stretham* crossed the equator on 21 June, beginning its southeasterly run to the Cape by the end of the first week of July. Rounding the Cape on 11 August, it set out across the Indian Ocean, maintaining the same latitude for several weeks and then heading northeast towards modern-day Indonesia. Though the prevailing winds were kind, with progress often measured at 30 nautical miles per day, it was not until 1 October that the western tip of Java was sighted. As the ship passed through the Sunda Straits between Sumatra and Java, it was still three months behind schedule. Any hope of reaching China that season faded with the passing of the southwestern monsoon, and the onset of the prevailing northeasterlies (against which progress across the South China Sea would have been practically impossible).

Missing the season's passage was a serious commercial setback for any East India trading voyage, and both Captain Myers and Christopher Brewster – the chief supercargo – would have been conscious of the potential consequences of their failure to meet the agreements they had variously signed with the Company. In an effort to make the delay as profitable as possible, Brewster and his assistants sought to take advantage of the trading opportunities that existed between these Indonesian islands and India. At Batavia (modern-day Jakarta, then the capital of the Dutch East Indies), they invested one chest of the Company's 'treasure' in a variety of exotic goods including agala (a fragrant wood), dragons' blood (an aromatic plant resin with reputed pharmaceutical properties), sugar, 'benjamin' (a perfume manufactured from the sap of the Sumatran benjamin tree) and bird of paradise feathers.[29] Startled at reports of French warships, the *Stretham* sheltered for some days in Malacca; yet this was not the most alarming of the anxieties pressing upon the ship's company. As it tentatively passed through the Straits of Malacca out into the Bay of Bengal on 27 December, the ship's journal records that 'at 4 yesterday Capn Myers departed this life having been ill some days', adding that the ship fired 22 guns as Myers was carried on shore and interred 'w.th all the Solemnity the Weat.r whold Permit, it raining and blowing very hard'.[30]

Thomas Flint – now in command – had sailed as chief mate with the *Neptune* in 1700, valuable experience for an officer on whom the heavy burden of command had unexpectedly fallen.[31] Even on less troubled voyages, the position of the captain on an East India Company voyage was delicate. He had supreme command of the ship and its officers; he was accountable to the ship's owners for the integrity of the vessel, for ensuring its safe passage, for determining its precise route and for safeguarding the lives of its crew. He had to take responsibility for the maintenance of discipline on board, for appraising reports of pirates and enemy ships and for evaluating the need for time-consuming maintenance. Moreover, he had to supervise the safe loading of the cargo for shipping back to Europe – a particular challenge when the goods in question were bulky but relatively light tea chests – and judge when the vessel was fully laden. But the captain was also responsible for delivering the commitments that the ship's owners had made to the Company, stated in an agreement known as the 'charterparty'. This specified the ports at which the ship should call, the cargos that it was to carry – in terms of tea, precise quantities of named varieties – and the basis upon which trade was to be conducted. The super-cargoes, as the Company's representatives on each voyage, enforced the terms of this agreement, and were held accountable by the Company's directors for any variation in the detail of the shipped goods. To this end, the supercargoes directing the trade of 1723 spent part of the return journey balancing their accounts, and preparing a letter to be sent to the directors 'to acquaint you of the reasons we had for Entering the Bohea Tea in the Invoices' in quantities higher than had been ordered.[32]

The *Stretham* sailed across the Bay of Bengal to Fort St George, the Company's fortified trading post at Madras (modern-day Chennai). Its arrival was noted tersely in the official consultation journal of the Fort's directors: 'the Stretham arrived the 10th Instant [that is, February] Captain Myers Dead'.[33] Soon after the ship's arrival, the journal evidences a serious failure of maritime discipline on board. Brewster and the other supercargoes lodged an official complaint against Richard Grimes, now chief mate of the ship following Flint's promotion. Grimes – they stated – was guilty of 'intolerable debauchery of all kinds', including threatening members of the ship's company, when drunk, 'that he would slitt their noses, and cutt their throats'. The situation had deteriorated to such a degree, the supercargoes represented (with telling priority), that 'it was not safe for the Comp[any]s Estate, nor for the security of the ship that he should longer continue in her'.[34] The Fort's council, representing the Company, wasted no time in dismissing Grimes from his post. Before long, the trou-bled voyage's fortunes took another hit. Worrying news was received from shipping returning from Amoy, detailing the unfavourable conditions that English merchants had recently encountered there. Eminent merchants of Madras offered their opinion that 'Canton is a much freer port [tha]n Amoy, & of quicker dispatch', opining that the 'Abuses of the Mandareens' at Amoy stood 'ready to swallow up the whole Profits of a Voyage'.[35] Once again, the *Stretham*'s supercargoes asked for the opinion of the Fort's council, whose members advised that if they had a ship of their own to send to China, 'they sh[oul]d rather choose Canton than Amoy'.[36] The instructions carried by the supercargoes gave them a contractual basis upon which they could allow the vessel to be 'forced to Canton', gesturing towards its destiny as the pre-eminent eighteenth-century tea port.

The presence in the settlement's harbour of a China-bound ship proved irresistible to an ambitious young member of the Fort's civil retinue. Charles Lockyer had been employed since September 1702 as an assistant accountant. A month after the death of the settlement's chief accountant, with the *Stretham* anchored nearby, Lockyer requested to be discharged, citing an 'Opportunity now presenting' which offered the poten-tial for increasing his 'small fortune'.[37] The Fort's council observed to the Company's London directors that 'Mr Charles Lockyer [was] discharged

13th April at his desire and went on the *Stretham* for China.'[38] With the favourable southwesterly trade winds now firmly established, the ship left Madras in mid-May with Lockyer on board, sailing back through the Straits of Malacca before pursuing a northeasterly course across the South China Sea. In early July 1704, it called briefly at the New Company's short-lived settlement at Pulo Condore (Con Son Island, off the south coast of Vietnam), where it offloaded some soldiers and their families transferred from Fort St George. These passengers were almost certainly delivered to their deaths, as the island's European settlers – including the Company's China 'President' Allen Catchpole – were massacred less than a year later.[39] At Pulo Condore the *Stretham* encountered the *Kent* and the *Eaton*, part of the next season's trading fleet, also bound for Canton. In a sure sign of things to come, the supercargoes of the *Kent* carried specific instructions to procure an immense tea cargo, the largest yet ordered for shipment to London. They were required to load nearly 90,000 pounds of singlo, 12,000 pounds of imperial and 24,000 pounds of bohea, an amount considered so vast that the Managers of the United Trade acknowledged that 'there is not a certainty of meeting with so great a quantity of Tea' in Canton. The three vessels headed northeast once again, sighting the coast of China on 6 August, coming to anchor in the mouth of the Pearl River near Macau two days later.

On your Arrival Insist upon the Following Termes

Canton, Lockyer acknowledges, had not long 'been in repute with the Company'.[40] Both Old and New Companies had invested considerable time, money and energy in vain attempts to cultivate permanent factories in China. The first attempt, in the southeastern port of Amoy in the late 1670s, was abandoned following the Old Company's perceived support of defeated Ming loyalist Zheng Jing (son and successor to the rebel military leader Zheng Chenggong).[41] Despite great hopes, New Company attempts to establish a base further north at Chusan had been abandoned at around the time of the *Stretham*'s voyage, leading to nothing except ill humour and mutual misunderstanding.[42] As for Canton, although the Old Company had occasionally attempted to trade there (most recently in 1690, when the disastrous visit of the *Defence* had ended in gunfire and death on both sides), it was the New Company which had successfully initiated trading contact with the visit of the *Macclesfield* in 1699.[43] Though there is no itemized record of its intended investments, its supercargoes carried very specific instructions to make 'Roome betwixt Decks for their Tea, since putting it in the Hold will be prejuditiall'.[44]

Following the union of the Old and New Companies agreed in April 1702, the United Company's Court of Managers dispatched four

List of Goods to be provided at Canton in China by ye Supra Cargo's of ye Kent proper for Europe

			Computatn. Computation of ye Size of Tonnage at Canton

Copper. in Barrs from Iapan or in want thereof in ye largest plates .. Sixty Tons — 60 — 2. 12. aG

Brass Cash ...... Forty Tons .... 40 — 1. 1.6oG

Quicksilver ...... Fifteen Tons .... 15 — 2.3 apouc

Vermillion ...... Five Tons .... 5 — 2.6 apouc

Tea Singlo .... Seventyfive thousand .... } 117 — 1. — }
Dr. Imperiall ... Ten thousand .... } pounds — 2. } apouc
Dr. Bohee ...... Twenty thousand .... } — 2. }

Green Ginger. ... Twenty Tons .... 20 16. —. — aG

Rubarb ...... (the finest & best pickd or none) (Six tons Computd to Cost in the) whole 6 200. —. —

We dont ty you to the Price of Rhubarb — but except you bring that which is very — fresh and new and well picked, otherwise bring none —

Peeces				
1500	Taffaties plain of One Colour Fifteen hundred pc.	2½	1. 6. — a peu
1500	Dr. Changeable ...... Fifteen hundred pc.	2½	1. 6. —
1750	Dr. Striped .... Seventeen hund & Fifty	3. —	1. 7. 9
1500	Gorgorons .... Fifteen hundred pc.	3¾	1. 8. 0
2500	Goshees Flowerd ..... Twenty five hundred p.	3. —	2. —. —
500	Sattins plain ...... Five hundred		
3000 { 1000	Dr. flowerd one Colour. One thousand } pc.	10	2. 3. 4
1500	Dr. flowerd Changeable Fifteen hundred		
500	Damask White or Goshees White Five hundred pc. —	1½	2. —. —
500	Dr. for Beds .... Five hundred pc. —	1½	2. 3. 4
1000	Pouses .... One thousand pc. —	2½	2. 5. —
2000	Hockins ye heaviest to be hd Two thousand pc. —	2	—. 2. —
1000	Masquerades .... One thousand pc. —	1¾	1. 8. 3
600	Pelongs dyed in 500 Colours Six hundred pc. —		

Silk Raw — if procureable at a cheap rate abt or under a hundred Tale a Pecul and very good to the value of Five thousand pounds Computed to be 22

ChinaWare to fill up the Vacancy.

These are the Particulars we think proper to be provided for Europe But if you shall not be able to purchase all those Sorts of Measured goods or the full quantityes of Each Sort, Or that you find some of the Species much cheaper or better than others, we allow you to encrease in such of them as you think most advantagious here, and to buy the fewer of other Sorts.

Observation

'List of Goods to be provided at Canton in China by the Supra Cargo's of the Kent, proper for Europe', 1703, manuscript. A typical early eighteenth-century 'List of Investments' annexed to the 'Instructions for the Supercargoes of the Kent'. The directors specify three types of tea here: 'Singlo' and 'Imperiall' (standard and premium green teas), and 'Bohee' (described by the British trade as 'black tea', though closer to what would be described today as 'oolong'). This darker tea represents only a fraction of the total anticipated tea purchase, suggesting the degree to which British consumption was dominated by the green varieties at this time.

ships to each of the trading centres which the two Companies had sought to cultivate (albeit with a persistent Old Company bias towards Amoy): the *Northumberland* to Chusan, the *Sidney* to Canton, and the *Stretham* and the *Mountague* to Amoy. But although the *Northumberland* traded successfully at Chusan in early 1704, the Company dispatched only two further ships from London to that port. As for Amoy, after the *Mountague*'s departure on Christmas Day 1703 it was to be 32 years before the Company made one final (abortive) attempt to trade there. The *Stretham*, as we have seen, ultimately joined the *Sidney* at Canton; Lockyer, its eloquent observer, noted approvingly that notwithstanding the directors' reluctance to relinquish their preference for Amoy, they have 'at last' chosen the 'more certain Trade of this Place [Canton], where a whole Fleet of Ships may be freighted without the least Danger of over-staying the Monsoon for a Cargo'.[45] Qing policy from this time also formalized the concentration of European shipping at Canton.[46]

Foreign ships arriving at Macau typically observed a series of formal steps ahead of the business of trade itself. Their agents would pay their respects to the authorities governing the Portuguese settlement and make contact with the representatives of the Canton customs office. These officials would conduct the chief supercargo upriver to Canton to open negotiations with the provincial customs superintendent, an individual whose title was generally transliterated as 'hoppo'. The *Stretham*'s chief supercargo successfully persuaded the hoppo's officers to perform the 'measurage' of the ship (a customs fee based on the vessel's size) while it was still anchored at Macau, a practice which Lockyer suggests gave English agents a greater bargaining power. Brewster's success in his negotiations is reflected in the reduction of the amount demanded from 1,500 'tael' to 900 (a 'tael' being a measurement of weight equivalent to about one and a third ounces, often used to signify a monetary amount based on the value of one tael of silver). The 600 tael thus saved was worth – at typical market prices in this period – over 2,000 pounds of tea.[47] The completion of these formalities was confirmed when the hoppo issued the 'chop', or permit, allowing the ship to proceed into the Pearl River. The ship's commander would arrange for a Macau pilot to come aboard for the nerve-wracking passage through the shallow waters of the delta, often with scores of sampans marking the narrow channel of deeper water.[48]

When the *Stretham* came to rest in the deep water anchorage to the south of Whampoa Island on 24 August – the furthest point that such ships could safely reach – the *Sidney* (in whose company the *Stretham* had left the Downs) was resting there, having also missed its intended passage to China the previous October.[49] Forewarned about the difficulty of trade that season, the *Stretham*'s agents wasted little time in transferring by pinnace the final 12 miles upriver to Canton and in renting a factory. Unfortunately for the recently arrived supercargoes, they discovered that they been beaten by their great commercial rivals, the Dutch East-India Company. As a result, 'goods were [priced] very high', with 'Tea scarce and in great demand for Batavia, as well by the junks bound thereto, as by the Dutch Ship sent on purpose to buy that commodity'.[50] Much depended on securing the assistance of the most influential local merchant firms, or 'hongs'. Even at this early stage in the China trade, certain hongs were developing considerable repute with the English supercargoes.[51] Lockyer recommended that supercargoes should 'find out one or two of the best Merchants (whose Names must be learnt from the last Ships that were there, before you go out) to be directed in what is further necessary', though he is prepared to recommend 'Linqua', 'Anqua' and 'Pinqua' as honest men 'for *Chinese*'.[52] Linqua and Anqua were to be the pre-eminent Canton merchants until the early 1720s.[53]

The supercargoes of the *Stretham* carried with them a generic set of instructions from the Company's directors, which contained a warning that

> The Chineeses are a subtill Cunning People and are very dexterous in putting Cheats upon all that Deal with them and must be managed accordingly, However they love to be respected & you must therefore carry your selves in such manner as not to affront them and yet to avoid being Cheated.[54]

Lockyer's *Account* makes it clear that it was not only the merchants who fell under suspicion. The linguists are 'all sharpers', those provisioning the ships (known by the Portuguese term *comprador*) are 'Knaves'; supercargoes are advised that they 'must expect to be daily visited by the greatest Sharpers in China' with goods to sell. Common tricks reported by Lockyer include the use of light weights in the measuring of commodities; rigged balances with arms of unequal length; distraction techniques (such as staged fights) to allow goods to be stolen from the factory; imitation chests and canisters with a smaller capacity than appearances would suggest; and the substitution of the contracted cargo for worthless items during the transfer from wharf to ship. Tea cargoes were vulnerable to unique threats. Good-quality leaves at the top of a chest might disguise a generally substandard consignment. Moreover, merchants at the beginning of a trading season often sought to mix fresh tea with the stale leaves left over from the previous year.

As a relatively new cargo, the question of how to judge the quality of the teas being offered for sale by the hong merchants was of particular concern. For the darker bohea leaves, Lockyer advises that:

> There are several ways to know the good from the bad; but in general the Judgment of the Buyer must direct. It ought to smell

and tast[e] well, look all of a colour, and be very dry, crisp, and brittle. In hot Water the best opens soonest, and the oftener it colours it, the stronger and better it is. Small black Leaves, and Dirt among it, are Signs of a bad sort.[55]

Supercargoes evaluating the green teas offered for sale were advised to 'chew it' and then observe the colour: 'the more it excels in Greenness the better it is'. Alternatively, different batches of tea could simultaneously be steeped in individual containers of hot water; that 'which holds

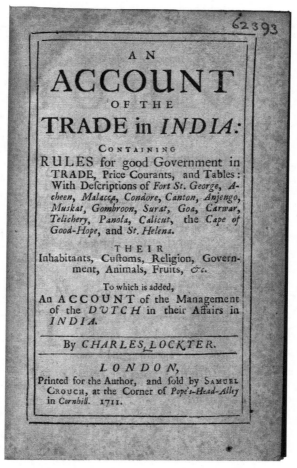

Charles Lockyer, title page from *An Account of the Trade in India* (London, 1711). Lockyer's *Account* was the first detailed description of the British trade with China (though, as its long title indicates, the business transacted in Canton forms only a small part of the book's wider interests). Throughout the eighteenth century, writers frequently used the generalized term 'India' (or – more specifically – 'East India') to refer to a vast swath of southern Asia, reaching from the South Asian subcontinent across the Malay peninsula and the Indonesian islands, and into China.

longest of a pale Amber Colour may justly be preferr'd; for the worst turns brownish'.[56] The real value of Lockyer's instructions may have been – aside from any genuine means of qualitative assessment – the provision of a series of practical, semi-theatrical steps by which European merchants might perform their 'expert' knowledge of the commodity, in a manner akin to an amateur wine connoisseur swirling a glass of claret and declaiming its colour, nose and bouquet.

The supercargoes of 1704 would nevertheless have been grateful for any tea, of any quality. Having initially been told that there was no tea for sale, the *Kent*'s supercargoes were finally able to acquire limited supplies of bohee and singlo, some of it shipped overland from Amoy, some of it requisitioned by the Canton authorities from the cargoes of the local Chinese junk trade (as the taxes raised from European cargoes ultimately made them more attractive to the provincial government). As the season drew to its close, the supercargoes had to conclude that 'finding we are not likely to come near our quantity of Singlo, nor to get any imperial Tea, makes us take all the goods we can get of any sort'.[57] Loading the contracted cargo onto the *Stretham* was complete by the end of the second week of December 1704; the supercargoes applied to the hoppo for the final chop allowing the ship's dispatch (when the final reckoning in terms of customs fees, and additional 'presents', would be levied). The ship's journal for 16 December records that 'our Supracargos and Passengers came down from Canton haveing Dispacht there business.' With the final chop in hand, Thomas Flint was again able to take on board a local pilot to guide the ship back to the deeper waters at the river mouth.

The *Stretham* sailed from Whampoa in company with the *Sidney* and the *Eaton* on 17 December, a little under four months after its arrival. As the ships manoeuvred over the first sandbar, they exchanged a nine-gun salute with the *Kent*, whose supercargoes were still struggling to complete the tea investments expected by the Company. Delayed further by the five-day celebration of the new year (13–18 January 1705), it was early February before the *Kent* finally reached the open water of the South China Sea once again. It carried just over 13 tons of bohea (more than had been ordered), but rather less than 12 tons of singlo (not much more than a third of the 33 tons its supercargoes had been told to procure), and no imperial at all.[58] By total weight, this represented less than 60 per cent of the anticipated investment. It was nevertheless still the largest tea cargo that the East India Company had ever shipped. The supply problems that the supercargoes encountered on the ground in Canton evidence the fierce competition between the various European companies courting the attention of tea; but they also suggest that the local supply chain, from farmers to hongs, was taken by surprise by the sudden increase in demand.

Detail of a 'Famille rose' punchbowl showing the western trading stations along the Canton waterfront, c. 1785, porcelain. This bowl, produced in China for the European market, depicts shallow 'sampans' at the Canton harbourside, before the warehouses and storage facilities associated with the European trade. Chinese merchants are identified by their hats and fans, whereas their European counterparts clutch staffs.

Notwithstanding its late departure from Canton, the *Kent* completed its return voyage long before the *Stretham*. Its arrival in Ireland was announced in London's *Daily Courant* on 3 October 1705, and it dropped anchor in the Thames on 20 November.[59] The *Stretham*'s journey home was less eventful than its outbound voyage; nevertheless, having reached the Straits of Malacca once again by mid-January 1705, it was detained for over a year on various matters of internal Indian trade, only passing the Cape of Good Hope on its journey back to London on 23 June 1706. Passing by St Helena in August, it finally returned to its port of departure in March 1707, after a period of some four years. It was to make two further voyages for the East India Company: to Madras and Bengal (1708–10), and once again to Canton (1712–14). It was probably then scrapped: four transoceanic voyages were generally considered to represent the lifespan of even the most seaworthy of East Indiamen.

Forced to Canton

Over its twelve years of active service as an East Indiaman, the *Stretham* witnessed the consolidation of a regular British tea trade at Canton. By then, the contexts for mercantile exchange had become well established. The supercargoes travelling with a season's shipping convened as an ad hoc 'council' (later formalized as the Company's 'Select Committee in Canton'), providing strategic and commercial oversight for each vessel's voyage. Building on the early knowledge recorded by Charles Lockyer, they quickly acquired significant expertise in terms of dealing with local officials, evaluating the quality of tea cargoes, cutting deals with merchants with whom they built ongoing relationships of trust and mutual respect, and troubleshooting the various unexpected twists that delicate matters of international trade and diplomacy occasioned.

The 'supercargoes journals' – a more or less complete archive from 1720 onwards – detail the everyday challenges of East India trading which supercargoes were required to manage. Matters of stowage and lading led them into difficult exchanges with the captains of East Indiamen anxious about the trim of their vessel, or the amount of water being 'drawn' (in other words, how low the ship was lying in the water). With a fortnight of loading still ahead, the *Macclesfield* – trading at Canton in 1724 – was lying so low that it was agreed that the ship needed to use the high spring tides to cross the two sandbars and complete the stowage of cargo in the deep water close to Macau.[60] When Daniel Small, in command of the *Duke of Cambridge*, advised the supercargoes council of 1723 that we 'cannot receive more goods on board without running the Risque of the whole', he was warned darkly that 'We must, and do, by these presents, acquaint you in the name and for the account of the Hon.ble United East India Company that yourself and owners are answerable for all losses that may accrue to the said Company by your breach of this article in your Charterparty.'[61] The ever-changing circumstances of taxation, measurage and other forms of financial claim made upon the British merchants by linguists, compradors, the hoppo and his officers required considerable and ongoing attention.

Occasionally, more strenuous diplomacy with higher provincial or imperial officials was required. This typically concerned matters of discipline (such as in 1722 when the gunner's mate of the *King George*, attempting to shoot a duck, fatally wounded a fifteen-year-old local boy).[62] At other times, the council was moved to make official complaints to these 'Superiour

Mandarines' about unfair local trading practices, such as when ships arriving for the 1721 season were informed 'of a Combination or Company the Merchants of this Place have erected themselves into'.[63] The supercargoes noted in their journal that bohea and singlo had been set at 'so exorbitant Prices as we can by no means come into, & as yet can see no probability of lowering them unless we can find some means to destroy this Combination of the Merchants'.[64] After a few days of brinkmanship, during which the supercargoes refused to enter any kind of arrangement for completing the formalities associated with commencing trade, the intervention of the provincial viceroy (the 'Chuntuck') resulted in victory for the supercargoes and those local merchants who had refused to affiliate to the 'Combination'.

It was nevertheless the availability of tea in the quantities and varieties ordered by the Court of Directors that remained the single greatest challenge for those responsible for acquiring the loose-leaf cargoes. Already anxious about securing their departure from Canton in good time to be assured of their passage back to the Cape of Good Hope, William Fazerkerley – chief supercargo of the council directing the trade of the ships of 1723 – recorded in his 'consultations' for 16 December that:

> We have been often pressing our merch^t Suqua to make what possible haste he could in the delivery of the Remaind.^{r} of the Teas we had contracted with him for urging that it now began to grow late and that it was high time to bring every thing to a Conclusion[.] We agreed with him the nett weights of the Teas he had deliver'd and found he was still indebted to us about fifteen hundred peculls [about 200,000 pounds] of the Bohea[.] He then told us that he had about one thousand more by him and that was all of our Contract that he had procur'd[.] that if we press'd him he must find the rest but he believ'd it would be difficult to find any that was good and that if he did we must wait some considerable time for it.[65]

Further negotiation led to the supercargoes accepting a smaller amount of a higher quality tea called 'congou' in place of the missing bohea, though Fazerkerley was clearly of the view that the merchants' knowledge of the ship's dependency on the northeasterly monsoon for the passage back to the Cape had placed him in a position of considerable weakness in concluding this arrangement. No sooner had this matter been resolved, a new – rather more delicate – issue arose, demanding Fazerkerley's diplomatic tact. One of the hoppo's officers had spotted a decorative clock on one of the ships, a privately owned trinket that the owner wished to sell (at profit) to a Canton merchant. The hoppo had other ideas: he wanted to send the clock to the emperor as a present; the ship was not to be granted its 'chop' permitting departure until the clock was surrendered. Anxious to avoid a delay to their departure, the supercargoes council decided to hand over the clock, having first purchased it at a fair price from its owner. The chop was accordingly provided; but as the ships were leaving, the clock was returned with no explanation. Shaking their heads wearily, we may imagine, the super-cargoes acknowledged that 'now we had neither time nor opportunity to dispose of it but to a great loss'. Nothing further remaining, the super-cargoes formally committed the East Indiamen back into the open ocean: 'We desire and order you to proceed with all Convenient speed for the Port of London where you go consigned to the Hon[oura]ble the Court of Directors of the United Company of Merchants of England Trading to the East Indies, heartily wishing you a safe arrivale thither.'[66]

FOUR

The Elevation of Tea

By the turn of the eighteenth century, tea was no longer an exotic and unfamiliar commodity in Britain, but was increasingly available in grocers' shops, as well as 'Indian' warehouses, China shops, coffeehouses, pleasure gardens and a host of diverse retail spaces. Although still expensive, tea was becoming more accessible to women and men of the middling stations of life. Tea, it seems, had arrived. But although tea was now readily available, it was still rather mysterious. What did tea mean? There were those who could tell you what it did to you: doctors, physicians, natural philosophers and botanists offered advice and research about the physiological properties of tea (as we will see in the next chapter). There were those who could tell you where it came from and how much it cost, including merchants, traders and shopkeepers. But in the new century, there was no agreement about the cultural meaning of tea or its history. The battle to understand tea in the first decades of the eighteenth century was a contest between rival poets and satirists, between tea lovers and tea haters, between those who saw this new beverage as a sign of corruption and the decay of values and those who saw it as a reforming peaceful supplement, the harbinger of civility. Through this dispute over the meaning of tea, new scripts were devised for its description, consumption and social purpose. And by this process, tea was elevated, but also domesticated: it was given a new British mythology.

Essaying Tea

The most important statement of the new English knowledge of tea was offered in 1699 by the clergyman John Ovington (1658–1731). Following his education at Trinity College, Dublin, and St John's College, Cambridge, Ovington was appointed chaplain to an East India Company ship on a voyage to India. Arriving in Bombay (Mumbai) during the monsoon in 1690, Ovington was less than impressed, finding the English factory there overwhelmed by 'Luxury, immodesty, and a prostitute dissolution of manners'. After a stay of several months, Ovington enthusiastically moved north to Surat, a port in Gujarat that had been ceded to England in the dowry of Catherine of Braganza in 1662. He remained there for two and a half years as the chaplain to the English factory, living in some splendour in the castle with the president, Bartholomew Harris. Surat was a rich and prosperous city, 'reckon'd the most fam'd Emporium of the Indian Empire, where all Commodities are vendible.'[1] With much time on his hands, Ovington composed an account of his experiences there, particularly among the Hindu, Muslim and Parsi communities. When he returned to London in 1693, his account of his travels, entitled *A Voyage to Suratt in the Year 1689*, created a very favourable view of the East India Company and its trading prospects. Through this success, Ovington found preferment in the Anglican church, being appointed both a chaplain to the king and to the living of St Margaret's, Lee, a wealthy parish in Greenwich, London.

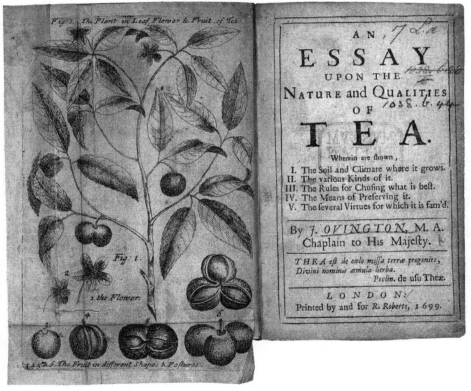

John Ovington, frontispiece and title page from *An Essay Upon the Nature and Qualities of Tea* (London, 1699). John Ovington was the chaplain to the East India Company's factory at Surat from 1690 to 1693, where he learned about tea from local Bania merchants and a Mandarin ambassador from China. On his return to London, Ovington published the first extended study of tea and its properties in English.

In Surat, Ovington had spent much time with the Bania (Bannians as he knew them), a Gujarati caste or community of merchants and traders who operated an extensive commercial system offering banking, intermediation, money-lending and financial services for both English factors and their Indian counterparts. The principal trade of Surat was silk and other textiles, but they also dealt in spices, pepper and diamonds. Through the Bania, Ovington also gained some knowledge of Surat's inter-regional trade with Siam (Thailand), China and Japan. Describing the food and comestibles of Surat, he offered an account of their *dol* (dal or lentils), and *dahi* (yoghurt), and made much of their love of tea, which he described as 'a common Drink with all the inhabitants of *India*, as well *Europeans* as Natives; and by the *Dutch* is used as such a standing Entertainment, that the Tea-Pot's seldom off the Fire, or unimploy'd'. Ovington observed that tea was 'agreeable' despite the heat of the climate, and was also an effective remedy, 'prevailing against the Headach, Gravel, and Griping in the Guts'. He said ''tis generally drunk in *India*, either with Sugar-Candy, or, by, the more curious, with small conserv'd Lemons . . . The *Chinese* among whom the Tea grows, take abundance of this Drink before their Meals, and are generally very plump and in very good likeing.' Though not a medicine exactly, Ovington observed that tea was conducive to a healthy life. Ovington was also a witness to the visit of a Chinese embassy, led by a 'Mandarine', a high-level envoy from Liampó (Ningbo) – an important Portuguese trading port close to the tea growing districts in the Fukien (Fujian) mountains. The emissary, Ovington says, 'brought with him several kinds of tea', which excited a great rivalry among those in the English factory. Some of the emissary's tea, he said with incredulity, was 'so valuable in *China* that a single Catte [a measure of weight equal to about 625 grams] of it was reputed a noble Present for the chief Ministers, and it was very rarely to be found, however he brought with him a Taste of it for our President, among several other kinds wherein he gave him a Morning Entertainment.'[2]

Ovington never went to China. But through his encounters with the Mandarin, and an unnamed 'Learned Physician, who had for some years lived in China', he fashioned himself into a man who know about tea: probably the most knowledgeable in Britain when he returned home. When he published his travels, he was the first to recognize that tea came in a number of distinct grades and preparations. Ovington described how there were three sorts of tea

that grew there, and were most frequently drunk among them, viz. Bing, Singlo, and Bohe. Bohe is a small Leaf and very young, and by its moisture, upon the score of its under-growth, requires more than an ordinary frixure [roasting], which makes it acquire that blackness visible in it, and which discolours the Water to a kind of Redness. The second is Singlo, which is a larger Leaf, because more grown. The third, which is Bing, is the largest of all; and is in *China* of a proportionable larger rate than the other two. Singlo obtains most among the *Europeans*; but Bohe among the *Chinese* has so much esteem and precedence above the other two, that in their Sickness they totally forbid them, but in their most dangerous Distempers instantly make use of this; and Experience convinces them of this Choice and Utility of that Leaf in their Extremities.[3]

Ovington offers here the first distinctive description of kinds of tea, specifying two forms of green tea, bing and singlo, and one 'red' tea, bohea. The physician gave some further evidence about the shrub from which tea was harvested, and the manner in which it was prepared. 'The Leaf is first green, but is made crisp and dry by frying twice, or oftener, in a Pan; and as often is taken off the Fire it is roll'd with the Hand upon a Table, till it curls.'[4] This was all new information in London, and valuable to the Company, to natural philosophers and to consumers.

In 1699, Ovington consolidated his renown as the tea expert in London by publishing a small octavo pamphlet entitled *An Essay upon the Nature and Qualities of Tea*.[5] This was an innovative attempt to methodize all English knowledge of tea by combining the available commercial, natural-philosophical, medical and moral discourse. It no doubt served a selfish purpose too, currying favour with the East India Company, which granted him a perquisite (as it had for his earlier books). At least one tea trader thought Ovington's pamphlet a useful advertisement for his products. A copy in the Huntington Library in California, once owned by a woman called Elizabeth Walter, contains a manuscript inscription stating that 'Richard Raper att ye Bell & Lyon next Mercer's Hall Cheapside sells all sorts of theas coffee & chocolett.'[6] The pamphlet also promoted his name among the royal court. Ovington dedicated his work to Countess Henrietta van Ouwerkerk of Grantham (d. 1724), the beautiful young wife of Hendrik van Nassau van Ouwerkerk (1672–1754), recently created the Earl of Grantham. The countess was well known for her forward-thinking taste and her love of oriental fashions. Ovington's address flatters her that

> 'Tis from Your innate Goodness only, and that condescending Temper which is so remarkable in You, that this Foreign Leaf dares presume to court Your Favour, and hope for a welcome Entertainment. For where can a Stranger, that was always bred among a People the most polite of any in the World, expect a kind Reception with more Assurance, than from a Person, whose Conversation is adorn'd with all that Civility that even China it self can boast of?[7]

Ovington figures tea itself as a 'tender leaf' courting the favour of the countess, personified as a stranger long-bred among a polite and civilized people, now seeking a 'kind Reception' among people who are similarly polite and civilized. Using the conventional language of compliment expected in a dedication, Ovington reinforces the association of tea with elite court culture.

For Ovington, tea itself is civilized and civilizing: there is nothing barbarous or corrupting about its approach to the British palate. This chimes with the wider 'discovery' of Chinese civilization in European philosophy and history in the late seventeenth century. Reports from expeditions, missions and trading voyages convinced European courts of the great extent and prosperity of the Chinese empire, of the sophistication and complexity of its culture and its extended and stable history. This posed a theological problem, for European scholars were forced to recognize that while China had a certified history extending back to the biblical era, the Bible – which supposedly offered a complete historical account of the world – took no notice of it. All this was greatly troubling to European historians, for they had habitually imagined Europe's encounter with the wider world as part of a narrative of civilizing Christian expansionism in which the heathen barbarism of the foreign knelt before European superiority, receiving the doubled benediction of colonization and Christianity. This narrative simply did not work in the case of China. Ovington's depiction of tea as a courtly emissary from this ancient and civilized culture who demanded respect and prestige reflects this impasse.

Ovington was clearly an avid student of Chinese history and of its luxury products, porcelain and tea among them. The purpose of his *Essay*, Ovington said, was to enhance the quality of information known about tea: it was an 'Account of its *Nature* and *Qualities*, to satisfy such as are its curious Admirers with the Knowledge of its Use'. This reflected his sense that there was increased demand for the product in Britain, where tea drinking was, he thought, widespread among scholars, merchants and courtiers. Having gained 'a singular Repute', tea deserved better treatment. Ovington offered more detailed information than that in his *Voyage to Suratt*, on tea cultivation, harvesting and manufacture, and on the varieties of tea. In the polite form of an essay pamphlet, Ovington sought to extend such knowledge to a wider non-scholarly audience.

In his tea curiosity, Ovington knew he was not entirely alone in London. There was a small group of people who were interested in knowledge about tea, and who possessed the critical language to make sophisticated judgments. The culture of the tea connoisseur was satirized in 1693 in a comedy by Thomas Southerne titled *The Wives Excuse*. Southerne depicts a foppish connoisseur, Mr Friendall, who has a taste for all sorts of rarified luxuries: not only strange teas, but rare wines and exotic snuffs. In his desire to appear fashionable, Friendall asks his women friends to take tea with him in 'the Fresko of the Garden' (cod-Italian for in the open air). He offers them a range of teas: 'The plain *Canton*, the *Nanquin*, *Bohe*, the *Latheroon*, the *Sunloe*, or which?' The women appear not to know or care which tea they have, and Friendall decides eventually on the 'the *Bohe*', explaining that '*My Bohe*, at the best hand too, Cost me Ten Pound a Pound.'[8] As Southerne's satire indicates, although there was some sophisticated knowledge about tea in London in the early 1690s, this was considered by others as obscure, esoteric and foolish: one of the fashionable learned follies in an age of luxury and corruption.

After Ovington's essay was published, British consumers became more adept at describing the different types of tea. While in the 1690s, tea merchants described their best wares in advertisements as 'extraordinary superfine Tea', by the first decade of the eighteenth century, East India Company sales were beginning to specify different parcels of 'Fine Singlo Tea' and 'Bohee Tea', and to note the difference between 'Green Tea' and 'Bohea Tea'.[9] By 1712, sales registered tea in five categories: bohea, pekoe, bing, congou and singlo; and by 1738, John Clarke, a grocer in Warwick-Lane in the City of London, was advertising a 'great Choice of the very finest and freshest Teas of all Sorts, viz. Hyson, Hissoon, Outchaine, Congo, Imperial, Powkae, Singlo, Pekoe, And all other sorts of Green and Bohea Teas'.[10] These distinctions, between teas of different manufacture and origin, and increasingly complex variety of flavour, aroma and appearance, reflected a growing sophistication in the market for tea, and also reflect greater curiosity about kinds of tea and modes of description and appreciation – although, as chapter Six explains, these English tea kinds bore little or no relation to Chinese taxonomies. It was in the nature of tea to seek out more sophisticated customers and reward them with both nuanced flavour and refined knowledge. The growth of a language of connoisseurship for tea is then part of its elevation out of the ordinary.

The Exaltation of Tea

Having made an entry into the English market as a polite and well-bred stranger, tea began to make itself at home. The 'tender leaf' underwent a course of interpolation, a complex process of analysis and description by physicians and natural philosophers, and by merchants and traders. But the imaginative reconstruction of tea was also undertaken within the cultural domain by poets, satirists, essayists and painters. The work of these men and women elevated and glorified tea by consolidating its association with elite culture, especially the world of high-status women, and further re-imagining it as a prestigious product associated with peace, refined sociability and the polite arts of conversation. A series of cultural productions, mostly poems, but also essays, plays and paintings, reiterated tea's high-society associations by elevating it to the gods, where it was the cherished favourite of the heavenly tea-table. This apotheosis re-focused attention on the earthly habits of taking tea, finding in the tea-table's circle of conversation and friendship an ideal of sociable equality.

The exaltation of tea (its elevation in authority, dignity and prestige) had begun already with Ovington's *Essay upon Tea*, which sported an epigram from Johann Pechlin's treatise on tea, *Theophilus Bibaculus, sive de Potu Theae Dialogus*, published in Frankfurt in 1684. Pechlin's epigram, translated as 'Tea is sent from heaven to the races of the earth, a herb equal to its sacred name', repeats the influential macaronic pun on the word 'Thea', deliberately confusing the word 'goddess' in Greek ('Thea') with the word used to mean 'tea' in early modern scientific Latin ('Thea').[11] Locke's friend Philip van Limborch, in his *Cento* poem on tea, also made use of this pun, mixing up the words 'tea' and 'thea' to make his poem work. English poets took the pun to new levels by reimagining it as a social and spatial construct, literally rethinking tea as the beverage of the gods. In the first four decades of the eighteenth century, a series of tea exaltation poems, published by poets both established and new, effectively consolidated tea within its own systems of meaning in British culture for the first time.

The first in this series of poems was entitled *Panacea: A Poem upon Tea: in Two Cantos*, published by Nahum Tate in May 1701 (although the title page stated 1700). Tate was the Poet Laureate, appointed by William III in 1693. He had already shown interest in the potential for using poetry to explore the origin of things: in 1686 he had translated a Latin epic poem by the Veronese physician Girolamo Fracastoro (1478–1553), *Syphilis; or, A Poetical History of the French Disease*, a poem first published in 1530 which described the origins of syphilis and the discovery of its cure. Fracastolo's invention poem inspired Tate to see the creative potential in poems on things. Tate was also a good friend of John Ovington, offering commendatory verses to his *Voyage to Suratt* in 1696, commending his 'search of Nature':

> Through her vast Book the World, a curious Eye
> May Wonders in each pregnant Page descry,
> Make new Remarks, which Reason may reduce
> To Humane benefit, and Publick Use.[12]

Both Ovington and his patrons in the East India Company would have praised and encouraged Tate's patriotic labours in commending the commodity in verse.

Tate's poem describes the historical origin of tea and the tea trade in Britain by appropriating and inventing complex mythological analogies for both. In the introductory verses, Tate recommends tea as an appropriate beverage for intellectually inclined people: his list includes statesmen, lawyers, physicians, natural philosophers, scholars, musicians and painters. For each of these kinds of men – the sons of muses – tea is proposed as a palliative and an inspiration. In Tate's verses, 'carousing in tea' is likened to supping from the Castalian spring, the magical fountain at Delphi that metaphorically inspired the poets of ancient Rome. The speaker of the first canto is a Wiltshire shepherd called Palæmon, a poetical name that recalls a shepherd in Virgil's *Pastorals*. Driven by curiosity, Palæmon has travelled the world, and, recalling Ovington, has returned to England with praise for the refined and civilized Chinese, bringing with him information and curiosities, including tea from China. Inviting his fellow 'swains' back to his 'grotto', Palæmon serves them tea, apostrophizing the 'genial liquor' in its silver tea urn and porcelain cups of Chinese origin. As his guests enjoy the tea and its physiological effects, Palæmon offers them an account of its origin: a 'charming history' of 'how this rare Plant at first Divinely sprung'.[13] Tate shows his awareness of Ovington's tea knowledge, versifying the cultivation of his three kinds of tea in China:

> There bloom'd the SOUMBLO, there Imperial TEA,
> (Names then unknown) and Sanative BOHE;
> All deem'd, in Honour to the Prophet's Shrine,
> Produc'd with Virtue, like their Birth, Divine,
> And sent a timely Cure of Publick Grief.[14]

As if this was not enough to assuage the hunger for tea knowledge, in the second edition, Tate added a nine-page prose appendix, 'An Account of the Nature and Virtues of Tea', loosely translating and redacting information from Pechlin's Latin treatise *De Potu Theae* (1684) and Ovington's *Essay*. With the supplement's survey of the available medical knowledge of tea, Tate's poem was now a complete guide to tea.

The two cantos of Tate's poem give separate accounts of the origin of tea. The first relates a tale borrowed from ancient Chinese history of a ruler known as King Ki; the second innovates by relocating the invention story to Graeco-Roman mythology. In the first canto, Ki rules the state with absolute authority, promoting sycophants and favourites, and devoting his time to pleasure, dissipation and displays of 'frantic Vice' and the 'Pomp of luxury' (such as bathing in a pool of wine). He rejects the advice of a loyal Mandarin officer who tries to warn him of the degraded state of the empire. Eventually the whole business of the imperial court is given over to nothing but 'Banquets, Music, Masques and Mimic Sport'. Finally, under the influence of a concubine called Amira, Ki removes himself to a specially constructed pleasure palace illuminated by ever-blazing lamps, where he

Nicolaes Aartman, *Interior with Company Drinking Tea*, c. 1740, pencil on paper. This drawing by the Dutch artist Aartman depicts a mixed group of men and women socializing over tea, assembled around a table in a large and well-appointed room. Tea drinking was especially associated with polite behaviour and conversation amongst women and men in the upper echelons of society in the eighteenth century.

riots in excess and enchantment night and day. In rebellion against Ki's excesses, the army eventually rises up and overthrows his rule. In Tate's verse history, the grateful but impoverished nation then solicit Confucius in his hermit's cave, who reveals to the people the healthful properties of tea. Tea restores health, contentment and prosperity to the land.

As Tate says in the preface to the poem, 'The Tale in the First *Canto* of this Poem was taken (as Romantick as it may seem) from the *Chinese History*, and, with very modest Fiction, accommodated to my Subject; to make the Discovery and production of the TEA-TREE more wonderful and surprizing.'[15] Tate's source for the tale of Ki is Louis-Daniel Le Comte's *Memoirs and Observations [of] the Empire of China*, published in London in 1697, translated from the French edition of 1696.[16] Le Comte's history is derived from his research in Chinese scholarship encountered during his extended sojourn in China as a member of the Jesuit mission. He details how Ki – a monarch now known as Jie, the seventeenth and last ruler of the Xia Dynasty (2100–1600 BCE) – was a tyrant who abused royal power, gave himself up to debauchery and was eventually overthrown. In memory of his fall, Le Comte explains, the Chinese celebrate an annual lantern festival. Tate's poem borrows many details from Le Comte's account of Ki, including his construction of a stately pleasure dome in his garden in which he spent days in libidinous riot with his concubines.

Tate's depiction of Ki further suggests an analogy between the history of China and of Britain: the overthrow of a royal ruler given over to riot and debauchery at court was strongly reminiscent of the Revolution of 1688, in which James II was deposed by William and Mary. Tate's representation of the act of rebellion against Ki recalls the Whig apologists for the revolution, who wanted both to justify their overthrow of a reigning monarch and to legitimate the resulting political settlement. According to Tate, the Chinese conspirators combine as friends of the 'Publick Good', and their 'Revolution' overthrows the king with peaceful ease.

> The conscious Prince from Empire thus retir'd,
> And all besides of Royal Race expir'd,
> The *Mandarins* assemble, to create
> A Monarch, to Reform and Rule the State.[17]

The new monarch is depicted as bringing reform and peace to the grateful nation. Confucius's gift of tea – a pacific and calming drink – is the appropriate beverage to heal the wounds of oppression and mend society. Tate's use of this 'Chinese' history moves beyond mere ornament: the canto celebrates tea as the Whig national champion, appropriate to the Whig ideology of polite and congenial virtue.

In his second canto, Tate offers a second mythic origin for tea, translated from Chinese history to classical myth. Tate imagines tea as the subject of a contest among the gods of classical Roman mythology, meeting at Jove's palace on Mount Olympus, as to which among them would be patron of tea. The neoclassical setting is ironic: like all of the modern hot beverages, tea was unknown to the classical world. A series of goddesses advance to state their case: Juno, as queen of the gods, claims her right to tea as the 'Queen of Plants'. Minerva, goddess of wisdom and the arts, claims tea as the reward of scholars and the inspiration of the arts: the 'sons of Isis and of Cam', she suggests, should be given tea as a reward for their industrious intellectual labours, delving deep in 'Learning's Mine'. The next to plead her case is Venus, goddess of love and beauty, who claims tea as the associate of youth and beauty. Cinthia, goddess of fertility and virginity, in turn declares tea is appropriate for women and for the cause of chastity, as a drink that will not compromise a woman's virtue. Thetis, a sea nymph, celebrates tea as one of the glories of the arts of commerce, imagining trade as the core of England's 'Ocean-Empire'. Salus, the goddess of health, pleads her case, arguing that tea can save mortals from disease: tea, 'this Reviving Plant', is the panacea, a remedy or medicine with the power to cure all diseases. The final contestant is Somnus, god of sleep, who makes the unconvincing claim that tea promotes pleasing slumber by inspiring more colourful and visionary dreams. With the gods' contention over tea showing no sign of ending, Jove starts up and declares that tea, 'A Plant that can so many Virtues boast / . . . merited the Patronage of All'.[18] Jove's intervention allows the poem to end with the tea-thea pun again: tea itself is a goddess.

In Praise of Tea

Numerous tea 'invention' poems followed Tate's lead, including verses by Peter Motteux, Ambrose Philips, Duncan Campbell and several anonymous poets, all offering fictional neoclassical histories of tea. These generally rest on the same scholarly historical irony, for the ancient Romans were as unaware of tea as they were of China. However, taken together, these poems work to elevate and domesticate tea and its culture of consumption. A friend of Tate, the accomplished poet and translator Peter Motteux (1660– 1718), wrote *A Poem in Praise of Tea* in 1704, although it was not published until 1712. It begins with the speaker describing a banquet of the gods, liberally supplied with drink by Bacchus, god of wine, in which the gods debate the comparative virtues of tea and wine. Hebe, goddess of youth and cupbearer to the gods, serves the goddesses tea to refresh them: an action that raises Bacchus's anger, as he complains about tea's 'want of strength'. Hebe in reply defends tea's healthful restorative powers, while Apollo, god of verse, praises its effects on the imagination and creativity, gives an account of its origins and healthful properties, and prophetically declares it to hold the nation's fate: tea brings health, liberty and peace. In the final stanza, awed by Apollo's defence, even Bacchus drinks 'sober tea at last'.[19] In Motteux's hands, tea is described as the appropriate drink for a modern, polite and commercial nation, such as that wrought by William and Mary after the Revolution of 1688. In an earlier version of the poem, probably written in 1701, Motteux's praise for William was more direct: in this earlier version, he explicitly celebrated the rise of tea as a sign of England's return to peace and prosperity after the turmoil and strife of Stuart rule. In this version, Motteux praised the role of tea in a moral reformation, specifically against drunkenness, instituted by William III. The broadly Whiggish reading of the politics of tea are encapsulated by the poem's final lines:

> Tea must succeed to Wine, as Peace to War:
> Nor by the Grape let Men be set at odds,
> But share in Tea, the Nectar of the Gods.[20]

Locating tea among the social world of the gods of ancient Greece and Rome remained a lively poetic trope over the following decades. Tea itself may have provoked the connection – its delicate flavours and clear bright colouration lent itself to refined discourse – but this neoclassical deification of tea was a radical cultural realignment of the exotic commodity. Rather than locating its context in Chinese history or philosophy, or understanding its

Tea tray, 1743, tin-glazed earthenware, painted in cobalt blue. This Delftware tea tray, made in London, was designed to carry the tea-things during the tea preparation. The painted and glazed image models appropriate tea-party behaviour: two elegant women entertain two men, their tea service sitting on the tray itself. A black servant wearing an exotic turban, evidently still a child, brings a kettle of hot water to the table.

effects according to Chinese medical principles, tea was given a new context within European myth and culture – indeed among the most prestigious classicizing Augustan mode of that European culture. Neoclassical myth-making about tea proved an enormously flexible, even irresistible poetic commonplace over the following decades. One anonymous Dublin poet, sometimes identified as James Dalacourt, published a poem addressed to his sweetheart (known only as Miss H----lt) entitled *The Tea-kettle: A Poem* (1730).[21] The poet imagines a summer scene in which Venus, taking her bath *au plein air*, is spied by Vulcan. Aiming to seduce her, Vulcan asks his friend Sol for advice about appropriate gifts – Sol suggests a copper tea-kettle as something befitting Vulcan's skills. Vulcan's metal tribute is received gratefully by Venus, especially when Sol visits her grove and makes it sparkle: the upshot is that she accepts Vulcan as her devotee. The poet hopes this narrative might work as an analogy for his own courtship of Miss H----lt

– swapping the gift of a copper kettle for a poem about one. The vogue for neoclassical invention poems about tea created new ways of understanding the beverage, including its flavours and preparation, and the sociable occasions on which it was served.

An important aspect of the elevation of tea was its association with politeness, with women, and with conversation. The convivial gathering of the tea-table, even in the most rarified strata of society, was the subject of considerable speculation. Alexander Pope's mock-heroic verse satire *The Rape of the Lock* (1714) ridiculed the follies of high society in Queen Anne's London and the tea-table gossip that attended it.[22] The poem is partly located at Hampton Court, the Thames-side palace west of London, where courtiers and maids of honour are shown to flirt, play cards, and 'taste *Bohea*' (IV, 156). Addressing Anne (whose regnal title, after the Act of Union in 1707, was Queen of Great Britain, Ireland and France), Pope proclaims:

> Here thou, great Anna! Whom three realms obey,
> Dost sometimes counsel take – and sometimes tea. (III, 7)

Tea, Pope observes, is the most characteristic social theatre of the royal court, though the precise nature of his mockery is hard to fathom. Here, as elsewhere, Pope makes a poetic figure carry the work of his satire. To some readers of these lines, Pope implies that the queen sometimes talks politics with statesmen and counsellors, and at other times retreats to the tea-table with her maids of honour, where conversation is polite but shallow. In such a reading, the tea-table, the realm of women and gossip, is opposed to the world of politics, the realm of male counsellors and affairs of state. But Pope's lines are curiously ambiguous, constructing a zeugma (a rhetorical device in which a single verb operates on two parts of a sentence, understood differently in relation to each other). As Pope's zeugmatic flourish indicates, tea and counsel can both be taken, but in different ways: tea is drunk, advice is followed. Equally, both produce a form of sociability, played out by company assembled around a table, in which information is exchanged.

Domesticating tea

The domestic tea-table, and its construction as a space of information exchange, played a no less important role in *The Spectator* (1711–14), the single most significant periodical of the early eighteenth century. The essays of *The Spectator* exerted considerable influence on ideas of polite behaviour, good taste and excellence in writing throughout the eighteenth century. In the tenth essay, published on 12 March 1711, Joseph Addison characterized the purpose of his new periodical venture:

> It was said of *Socrates*, that he brought Philosophy down from Heaven, to inhabit among Men; and I shall be ambitious to have it said of me, that I have brought Philosophy out of Closets and Libraries, Schools and Colleges, to dwell in Clubs and Assemblies, at Tea-tables, and in Coffee-houses.[23]

Addison proposes that *The Spectator* turn philosophy away from abstruse and scholastic disputation towards the study of practical ethics in the polite and everyday world. He imagines the descent of philosophy as a movement that is at once spatial and social: philosophy should be ushered from closets and libraries, schools and colleges into a new life dwelling in clubs and assemblies, tea-tables and coffee-houses. These four latter forms of urban sociability are repeatedly championed by *The Spectator* as the location of the new polite urbanism. Addison imagines, in this way, a new purpose for tea-table conversation: philosophizing. He continues:

> I would therefore in a very particular Manner recommend these my Speculations to all well-regulated Families, that set apart an Hour in every Morning for Tea and Bread and Butter; and would earnestly advise them for their Good to order this Paper to be punctually served up, and to be looked upon as a Part of the Tea Equipage.

The Spectator, Addison hopes, will become central to each family's everyday routine, so that it is considered almost part of the tea equipage. Alongside the cups, saucers and teapot, reading *The Spectator* should be, he argues, a necessary aspect of the social act of tea consumption. Numerous essays reinforce this message: families and groups of friends should assemble at the tea-table every morning for tea and bread and butter, and to read *The Spectator*. These groups – mentioned in twelve or thirteen further essays – usually comprise both men and women, although groups consisting of young women alone are also discussed.[24] In these scenes, groups of people read *The Spectator* aloud to one another, and over their tea debate the moral question posed by the essay. Morning tea is not about the tea, not about quenching thirst, but rather is the occasion for associated social practices: these are primarily polite and conversational, but are also concerned with reading literature and debating ideas.

In *The Spectator*, the tea-table is conceived as a social space, one especially associated with the polite world of women. Clubs and coffeehouses were open only to men and were virtually inaccessible to women of propriety. Addressing the company assembled at the tea-table, by contrast, allowed Mr Spectator to comment on matters of interest to women. In an early essay (No. 4), Mr Spectator explains that *The Spectator* will have a particular focus on the 'fair Sex', as he calls it: in a way, this focus on women and their manners is what was innovative about his new periodical venture. But he cautions that, in his focus on women, he will neither ridicule female manners nor condescend to them. Rather, he wants to examine their codes of behaviour and moral qualities, and to criticize fairly what he sees, with an eye for improvement: in his words, he will 'not lower but exalt' women. 'I shall take it for the greatest Glory of my Work, if among reasonable Women this Paper may furnish *Tea-table Talk*.'[25] Mr Spectator wants the kind

The Tea-table (London, [*c.* 1720]), etching. The tea-table, long associated with polite domestic sociability amongst women, aroused anxieties as the seat of gossip and scandal. In this satirical print illustrated by explanatory verses, a party of women chat over their tea, while Envy drives Justice and Truth from the room. Male eavesdroppers hover outside the window and under the table.

of philosophical debates he discusses in the essays to become the subjects of conversation around the tea-table.

Conversation is central to the activities of the tea-table, at least as Mr Spectator sees it. Visual evidence also testifies to this connection. An engraved print published around 1720, entitled *The Tea-table*, depicts six women taking tea in a lavishly decorated room, celebrating the tea-table as a place of talk. On the table is an assortment of objects associated with the ritual of taking tea, such as a tray with spare cups and a spoon, as well as a series of fashionable objects, among which are a fur muff, a fan and a book, open to reveal its title, *Chit Chat*. This was the name of a fashionable play from the year before by Thomas Killigrew, but it also implies that the conversation was common small talk, light and familiar.[26] While the women chatter, they drink tea: one is pouring from the pot and others are holding their handleless cups between forefinger and thumb, as was proper in the period. The hostess's collection of porcelain is displayed proudly in an alcove in the corner of the room, including cups, saucers, plates, a bottle, drinking vessels, a mortar and pestle, and a coffee pot. Tea and the tea-table, this plate argues, was a place for the consumption of precious commodities (tea, porcelain, fashion) alongside a social performance of good manners and polite conversation. Similar scenes were painted on fans and even porcelain: a tin-glazed earthenware tea-tray from 1743 in the Victoria and Albert Museum depicts a tea-party scene with a black servant-boy bringing a kettle of hot water to the table, around which two men and two women are gathering to drink.

Conversation and Gossip

The imaginative reassignment of the tea-table to the realm of polite conversation worked so well that many commentators reckoned talk to be more important than tea. Samuel Johnson, later in the century, joked that tea drinkers used their habit as 'a pretence for assembling to prattle, for interrupting business, or diversifying idleness'. He went on: 'they are brought together not by the tea, but the tea-table.'[27] A satirist argued in 1707 that tea was secondary to the talk it occasioned: describing how tea-drinking women were 'letting a loose to their Passions and their busie Tongues, which are the Ambassadors of their evil Intentions . . . and Backbiting the whole World, is the chief Diversion among 'em, and Scandal the principal Dish of the Collation'.[28] The dramatist Colley Cibber observed that while tea was itself a sober and innocent drink, nonetheless, in the social form of the tea-table, it seemed to encourage the exchange of gossip and slander. A character in his comedy *The Lady's Last Stake* (1708) exclaimed: 'Tea! Thou soft, thou sober, sage, and venerable Liquid, thou innocent Pretence for bringing the Wicked of both Sexes together in a

Formerly attributed to Nicolaes Verkolje, *Two Ladies and an Officer Seated at Tea*, c. 1715, oil on canvas. A gentleman in a red coat offers snuff to two women sharing an intimate tea party. They are seated around an ebony tea-table displaying a blue-and-white porcelain tea-set comprising three cups and saucers with silver teaspoons, a sugar and a slops bowl, a brown stoneware Yixing teapot, and a shiny metal kettle.

Morning; thou Female Tongue-running, Smile-smoothing, Heart-opening, Wink-tippling Cordial.'[29]

This argument – that the tea-table encouraged gossip – was rehearsed in an anonymous poem called *Tea, a Poem: In Three Cantos*, published in 1743. Although the poem defends tea itself as the 'Best of Herbs', the tea-table assembly is identified as a source of destructive scandal. Emulating Pope's *Rape of the Lock*, the poet adopts the mock-heroic mode to satirize the polite discourse of the tea-table. In the second canto, the poet describes a neoclassical 'Temple of Tea' at which obedient votaries gather to exchange gossip under the watchful eye of the 'saucy Virtues', Folly and Envy. At the altar, the twin goddesses of Scandal and of Pride lead the slaughter of Reputation, who expires while calling fruitlessly to be rescued by Truth. The gossipy gathering at the tea-table continues:

Now all inspir'd, with fell malignant Rage
(For so the *Goddess* bids) with Warmth engage;
Belles meet with *Belles*, asperse each others Cloaths,
Prude jostles *Prude*, and *Beaux* encounter *Beaux*.
Determin'd all, to conquer, or to die,
Gloves, Sword-knots, Fans, in rude Confusion fly.
The Tumult thickens; now they loudly jar,
All furiously involv'd in equal War!
By Turns all conquer; all the Vict'ry claim,
Triumphant those, who most can mangle Fame.[30]

Tea-table sociability, the anonymous poet suggests, encourages the exchange of gossip, figured as a malignant force, ruinous to virtue, destructive of reputation, driven by base motives and obsessed with the shallow concerns of fashion and appearance.

The engraved image of *The Tea-table* (1720) also makes this connection between women, the tea-table and gossip. The engraving originally illustrated a series of essays published in a newspaper, Nathaniel Mist's *Weekly Journal and Saturday Post*. The second essay in the series comprises a poem on the tea-table, the lines of which were subsequently printed below the plate by the Cornhill print-seller John Bowles. The verses launch a trenchant attack on the moral status of tea-table conversation, describing it as the seat of female empire, as the source of gossip, the place that manufactures scandal, slander, falsehoods and lies:

How see we Scandal (for our Sex too base)
Seat its dread Empire in the Female Race,
'Mong Beaus & Women, Fans & Mechlin Lace.
Chief Seat of Slander! Ever there we see,
Thick Scandal circulate with right Bohea.
There Source of blackning Falshoods, Mint of Lies,
Each Dame th'improvement of her Talent tries,
And at each Sip a Lady's Honour Dies.[31]

The engraved image represents the verse's argument by an iconographic allegory, unfolding around the women gathered at the tea-table. Beneath their table, a tea-drinking and horned man lurks, seemingly representing the eavesdropping incarnation of scandal: two more men listen at the window, literally under the eaves. Meanwhile Envy, depicted in emblem-book fashion as a filthy, topless hag carrying a viper and a thorned club, drives two women out of the room: Justice, carrying her scales, and Truth, not quite as naked as she ought to be. It seems that rather than the location of polite and rational debate, the tea-table was also subject to the more

Tea chest, *c.* 1750–77 (Paris), Japanned wood (vernis Martin), pink silk lining, japanned tinned iron. Although made in France, designs with Chinese motifs decorate the exterior of this ornate varnished tea chest. Inside, nestling in the pink silk lining, are three tea canisters, made of metal varnished to look like Japanese lacquerware. The tea chest can be locked, suggesting that the contents were highly valued by their owner.

unruly energies of gossip and scandal. Although the 'tender leaf' was ushered into the English world by Ovington as a polite and deferential stranger, its effects on the domestic world were at times more diverse and disruptive.

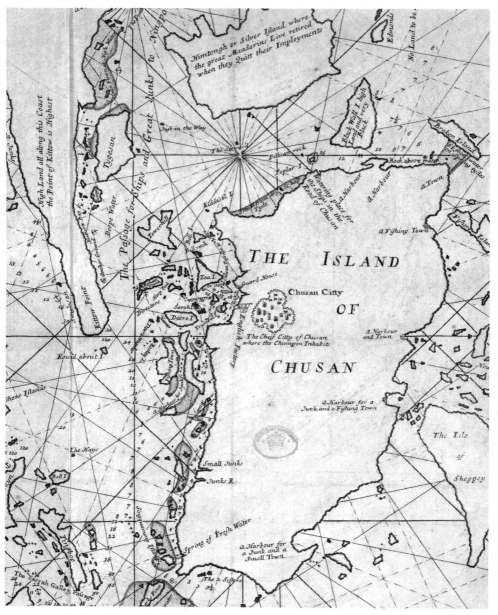

Detail of 'A Large Draught of the North Part of China. Shewing all the Passages and Chanells into the Harbour of Chusan'. This map was printed in the third book of John Thornton's oceanographic masterpiece *The English Pilot* (London, 1703). The map is derived from a manuscript chart produced by Captain John Roberts and James Cuninghame in autumn 1701, during the New East India Company's abortive mission to establish a Chinese base on Zhoushan. 'Tea I[sland]' can be seen to the south (that is, to the left) of 'The Island of Chusan', with its 'English Factory' and 'Cheif Citty'.

FIVE

The Natural Philosophy of Tea

The urge to understand tea in eighteenth-century Britain was an intermingling of intellectual and cultural currents. Broader anxieties and ambitions dominated: an uncertain fascination with distant civilizations, a monumental programme to classify and order the entire natural world, a resolute determination to comprehend and instrument the utility of global resources and manufactures, a lust for maximizing commercial efficiency and profit. Three related disciplines of scholarly and professional endeavour were at the confluence of these desires. Botanists sought encounters with live specimens of the tea plant in order to locate its exotic anatomy within prevailing systems of Enlightenment taxonomy. Physicians experimented with tea's medicinal virtues – in the laboratory and on their patients – in order to test traditional Asian (and newer European) claims concerning its panacean properties, as well as the range of counter-arguments positing its enervating and emasculating effects. Horticulturists dreamed of growing tea for themselves, of learning the secrets of its cultivation, harvest and processing – even of inaugurating western tea plantations that could capitalize on Europe's habit while undercutting Chinese suppliers.

Yet tea – in so many ways gentle, pliable, understated – proved curiously resistant to these attempts to pin it down. Well into the nineteenth century, students of botany could not quite decide whether the multiple varieties of tea on the British market came from one or more species of the shrub. Aggressive medical debates persisted about the physiological benefits and drawbacks of tea consumption – particularly when taken in excess, or by women, or by the labouring poor. Gardeners and their patrons tried and repeatedly failed to import and propagate *Camellia sinensis*; and when they eventually succeeded, the aim of instituting its agricultural production in Europe or America was never meaningfully realized. Leaf tea was increasingly commonplace in the shops of British grocers and on the tables of British families; but knowledge concerning the plant from which it was made remained implacably mysterious, often controversial, frequently unsettling.

Immediate Encounter, Remote Taxonomy

Almost as soon as European botanists became aware of tea's existence, they began to locate it within their own frameworks of understanding. In his accomplished *Pinax Theatri Botanici* (Illustrated Theatre of Botany, 1623), the Swiss herbalist Gaspard Bauhin (1560–1624) incorporated 'tea, a herb [that grows] in Japan' among the 'Foeniculum' within his order of umbelliferous plants (the classification did not stick: *'Foeniculum'* now refers to a genus of plants including fennel, or *Foeniculum vulgare*).[1] An inveterate mapper of new species, Bauhin's reference had been gleaned from van Linschoten's *Voyages into the Easte & West Indies* of 1596 (see chapter One). As an early modern natural historian, Bauhin's book-bound approach was as much to compile incidental descriptions of exotic rarities from the treatises of travellers as it was to examine physical samples: via the careful sifting and cross-referencing of available evidence, synthetic truths about nature could be distilled. In any case, neither Bauhin nor his successors during the following half-century had the opportunity to examine botanically meaningful specimens of tea; they relied instead on the printed accounts of visitors to China and Japan, and on the twigs, flowers and seeds that accidentally found their way into crates of leaves shipped for the purposes of infusion rather than inspection. The information that could be siphoned from these channels was necessarily haphazard and incomplete. What scholars really craved was someone on the ground, someone who could examine tea at first hand and secure examples of its foliage and florescence for preservation and examination.

One of the first Europeans to record access to Chinese plantations was the French Jesuit Louis-Daniel Le Comte (1655–1728), who witnessed tea under cultivation during the late 1680s. Le Comte travelled throughout East Asia both under the auspices of the religious mission led by Father Jean de Fontenay (1643–1710), and as a 'corresponding member' of the French Académie des Sciences. In his *Nouveaux mémoires sur l'état présent de la Chine* (New Memoirs on the Present State of China) – a text notable for its role in contemporary theological controversies concerning the relationship between Confucianism and Christianity – Le Comte documented how in *'Fokien'*

> they first made me observe *Thee* upon the declining of a little Hill; it was not above five or six foot high, several Stalks, each of which was an inch thick, joyned together, and divided at the top into . . . many small Branches, [which] composed a kind of

Cluster, much what like our Myrtle. The Trunk, tho' seemingly dry, yet bore very green Branches and Leaves. These leaves were drawn out in length at the point, pretty strait, an inch, or an inch and an half long, and indented in their whole Circumference.[2]

The opportunity to detail and corroborate these observations further was apparently curtailed, the writer complaining that 'I had but a quarter of an hour to examine the Tree.'[3] Yet even if they would have to wait for others to produce a minute botanical description, Le Comte's readers – both at home and abroad – were tantalized with the promise of a more extensive and complex understanding of tea than had previously been possible. Among Le Comte's more significant insights was the inception of a European descriptive register for categorizing the multiple varieties of processed leaves. Inferring that the tea 'which they commonly drink in *China*, hath no particular Name, because it is gather'd hand over head in different Territories and Soils', Le Comte then itemized two superior types of leaf, used by 'Persons of Quality' and associated nomenclaturally with their *terroir* of origin. '*Thee Soumlo*' he describes as a green tea with a fleeting 'pleasant' taste and a scent 'a little of Violets', while '*Thee Voüi*' generates a 'delicious' infusion 'inclining to black'.[4] These two basic categories, contemporaneously labelled by John Ovington in England as 'Singlo' and 'Bohea' tea, were to delight consumers and to confuse taxonomists for decades to come.[5]

The realization that dried leaf tea was not an homogenous product but instead a differentiated and gradated commodity was to have an impact not only on the world of British business but on that of British botany. Soon after the translation of Le Comte's *Mémoires de la Chine* went on sale in London bookshops, the English natural historian James Petiver (*c.* 1665–1718) was badgering a recent acquaintance for favours from that distant empire. 'Being assured you design for China', he wrote early in 1698 to James Cuninghame (see Introduction), 'I make bold to give you a short Epitome of such plants as are mentioned to grow there which I formerly extracted from [John] Ogilby's translation of [Johan] Nieuhoff in the *Embassy from the Dutch East India Company*'. Listing 80 species for which he importuned his friend to forage, Petiver demanded in relation to item fifteen, 'Thea or Cha' – 'Its flower is white, with yellow thrums and Blackish seed' – that Cuninghame 'inquire what variety their is of it & wherin the Bohe Tea differs from the common'.[6] During his subsequent voyage Cuninghame compiled a field book, its records arranged chronologically and by territory – Mallorca, Java, China, Mallaca, the Cape, Ascension Island – documenting in its author's best botanical Latin the local flora more or less as they were encountered on the ground.[7] The now-faded notes that Cuninghame penned in these octavo booklets (hand-folded from larger folio sheets, then cut to produce eight leaves) indicate that on the islands of 'Emuy' (Xiamen) and 'Colonshu' (Gulangyu) he was able to identify specimens of 'Tea, Planta floribus et foliis serratis Urticus subtus albicantibus' ('Tea, a flowering plant, with leaves serrated like nettles and whiteish underneath'), and seeds from 'Flores Tea Singlôo' ('the flowers of Singlo Tea').[8] More remarkably, the same manuscript itemizes more than 700 local plants that Cuninghame had delineated and coloured by local artists during his stay, and which he exhibited at the Royal Society on 25 October 1699 following his return to London.[9]

Despite the considerable botanical achievements of his expedition, Cuninghame was yet to answer Petiver's key question concerning the relationship between bohea and 'common' (green) tea. This would have to wait for his next trip. After a brief spell in Britain during the winter of 1699, Cuninghame set sail in the service of a New East India Company project to found a permanent Chinese factory under the leadership of President Allen Catchpole (d. 1705).[10] The settlement was to be inaugurated on Chusan (Zhoushan), the dominant island in an East China Sea archipelago which had been strategically chosen on account of its position as the gateway to the major trading seaport of Limpo·(Ningbo), and thence up the Yangtze River (past Shanghai) to Nanking (Nanjing). As official surgeon, Cuninghame received a salary of £30 per annum, with a further annuity of £10 so long as he kept a servant (a perquisite he presumably lost when his man Edward Parker was dispatched home by the President in 1701 'for his notorious & scandalous immoralities').[11] The Chusan factory, designed optimistically by the New Company to function both as a staging post for inaugurating its 'Japan Trade', and to supply 'a Considerable Vent for our woollen manufactures' (the hope being such goods would prove more marketable in northern China than they had done at Canton or Amoy in the south), proved catastrophic.[12] The President and Council of the nascent colony stuck it out for just sixteen months between October 1700 and February 1702 (although Catchpole made further abortive attempts to revive the enterprise until fully abandoning it in December 1703).[13] Cuninghame, perhaps not overly employed in his professional capacity, exploited this chance to research the local geography and natural history – indeed, he remained on the island for a year longer than most of his colleagues, until February 1703.

Cuninghame's ship the *Eaton* landed at Chusan on 11 October 1700, and he lost no time in exploring his surroundings. A long letter to Petiver composed just before the end of the year reported the natural prosperity of his new home. 'The Island . . . in general abounds with all sorts of Provisions, such as Cows, Buffelos, (Horses & Asses) Goats, Deere, Hogs Wild & tame, Geese Ducks & Hens; Rice, Wheat, Calavances [pulses] & some Beans, Coleworts [cabbages], Turneps Potatoes, Carrots, Spinach & Beetes, small Oynons, Leeks & Garlick.' Moreover, Cuninghame described how 'I have made severall progresses upon this Island 5 or 6 miles off, where I have found the Tea grow plentifully on the tops of the Hills in small shrubs amongst the Pines' – even if Chusan tea, it transpired, 'is not in that esteem with what grows on more montanous Islands'. Accompanying this written missive of 20 December 1700, Cuninghame enclosed (among other things) 'a quare of Paper containing about 150 Specimens of different Plants'.[14] When they reached Petiver in London on 15 July 1701, the apothecary judged the package 'highly acceptable'. His reply remarked particularly upon the 'crenated Leaves' of the 'Thea', a morphological characteristic that he deemed typical of Cuninghame's 'Chusan shrubs'.[15]

Tea was prominent within the Chinese landscape that Cuninghame encountered. On a hydrographic chart of the archipelago that he surveyed with Captain John Roberts in the autumn of 1701, the English label attributed to Dapan Shidao (lying across the main harbour to the south of Chusan) is 'Tea Island'.[16] Direct exposure to tea in its natural habitat ultimately enabled Cuninghame to crack James Petiver's enigma. After twelve months of observing the ecological and agricultural cycles of the island's flora he dispatched to London a fuller account of the nature and cultivation of tea:

> The 3 Sorts of Tea commonly carryd to England are all from the same plant, only the Season of the Year & the Soyl makes the difference. The Bohe (or Voüi, so calld of [the Wuyi] Mountains in the Province of Fokien, where it is chiefly made) is the very first bud gathred in the beginning of March, & dryd in the shade. The Bing Tea is the second growth in April: & Singlô the last in May & June, both dryd a little in Tatches or Pans over the fire. The Tea Shrub being an Evergreen is in Flower from October to Januarie, & the Seed is ripe in September & October following, so that one may gather both flowers and seed at the same time.[17]

Cuninghame's epistolary description of tea (alongside other aspects of Chusan life and natural history) rapidly found its way into the public realm: in 1702 it was printed in the *Philosophical Transactions*, the pre-eminent scientific journal of the period, which was closely associated with the research efforts of the Royal Society.[18] His information that 'the Season of the Year & the Soyl makes the difference' when it comes to the '3 Sorts of Tea commonly carryd to England' no doubt relied in part upon information gathered through translated conversation with farmers and merchants, but Cuninghame had also closely inspected tea trees for himself and appears to have witnessed the processing of the harvested leaves on Chusan (he certainly recorded that among the island's limited 'Manufactories . . . they make some Tea, but chiefly for their own use').[19] He signals too – though perhaps is less conscious of its significance – the role played by methods of preparation: bohea is 'dryd in the shade' (to allow fermentation), whereas singlo and bing are 'both dryd a little in Tatches or Pans over the fire' (arresting oxidation and preserving verdure). Cuninghame was the first British traveller to observe, document and collect Chinese plants in any meaningful detail – and the scientific value of his fieldwork was underlined the following year when 'Thea CHINENSIS vera potulenta' ('the true, drinkable CHINESE tea') was included in a catalogue of specimens prepared on his behalf for the *Philosophical Transactions* by Petiver.[20] Around the same time, Petiver commissioned an engraving of Cuninghame's tea cutting for the third 'decade' of his *Gazophylacii Naturae et Artis* (Treasury of Nature and Crafts); the plate upon which it is depicted also illustrates an elaborate chair carved from the roots of a tea tree, gifted by the governing 'Chumpeen' of Chusan to the New East India Company (which in turn donated it to John, Baron Sommers (1651–1716), then President of the Royal Society).[21]

James Cuninghame's botanical declaration concerning the specific origins of various leaf teas shipped to Europe could not have been clearer: they 'are all from the same plant'. As well as appearing in the *Philosophical Transactions*, this claim was quoted verbatim in the second edition of John Ovington's *Essay upon the Nature and Qualities of Tea* (1705) (indeed, it is the only significant addition to the reissued *Essay*).[22] Moreover, the most influential early eighteenth-century European treatise on tea, that of Engelbert Kaempfer (1651–1716), contained nothing to contradict Cuninghame. Kaempfer had travelled through much of Asia (although not China) between 1683 and 1693, encountering tea in Japan, whence he brought back with him what are now among the oldest surviving European specimens of *Camellia sinensis* (Kaempfer's collections were purchased by Sir Hans Sloane, and like Cuninghame's form part of the Sloane Herbarium at the Natural History Museum in London).[23] The account of tea in his *Amœnitatum Exoticarum* (Exotic Delights) of 1712, if more extensive than Cuninghame's, is essentially consistent with that of his British contemporary once local differences of geography and culture are set aside. Like Cuninghame, Kaempfer identifies three distinct phases of the tea harvest – which in turn generate three different grades of leaf – before enumerating the arduous processing routine that centres around 'roasting-houses, or laboratories publick, built for this very purpose'. In this undertaking his sympathies are evidently with the Japanese 'Tea-preparers [who] complain mightily of the unhappiness of their profession, for nothing they say, can be got cheaper in the Country than Tea, and yet no work is more tiresome and fatiguing'.[24] Kaempfer's understanding of tea categorization is (familiarly) that it depends upon the agricultural situation, the time of gathering and the method of processing the leaves, and the manner of their preparation and infusion once dried. Although his typology of tea differs from the contrasts to be observed

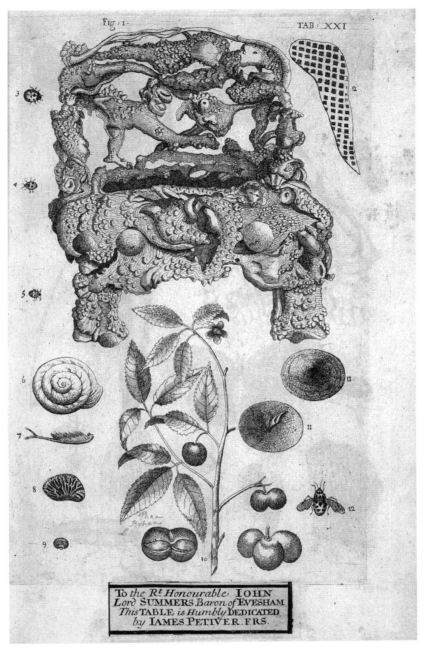

James Petiver, *Catalogus Classicus et Topicus, Omnium Rerum Figuratum in V. Decadibus, seu primo volumine Gazophylacii Naturæ et Artis* (London, 1709). This plate comes from the third 'decade' of James Petiver's *Gazophylacii Naturae et Artis* (Treasury of Nature and Crafts) (1709). Figure 10 (marked in pencil 'Thea Bohea') is an engraving of a tea specimen sent to Petiver by James Cuninghame from Chusan in 1700–1701. Above this, Figure 1 depicts a chair carved from the roots of a tea-tree. The chair was given by the provincial ruler (or 'Chumpeen') of Chusan to the East India Company, which donated it in turn to John, Baron Sommers, then President of the Royal Society (and the dedicatee of Petiver's plate).

Camellia sinensis, c. 1700 (China), dried vegetable matter mounted on paper. This dried sample of tea was collected by James Cuninghame on the island of Chusan in the early eighteenth century. The specimen clearly retains its crenellated leaves, pale flowers and dried fruit. Cuninghame's original handwritten label is also preserved.

Camellia sinensis, 1690s (Japan), dried vegetable matter mounted on paper. This dried sample of tea, collected by Engelbert Kaempfer in Japan, is among the oldest surviving European tea specimens, and is now in the Sloane Herbarium at the Natural History Museum.

between Chinese bohea and singlo – he talks instead of '*Imperial tea*' or '*Ficki Tsjaa*', '*Chinese[-style] Thea*' or '*Tootsjaa*', and 'coarse tea' or '*Ban Tsjaa*' – there is no intimation that these are anything other than the products of a single plant.[25]

Despite the pioneering botanical and anthropological efforts of Le Comte, Cuninghame and Kaempfer, the European experience of consuming two markedly different types of tea – green and bohea – persistently militated against an acceptance that they were derived from one species of shrub. Indeed, in 1759 (half a century after Cuninghame's Chusan adventure) the English natural historian Sir John Hill claimed to have identified a genuine distinction. Observing 'among my CHINA Plants, two Specimens under the name of Tea, which differ obviously', he recorded of bohea that it has 'shorter and darker Leaves, and in each Flower six Petals', while green bears 'longer and paler Leaves, and in every Flower nine Petals'.[26] Partly on the basis of Hill's ascription (and disregarding the author's equivocation that 'perhaps it is an Error'), Carl Linnaeus (1707–1778) outlined two separate species, '*Theæ Bohea*' and '*Theæ viridi*', in a dissertation on 'Potus Theae' (The Tea-drink) defended by his student Pehr Cornellius Tillaeus on 7 December 1765.[27] Such was Linnaeus's authority within the contemporary scientific world as the arbiter and custodian of his influential system of botanical classification – based on the observation of and discrimination between sexual characteristics – that this division of tea using two specific binomial designations was soon widely accepted by those who had no opportunity to examine specimens of the plant for themselves.

Nonetheless, there were naysayers prepared to contradict Linnaeus's distinction. One of his most cherished English correspondents, John Ellis (*c.* 1710–1776) – himself no friend of Hill – as well as one of his many great admirers, John Coakley Lettsom (1744–1815), both gently sought to correct the professor's error. In 1768, Ellis wrote privately to Linnaeus – on the evidence of Thomas Fitzhugh (1728–1800), a trusted East India Company factor recently returned from China – that 'you must have been imposed on by Dr Hill'; while in his published *Directions for Bringing over Seeds and Plants from the East-Indies* (1770), he insisted that 'the green tea and the bohea tea are . . . one and the same species'.[28] Two years later, Lettsom's *Natural History of the Tea-tree* repeated the mantra that 'There is only one species of this plant; the difference of green and bohea Tea depending upon the nature of the soil, the culture, and manner of drying the leaves.'[29] Yet Linnaeus did not publicly alter his deposition, and somewhat bizarrely Lettsom himself would later publish engravings of the two 'species' in the much enlarged but not particularly improved second edition of his *Natural History* in 1799. Even in the nineteenth century, the popular but respectable horticultural writer John Claudius Loudon catalogued both '*Thea viridis*' and '*Thea bohea*', despite acknowledging (as Cuninghame had known and Ellis had repeated) that the distinctions in appearance, aroma and taste between green and black tea were functions of the different manufacturing processes.[30] Only when Robert Fortune (1812–1880) achieved unprecedented access deep into mainland China during the 1840s did the truth that Cuninghame had so plainly communicated a century and a half earlier become incontrovertible. Fortune confirmed that any plant could be used to produce 'green' or 'black' leaf tea, and its monospecific nature was contemporaneously corroborated by Samuel Ball, a former East India Company Inspector of Teas (who also correctly allowed for multiple varieties of the species).[31] Tea had long relished being unknown, evasive, duplicitous. It took two centuries of endeavour for European botany fully to comprehend and assimilate within its own systems of taxonomy this oriental enigma.

Advocates and Accusers

Tea has always been experienced as a plant that imposes subtle but discernible physiological effects upon its consumers. Like botanists, early modern medical practitioners were keenly interested in tea's natural properties. Its instrumentation and mythologization in China constructed it as a remarkable aliment, conferring longevity upon and alleviating illness in its adherents. These claims reached European ears with the very first murmurs about the beverage, surfacing (for example) in Giovanni Battista Ramusio's conversations with Hajji Mohamed (see chapter One). Ramusio reports Mohamed's relation of the Chinese lore that 'taking one or two cups of this decoction whilst fasting alleviates the fever, [and] maladies of the head, of the stomach, of the sides, and of the joints' (it is also said to relieve the gout and indigestion).[32] Over the course of the next century this catalogue of cures became commonplace in tea literature, appearing in botanical treatises such as Robert Lovell's *Pambotanologia* (1659), and thence into the promotional materials of apothecaries and grocers: Thomas Garway's broadsides on tea, for example, draw explicitly on Lovell's optimism.[33] Physicians seemed inclined to agree – the irascible Dutch 'tea doctor' Cornelis Bontekoe prescribed enormous quantities of dilute tea on the basis that its warm, liquid properties enhance the circulation of the blood and banish bodily impurities.

In the early modern marketplace – as today – the authenticating association of unlikely pharmacological properties with a costly and exotic article of diet became both central to its intellectual allure and fundamental to its rapid acquisition of fashionabilty. Nonetheless, by the later seventeenth century there was a lively debate to be had about the validity of the sometimes outlandish assertions that circulated concerning tea's healing powers. The Danish naturalist Simon Paulli (1603–1680) was among those who dared to suggest that pro-tea discourse was inherently mendacious. Tea 'corrupts our Regimen, and impairs our Health', he deposed (in the words of an eighteenth-century British translation); it achieves nothing that cannot be matched by infusions of benign local herbs such as betony. Moreover, in Paulli's view tea-inculcated debility rapidly transfers itself from the body corporeal to the body politic: the 'raging epidemical Madness of importing *Tea* into *Europe* from *China*' is deemed as sure to prove financially as physically ruinous.[34]

Medical ideations of tea were never far removed from the interlocking social and economic concerns with which it was associated. Writers were often conscious of this tendency. The Scottish physician Thomas Short (c. 1690–1772) took as the starting point for *A Dissertation upon Tea* (1730) his sense that the drug polarized pharmaceutical opinion, and he was scathing about the irrational prejudices that produced this divergence. 'Some ascribe such sovereign Virtues to this Exotick, as if 'twas able to eradicate or prevent the Spring of all Diseases', he complained, while 'Others, on the contrary, are equally severe . . . accounting it no better than a slow, but efficacious Poyson'.[35] As a corrective, Short promised a balanced and detailed enquiry into 'a Liquor' that 'has so singularly prevail'd in *England*, for these forty or fifty Years past, among all Persons (except of the very lowest Rank)'. Advocating the practice of intellectually informed consumption, Short opines that 'our Examination and Understanding should . . . bear some Proportion to the Use and Preference we have made of it'. His own account is structured upon a combination of bookish natural history and first-hand chemical and medicinal experimentation.[36]

Short's basic argument is that tea's 'astringent' quality tautens bodily tissue, while the water in which it is infused quickens the blood and augments circulation. The effects can be detrimental for some subjects in certain environments – asthmatics, convalescents and idlers, for example. But Short ultimately enumerates such an overwhelming succession of benefits that his opening protestations of objectivity seem at risk of insincerity. Tea can dispel headaches, vertigo, drowsiness, ocular infections, pleurisy and pneumatic disorders, hangovers, constipation, oedema, colds and catarrhs. It is even 'an antidote against chronick Fear or Grief'.[37] Moreover, in a reversal of Paulli's polemic, Short explicates the parallel benefits that accrue to state and society – as well as to individuals – via the widespread habit of tea drinking. Tea generates an increase in corporate tax revenues; it stimulates ancillary enterprises that variously supply items of tea equipage or sites for tea consumption; it inculcates a culture of sobriety that unmistakeably promotes 'Business, Conversation and Intelligence'.[38]

Short's *Dissertation* struggles to achieve the mature equivocation concerning tea's properties that had been promised, the writer finding himself unable to tame his enthusiasm for its apparent advantages. In a revised version published some two decades later as *Discourses on Tea* (1750), it transpired that twenty years of further experience (both of drinking tea and of ageing in body) had done little to dampen Short's ardour, although he now more openly recommended tea as an article of diet rather than as a specific medicine.[39] The young medic Thomas Percival (1740–1804) was soon to invert Short's position. In 'Experiments and Observations on Astringents and Bitters', first published in 1767, he declared himself energetically to be 'against the general and too frequent use of tea'; even if, he conceded, 'candour obliges me to acknowledge, that it is capable of being applied to very important, medicinal purposes' (for example in relation to its alleged 'sedative powers').[40] For Percival, tea's ills far outweigh any goodness, and in no sphere of well-being is it judged so pernicious as the proper operation of the nerves. Tea is charged with 'the introduction of a numerous class of nervous ailments, in a great measure unknown to our ancestors, but which now prevail universally', thunders Percival: 'hypochondria [depression], palsies, cachexies [malnutrition], dropsies [oedema], and all those diseases which arise from laxity and debility'. Moreover, far from being a sobering beverage, tea encourages among its adherents an 'excess in spirituous liquors': after all, 'the lowness and depression of spirits it occasions, renders it almost necessary to have recourse to what is cordial and exhilarating'. As such, the ever-extending fashion for taking tea is undermining traditional social certainties. 'The hysterics, which used to be peculiar to the women, as the name itself indicates, now attacks both sexes indiscriminately', Percival bewails ('hysteric' literally means 'of the womb'); while from tea-induced alcoholism 'proceed those odious and disgraceful habits of intemperance, with which too many of the softer sex of every degree, are now, alas! chargeable'.[41] Tea, it turns out, (directly) turns robust masculinity into enfeebled femininity, while perversely (and indirectly) exposing feminine delicacy to masculine immoderation.

Percival grounds his critique in processes of laboratory experimentation and medical observation that lead him to conclude that tea is astringent and antiseptic, and therefore generally inimical to (if on occasion pharmacologically useful for) bodily health. There is however some slippage between his natural scientific judgement as a physician and his social scientific evaluation as an elite observer of contemporary life. This sense of permeability between researched knowledge and ideological ends occurs everywhere in tea discourse from the middle decades of the eighteenth century. In *The Good and Bad Effects of Tea Consider'd* (1745), for example, the apothecary Simon Mason expresses scepticism about the beverage's curative virtues and recommends sage-leaf infusions instead. Yet his real target appears not so much the misselling of tea as a universal medicine ('could we believe what is said of it, we should meet with no Distemper but what it is good for'), as the 'modern Depravity' of gossipy afternoon tea parties.[42] Meanwhile, James Kirkpatrick (1696–1770), the British editor of

Samuel Tissot's *Essay on Diseases Incident to Literary and Sedentary Persons* (1768), took issue with the Swiss physician's argument that tea's blood-thinning properties de-optimize digestive processes already restrained by physical inertia, and so prove 'hurtful to studious men'. 'The tea-pots full of warm water I see upon their tables,' laments an anxious Tissot, 'put me in mind of Pandora's box, from whence all sorts of evils issue forth'.[43] 'Our author has certainly accumulated here the utmost that can be supposed in the prejudice of this poor oriental leaf', Kirkpatrick retaliates in a long footnote; for 'having almost daily used it myself, and not seldom twice-a-day, for the greater part of full sixty years . . . [I] find nothing deterring in it'. Nonetheless, the editor cannot help but append one 'serious objection to the too extensive use of tea, and that is, to the too frequent consumption of it by washer-women, chair-women [char-women], and other laborious females in the lower class of life'. A far better refreshment following 'their hard work' than the 'corrupt dirty sort of tea' that such labourers' wages can afford would be 'a moderate quantity of good malt liquor'; besides, a draught of ale precludes any 'apology for introducing a cup of gin, or some fiery spirit, which tea does'.[44] Once again, tea is assigned a complex network of physical and social functions and effects: it somehow both enfeebles and enlivens, it signals aspiration but produces insubordination, it is a sober potion that provokes intoxication.

It was the London physician and philanthropist John Coakley Lettsom who would prove the most diligent student of tea during the final third of the eighteenth century.[45] *The Natural History of the Tea-tree, with Observations on the Medical Qualities of Tea, and Effects of Tea-drinking* (1772) re-organizes and expands Lettsom's doctoral thesis of 1769, which had been written and printed in Latin.[46] The book supplies as its first part a minutely detailed 'Natural History' (which includes the gentle rejoinder to Linnaeus), and as its second 'The Medical History of Tea'. Like Thomas Short, Lettsom's stated objective is a dispassionate and accurate under-standing of tea's virtues and drawbacks, avowing that 'in treating of this substance, I would not be understood to be either a partial advocate, or a passionate accuser'. His evidential basis is a familiar mixture of laboratory work and user testimony. Tea's antiseptic qualities are attested via its prolongation of the putrefaction process in newly slaughtered beef, while its sedative powers are indicated by the terminal effect when a distillate 'of the best and most fragrant green Tea' is applied to a frog's 'ischiatic [hip] nerves laid bare'. Lettsom then reports a series of alarming narratives concerning the fates of tea brokers and their servants who are long exposed in confined shops and warehouses to 'the fine dust of Tea', which appar-ently induces 'a spitting of blood', not to mention (in one instance) 'violent giddiness, head-ach, universal spasms, and loss of speech and memory'. Elsewhere the negative impact of tea accrues to more conventional methods of ingestion. Lettsom describes an acquaintance with 'a remarkable delicacy in feeling the effects of a small quantity of fine Tea': a single dish 'affects his stomach with an uneasy sensation', 'entirely takes away his appetite for food at dinner' and 'deprives him of sleep for three or four hours'. Indeed, it is claimed, 'opium has nearly the same effect upon him as Tea' (albeit 'in a greater degree').[47]

Nowhere however is tea's potentially ruinous nature more manifest for Lettsom than in 'all that train of distempers included under the name of nervous, [which] are said to be, if not the offspring, at least highly aggravated by the use of Tea'. Patients so affected find themselves 'constantly seized with great uneasiness, anxiety and oppression, as often as they take a single cup'. One poor 'young man of a delicate constitution' found that 'fine green Tea' induced feelings of 'dejection and melancholy, with loss of memory, tremblings, a proneness to great agitation from the most trifling circumstances, and a numerous train of nervous ailments'. Aside from the obvious discomfort and inconvenience of these unpleasant side effects, Lettsom's concerns about this 'fashionable herb' key directly into the period's social anxieties about how best to police an individual's 'sensibility', that web of impulses imagined to connect the human faculties of physical, moral and emotional feeling. Alarmed by the 'effeminacy' precipitated by a combination of 'disease' and 'the general use of Tea', Lettsom obliquely but unmistakeably opines that 'Desire is not always proportioned to bodily strength: it may be strongest when the corporeal strength is at the lowest ebb.' Even without the assistance of alcohol, in other words (for such had been Percival's proposition), tea engenders sexual dissipation among its devotees, rendering their bodies unhelpfully susceptible to the most voluptuous 'vice' of 'the present age'.[48]

For all Percival's and Lettsom's pessimism about tea's capacity to lower the spirits and to distort the body's nervous fabric – and it must be acknowledged that many of the symptoms they enumerate are known consequences of high caffeine dosages – the journal of James Boswell indicates that users often experienced quite different effects. Habitually depressive, Boswell recorded on 13 February 1763 (during a period of convalescence after a bout of gonorrhoea) his successful self-medication when feeling 'low-spirited', 'dull' and 'miserable':

> Green tea . . . indeed is a most kind remedy in cases of this kind. Often I have found relief from it. I am so fond of tea that I could write a whole dissertation on its virtues. It comforts and enlivens without the risks attendant on spirituous liquors. Gentle herb! Let the florid grape yield to thee. Thy soft influence is a more safe inspirer of social joy.[49]

For Boswell, it is the mildness with which tea 'comforts' the drinker (it is 'kind', 'gentle', 'soft', 'safe') that is remarkable. None of the traumatic manifestations charted by Lettsom are implied here. Yet even in this personal paean, broader concerns intrude, invoking 'the risks attendant on spiritous liquors'. Over and over again, the investigation of tea's psychological properties returned its students to perceived instabilities of mind, body and soul.

During the second half of the eighteenth century, tea became so fully enmeshed within Britain's daily diet and routines that it was instinctively reproduced as a touchstone for assaying innumerable physical, moral and social anxieties. Indeed, at times it appears to be the excuse for their regurgitation. For John Coakley Lettsom, tea's attack upon weaker consumers transcends 'corporeal' debilitation: they are rendered liable to mental instability, ethical decrepitude, crisis of identity. Nonetheless, it is also the case that Lettsom cannot help observing (like Boswell) how tea 'enlivens, refreshes, exhilirates' its imbibers, among whom it abates the incidence of 'inflammatory diseases'. Moreover, tea's potential destructiveness is offset by its capacity to bind Britons together in 'the pleasure which arises from reflecting how many millions of our fellow creatures are enjoying at one hour the same amusing repast'.[50] As Lettsom inadvertently demonstrates, tea continued to resist conclusive medical definition. Instead it bore the burden of over-determination, as an unprecedented transformative reach – in multiple spheres of life – was ascribed to and experienced through a simple, foreign, herbal infusion.

Growing Green, Saving Silver

Eighteenth-century botanists and physicians across Europe struggled to comprehend tea, and the geographical inaccessibility of live specimens was undoubtedly one major impediment. For horticulturists with an eye to both intellectual prestige and commercial profit, this represented a worthy challenge. The achievement of early travellers to China such as James Cuninghame had been to examine the plant in its native habitat, and to procure cuttings in flower and fruit; but by the mid-century the quest was on to cultivate tea trees on British soil. As the historian of science Londa Schiebinger has observed, eighteenth-century 'botany – expertise in bioprospecting, plant identification, transport, and acclimitization – worked hand-in-hand with European colonial expansion'.[51] Tea was one object of this mutual endeavour. At the outset of their correspondence in the late 1750s, Carl Linnaeus and John Ellis eagerly exchanged ideas about how 'to bring exotic seeds from China, and other distant parts of the world, in a vegetative state' and 'likewise the best method to preserve the plants alive, in so long voyages and so many different climates'.[52] The practical difficulties were immense, of course: securing a horticulturally skilled contact on an East Indiaman was tricky enough before one considered the problems of acquisition in Asia, or storage and sustenance throughout a six-month journey that travelled across oceans, round the horn of Africa and twice over the equator.[53] Yet the enthusiasm of these two men for vicarious intercontinental plant-hunting was unbounded, and Linnaeus made it clear from the start where his priorities lay. 'I would especially recommend your attention to bringing over a living plant of the Tea' from China, he wrote in December 1758, for 'I am very sure that this plant would bear the open air in England, as it thrives at Pekin, where the cold is more intense than in Sweden. Pray do not forget this request of mine.'[54]

Over the next year or two, Ellis and Linnaeus persistently debated alternative systems for the transportation of seeds (not least those of the tea tree), the Englishman preferring to encase them in waterproof and airtight globules of beeswax or tallow, the Swede opting to recommend containers embedded in protective salts. Not surprisingly it was the Londoner who enjoyed the greater opportunities for persuading merchants and sailors to pilot these methods. In 1760 his friend Thomas Fitzhugh sent home aboard a China ship a large quantity of 'Tea seeds inclosed in wax' which Ellis triumphantly distributed not only to Linnaeus, but also to 'to each of our governors of provinces from New England to Georgia; so that I hope to establish Tea in America, by that means, in time'.[55] On this occasion, however, horticultural ambition was not to germinate. Having (one presumes) patiently watered and watched his samples for some time, Linnaeus wrote in April 1761 that 'I return you thanks for the Tea seeds; but they are not yet come up, nor perhaps ever will . . . I fear your seeds will not grow, not even those sown in America.'[56] Two months later, Ellis despondently accepted this judgement. 'I am in fear that our Tea seeds will not grow, though we did not expect them to appear till the middle of this month', he conceded; 'however, I am not discouraged from proceeding in such useful experiments.'[57]

As the plan 'to establish Tea in America' indicates, Ellis's appetite for exotic plants was not just theoretical. Cultivation in the transatlantic colonies would both boost American agriculture and staunch the drainage of British silver into Chinese coffers. In the words of the historian Richard Drayton, 'an ideology of [agricultural] development . . . was fundamental to the making of the British Empire', an endeavour predicated partly upon what elsewhere has been described as 'scientific imperialism'.[58] Linnaeus's intentions for Sweden were not dissimilar. As early as 1746, he had in the same breath complained of tea's physiological destructiveness – 'it makes the flesh in the body loose, the nerves flabby, the head stupid, and the body feeble' – but celebrated its economic potential. 'Let us bring the Tea-tree here from China!' he exhorted. 'If one used just half the money that in one year alone leaves the Realm for Tea, then one would without fail gain so much Tea through Tea plantations here in the Country that in the future not a pence would leave us for those leaves.'[59] For over fifteen years thereafter Linnaeus's schemes faltered. Aside from Ellis's lifeless seeds there was a tree that turned out to be the wrong species of *Camellia* in 1757, and a specimen eaten by Gothenburg rats in 1761; but in August 1763, news of a returning ship under the command of Carl Gustav Ekeberg sent him into paroxysmal delight. Writing from Uppsala in response to a report that tea trees had been safely landed in Sweden, Linneaus promised with tremulous extravagance, 'Truly if it is Tea, I shall make your name, Mister Captain, more eternal than Alexander the Great . . . If it is true Tea Trees, I beg you, Mister Captain, for God's sake, for your love of your Fatherland, for the natural sciences, and for all that is holy and famous in the world, treat them with the most tender care.' When the plants reached him, they were indeed 'true Tea Trees', although they were also decidedly dead. But an initially distraught Linnaeus rode his luck, and immortality still beckoned for Ekeberg. The captain had wisely held back a further ten seedlings, which he now dispatched with his wife by cart to Uppsala, where they were lovingly received into the professor's famous botanic garden.[60]

While Linnaeus was able to celebrate his acquisition of the first certified tea tree in Europe, his frustrations were not at an end: indeed, his success would prove fleeting. Two years after Mrs Ekeberg had completed her delivery, Linnaeus wrote to Ellis that 'my Tea-tree is thriving, but still without flowers; nor have I yet dared to expose it, in the open air, to the cold of our winters, having only a single plant.'[61] Around the same time he appears to have resigned himself to the idea that it would not blossom in Sweden at all, for Ellis felt able to open negotiations about buying the Uppsala tea plant for any one of a number of wealthy English collectors.[62] The deal did not proceed, but in any case Ellis's own Canton contacts were about to come good. When the 1768 ships came in, Ellis was able gently to boast that 'Mr Fitzhugh, Factor to the East India Company for many years in China, who has been in the tea country, has just arrived, and has brought a Tea-tree home alive.' (It was at this moment that Fitzhugh was also able to confirm Ellis's botanical suspicions about 'the species of tea, green and bohea': he 'declares it is but one and the same plant'.)[63] As if this victory were insufficient, the following winter Ellis could casually divulge to Linnaeus that 'I have raised a Tea plant from a seed that happened to lie in the bottom of a tin canister from China, which I received this time twelve month.'[64] By the early 1770s, moreover, Ellis had established a regular supply of tea trees and other China exotics, thanks in no small measure to the assiduity of James Bradby Blake (1745–1773), an ambitious young botanist and the East India Company's newly resident factor at Canton. It is presumably Blake's efforts that are acknowledged in one of Ellis's final letters to Linnaeus, which notes the 'many young Tea trees brought over this year . . . from China'.[65] Indeed, Blake had raised tea from seed in Canton, and confirmed for Ellis that mature plants could withstand the winter snows of China and therefore need not be maintained in hot-houses in Britain.[66] Blake made copious notes on native flora, and commissioned beautiful watercolours of them from a local artist, Mauk-Sow-U; only premature death prevented him from becoming the century's most significant European documenter of Chinese natural history.[67]

While Ellis co-ordinated the procurement of tea trees from China to Britain, he recognized that his Gray's Inn residence in the city – and perhaps his amateur (if no doubt considerable) skill as a gardener – was not conducive to assuring their survival. His practice was therefore to send newly arrived or raised specimens in two directions for safe-keeping: east of London to the commercial nursery ground of James Gordon (c. 1708–1780) at Mile End; and west of London to the royal garden at Kew, under the direction of William Aiton (1731–1793). Gordon was entrusted with Fitzhugh's gift in 1768; and whether propagated from this or later examples, by the autumn of 1772 the nurseryman was advertising for sale 'handsome and elegant Plants of that very rare uncommon Exotic, the true green Chinese Tea-Tree, naturalized to this our Northern Climate in their Meridian Perfection and Exuberance of Health'.[68] Aiton meanwhile had been approached to safeguard Ellis's own seedling of 1769, which three years later (again in 1772) was lauded in the preface to Lettsom's *Natural History* as 'the largest Tea plant in this kingdom'.[69] Presumably via the agency of one of these horticultural technicians, a thriving shrub was transplanted into the gardens of Syon House, the London estate of Henry Percy (c. 1712–1786), Duke of Northumberland. Quick not only to construct a sense of national pride predicated upon the (supposed) scientific acumen of one of the King's favourites, but also – like Linnaeus and Ellis during the previous decade – to spot a potential game-changer for Britain's international trading prospects, the *London Evening Post* reported in October 1771 that

> The Duke of Northumberland, who had been happy beyond all other persons in the perfect cultivation of the most scarce plants, has at this time a tea tree in full flower. It is the first that ever flowered in Europe. This shrub grows from cuttings like a willow, and probably it will prove hardy enough for the open air with us; if so, as it is a very quick grower, we may soon have tea of our own production, and save some of our silver.[70]

By the early 1770s therefore, British natural philosophers could finally study tea close up. Northumberland's flowering tree was drawn and engraved by John Miller (1715–1792), one of the most celebrated botanical

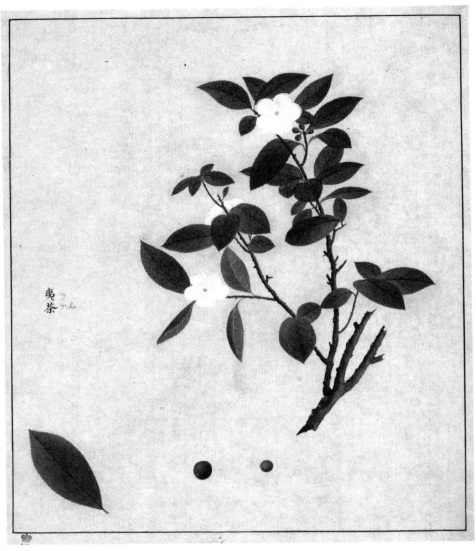

Mauk-Sow-U, *Tea, c.* 1770, watercolour. This watercolour was commissioned around 1770 by the British naturalist and East India Company Factor at Canton, James Bradby Blake. Blake's requirements for the accurate botanical depiction of leaves, flowers and fruit here encounter the flattened perspective of contemporary Chinese painting. The Mandarin character for tea is clearly legible to the left.

John Miller, 'Green Tea, Publish'd according to Act of Parliament', 10 December 1771, in John Coakley Lettsom, *The Natural History of the Tea-tree, with Observations on the Medical Qualities of Tea, and Effects of Tea-drinking* (London, 1772). John Miller's botanical engraving of 'Green Tea' was the frontispiece to Lettsom's influential *The Natural History of the Tea-tree*. Taken from the life in the gardens of Henry Percy, Duke of Northumberland, at Syon Park, this therefore portrays the first documented flowering of *Camellia sinensis* in Europe. This landmark event was reported in the *London Evening Post* in October 1771.

draughtsmen of the period, and the image was selected by Lettsom as the frontispiece for his book (dedicated, naturally, to the Duke). That the venues in which the plant first conspicuously bloomed in Britain should be the royal and noble gardens of some of the most powerful men of the age is only to be expected. A mainstay of both international commerce and domestic taxation, tea was now an everyday ritual in the lives of the polite and middling sorts: to own the means of its production (albeit symbolically), in the form of a live *Camellia sinensis* shrub, was to appropriate and display the globalized wealth and national prosperity that it connoted. Yet this neat conclusion does not tell the whole story. Aside from neglecting the vital energies of men beyond Britain, it neglects the insistent reluctance of tea throughout the eighteenth century to submit to Western understanding – to the 'epistemological authority' of the 'empire of knowledge'.[71]

For all that tea shrubs were now available in London to scrutinize, to touch and to paint, they had travelled such a distance from the contexts of their agricultural cultivation and processing that relatively little could be done with them. No 'tea of our own production' (as the *London Evening Post* had anticipated) is known to have resulted from the horticultural experiments of the 1760s and '70s: it would be two centuries and more before Cornish tea entrepreneurs Tregothnan could proudly claim to put 'the English into English tea for the first time in history'.[72] Meanwhile, John Ellis's public and 'ardent wish before I die to see the Tea tree of China established in North America' would also come to naught.[73] It was neither on the Scandinavian plains of Scania earmarked by Linnaeus, nor in the rainforests of Carolina and Georgia identified by Ellis, that European-owned tea plantations would be finally established. That shared if disparate dream would only be realized over half a century after their deaths, in what was for them the unimagined context of the Assam hillsides in nineteenth-century British India. For now tea would continue to be sourced from China, a known unknown, unerringly exotic.

SIX

The Market for Tea in Britain

It is early on Sunday evening, just two days before Christmas in 1759. Despite the lateness of the hour, the small grocery owned by William Proedd on Holborn Bridge is choked with customers purchasing spices, cereals, coffee, chocolate and tea. Running the shop alone, the grocer's 'boy' – William Bridgewater – is busy opening canisters containing the various dried goods that the shop dispenses, precisely measuring small quantities of nuts, dried fruit, starch and moist sugar, and wrapping them in squares of paper for the convenience of the clientele. In the midst of the clamour of raised voices, the handling of loose coinage, the tearing of wrappers, a young woman – Elizabeth Blake – does her best to pass unnoticed, observing the large chests on the shop's floor containing the grocer's valuable stock of tea leaves. She is the daughter of a poor widow who sells cheap clothing at Rag Fair near the Tower of London, and is later described by an acquaintance as 'an honest girl', though with 'not so much wit as other girls have'. Bridgewater, busy behind the counter, has not noticed the unfamiliar face in the crowd or the nervous figure crouched over one of the chests – but his regulars are more observant. 'That girl', they warn him, 'is doing what she should not do'. Alert to the vulnerability of the shop's stock to petty theft, Bridgewater raises his voice: 'What are you at?' he demands, crossing the shop to take better measure of the situation. When searched, Blake is found to have concealed in her apron 10 ounces of green tea, valued at sixpence. Mr Proedd is informed, and demands that a constable be summoned; while they wait, a distressed Blake fabricates a story involving an unknown woman in the shop putting the tea into her apron. 'I never saw that woman in my life before,' she asserts desperately. 'I was only here to look for my mother.' Three weeks later, in her trial for petty larceny at the Old Bailey, this story is granted no credence. Blake is sentenced to be whipped for her misdemeanour.[1]

Tea's infusion within British shopping habits was as subtle as it was comprehensive. Blake's attempted theft of a handful of tea – drawn from the published *Proceedings* of the Old Bailey trial – is an unremarkable mid-eighteenth-century story. It offers a glimpse of a city in which tea, 50 years after its first appearance in London shops, had embedded itself within the behaviours of the metropolitan populace: its patterns of consumption, the retail practices of grocery, and the background noise of low-level crime. Tea's emergence as a regular item of eighteenth-century grocery in the shops of the metropolis is most strikingly evidenced in the everyday cultural detritus which it occasioned: prosecutions for tea theft at the Old Bailey; the presence of tea-related motifs in the elaborate signs which identified shops in a city before street numbering; newspaper advertisements announcing the commodity's availability; the designs of the decorative trade cards distributed by city tradesmen; the listings of 'tea dealers' in London trade directories; the inclusion of tea in the itemized receipts issued by shop owners to favoured customers whom they had granted lines of credit.

As tea moved through the various stages of its metropolitan distribution chain, it was serviced by the many thousands who depended on the trade for their livelihood. Tea was transported from recently arrived East Indiamen to London's 'Legal Quays' in shallow boats, where it was landed by porters working for the wharfingers who owned those quays. Following its assessment by the customs officers who weighed and collected duties on these imports, tea travelled in the carts of carmen to the East India Company's warehouses, where the warehouse keepers directed its porterage, storage and security. In advance of the biannual East India Sale, the tea's condition was assessed by professional tea brokers before being resealed in its chests by gangs of warehouse labourers. The wholesale dealers who purchased tea at the sale either stored it in their own warehouses, or rented storage space from the Company itself. The tea was carried by waggoners from the wholesalers to the many thousands of small retailers in the city and beyond, in whose shops it was exhibited to potential customers in tin canisters or small wooden chests. Finally, shop boys like William Bridgewater folded small amounts of tea within paper wrappers and placed them into the hands of its consumers.

From Ship to Shore

A dependable supply of tea from Canton was of increasing importance for the prosperity of the city of London, the financial security of its largest trading company and the livelihood of its working population, not to mention the daily domestic routines observed in its dwelling places. Perhaps for these reasons, the imminent arrival of an East India Company ship was often heralded in London's newspapers long before it had dropped anchor in the Thames. Only rarely were the ships brought into the Pool of

John Boydell, *A View of the Blackwall Looking Towards Greenwich*, 1750, hand-coloured etching. Recently arrived merchant ships anchored at Blackwall Reach on the Thames, near the entrance to the Blackwall shipyard (where other ships are depicted at various stages of construction in dry docks). The cargo of the merchant ships is being transferred by shallow 'lighters' to the London Custom House (not shown). In the distance, the buildings of the Greenwich Naval College can be glimpsed.

London: East Indiamen were generally considered too large to proceed into this congested stretch of the Thames. For most of the eighteenth century – until the opening of Brunswick Dock in 1789 afforded dedicated space set apart from the main channel – they typically moored in the river at Blackwall Reach, near the Blackwall Yard, where most of the ships had been built.[2] An engraving of this stretch of the river of 1750 by John Boydell (1720–1804) depicts the constant passage of small boats servicing recently arrived East Indiamen, while in the nearby dry docks ships are built and repaired. The high market value of East India merchandise made the ships dangerously vulnerable to the theft of their cargo (a large quantity of tea was stolen over a period of several days from the *Harrison*, for example, as it lay at Blackwall in 1729),[3] and it was in the Company's interests to transfer the tea as quickly as possible into secure warehouse storage. But until the late eighteenth century, all imports into London had to be funnelled through the bottleneck of the London Custom House on the City's Legal Quays at Billingsgate in order to be registered, and the appropriate customs duty levied. Such were the risks of petty theft that an officer was appointed, known as the 'husband', to safeguard the passage of incoming tea from ship to warehouse. Chest by chest – in a mirroring of the role of the sampans on the Pearl River delta half a world away – the tea was transferred from the oceangoing vessel into small, manoeuvrable, shallow-keeled boats called 'lighters'. These privately owned craft

Samuel Scott, *A Thames Wharf, c.* 1757, oil on canvas. A busy Thames-side wharf – sometimes identified as the 'East India Wharf' – with various goods of international trade (the cargo, the artist suggests, of the merchant ships at anchor nearby). Among the various barrels and cases, a light-coloured container, bound by rope, bears the distinctive merchant's mark of the East India Company together with the numerical designation '316'. The mechanism of a tread-mill-operated crane can be seen behind the figures on the wharf, while above a barrel is lifted into a warehouse.

– operated by 'lightermen' – conveyed the cargo the final few miles upstream into the City of London.

The Legal Quays were a legacy of Elizabethan attempts to regulate the landing of foreign goods. They comprised a congested series of approximately twenty privately owned wharves – separated from each other by river steps – located on the short stretch of the north bank of the Thames between the Tower of London and Billingsgate Dock, just downstream from London Bridge.[4] Here the Company's shipments were landed, and typically housed temporarily in a small warehouse on the quayside known as 'East India Wharf'. A mid-eighteenth-century painting by Samuel Scott (1702–1772) in the collection of the Victoria & Albert Museum may depict this very scene (the painting's title, when purchased, was *The Old East India Wharf at London Bridge*, though there is some uncertainty about the precise location illustrated). Various cargoes are depicted on the wharf, including a bale stamped with the merchant's mark of the United East India Company. In the foreground, a treadmill-operated crane has been loading some of these items onto a horse-drawn wagon, while – high above – a barrel is being lifted into the second storey of a riverside warehouse.

Such was the volume of merchandise passing across the quays on a daily basis that organization was often haphazard and chaotic.[5] The movement of tea chests on the quayside, and their transferral from the Custom House to the Company's warehouses, thus represented another risk to the integrity of the precious East India cargo. Notwithstanding their careful packaging, the long sea voyage often resulted in minor damage to tea chests that compromised their secure containment of the dried leaves. Workers at the quayside conventionally collected the spilled tea for their own consumption but the porters who shunted the chests, and the carmen who transported the tea to the Company warehouse once it had been cleared by Custom House officials, were occasionally accused of deliberately damaging the containers in order to increase the spillage rate. So concerned were the Company's directors in the late 1740s that they commissioned the attorney-general to prosecute their interests in the Old Bailey trial of William Martin, a carman accused of stealing half a pound of tea. The attorney-general suggested that the magnitude of the problem extended well beyond this specific case: 'the Carmen, when they took the Tea in order to carry it to the Warehouses, they considered how much Money it produc'd, they bored Holes in the Chests; one saw another do it; at last it became universal.'[6]

Behind the Legal Quays were the important city thoroughfares of Thames Street and Tower Street, along which wagons transferring cargoes from the Legal Quays passed in a continual stream. They – and the narrow alleys which connected them – were lined with warehouses and businesses specializing in the processing of incoming cargoes, such as sugar refineries and distilleries. Throughout the early decades of the eighteenth century, the Company stored its cleared goods in warehouses which lay adjacent to its Leadenhall Street centre of operations, East India House (now the site of Richard Rogers's striking headquarters of the British insurance market, Lloyd's of London).[7] Though this was conveniently located less than half a mile from the Legal Quays, as the market expanded it quickly became clear that dedicated premises were required. Additional storage space was leased in the parish of St Helen's, Bishopsgate, and by March 1734 the Court of Directors had commissioned the construction of new purpose-built ware-houses accessed via Fenchurch Street, a short distance to the east.[8] By the mid-century, however, the Company's directors were again using additional storage, being obliged to seek permission from the Treasury to store bonded tea in leased warehouses south of the river in Rotherhithe.[9]

The Fenchurch Street premises grew organically across the second half of the century into an extensive complex of interconnecting multistorey warehouses. By the late 1780s they stretched as far as Crutched Friars to the south, and Jewry Street to the east. A satellite warehousing site had also been established just outside the City boundary, a short walk away on the other side of the Minories around Haydon Square, and before the turn of the nineteenth century the Company had constructed another immense facility to the north in New Street and Cutler Street.[10] These new six-storey warehouses alone had a capacity estimated at some 650,000 chests of tea.[11] The vast geographical area which these facilities spanned is shown clearly on a map of 1806, produced as part of a survey of the Company's estate commissioned by the Committee of Warehouses in 1799.[12] In the early nineteenth century they were serviced by several thousand labourers, forming the largest civilian manual workforce in the city.[13] An estimate provided by the Company's accountant in early 1767 suggests that over 7 million pounds of tea was at that time in storage; this had risen to 50 million by the mid-1820s.[14] Given that chests ranged in capacity from around 40 to 70 pounds of tea, it is surely no exaggeration to imagine well in excess of half a million chests piled high in these cavernous warehouses by 1800. Ensuring adequate rotation of the stocks was a perpetual headache, as tea brokers quickly spotted when the Company was trying to introduce old stock into its sale. Indeed, the alleged attempt to foist large quantities of mouldy tea – effectively unsellable in London – onto the colonies of North America was one of the immediate causes of the Boston Tea Party (see chapter Ten).

The movement of tea chests through these warehouses afforded regular opportunities for small-scale pilfering, usually occasioned by workers gathering the sweepings from the warehouse floor or dipping their hands into open chests.[15] As the registers of the Company's Committee of Warehouses have not survived, the incidental details noted at Old Bailey trials breathe life into the historical record. It is clear from these accounts that the East India Company was required to invest heavily in security measures to keep their workers under surveillance. Each warehouse had a 'gate keeper' who monitored the comings and goings of the labourers, a 'watchman' who observed them and a number of 'commodores' (or gang leaders) who directed their work.[16] Workers were not allowed to carry any of their own tea into the warehouse; any found concealed about their person could thus be deemed to be the property of the Company.

No in Plan	Where situated	How occupied
1	East India House	Stationary Warehouse
2	Saint Helens	Private Trade Baggage & Cloth
3	New Street	Tea & Drug. Bengal, Coast & Surat
4	Leadenhall Street	Coast & Surat Warehouse
5	Billiter Lane	Private Trade Warehouse
6	Lime Street Square	Military Fund Office
7	Fenchurch Street	Tea & Drug Warehouses
8	Jewry Street	Tea & Drug Warehouses
9	French Ordinary Court	Tea & Drug Warehouses

No in Plan	Where situated	How occupied
a	Crutched Friars	Company's Mint
b	Crutched Friars	Tea & Drug Warehouses
c	Seething Lane	Tea & Drug Warehouse
d	Somers & Lyons Quay	Wharf & Export Warehouse
e	Hayden Square	Tea & Drug Warehouses
f	Hayden Square	Tea & Drug Warehouses
g	Cooper's Row	Tea & Drug Warehouses
h	Ratcliff	Salt Petre Magazine

Details of *General Plan of Part of the City of London shewing in what Situation the Buildings are Erected*, 1806, manuscript. The East India Company's numerous warehouses and storage facilities are marked on this plan of central London, which accompanies a thorough survey of the Company's estate prepared at the turn of the nineteenth century. The names by which these warehouses were known by the Company's powerful Committee of Warehouses are given in the key.

Once inside, labourers were – by strict order – not allowed to leave until the specified time; the importance accorded the procurement of a clock for the Fenchurch Street premises (recorded in the court minutes for 18 May 1737) indicates the new practices of chronologically determined work discipline that the Company's directors were keen to enforce.[17] On leaving the buildings, labourers were regularly frisked by a Company officer called the 'rubber down', or otherwise by an officer of Excise known as the 'King's Locker'. This was when most small-scale theft was discovered, such as the one and a half pounds of singlo tea found in the breeches of John Quincey on 2 April 1761.[18] In August 1793, an excise officer performing a 'rubbing down' of Daniel Serjant at one of the Fenchurch Street warehouses 'found something bulky with my hand passing, and I gave it a pinch with my hand, and I found it was tea'. His fellow officer smirkingly observed to the captured thief that 'you have got something between your legs that does not belong to you' – this was soon revealed as a bag containing 18 ounces of congou.[19]

Consignments of tea (usually chests, but also – especially in earlier decades – tubs or canisters) were catalogued on entry to the warehouse, where they were inscribed with the name of the ship on which they had been carried, and a designated number. The combination of these two pieces of data conferred a unique identification upon each container, by which it could be cross-referred in Company records by senior management. Tea consignments were usually stored according to their variety in specific warehouses or on particular floors of warehouses.[20] Ahead of an 'East India Sale' – and under intense surveillance – a large number of chests ('many thousand' by the end of the century, according to an overseer testifying at a trial of September 1793) were prepared for each warehouse 'show day'. The wooden lids were prized open, the thin tutenague foil wrapper within which the tea had been sealed 6,000 miles away in Canton broken and independent tea brokers invited both to inspect the condition of the chest (to determine how the cargo had been handled and whether it bore any signs of damage by water or vermin), and to handle the dried tea (to assess its quality, freshness, the size of the leaves, the consistency of its manufacture).[21] According to warehouseman John Tadmire, 'the brokers come, and the chests are opened for them to take samples, and then a sheet of paper is put over to cover it, and lead over that, and then the wooden lid put on, and then that is nailed down'.[22]

A handwritten document in the papers of late eighteenth-century grocer Davison Newman, preserved at the London Metropolitan Archive, sheds some light on the way that tea was graded. Entitled 'Brokers Marks & Characters', it is a crib sheet by which company agents could interpret the shorthand notation employed by the professional tea brokers. The sheet details two systems: those used by Henry Bagshaw (later appointed by the

Valentine Davis, *East India Warehouse at the North East Corner of Crutched Friars on the Site of the Navy Office*, 1806, watercolour on paper. A view of a small part of one of the East India Company's extensive warehousing facilities in the City of London. The artist is at pains to emphasize the clean lines and symmetry of the warehouse design, suggesting at once its functionality and its orderliness. Six storeys can be seen, with space maximized through the use of a half-basement level, to which natural light is provided via a light-well at the foot of the building.

East India Company as Inspector of Teas in Canton) and by John Popplewell (who ran a London-based tea brokerage in the late eighteenth century) respectively. Bagshaw's scale allows for eleven tea grades, ranging from 'Fine' to 'Musty & mouldy' (passing through such categories as 'Good midling' and 'Very ordinary' on the way). Popplewell adopts a less ambitious six-point scale (from 'Fine' to 'Ordinary'). A long list of additional 'characteristics' might further describe a batch of tea; thus 'os' is used in both systems to indicate 'Odd smell', 'w' designates 'Woody', and 'f' denotes 'Flaggy' (indicating soft or limp leaves). Other marks are employed to describe various degrees of 'Burnt flavour' ('B', with extreme cases warranting 'vB') or smokiness ('sm'). Still further symbols demonstrate the brokers' ability to identify samples where leaves of different varieties have been mixed: thus 'cL' indicates that 'Among Singlo & Hysons are Blooms', and 'B' (confusingly, the same symbol as 'Burnt flavour') classifies those consignments where 'Among Souchong & Congou are Bohea'.[23] These symbols – or others like them – were used to annotate the sales catalogue that buyers carried into the sale itself. Tea, at the moment when it was about to reach its British consumers, thus had to submit to the interrogation of these assessors. By the time it proceeded into the theatre of its marketplace, it bore their 'marks' and was forced into their taxonomy.

Declaring Tea on the London Market

The twice-yearly sale of the East India goods – convened in the Sale Room of East India House – was one of many commercial rituals by which the passing of London's mercantile year was measured. This was a time-determined auction, a 'sale by candle', in which the lots were various quantities of East India cargoes: textiles, spices and – of course – tea. Each tea lot (or 'break') was a grouping of chests assembled by the Company's Committee of Warehouses, organized by the variety of the tea that they contained, their capacity and the ship on which they had been transported from China. The offer (or 'put-up') price of a break was typically the Company's cost price (including allowances for shipping, the commissions of the supercargoes, insurance and the import charge).[24] The amount by which its price was 'bid-up' during the sale to find a market rate thus represented the Company's profit. Through a system that was firmly in place by the 1740s, and probably well-established decades earlier, the only bidders were licensed tea brokers, making purchases on behalf of their 'principals'. At the beginning of the bidding for each lot, a one-inch candle would be lit. Brokers with whom the bidding rested at the moment each candle burnt out would be bound to arrange with their principal for the purchase of the goods at the going rate.[25] Just as with the most familiar modern incarnation of time-limited sales – the online auctions facilitated in the Internet

Augustus Charles Pugin and Thomas Rowlandson, *Interior of Sale Room in East India House, during sale,* 1808, aquatint on paper. Pugin's precise architectural interior – with its emphasis on the classical statues in their niches, and the sunlight streaming in through the ceiling light – is then transformed by Rowlandson's figures into the occasion of an East India sale. The professional brokers are shown competing eagerly for each lot. Down below, Company officials direct the sale, while the deals are recorded by a small team of clerks.

saleroom eBay – regular bidders developed techniques for winning a sale. A participant in a seventeenth-century candle sale (though not an East India sale), one 'cunninger than the rest', informed Samuel Pepys that 'just as the flame goes out the smoke descends . . . by that he do know the instant when to bid last, which is very pretty'.[26]

The sale's prominence in London trading life justified its inclusion in Rudolph Ackerman's *A Microcosm of London* (1808), a portrayal of London's commerce and culture consisting of a series of vivid coloured engravings with accompanying interpretative text. While the depictions of the architectural spaces were designed by the Paris-born draughtsman Augustus Charles Pugin (1762–1832), the responsibility for populating these spaces was assigned to the English caricaturist Thomas Rowlandson (1756–1827).[27] The artistic tension this occasions in the depiction of 'India House, the Sale Room' captures something of the way in which the energy, volume and competitiveness of the bidding undercut the fashionable sobriety of the room itself, with its modest neoclassical styling. Whereas Pugin seems to have been keen to represent the Company's business as the noble, civilizing achievement of imperial London, Rowlandson's figures suggest the ruthless world of commodities trading by which its profits were determined. The brokers are depicted (for the most part) as lean, earnest, even aggressive. While some sit on the tiered steps of an indoor amphitheatre intently studying their sales catalogues, others – gesturing or pointing wildly – stand on raised platforms, where they contrast pleasingly with the sobriety of the classical statues arranged in niches around the room's vast circular skylight. The auction caller stands at the raised dais at the front, on the left-hand side of the engraving, while the chairman reclines self-indulgently below the clock that regulates the sale. The anonymous tea dealer who published *Tsiology* in 1826 acknowledged that during the sale 'noise and confusion reign':

> To the uninitiated a Tea sale appears to be a mere arena, in which the comparative strength of the lungs of a portion of his Majesty's subjects are to be tried. No one could for an instant suspect the real nature of the business for which the assemblage was congregated.[28]

According to this author, the noise suggests not chaos (the naive supposition of the 'uninitiated'), but rather the health and energy of the tea market itself.

In a practice established by the 1680s, these East India auctions took place in March and September each year, though the Company often delayed the start of a sale – or adjourned it partway through – as it saw fit. The progress of each sale featured regularly in newspapers. From these casual observations, it is clear that sales were often many weeks in duration, typically with hiatuses in the proceedings when auctions for a particular group of commodities had ended.[29] Unfortunately, while details of the early sales until 1705 have survived, the volumes comprising the Tea and Chinaware Ledger on which this information was subsequently recorded as the trade expanded were destroyed in the mid-nineteenth century.[30] Detailed information exists for just one extensive tea sale, beginning on 1 September 1719.[31] In this single case, full details concerning the lots, offer prices, sale prices and purchasers was collated, printed and published, apparently at the instigation of Samuel Proctor – a minor participant in the auction – who had been a buyer at East India sales since the late seventeenth century.

Nearly 5,000 chests (together representing over 180,000 pounds of tea) were sold at the sale of September 1719, primarily the cargoes of two ships – the *Carnarvan* and the *Hartford* – both of which had traded at Canton in 1718. The chests were grouped into some 1,600 separate lots, with sales totalling nearly £125,000. These figures were typical for tea sales in this period, though small in comparison with those of later decades.[32] Tea was purchased at the sale by fewer than 200 individuals, most of whom spent several hundred pounds on several tea varieties. Analysis of the data suggests that some purchasers were acting for small retailers, winning just one or two lots for direct sale to the public. At the other end of the scale, a large number of buyers incurred a significant financial obligation, as much as £8,000; businesses with this amount of purchasing power – or the ability to raise the necessary credit – were presumably tea wholesalers who would sell the tea on to retailers nationwide. Such businesses maintained their own warehouses for the storage of tea, though it could also be retained in Company storage in return for a rental payment. In the mid-range was a group of purchasers who may have been active both as retailers, and as small-scale dealers. These included the young Collet Mawhood (d. 1758), the proprietor of what would become a well-known tea business operating under the sign of the Golden Lion and Unicorn in the Strand.

Over the duration of the September 1719 sale, Mawhood made purchases totalling £1,500, investing in both green and 'black' (or oolong) teas. This sale offered two green teas under names which had become familiar in London shops: a common green sold as 'singlo', and a premium variety known as 'bing'. According to eighteenth-century texts, 'singlo' was an Anglicized version of a specific tea growing region, the 'Sung-lo Hill' (probably Song Luocun in Zhejiang province). Its leaves were of relatively small size, and were considered to make a strong tea; its popularity in the earlier decades of the century is suggested by Mawhood's investment of £640, comprising 30 chests in total, including some presumably deemed to be of exceptional quality for which he was willing to pay more than double the offer price. Bing was produced from a larger leaf and – as a result – could be less densely packed; this usually resulted in higher prices on the London market.[33] It appears to have been regarded as a premium product in the early decades of the eighteenth century, perhaps through its reputed association with the habits of the Chinese emperor ('bing' – probably derived from a Han word signifying 'power' and 'authority'– was often glossed in tea advertisements as 'imperial'). Bing faded from view towards the mid-century, though an apparently similar tea described as 'bloom' was occasionally available in later decades.[34] Mawhood bought none of this tea. Indeed, it is intriguing that even though green tea was consumed in greater quantities than black until the 1740s, Mawhood was willing to spend more on his black tea investments.

The higher grades of green tea generally became designated from the 1730s as 'hyson', a term possibly originating from *hei-chun* ('bright spring'), a Cantonese phrase relating to the season of its harvest, or otherwise from 'Xiuning', the village in Anhui province most closely associated with its cultivation.[35] The term was used in popular literature to denote the highest-quality green tea available. Betsy Thoughtless, the eponymous heroine of a novel by Eliza Haywood, is tempted from her sedan chair into the house of a wealthy acquaintance with the promise of a sample of 'a Canister of some of the finest Hyson in the world'.[36] 'If I had been going to steal tea,' protested George Bristow at his trial for theft from the Company's warehouse in July 1795, 'I would not have taken [the cheaper] bohea tea, I could have taken hyson tea, which is worth half a guinea a pound.'[37] The common singlo gradually came to be replaced by another lower grade tea, 'twankay' (conceivably a corruption of 'Tungxi', another tea producing region in Anhui), though for many decades leaves under both designations were traded in London.[38]

Of the so-called black teas at the September 1719 sale, the basic standard was defined as 'bohea', a ubiquitous designation which led to its frequent use as a label for all non-green teas. Samuel Johnson defined the term in his *Dictionary* as 'a species of tea, of higher colour, and more astringent taste, than green tea'.[39] A corruption of the name of an important area for oolong production in China's southeastern Fujian province (the Wuyi Mountains), bohea had entered English usage in the last decade of the seventeenth century when Company directors became aware of an alternative to standard (green) tea. Presumably indicating the higher consumption of green tea, bohea was sold in September 1719 in much smaller breaks comprising single large chests of 69 pounds, rather than the six-chest lots (totalling 204 pounds) of singlo. Mawhood's investment of around £280 is significant, though still only half the money he spent on singlo, the basic green tea. It may have been that he regarded the prices that the bohea lots were reaching to be too high, as he wisely appears to have reserved money for some of the finer black teas which were to sell at similar rates. Names such as 'congou' (usually traced to the Chinese *gongfu* – popularly 'kung fu' – meaning 'work') and 'souchong' (probably from *xiaozhong* meaning 'small sort', a reference to the leaves from which it was produced) identified the progressively finer grades of black tea, though there was contemporary suspicion that unscrupulous dealers took advantage of the relative inexperience of small retailers and their customers by selling common bohea under these terms.[40] Although there was no souchong at the September 1719 sale, Mawhood secured 604 pounds of congou at a decent rate of 15s. 9d. per pound (the same average achieved in the sale for bohea), an investment of nearly £480. Most prized of all the black teas was 'pekoe', made from the very youngest leaves of the tea plant and (in its finest form) including partially opened leaf buds (the name itself is commonly associated with Min words which describe the fine hairs these young leaves bear). This tea, according to Thomas Short (writing in 1730), 'has the most pleasant and delicate Flavor of all'.[41] Mawhood acknowledged the limited market for this rather dainty variety with the purchase of a single lot of two small chests totalling 90 pounds, for just under £75.

Finest Teas of All Sorts

While tea was sporadically available in limited quantities in the later decades of the seventeenth century, its comprehensive arrival in the shops of London can be dated to the first decade of the eighteenth century. The widespread uncertainty concerning the commodity's qualities and uses was reflected in handbills and newspapers advertising its availability in a wide range of retail premises: grocers, mercers, apothecaries, chandlers, haberdashers and linen drapers. Even the earliest of these advertisements made use of the specialist terms which were becoming regular components of the mercantile jargon of East India trading. Thus Samuel Walter issued a notice in 1701 advertising the availability of bohea at his druggists at the sign of Queen Elizabeth's Head in Cheapside.[42] An advertisement in the *Post Man* for 2 May 1704 announced the availability of 'Excellent BOHEE TEA' for sixteen shillings per pound from 'the druggist near St Magnus's Church' (in later appearances named as the business of 'Robert Fary').[43] This had fallen to twelve shillings when re-advertised in late September, suggesting something of the volatility of the retail market for tea.[44] An announcement in the *Daily Courant* for 18 August 1707 stated that 'Singlo' was offered for sale at the Marine Coffee House in Birchin Lane, whereas Thomas Doyly – a linen draper of Covent Garden – claimed superior knowledge of the commodity by offering tea 'with or without the Flower' (referring to white immature leaves rather than the tea flower itself) in a notice placed in the *Post Man* on 20 January 1705.[45] Bing was offered for sale at Garraway's Coffee House in Exchange Alley near the Royal Exchange in a notice in the *Daily Courant* for 13 July 1709, while Lawrence Green advertised in the same newspaper on 3 May 1708 the availability of 'Imperial Tea, a good sort' at his grocery in Fetter Lane in Farringdon.[46]

The extensive vocabulary which became associated so quickly with the new commodity is suggestive both of its rapid rise in popularity and its growing modish appeal. One might draw a comparison with the remarkable speed with which manufacturers and retailers of the last quarter-century have introduced contemporary consumers to the technical terminology associated with the miniature architecture of smartphones, the varieties of New World wines or Italian-American preparations of coffee. We might nevertheless imagine that Humphrey Broadbent – the self-styled 'Domestick Coffee-Man' – typified the bemusement with which some regarded the new trade by the early 1720s: 'of Tea there are but two Sorts', he opined incisively, 'Green and Bohea; a pravalent Curiosity after Novelty, especially in matters of sensual Gratifications, almost continually Multiplies new kinds or distinctions of this Plant upon us.'[47]

Notwithstanding tea's early eighteenth-century availability in shops belonging to various trades, it soon became regarded principally as a regular item of grocery. Although an ageing Collet Mawhood was stubbornly defining his shop on the Strand as a 'druggist' as late as the 1750s, he was very much an exception.[48] By the mid-century a tea retailer was most likely to define the nature of the business as 'Grocer and Tea Dealer', though in the second half of the century the more specialist term 'Seller of Fine Teas, Coffee and Chocolate' became an increasingly popular moniker. Tea – or at least the containers in which it was shipped – was quickly integrated within the coded visual iconography of the eighteenth-century street via the symbolic apparatus of the period's elaborate shop signs. In an indication of the importance of sugar in their businesses, many grocers of the early eighteenth century traded under the sign of the 'three sugar loaves' (a reference to the way in which sugar was prepared for retail by being set in conical moulds), but the British Museum's extensive collection of trade cards from this period shows that grocers who sold tea also added symbols relating to this new commodity. The 'three sugar loaves and tea canister', in particular, acquired the status of a semi-fixed symbol for such an establishment. Indeed, the synthesis of these two commodities in shop signs is suggestive of wider British cultural practices in which a growing quantity of sugar was added to infusions of tea. As Sidney Mintz has argued, hot beverages are particularly amenable to dissolving large quantities of 'palatable sweet calories'; the fourfold increase in per capita annual sugar consumption in Britain across the eighteenth century was thus closely connected with the success of tea.[49] If Britain was increasingly an important zone for transcultural encounter, the humble grocer's shop of the mid-century was the space that staged the remarkable meeting of sugar from the Caribbean and tea from China. To adopt the nomenclature of eighteenth-century trading, the typical British cup of tea contained the products of both the West and the East Indies, commodities growing in lands separated by 10,000 miles.

Though a small number of successful 'tea men' occupied large retail premises within which customers might encounter an array of varieties, the vast majority of establishments selling tea in eighteenth-century towns and cities were small shops which attracted their custom from those living in the immediate neighbourhood.[50] While the very smallest establishments – particularly outside London – perpetuated the traditional practice of selling goods to passers-by through an open window, metropolitan grocers of the eighteenth century appear to have run their businesses within an interior space.[51] These shops were typically housed in the front ground-floor room above which the proprietor's family lived; a separate 'counting room' often adjoined the main shop, a space within which the proprietor maintained the business's account books and stored the day's takings in secure cabinets. Dried groceries were arranged on the shop's shelves – or even on the floor – in separate labelled tin canisters; customers typically asked the grocer (or the 'boy') for a specific amount which would be taken to a raised counter at the rear of the shop to be measured precisely using a set of balances and packaged in a paper wrapper. Sales of tea – as with all goods subject to the levying of an excise duty – were documented minutely in the shop's books to await the regular (though designedly unpredictable) inspection of the excise officer assigned to the area in question. The officer carefully 'gauged' the weight of tea contained in each canister and compared this with the records maintained on the premises. A mismatch between the amount of tea passing through the grocer's books and that which the officer calculated as remaining in stock required investigation: too much indicated that the grocer had an illicit supply of black-market tea; too little might suggest that the grocer had been the victim of petty theft.

Small shops often had a 'shop boy' or porter, who served customers, fetched tea from nearby warehouses and delivered groceries to customers who were unable (or unwilling) to attend the shop in person. Easy access to a valuable dried commodity like tea proved too great a temptation for many individuals employed to perform menial tasks in these businesses, and some demonstrated considerable ingenuity in hiding their thefts. In October 1758, Edward Thackerill was sent to the gallows for stealing one hundredweight of tea from his employer, John Walker, over a period of seven years. The small amounts that he took on a regular basis from the stocks in Walker's shop were hidden from both proprietor and excise officer by means of the careful placing of weights in the appropriate canisters: 'every time the officer came to weigh, he kept putting in weights till it amounted to an hundred weight and odd'. This is not the only case in which knowledge of the regular rhythms of tea retail provided insiders with the opportunity for light-fingered work. At a trial of 1765, it was alleged that Benjamin Watkins, employed as a porter at the shop of Joseph Fisher of Carnaby Street, regularly took advantage of the confusion occasioned by the delivery of fresh tea from the shop's wholesale dealer – 'when the shop was crowded with goods' – to roll canisters into an adjoining passage and remove handfuls of tea.[52]

The canisters in which tea was kept were not the decorative containers associated with domestic storage: in fact, they were often large and heavy, permanent features of the shop furniture which were restocked with fresh tea leaves on a regular basis. Their weight often presented significant practical problems for those minded to steal them. A witness questioned at a trial of 1780 concerning a canister which had been 'dragged . . . out of the shop' of John Sealy and Bolton Hudson, deposed that it had 'stood in a corner within reach of the door for many years'. A canister stolen in 1747 from the shop of Joseph Hurst in Goodman's Fields, Whitechapel, was considered to be so heavy that an accomplice to the crime was asked in the trial: 'These were large canisters, how did you carry them?' His response is as vivid as it is practical: 'I flung away the top, and carried it as well as I could.' The smallest shops might only carry the cheapest grades of bohea and singlo. Shops with a more expansive trade, however, typically stocked a wider range of teas graded according to quality; no fewer than ten canisters containing different varieties of tea were stolen from another Whitechapel grocer, John White, in the early hours of 7 October 1744.[53] Indeed, the range carried by some larger establishments clearly necessitated careful labelling: a trade card issued by 'D. Hernon, Grocer' near Somerset House in the Strand in 1770 includes a depiction of a container marked 'Hyson no. 8', an indicator of the supposed quality or character of its contents.[54]

The notices placed in the weekly and daily newspapers by London tradesmen provide evidence of tea's emergence in London shops in the first decade of the eighteenth century. But advances in large-scale print production, and the availability of cheap paper, provided eighteenth-century shopkeepers with additional opportunities to market their goods. The distribution of trade cards by shopkeepers became – by the mid-century – the hallmark of the business of an entrepreneur, and were all but ubiquitous as the century neared its close.[55] Although it is evident that shopkeepers typically distributed their cards to potential customers or suppliers as forms of advertisement, it would appear that they were also used as branded stationery. Many of the surviving trade cards issued by sellers of tea were provided as receipts, or issued as monthly or quarterly 'tea bills' itemized for wealthy customers. There is also evidence that some establishments printed their trade cards on thinner material, which they used as the paper wrapper in which tea was packaged for customers.[56]

Though Ambrose Heal – the noted early twentieth-century collector of trade cards – was keen to claim that they were untainted by the 'unseemly parade' of the modern sales puff (being nothing more than 'a straightforward announcement of [a shopkeeper's] wares'[57]), the design of these trade cards is revealing of the way in which tea was marketed by grocers across the century. The majority of trade cards dating from 1720–60 are embellished versions of the establishment's street sign. Thus the trade card of Parkinson, a Hay Market 'Tea Dealer & Grocer' which sourced its tea 'from Twinings', occupies a simple frame dominated by a drawing of the 'three Golden Sugar Loaves'.[58] 'Raitts Tea Warehouse', trading from premises on St Martin's Lane in the 1750s, had a similarly simple card depicting the shop's 'Green Canister' sign.[59] The canister which is used to depict the shop sign of William Chance ('the Green Tea Canister & Golden Sugar Loaf'), trading in the mid-eighteenth century in Fetter Lane, is labelled 'FINEST TEAS OF ALL SORTS'. Others – such as that used for a tea bill issued by John Dawson on 30 June 1741 – contain multiple canisters variously labelled 'congou', 'pekko' or 'bloom'.[60]

Increasingly from the late 1740s, it would appear that grocers began to market their tea visually as an exotic commodity brought to London by

Parkinson from Twining's, Tea Dealer & Grocer, at the Three Golden Sugar Loaves, in Rupert Street near the Hay Market, London, c. 1740, etched trade card. This advertisement for Parkinson's grocery business – probably dating from the mid-eighteenth century – clearly trades on its tea being sourced via Twining's. The design itself is a stylized version of the shop's sign, itself a relatively commonplace emblem marking the place of business of a grocer.

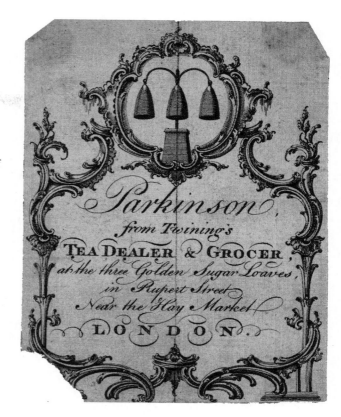

Raitts Tea Warehouse, at the Green Canister, in May's Buildings, St Martin's Lane, London, is sold all sorts of fine teas, coffee, and chocolate, wholesale & retail, c. 1757–8, etched trade card. A mid-eighteenth century advertisement for a tea business – rather grandly termed a 'Tea Warehouse' – on St Martin's Lane in Covent Garden. The embellishment at the head of the trade card is based on the shop's sign: the Green Canister.

the remarkable transoceanic reach of British mercantile activity.[61] The trade card of John Heigham Gresham (whose premises were to be found under the 'Green Canister' adjacent to the church of St Martin's-le-Grand) is a relatively early example of this development. Two small canisters are depicted, one marked 'Fine Hyson Tea', the other 'Fine Congou Tea'. Between them – in a frame also suggestive of a canister – three oriental figures appear: two hold parasols, and two appear to be holding some kind of organic matter: a rather fanciful representation of Chinese agricultural labourers engaged in the collection of the tea harvest. A simple Chinese landscape is also imagined in the card of Jane Taylor & Son, China and Glass Sellers in Pall Mall, of the late 1750s, in which two figures engage in conversation in a rural setting. The pointed hat and loose garments identify one of these figures as stereotypically Chinese; he is drawing the attention of his companion (whose tail coat and walking stick demonstrate to be a wealthy European merchant) towards two large tea chests, covered in 'Chinese' letters. A solitary figure, meanwhile, appears in a whimsical scene depicting the shop sign for John Harling's business in the Strand ('the China man and Tea Tree') on the reverse side of a tea bill issued on 10 August 1764.[62]

From the 1770s, the majority of the surviving trade cards produced for businesses selling tea make use of a series of stock images representing oriental gardens, tea bushes, pagodas, harbours, Chinese labourers and merchants. Some incorporate these symbols within existing designs. Thus James Randall, claiming to be 'the successor to Collett Mawhood', issued in the mid-1770s a trade card consisting of a decorative frame featuring various tea-related symbols including tea chests with Chinese letters, a tea tub and a Chinaman who points across the frame to a canister labelled 'Finest Plain Green Tea'. Others develop intricate engravings of oriental scenes; many of these are clearly mass-produced by printers marketing their services to shop owners, and contain a central cartouche into which the name and address of the particular business is inserted.[63] A typical example is the trade card of William Barber, a tea dealer who traded from 21 Leadenhall Street in the early 1790s. An apparently well-to-do Chinaman reclines drinking tea in the midst of an ornamental landscape; in the background, a labourer is watering a tea bush, while mountains and a tall pagoda rise on the horizon.[64] In another mass-produced design popular at the turn of the nineteenth century, a Chinese merchant sits on a chest of hyson, pointing at the name of the grocer whose business he is promoting; in the background is a depiction of a Chinese harbour, with a European East Indiaman setting sail.[65] More unusually, some trade cards depict scenes on the Thames, the tea cargoes illustrated as they are landed. Thus the business of J. Fisher, a grocer at 29 Jermyn Street in Covent Garden, is presented under a design depicting Britannia, seated on a lion, receiving the goods at the Legal Quays. An amalgam of these themes is provided

Wm Barber, Tea Dealer, No. 21 Leadenhall Street, London, c. 1789, etched trade card. A trade card for tea dealer William Barber, dating from the later years of the eighteenth century. In the foreground, a woman with a fan drinks tea with a Chinese man (his nationality represented via the usual stereotype of the pointed hat). On the right, another Chinese man waters a tea bush. The landscape beyond is suggestive of the mountainous terrain of the tea-growing districts of southeastern China. The pagoda on the left is another stock European symbol for China. The grasshopper – an image long associated with mercantile activity in London – may refer to the business's shop sign.

in the trade card of George Harris, a Bristol tea dealer, which fancifully imagines the East India House located on the banks of an oriental harbour on the waters of which a European ship sails.[66] This design in particular seems to make explicit a connection which others imply: the Pearl River and the River Thames, Canton and London, harbour cities located at the end of winding river estuaries. Through the reach of international trade – the passage of the East Indiamen – the tea trade invites its customers to establish, in the act of consumption, a series of imaginative connections between London and its distant counterpart.

The trend towards ever more complex and artful advertisements, in which retailers emphasized the mysterious contexts within which tea was cultivated, harvested and manufactured, can be related to the contemporary fashion for chinoiserie, a movement which extended beyond tea, but which tea helped to inaugurate (see chapter Seven). It suggests that grocers in the later decades of the eighteenth century were interested not so much in finding new tea drinkers as they were in attracting customers from other tradesmen. This apparent exoticization of tea thus paradoxically demonstrates its increasing naturalization in Britain. Evidence offered by these 'sellers of fine teas' indicates that eighteenth-century consumers were

J. Fisher, Grocer and Tea Dealer, No. 29 Jermyn Street, Covent Garden, c. 1791, etched trade card. This late eighteenth-century trade card for the grocery business of J. Fisher depicts a harbour-side scene in London, where Britannia – seated on a lion skin – receives the goods being brought from around the world. The building on the left might represent the London Custom House, or the nearby Tower of London.

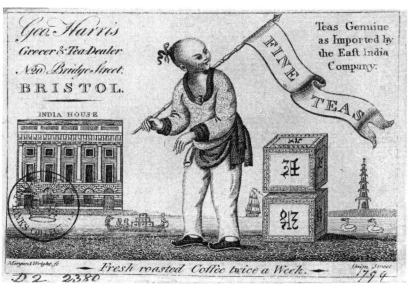

Geo. Harris, Grocer & Tea Dealer, N. 20 Bridge Street, Bristol, c. 1799, etched trade card. The design of the trade card advertising the business of Bristol-based tea dealer George Harris combines symbols referring to both Canton (pagoda, sampan) and London (the India House). The image appears deliberately to conflate the Pearl River and the Thames. The design is dominated by a Chinese figure holding a banner advertising the establishment's 'Fine Teas'.

increasingly being asked to re-interpret their own newly acquired cultural practices – their consumption of the produce of empire – as the luxurious (yet commonplace) habits of the inhabitants of a trading superpower. These shopkeepers were engaging in a collective appeal to persuade their customers that the refinement of a taste for tea – be that through their selection of 'Hyson no. 8' or the 'finest plain green tea' – made them participants in a trade which established transglobal connections between two imperial civilizations.

Richard Collins, The Tea Party, c. 1727, oil on canvas. Family tea was an occasion for the conspicuous display of prized possessions and polite behaviour. This anonymous family proudly display their tea service and their successful performance of the tea party ritual. On the tea-table, a made-up silver tea-set comprises a teapot on a stand, jug, sugar bowl with lid, sugar tongs, slops bowl, spoon dish with teaspoons and tea canister, together with four blue-and-white porcelain teacups and saucers.

SEVEN

The British Way of Tea

A family is taking tea, gathered around a rectangular wooden table: a woman, her husband and two daughters. The family is prosperous, and serious about advertising their wealth. The woman is dressed in a lustrous black silk gown, fabric spilling out behind her, with a gold apron and delicate lace cuffs, handkerchief and cap. Her husband shows his state of leisured relaxation by wearing a loose red gown over an unbuttoned shirt, with a soft turban-like cap known as a banyan, proclaiming his status as a gentleman at leisure at home. Sheltering under an arm of each parent is a child, dressed with loose hair and plain clothes. Both parents are drinking tea, as is the elder daughter, herself dressed in a blue gown with a white lace panel. The only member of the family not drinking tea is the younger daughter, dressed in a plain white gown. She is eating a piece of bread and butter – the sole dairy product on show, for there is no milk or cream. The family's spaniel puppy plays on a stool in the foreground. This scene is depicted in a painting entitled *The Tea Party* by Richard Collins (active 1726–1732), dated to around 1727 and now in the Goldsmiths' Hall, London (another version, including only one child, is held in the Victoria & Albert Museum). Tea drinking is the occasion for the family portrait, but the polite domestic event of drinking tea is embedded within a wider circle of social and cultural ideas.

Conversation Pieces

Collins's painting celebrates this family's self-presentation of genteel domestic civility, shown in and through their calm and polite 'tea party'. But it is also a spectacular display of conspicuous consumption, lavishly recording in paint the apparently unremarkable exercise of tea drinking, as if to show to all viewers this family's prosperity and social achievement. Gathered around the tea-table, they also display all the material objects of the tea equipage needed in 1727 to make tea properly. The tea service, which may belong to the artist's studio, is not a uniform set, and seems to have been assembled over a period of time. There is a silver pear-shaped teapot with a swan or dragon-mouth spout and a black ebony handle, sitting on a silver stand above a spirit lamp, to keep the contents hot. Also in silver are an octagonal covered jug with an ebony handle for hot water, an octagonal tea canister, a sugar bowl with cover, a pair of sugar tongs, a spoon boat with three teaspoons and a slops or waste bowl. In form, these silver items follow fashions established some decades earlier.[1] In the lustrous polished silver, Collins shows a reflection of two bright windows, and perhaps the ghostly shadow in front of them of the painter or viewer. While the tea is prepared using these silver dishes, the family consume it in fine blue-and-white china cups and saucers. Like the tea, the china is Chinese in origin. As was typical of the period, the cups do not have handles, and – when full of scalding tea – are held in various ways between the thumb and forefinger by the rim and base: the family show the three different methods acceptable to polite society. Everything about this conversation piece displays the sitters' immaculate taste in a discreet domestic setting: the tea-set, the clothes, their pose, their handling of the cups, the lapdog and the children. The group is shown performing their successful achievement of the role of a prosperous family in the middle stations of life. Even the form of the painting – a conversation piece, a new form of portraiture in which the sitters are shown in sociable groups in everyday situations – adheres to this agenda.[2]

Tea drinking was among the most common activities illustrated in conversation piece painting: an occasion for socializing, involving women and men in domestic settings. Arthur Devis's *Mr and Mrs Hill* has two sitters isolated in a fictitiously large and empty domestic setting, a space imagined rather than real, designed for proclaiming their bourgeois marriage. Both the human subjects here, their faces proud in rectitude and propriety, are shown in poses suggestive of genteel leisure: Mr Hill's hand in his waistcoat, Mrs Hill attending to the tea-things, sugar tongs in her hand. The tea-table behind her exhibits, in engaging detail, the couple's tea equipage: a set of seven small porcelain teacups and saucers, a sugar bowl and a larger slops bowl, alongside a silver water jug and a Yixing stoneware teapot, understood at the time to be recommended by Chinese authorities as superior for oolong or bohea tea preparation. The Hills' collection of china also includes a giant porcelain vase used ornamentally in the fireplace. In these conversation pieces, tea and the tea equipage, especially the porcelain, is located within a sociable performance of taking tea, reinforcing the spectacular display of proper domesticity in the middle station.

Conversation-piece paintings and tea-preparation guides show how the quotidian sociable activity of tea drinking was meaningful in the polite culture of eighteenth-century Britain. A tea party was not simply an event in which a refreshing hot beverage was consumed, although it was always that too. Rather, drinking tea became part of an elaborate performance in which the tea joined with human actors, the props of the tea equipage and the stage of the tea-table in a performance whose meaning was always in excess of the assembled items. The art historian Marcia Pointon observes that porcelain had become a 'status symbol' and as such, 'the central focus of a highly evolved series of competitive social rituals'. She concludes that 'Tea drinking is a paradigmatic case of a cultural phenomenon in which economics and performativity are inextricably bound up with represen-tation and self-presentation.'[3] In examining the tea party as a performed event, the historical particularity of the experience must be noted, and it should not be assumed that the event is congruent with the 'rules' of morn-ing or afternoon tea in our own period. The small and reassuring rituals of afternoon tea as it is now understood – putting the milk in first, warming the teapot, taking the teapot to the kettle – were almost unknown in the eighteenth century. Even in the eighteenth century, the tea-party perform-ance was a highly mediated one, an event about which numerous writers, satirists, essayists and painters battled to establish and contest scripts and tropes. The ironic phrase the 'British way of tea', as used in this chapter, suggests how the sociable event of taking tea in Britain was codified and ritualized in this period, somewhat like the *chanoyu*, the Japanese way of tea or tea ceremony (though, of course, almost nothing like it in practice).[4]

The Ceremony of Tea

Tea assemblies were a social duty within the family, located within the chronological and spatial organization of the family household. In the early eighteenth century, in households of the upper echelons of society, tea was commonly served in the morning as part of the ritual of social visiting, although it could be consumed at any time. In a private family of the middle station, tea was offered to the assembled family members and their guests as their 'morning repast', between eight and ten o'clock. Break-fast tea could take longer. A correspondent in the *London Chronicle* in 1765 complained that his wife wasted the whole morning, 'the prime part of the day', at the tea-table: 'she cannot prevail with herself to rise from bed before nine in the morning at the earliest . . . Tea is such a consumer of time, that it is past eleven o'clock before breakfast is over, and the manifold apparatus for the brewing it are all deposited in their proper places.'[5] Many families also took tea together, with invited guests, after divine service on Sunday afternoons, and in the evenings. A guide to tea addressed to the 'fair sex' advised that 'The morning (earlier the better) [was] the properest time; especially when to be taken in Quantity: In small Quantity, if drunk imme-diately after dinner: Two or three Hours after, more freely if you please.'[6]

Arthur Devis, Mr and Mrs Hill, 1750–51, oil on canvas. A wealthy married couple display their porcelain as an important marker of their status and propriety, in an otherwise strangely minimalist eighteenth-century interior. On the table is a tray with seven teacups and saucers, together with a sugar bowl and slops bowl, a silver jug and a brown stoneware teapot. A magnificent porcelain storage jar with a lion-topped lid stands in the unused fireplace.

Tea was served in the public-facing rooms of the household, such as the drawing room or even in specially decorated tea salons (as the conversation-piece paintings suggest). But equally, tea was also served in the private and domestic spaces within the household, such as the dressing room or bedroom, where women might entertain each other without chaperones.

Tea preparation was one of the few tasks that women or men of the higher stations were proud to be seen to perform themselves. In general, women in the middle classes and above were not expected to undertake manual labour in the home, especially activity associated with food service. What did fall into their purview were certain forms of high-value activities such as the direction of domestic labour and the formulation of medicines for the family.[7] When tea sociability emerged in the seventeenth century, tea's association with high-status women, its expense and its reputation as a sanative or remedy meant that tea making generally fell within the tasks of the women of the family. When the family and friends assembled for tea, the ranking or hosting lady (or sometimes gentleman) made and served tea with her own hand. The actual act of making tea occurred in the presence of the audience of assembled family and guests: the hostess took from the tea caddy a sufficient quantity of tea leaves and added it to the teapot, into which she then poured hot water from a large kettle, brought into the room by a servant. In Joseph van Aken's conversation piece *An English Family at Tea* (1720), the family's dry tea stocks are kept in a specially made chest, holding two separate porcelain tea canisters to protect the different kinds of tea from destructive odours. Such tea canisters were also imitated in silver or wood, sometimes in elaborate sets marked for green and bohea tea. Tea chests were lavished with ornate decoration, lacquered, japanned, painted and equipped with locks, such as that in van Aken's painting and

Joseph van Aken, An English Family at Tea, c. 1720, oil on canvas. Van Aken's depiction of tea-making reinforces the distinction between front- and backstage functions in the domestic family home. While a serving woman pours hot water ---from a metal kettle to the stoneware teapot on the table, a gentlewoman of the family has unlocked the tea chest and tips a serving of the expensive commodity from the tea canister to its lid, ready for preparation. Tea making was among the only examples of food preparation undertaken by members of the family, rather than their servants.

other surviving examples. Some accounts testify that the tea chest, or the canister itself with its high-value contents, was kept under lock and key, accessible only to each particular owner within the family. In this way, tea functioned differently from almost any other consumer commodity in the household.

In making tea, the most scrupulous care had to be taken at each stage. Even the water was subject to curious consideration. In an appendix added to the second edition of his *A Poem upon Tea* (1702), Nahum Tate offered some 'Observations for Making Tea'. He gave advice about the quality of water to be used, arguing that the finest tea was made with the purest and softest water, such as rainwater. He noted, nonetheless, that hard water from a pump or conduit made a 'brisker Drink' ('brisk' meaning fresh, lively and exhilarating). He further advised that the water be allowed to cool slightly before the tea was made – 'when it has boiled let the Agitation be over' – before being poured onto the leaves. Even so, each kind of tea performed differently under these directions.

> Your Singlo and Imperial Teas, are to be made by Infusion only;
> the least scalding of them being prejudicial both to their Taste
> and Colour. The *Bohea* will bear heating or boiling over again,
> and still drink well.[8]

According to Tate, while bohea's robust flavours will tolerate reheating or even repeated boiling, the more refined green teas, such as singlo and imperial, should be made by infusion in water below boiling point. 'Taste and Colour' are the goals of the subtle and evanescent flavour landscape of tea in its fluid form.

Having steeped for several minutes, tea was poured into tea bowls, usually made of porcelain. In the early eighteenth century, tea bowls were small and without handles, usually of a size that would contain no more than three of four tablespoons of liquid, requiring repeated refills through the tea service. Between successive pourings, any remaining cold tea was poured into a waste basin, known as a slops bowl. Tea parties required careful management of refills and reheatings, both in the cup and the teapot. Nahum Tate offered some advice about sugar:

> The natural Way of drinking Tea, (especially the *green* sorts) is
> certainly without Sugar, and too much dulcify'd [sweetened],
> their Medicinal Virtue is taken off, which our Author says, is
> not hindered by a little Sugar, and so rendered more Balsamick.
>   Note, The Refinedness of your Sugar is always an Advantage
> to your Tea-Liquor, both for Colour and Flavour. But with your
> *Bohe*, more Sugar is not only agreeable, but requisite.[9]

Tate, like most eighteenth-century tea preparation guides, gives no instructions for the addition of milk or cream, although there were recipes for tea boiled in milk for medicinal purposes. Items described as 'milk potts', 'milk jugs' or 'cream ewers' began to be listed among porcelain tea sets from around the 1760s, sold with breakfast wares.[10] But tea in the early eighteenth century, whether green or bohea, was typically consumed without milk.

A full description of the British tea ceremony, however, would properly begin well before the time for tea, before even the arrival of the family and guests at the tea-table. We could think of the performance of the tea ceremony as having a frontstage and backstage, with different actors and actions, and different chronological locations, involved in each.[11] Although tea was made by the ranking woman of the family, this act was an idealized recital of labour. Preparations for the proper performance of tea involved the family's servants in cleaning and setting out the tea equipage and the presentation of non-tea consumables (sugar, bread and butter). The servants were also responsible for heating and carrying the hot water to the tea-table assembly, bringing the backstage functions into the frontstage action. Even further backstage were the miscellaneous duties of service in maintaining the fire, and beyond that, the provision of the tea-table commodities to the household by the tea man and the grocer through the agency of the steward or the housekeeper.

Robert Dodsley, a footman turned poet who later rose to wealth and cultural prominence as a bookseller, described the 'Time of drinking Tea' from the point of view of a servant.

> The Kettle fill'd, the Water boil'd,
> The Cream provided, Biscuits pil'd,
> And Lamp prepar'd; I strait engage
> The Lilliputian Equipage
> Of Dishes, Saucers, Spoons, and Tongs,
> And all th' *Et cetera* which thereto belongs.
> Which rang'd in order and Decorum,
> I carry in, and set before 'em;
> Then pour or Green, or Bohea out,
> And, as commanded, hand about.[12]

The immaculate presentation of the tea equipage, 'rang'd in order and Decorum', Dodsley reminds us, is a function of its owner's taste, but also of the almost unseen labour of those in service. Tea-table assemblies were a moment of domestic choreography when the frontstage performance synchronized with the backstage labours, and moreover, in which those backstage labours could be effaced. Van Aken's *An English Family at Tea* depicts the moment the servant arrives with the water kettle, temporarily

A Family Being Served with Tea, c. 1745, oil on canvas. While one woman plays the harpsichord, three members of the family, and their two lapdogs, are served with tea. At a tripod table, a *famille rose* porcelain tea service on a silver tray, with matching teapot, five cups and saucers, a slops bowl and a sugar bowl, has the attention of the ranking woman in the family, seen here adding a lump of sugar to one cup. A male servant brings a shiny tea-kettle from the brazier to the table: the anonymous painter, with his easel, is reflected in its shiny metal surface.

crossing from backstage to frontstage, an insouciant expression of casual boredom on her face. A successful performance of 'the tea party', van Aken suggests, would maintain the illusion that only the specific activity of making tea requires labour of any kind, to be performed by genteel womenfolk, even though there were constant reminders of the role of the servants.

Scripting the Tea Performance

The sociable tea gathering was extensively modelled in poetry and satire in the first half of the eighteenth century. From the outset, serving tea was understood to be an important social occasion, at which appropriate codes of behaviour had to be observed, and for which an elaborate tea equipage was absolutely necessary. By the mid-eighteenth century, when tea consumption in Britain had become common among the middling sort, its longstanding association with the polite elite and with women was elaborated in new ways. Duncan Campbell, in *A Poem upon Tea* (1735), observed that tea preparation was an elegant and feminized activity:

> 'Tis brew'd and manag'd by the nicest Hands,
> And in China Mash-pot by them stands:
> From them they draw it in transparent Cups,
> Season'd with Sugar, instead of bitter Hops.[13]

By the early eighteenth century, such associations between tea and women and polite behaviour were profound. This is not to say men did not drink or serve tea, but that drinking tea was associated, in culture and politics, with the social world of women and its values. Tea drinking was feminized, though not necessarily feminizing; in the same way, tea itself, and the porcelain tea equipage, was also feminized. Campbell literalizes this gendered specificity by having two separate advisory prefaces, one for men and one for women, advising men that both tea and love belong properly to the 'fairer sex'. Campbell praises tea as 'the Liquor of the Fair and Wise / It chears the Mind without the least Disguise', preferring it especially to wine, which 'intoxicates and wrongs each Sense'. Tea drinkers gathered sociably together are politer and kinder, Campbell argues, because of the tea.

> [Tea] makes its Lovers to each other kind:
> It makes them smile, and sip like pretty Bees,
> Talk of *Marriages*, *Births*, and *Pedigrees*,
> *Sweet-hearts* and *Husbands*, and their Children dear,
> As like *Papa*, as ever they can stare.

The good-natured hum of tea-table chatter is a scene of convivial civility, at which agreeable politeness is the rule.

> Thus, Madam, home --- at, at her Table plac'd,
> Looks round her, smiling on each welcome Guest:
> Pray, Ladies, what d'ye drink, *Bohea* or *Green*?
> The Ladies, reply with an Air serene,
> Madam, what e'er you drink, be it both, or either,
> *Bohea* or *Green*, or mix'd if you had rather.[14]

Complaisance and serenity are the key here: a tea-table gathering in which the proper forms of society are observed without the dissension and tumult associated with wine drinking.

In *Tea, a Poem: In Three Cantos* (1743), the anonymous poet develops a verse inventory of each element of the tea-table. In the first canto, the poet celebrates tea as the harbinger of civilization and prosperity. Imagining a tea party at which women gather after religious service on Sunday, the poet describes tea in its domestic location, examining the tea equipage with a mock-heroic attention to the luxurious and exotic tastes betrayed by those items. The description begins with the tea-table itself:

> TEA's sacred *Altar*, be it neat and new:
> Nor mind what Forms old Fashions did produce,
> A Round's now best, because the most in Use.
> For its politest Look, and nicest Grain,
> *Mahogany* does now, unrival'd, reign;
> That Wood, as fittest, *Fashion* does prefer,
> Obey her Dictates, and you cannot err.

Whether fashion dictates a round or oval table, the poet describes its refined appearance, made of expensive exotic wood and, as he goes on to explain, inlaid with an intricate veneer image. Next to be noticed are the teapot and the tea urn, made of China or porcelain, translucent and elegant.

> Prepar'd the *Table*, let the TEA-POT share
> Your applicated Thought, and ardent Care.
> Be curious here, the noble Subject well
> Deserves the Trouble of the nicest *Belle* . . .
> Let *China's* fine transparent Earth compose
> The stately Urn, with Elegancy chose.

Careful and attentive tea-table preparation, the poet cautions, is an accomplishment expected of the proper young woman of the polite classes. Alongside the teapot, the poet places the tea bowl and saucer, also in porcelain:

> Nor let or *Dish* or *Sawcer* be forgot,
> They claim an equal Notice with the *Pot*,
> Form'd of the same refin'd material Mould,
> Neat be their Structure, elegantly bold,
> Nor large, nor small: Observe a Medium due;
> Fashion consult; none dictates half so true:
> If she commands, see mimic Flowers arise,
> Rich, in the Splendor of a Thousand Dyes,
> Swell on their Surface, with a pompous Show,
> And golden Circles round the Borders glow.

The poet admires the decorative scheme of these delicate porcelain vessels, adorned with intricate floral imagery and enamelled gilt borders. Finally, attention turns to the tea-kettle, made of silver or copper, and set above a lamp designed to keep its contents hot:

> Let polish'd Silver from the *Indian* Mine,
> Or finest Copper form the favourite Shrine:
> High on a *Lamp,* let the fair Fabrick rest.[15]

As well as reiterating the functional status of each item in the tea equipage, the poet also records that the form and appearance of each is dictated by fashion and luxury. Moralists warned that the consumer desires aroused by such objects had the power to corrupt and debase unwary virtue.

The items of the tea equipage – sometimes known as the 'tea-things' after 1740 – were just things, objects to be used in making and serving tea, but as such they were invested with considerable symbolic weight and cultural capital. Each item of the tea equipage could be purchased in a dizzying variety of shapes and forms, at different levels of quality and expense. As such, an individual's tea equipage was an expressive example of the exercise of their aesthetic judgement, a spectacle of personal taste. Moreover, as tea, its equipage and the sociable tea party were all associated with women, the representation of these things was freighted with anxiety and unease, attracting the attention of satirists and moralists alike. Indeed, an important poetic trope emerged, exploring the symbolic equivalence between women and their tea-things. Ambrose Philips, in his poem *The Tea-pot* (c. 1725), experimented with the neoclassical tea myth described in chapter Four. In this one-page broadsheet poem, he depicted Venus competing with a mortal woman whom she suspects of seducing Mars, god of war. Juno, goddess of marriage, proposes to punish the mortal virgin, who has dared to tempt a god, by reducing her to a porcelain tea thing, destined to serve other women for ever: 'Into a Tea-pot's Figure *thrown / Shall still attend and serve her own*'. The poem subsequently imagines the 'Maid's' transformation into a teapot: her arm congealed into a handle, her mouth and lips the opening and lid, her nose the spout, until 'by *Juno*'s Hand, / The Nymph a finish'd Teapot stands'.[16]

The same idea is pushed even further by the anonymous poet of *Tea: A Poem; or, Ladies into China-cups; A Metamorphosis* (1729), which depicts a tea-table located in the heavens, at which a group of goddesses sit to chat and gossip. Incensed by cruel treatment from their husbands and lovers, the goddesses decide to create a woman, Pandora, from clay trebly refined (like fine porcelain), and to invest her with all their special powers. The goddesses send Mercury to 'India' for 'a Weed call'd Tea', using the term 'India' loosely to suggest all Asian destinations, but also to reflect the fact that the East India Company imported Chinese tea into Britain. The poem describes the effects of tea on the goddesses, noting that it makes them quarrelsome and defamatory. Pandora takes their pot of tea down among the mortals, where the vapours of tea incite women to scandalize and rail, until even the goddesses Venus and Juno are objects of malicious gossip. Descending to earth on invisible clouds, the goddesses visit earthly tea-tables, and cause the gossiping women, whenever they try to take a sip, to drop their cups of tea, which shatter on the floor and bespatter their clothes. In the final Ovidian image of the poem, the broken china cups are made whole again as emblems of the women's manners and virtue: lustrous and beautiful, but also fragile and transparent.[17] In this equation of female manners and porcelain, the poet responds to Pope's *Rape of the Lock* (1714), in which the heroine Belinda's virginity is described as being like a piece of china:

> Whether the Nymph shall break *Diana*'s law,
> Or some frail China Jar receive a flaw.

At the end of the poem, after Belinda's lock has been cut, and her virginity compromized, the equation between women's sexuality and fragile porcelain is reiterated:

The GIRL in STILE.

Henry Kingsbury, *The Girl in Stile*, 18 January 1787, hand-coloured etching. A fashionably dressed courtesan, a kitten at her side, drinks tea in an affected manner. The tea has been prepared by a black servant in livery, who is shown adding hot water from a generous urn to a teapot. An exotic parrot in a cage, and a rather lubricious painting on the wall, complete the room's decoration. Tea retained its association with women and luxury long after its consumption in Britain had become almost ubiquitous.

Not louder Shrieks to pitying Heav'n are cast,
When Husbands or when Lap-dogs breathe their last,
Or when rich China Vessels, fal'n from on high,
In glittering Dust and painted Fragments lie.[18]

The deployment of this image of women's sexuality as fine china – beautiful, valuable, but fragile – has troubled many readers, redolent as it is of historically enduring discourses of misogyny.[19] Benjamin Franklin made the joke again in 1750: 'Glass, China and Reputation, are easily crack'd, and never well mended.'[20] As these satires have suggested, many observers rejected the high regard in which the British way of tea was held in eighteenth-century culture. The tea ceremony concatenated a whole range of cultural anxieties, focused variously on its many tiny rules and observances, on its aestheticized concerns with porcelain and the tea equipage, and more generally on the mistrust of exotic luxury and of consumer culture, and on the domestic reverberations of empire.

The Rage for China

To drink tea in the early eighteenth century invoked the use of another import from China: porcelain. All porcelain came from China, like all tea. Porcelain was not necessary for tea consumption, since much of the tea equipage, including teapots, kettles, jugs and sugar bowls, could be made of silver or other metals; and in these items, British manufacturers were as competitive as any. But as tea was served hot, many people considered metal inappropriate for tea dishes, as it was a good conductor of heat and so uncomfortable to the lips. When tea and coffee first entered the British market in the seventeenth century, there was no domestically manufactured pottery that could stand the thermal shock of hot beverages. Drinking tea in British earthenware pottery, even when glazed, physically degraded the dishes, quickly causing cracks and crazing. Though thin and fragile, porcelain's resistance to hot liquids was greatly admired. Thomas Tickell caught this paradox well in a poem of 1722, describing:

some frail cup of *China's* purest mold,
With azure vernish'd, and bedropt with gold, . . .
The tumults of the boiling *Bohea* braves
And holds secure the Coffee's sable waves.[21]

The story of tea is in this way also the story of porcelain: the two Chinese products locked in a commercial embrace.

Porcelain is a ceramic of uncommonly high quality, produced by firing a refined form of clay in a kiln at very high temperatures, between

1,300 and 1,400°C. The result is a ceramic that is strong and hard, white and translucent in appearance, with a tough vitreous surface, highly resistant to stain and heat stress, and possessed of a distinctive ringing resonance when tapped. These characteristics made it an object of intense desire in early modern Europe. Porcelain itself had a long history in China, where it evolved from older forms of earthenware pottery, so that by the end of the Song dynasty (960–1279) a true porcelain had been created. This was a process of gradual technological refinement: a combination of sourcing the appropriate mix of high-grade primary resources, kaolin and petuntse (the English words for which were transliterated from Chinese), achieving consistent firing in innovative 'dragon kilns' designed to reach ultra-high temperatures, and developing a large-scale and highly skilled workforce. By the beginning of the eighteenth century, the town at the centre of the Chinese porcelain industry, Jingdezhen, produced more than 3 million porcelain items every year, large numbers of which were exported all over the world.

The first imports of porcelain to Britain predate tea, and were imported by indirect routes. The earliest reflected Ottoman tastes, probably imported overland on the Silk Route, while later examples arrived on Portuguese ships or by Dutch privateers. Nonetheless, very limited quantities of blue-and-white Chinese wares had found their way to Britain by the early seventeenth century. Aristocratic families established some substantial collections: Alethea Howard, Countess of Arundel (1582–1654), for example, displayed a collection of blue-and-white *kraak* ware, and white *blanc de chine*, in a dedicated chamber she called her Pranketing Room. As Juliet Claxton has showed, this room was a highly specialized location for banqueting and other elite sociable gatherings, in which the display and use of exotic and expensive porcelain played an important part.[22] The most influential seventeenth-century proponent of Chinese porcelain as a decorative feature in the domestic interior was Mary II (1662–1694). When she returned from the Netherlands in 1689, she brought with her a large collection of china, both for use in tea consumption and for display. At Hampton Court, she displayed massed arrays of both Chinese porcelain and Dutch faience 'Delft' wares to impressive effect in a specifically designed china closet or *Porzellankammer*. Porcelain was displayed everywhere in such rooms: on shelving, over doors, on pedestals and on lintels and mantelpieces. Such spectacles, inspired by Queen Mary's experience of Dutch decorative schemes, were characteristic of the palaces of the Protestant House of Orange.[23] Aristocratic women followed the Queen in this patriotic Whig fashion for massed displays of Chinese porcelain. Sarah Churchill, the Duchess of Marlborough, collected Dehua *blanc-de-chine*, while Henrietta Howard, Countess of Suffolk, and Margaret, Duchess of Portland, both had notable collections of Chinese blue-and-white porcelain.

Bow Porcelain Factory, London, teapot, c. 1750, soft-paste porcelain painted in underglaze blue. English porcelain imitated the decoration and design of Chinese products. This teapot was made at the Bow Porcelain Factory at its New Canton factory in Bow, a village 4 miles east of London, only a few years after the first successful imitation of porcelain in Britain.

Chinoiserie, the taste for Chinese decoration, was associated especially with the aesthetic of elite women, and with the domestic spaces in the home reserved for them. Elizabeth Montagu (1718–1800), the 'Queen of the Bluestockings', decorated a salon in the Chinese taste in her London town house in Hill Street in the late 1740s.[24] Montagu used her 'Chinese room' to entertain a circle of intellectually engaged women and men who came to identify themselves as 'bluestocking philosophers'. In decorating her 'Chinese room', Montagu was aided by her brother, Captain Robert Robinson of the East India Company, who had made a series of voyages to Madras and Canton, bringing her rare items of Chinese porcelain and other 'oriental' objects she could incorporate into her decorative scheme. Chinoiserie was not without its detractors: some accused it of being a debased and luxurious taste, selfishly encouraged by the mercantile interest, at once both impiously pagan and morally fake. But, as Montagu was aware, the vogue for 'Chinese taste' allowed her to create a gently feminized space in which her women friends might be at home with their intellectual ambitions; at the same time, it accurately reflected her status as a wealthy landowner and a 'sociable creature'. Intriguingly, Montagu conjectured that the Chinese room allowed her to play new roles. Writing to her husband in 1751, she imagined herself as a Qing empress: 'I have a great mind to sit this Winter like a true Empress of China in retired state with nodding mandarins about me. I think I have a Chinese Palace & why may I not have the rest of her Chinese Majestys prerogatives?'[25] Chinoiserie represented on the one

Pattern plate, Jingdezhen, China, *c.* 1790, porcelain decorated in polychrome enamels and gilding. Chinese export porcelain commissioned with European armorial decorations commanded high prices. A design for armorial bearings, or indeed any other image, was sent to China, where it was either transmitted to Jengdezhen to be incorporated into the glazed wares or, if in Canton, enamelled onto a plain piece of porcelain, which was then fired again. The whole process, between commissioning and receiving an order, could take two or three years. This pattern plate allowed European families to choose the decoration of their porcelain service.

hand a thoughtful and engaged response to the exotic experience of Chinese taste, whether for porcelain, tea or other exotic commodities; but on the other, it rendered these items into a shallow decorative scheme that refused to engage with the more morally complex, and even exploitative, aspects of Europe's economic and cultural encounter with China.

One visitor to Montagu's Chinese room soon after it was completed was Marie-Anne du Boccage (1710–1802), a celebrated French dramatist who sojourned in London in 1750. Du Boccage was charmed with the manner of English morning socializing, which brought together a diverse range of people, she said, over 'exquisite viands' and luxurious tea things:

> We breakfasted in this manner today at Lady MONTAGU's, in a
> closet lined with painted paper of *Pekin*, and furnished with

the choicest movables of *China*: A long table, covered with the finest linen, presented to the view a thousand glittering cups, which contained coffee, chocolate, biscuits, cream, butter, toasts, and exquisite tea. You must understand, that there is no good tea to be had anywhere but at *London*. The Mistress of the house, who deserves to be served at the table of the gods, poured it out herself; this is the custom.[26]

To this French intellectual, one of the most striking aspects of the British tea ceremony was the role played in it by the 'Mistress of the house', who, belying her wealth and influence, chose to pour the tea herself.

The market for Chinese porcelain, as it was for tea, was in the hands of the East India Company, either officially, or through the 'Private Trade' of its supercargoes. Porcelain was comparatively heavy and fragile, but it was impervious to water damage, unlike the valuable but bulky commodities of tea and silk. This made it a valuable complementary cargo in the Company's Indiamen. Packed low in the hold, the tubs of porcelain were filled up with sago to reduce breakages: the sago was not expected to be in any condition to be sold on arrival. As the East India Company increased the number of its voyages to China in the early eighteenth century, quantities of porcelain 'China-ware' also increased.[27] In 1705, Company orders for the frigate *Oley*, bound for Canton, directed it to purchase 30 tons of silk, 100 tons of tea (60 singlo, 15 imperial, 25 bohea), and 10 tons of China-ware.[28] This was a considerable quantity of what was a durable commodity. In 1710, a Court Minute detailed the quantity of China-ware that was to be offered at the next Company sale in April, where it was proposed to sell 180,000 cups and saucers, 27,000 plates, 26,000 bowls and dishes and 4,000 teapots, among other items. Prices achieved in auction sales like this one suggest that a simple utilitarian Chinese export cup and saucer could be purchased for about twopence wholesale.[29] Huge quantities of Chinese porcelain were imported later in the century. In 1734 alone, more than a million pieces were imported, though precise numbers are difficult to quantify as individual items were not recorded in the dispatch books.[30] Many of these were ordinary everyday wares, reproducing a limited number of Chinese patterns. These tea dishes and saucers, though mundane compared to the elaborate vessels and dishes displayed in aristocratic *Porzellankammer*, remained a high-status commodity, distributed through the expanding luxury market in England's cities. At East India Company sales, porcelain was grouped in large lots for sale to trade buyers – known as 'China-men' – who distributed and sold the items on the retail market around Britain, and also by export to its colonies.[31] Peter Motteux, the poet of tea, sold both Chinese porcelain cups and Chinese tea at his 'India Warehouse at the sign of the Two Fans' in Leadenhall Street, close to East India House.

Richard Steele, in *The Spectator*, 'found his spacious Warehouses fill'd and adorn'd with Tea, *China* and *Indian* Ware'.[32]

The most notable increase in East India Company imports of porcelain and tea occurred at the same historical moment, in the first decades of the eighteenth century. These were important decades for tea culture, as consumption increased sharply, and it was subject to increased mediatization in poems and satires that followed Ovington's *Essay upon Tea* (1699). These were also important decades for porcelain, which was imported in noticeably larger quantities from the 1690s onwards. Histories of tea often assume that tea beseeched porcelain; which is to say that the hot beverage required the importation of appropriate vessels to drink it from, since domestic wares were inadequate. The evidence in the ledgers, however, suggests that the reverse may also have been true: that the desire for Chinese porcelain encouraged a taste for something appropriate to do with it, and that something, increasingly, was to drink tea out of it. Taste for one Chinese product enhanced the taste for another.

Chinese porcelain's unique qualities – whiter and brighter, lighter and harder, resistant to hot liquids and flavour taint – made it something of a disruptive technology, unsettling local pottery manufacturers in Europe and causing intense cycles of imitation and reform. Across the Continent it transformed the coarse brown earthenware that had been the dominant pottery of any quantity since the Roman period, inspiring inferior tin-glazed faience earthenware imitations such as majolica and Delftware. The competition with porcelain also drove local manufacturers, and European heads of state, to seek domestic surrogates or imitations.[33] The first to find success was that promoted by Frederick Augustus I (1670–1733), Elector of Saxony, at Meissen, near the German city of Dresden in Saxony, in 1709. The breakthrough was made after discoveries of kaolin and petuntse allowed a 'true' hard-paste porcelain recipe to be achieved, which were fired in higher-quality, high-temperature kilns. European knowledge of porcelain and its 'secrets' was greatly enhanced by the publication of a description of the Jingdezhen system in a series of letters written by a Jesuit missionary, François Xavier d'Entrecolles, in 1712, which were finally published in 1735.[34] By 1760, more than 30 rival European porcelain factories had been established.

In England, the first porcelain manufactories were in London, at Bow, Limehouse and Chelsea, in the mid-1740s. While the latter concentrated on figurines and other art manufactures, the Bow porcelain factory was established to produce wares to rival those offered in the East India Company sales, especially tea dishes and teapots. In 1748, a consortium of London merchants established a factory to exploit an innovative recipe for a soft-paste porcelain made using calcined bone ash, kaolin and potter's ball clay, a recipe that led to the development of fine 'bone china'.[35] The works were established at a place they named 'New Canton' in imitation of the East India Company factory in China, on the Bow Back River of the River Lea, only a mile or so from where this book has been written, underneath what is at present a Porsche car showroom. The location was carefully chosen: it was close to London (the principal market for porcelains); was accessible for waterborne transport (the most suitable mode for fragile goods); and was near to the abattoirs and slaughterhouses of the city's meat market (the source for the raw material of bone). The project was also encouraged by tax advantages, as domestic wares would avoid the high import duties on 'painted' porcelain. The Bow porcelain manufactory sought to compete in the sale of ordinary tea wares in blue-and-white, selling them at auction sales but also through their own warehouse at New Canton and at sundry china shops across the capital. In 1753, a 'Bow China Warehouse' was opened near the Royal Exchange on Cornhill, in the centre of the City, 'for the convenience of all Customers in both Town and Country; where all sorts of China will be sold'.[36] In the longer term, the Bow porcelain factory failed to survive its founders, closing in 1776. However, bone china itself continued to be manufactured and was perfected by other potteries in the later eighteenth century, especially those in Derby and Stoke founded by Josiah Spode and Josiah Wedgwood.

The Emperor's Tea Poem

European porcelains were a creative, technological and scientific response to the disruptive influence of Chinese porcelain in commercial and social life. In this way also, porcelains resemble the effects of tea on British culture. The relish for chinoiserie, whether tea or porcelain, demanded change in the client culture, creating new hybrid forms of behaviour and knowledge – including the British way of tea. Among the most extraordinary examples of the desire for Chinese things was the publication on 14 July 1770 in the *Public Advertiser* (a London newspaper) of a poem on tea written by the Chinese emperor himself. The Qianlong Emperor, whose name was then transliterated as Kien-Long, reigned from 1735 to 1796 as the fourth emperor of the Qing dynasty. Celebrated as a scholar and connoisseur of arts and culture, under his leadership the imperial court had become a very significant patron and collector, enlarging imperial workshops, collecting antiquities and building palaces. Among his own accomplishments was a taste for poetry.[37]

The Qianlong Emperor's poem presented an account of tea preparation, but also described the meditative Confucian approach to tea drinking in China. In the Chinese way of tea, tea drinking was embedded within a ritual and synaesthetic appreciation of other natural beauties. Qianlong's poem instances a tea drinker's delight in seeing and smelling a Mei-hoa flowering plum (*Prunus mume*) and a Fo-shou Buddha's hand fruit (*Citrus medica* var. *sarcodactylis*). The proper preparation of tea was minutely observed. The Qianlong Emperor advised:

> let there be placed on a moderate Fire, a Tripod Boiler whose Form and Colour, shall show it to have been well-seasoned by long Service; it should be filled with the limpid Water of melted Snow, and warmed to that Degree which suffices for whitening the finny Tribes, or reddening the Shell of the crustaceous Kind: Then pour it into a Cup made of the Porcelain of *Yvay* [Yue]; let it stand till the Vapours which, at first, will rise in Abundance, and form a thick Cloud, shall have gradually thinned into the Appearance of light Mist: Then you may, without Precipitation, sip this delicious Liquor.[38]

The purpose of tea drinking, the emperor continues, is exactly 'the Calm which steals upon the Senses from a Liquor so prepared': he describes how, sitting in his tent on a military campaign, tea can soothe the mind and allow meditative reflection on the activities of the day.

Emperors and kings did not often publish poems in the eighteenth century. It must have come as something of a surprise for readers of the *Public Advertiser* to read an article entitled 'A PROSE-TRANSLATION of an ODE on TEA. Composed by Kien-Long, the present Emperor of *China* and *Tartary* in the Year 1746'. The translator introduced the poem as a 'Curiosity' – an 'Oriental Composition' from 'so eminent a Hand' as the emperor – and noted that it had been discovered in France 'stamped upon Sets of Tea-Cups of a particular Kind of Porcelain' owned by Henri Léonard Bertin, the sinophile secretary of state who had once administered the French East India Company. The Emperor's 'Ode on Tea', as it appeared in the London press, was probably translated from the French translation made by the Jesuit missionary Jean Joseph Marie Amiot (1718–1793), who had gained the confidence of the Qianlong Emperor during his long residence in Beijing.[39] A superior verse translation was published two years later in 1772, in the same newspaper, and yet another appeared in 1773 from Sir William Chambers, all from Amiot's French version.[40] The emperor's tea poem gained a certain notoriety: while knowledge of Chinese tea philosophy excited some scholars and poets, satirists also observed a ridiculous gap between the writer's elevated status and the apparently mundane topic of the verses. As such, numerous 'emperor poems' circulated in the later decades of the century, each more absurd than the last, exploiting the disparity between Chinese and English culture.[41] One example was Peter Pindar's 'Ode to Coffee in the Manner of Kienlong', first published in 1792: it imitates the 'Ode on Tea' by describing coffee preparation in some detail,

Beijing Zaobanchu (Workshops of the Imperial Palace), bowl with lid [inscribed with 'Three Purity Tea' poem], 1746, porcelain, blue enamel on white enamel ground on copper. This Chinese porcelain tea bowl with lid is decorated with a poem about tea composed by the Qianlong Emperor. The poem, which celebrates the preparation of tea within a meditative and sensory framework, was first published in English in July 1770 in *The Public Advertiser*, a London newspaper.

and deflating the Qianlong's tea reverie by describing the poet-statesman drifting off to sleep, dreaming of his ministers.[42] As these satires suggest, the emperor's scholarly tea aestheticism, embedded in Confucian philosophy and Chinese cultural politics, was incommensurate with what was by then the almost ubiquitous, and decidedly ordinary, experience of the British way of tea.

William Dent, *Catlap For Ever, or, The Smuggler's Downfal*, 1784, etching. Prime Minister William Pitt addresses a group of women outside the East India House on Leadenhall Street in central London. The tea chests on which he stands are themselves placed on top of the prone figure of Charles James Fox, leader of the faction opposing Pitt in Parliament. Pitt's speech, and that of many of the other figures in the drawing, makes reference to the recent passing of the Commutation Act by which the excise levied on tea was to be replaced by an additional tax on windows.

EIGHT

Smuggling and Taxation

By the mid-1780s, tea had become a weighty political issue. A satirical cartoon printed by William Dent in early July 1784, entitled 'CATLAP FOR EVER, OR, THE SMUGGLER'S DOWNFAL', depicts Prime Minister William Pitt standing on top of tea chests marked 'Bohea Tea Duty Free' and 'East India Bill'.[1] Behind him, framing his youthful profile, rises the facade of East India House, propped up by artificial buttresses labelled 'prerogative' and 'monopoly'. Pitt, in line with prevailing satirical commonplaces, is a gaunt and aloof presence who appears unmoved either by a broadly supportive group of raucous women stood before him (one of whom calls him a 'little cock of wax'), or by the well-dressed bald man on his right who shakes his fist and heckles him with the words 'Dam[n] your Catlap – give us Windows, Coals and Candles or, my eyes and limbs, I'll thump your bread basket.' 'Catlap' was a slang coinage of the 1780s, referring to an insipid liquor fit only for consumption by cats. The joke on which this cartoon plays is the idea that tea – in one strand of cultural understanding, at least – is a species of 'catlap', a concoction which is bland, inoffensive, unobjectionable, valueless. Pitt's words, in common with those of the bald man, allude to a connection between tea on the one hand and windows, coals and candles on the other. But for him, tea is a 'weed so nourishing that it may be called the Manna of females'; and while 'the loss of Daylight, Firelight & Candlelight' is the price that the people have paid for 'reducing the price of Tea', this inconvenience can easily be overcome by a 'drop of Gin'. Lying on the ground at the bottom of the image is the thick-set figure of Pitt's great political adversary, Charles Fox, crushed by the weight of the tea chests on which Pitt stands. 'Push him off or he'll squeeze my lights out,' Fox cries, his words playing on the cartoon's interest in illumination (and its extinguishment). The relationship between commodity and politician is symbiotic. Pitt – diminutive, birdlike – has made use of the heavy chests of Tea to give him the political weight necessary to crush his opponents, and to deliver a populist victory. Tea – equally – has enlisted Pitt's political savvy to enable the next stage of its conquest of British taste. 'CATLAP FOR EVER', tea victorious.

Identifying tea as 'catlap' had a prevailing satirical currency in the mid-1780s. Indeed, readers looking up the meaning of the term in Francis Grose's *Classical Dictionary of the Vulgar Tongue* (1785) would find it defined – straightforwardly – as 'tea'. It is possible that such usage had its roots in a simple derision of tea's lack of a bold flavour. But confusingly Grose's *Dictionary* also uses 'tea' to define the more political term 'scandal broth'.[2] This equivocal resonance of 'tea' – echoing in the body politic wider debates about its healthfulness for the individual drinker – seems to offer a way to make some sense of Dent's caricature. By the 1780s Pitt, and indeed the East India Company, stood to benefit from tea being regarded as 'catlap': gentle, innocuous, unthreatening, an unremarkable part of everyday life. Unfortunately, and to their distaste and detriment, tea had nevertheless become politicized. Rather than a gentle aliment, it was (in political, commercial, and legal terms) 'scandal broth', an active, destabilizing agent in political and cultural change. Dent nevertheless depicts Pitt as a shrewd operator. While he is keen to have tea understood more widely as 'catlap', he is also eager to harness its political power to his own advantage. To understand fully tea's dual role as both 'scandal broth' and 'catlap', we must travel outside the limits of London's sphere of commercial and political influence, and beyond the mercantile reach of the East India Company. The Company's trade, it is true, played a fundamental role in establishing the British taste for tea. But that story is a predominantly metropolitan account, which favours the contexts of London: its commercial institutions, its offices of state, not to mention the fashionable habits of its elite and middling sorts.

Tea's infusion within British culture may have begun in London in the last decades of the seventeenth century, but by the mid-eighteenth century increasingly domesticated patterns of preparation and consumption were in evidence across the country. Whatever its charter stated about its rights to trade, the East India Company had no effective monopoly on the nationwide retail of tea. Moreover, it had very little market freedom by which it could persuade provincial grocers to choose its products over the cheaper alternatives transported to Europe by the East India Company's competitors and conveyed illicitly to Britain. Given that the European companies eschewed the cheap bohea favoured by British merchants, it is highly likely that most of this untaxed tea was higher-quality congou. East India Company tea was drunk outside the capital, of course; the official provincial distribution networks were dominated by an increasingly closed oligopoly of London-based tea wholesalers. But for much of the eighteenth century this legal tea had to compete with the vast quantities of untaxed leaf smuggled (or 'run') into Scotland and the northern English counties, the coastal districts of Wales, the far western and the closer southeastern regions of England. The widespread uptake of contraband tea by consumers was driven by simple economics: smuggled tea was much cheaper than its legal cousin. East India Company teas were expensive not because of corporate inefficiency, or of profiteering on the supply chain, or because British supercargoes failed to compete successfully in Canton. For while it was true that these considerations were often alleged by the tea trade's critics to have inflated the market price of tea, their impact was minimal. What really drove the high retail price of tea was the British government's desire to raise revenue on this burgeoning article of consumption, at a rate which effectively doubled its retail price by the mid-century.

In raising taxes on the home consumption of tea, the British government unwittingly facilitated its movement onto tables far from the hallowed courts of Leadenhall Street, for it allowed tea to inveigle its way onto the countless fast ships that traded directly into small ports all around the country's coast 'in Defiance of the Laws of Customs and Excise', enabling the emergence of rural marketplaces that played an important role in coastal economies.[3] By making itself available to retailers in quantities and at prices hitherto unseen, tea found a ready market unconcerned about the loss of excise to the Treasury. But there were also wider cultural resonances of tea smuggling. In redefining itself in these contexts as illegal, prohibited, dangerous – as 'scandal broth', we might say – tea was able to break the connections between tea drinking and the fashionable habits of the metropolis. Drinking smuggled tea beyond the city's grasp was an act that by its very nature resisted the power both of the state and of London's merchants, stockbrokers and financiers. Tea demarcated a terrain on which the political and financial sovereignty of London confronted the independent desire and will of the country's wider population. This toxic brew redrew the habits of millions – but in the opinion of those with a vested interest in the legal trade, at least, it occasioned civil unrest, the indulgence of immorality and the bare-faced derogation of the state's executive power. Boldly establishing itself as an illegal black-market drug was a high-risk manoeuvre; but tea was protected from punitive legislative action due to the financial revenue which the Treasury collected from trade in the legal product. Pitt's great political achievement for the interests of the London trade in causing 'THE SMUGGLERS DOWNFAL' was therefore to allow tea to redefine itself once again – not as a healthful tonic, or as a fashionable exotic, or as an exciting narcotic, but rather as 'catlap'.

Goods to Declare

Time and again during periods of high national expenditure, it was to the trinity of modish exotic commodities – tea, coffee and chocolate – that parliamentary attention turned. The first attempt to tax tea consumption predates the beginning of a regular tea trade, and was a part of the first tranche of revenue raising following the restoration of the Stuart dynasty in 1660.[4] The tax was incurred not at its moment of importation as an item of international trade, but rather at its moment of local 'manufacture' as a drink. This 'excise' (or 'inland duty') was levied at a rate of eight pence per gallon, later doubled in legislation of 1670.[5] In practice – perhaps unsurprisingly – this early attempt to raise revenue on tea was an abysmal failure, and the excise was replaced in 1688 by a customs charge fluctuating in the years that followed between one and five shillings for every pound imported.[6] But tea merchants had not heard the end of the excise. Initially an innovation of the Commonwealth government during the Protectorate, these inland duties enjoyed a new vogue in the early decades of the eighteenth century.[7] Robert Walpole, prime minister from approximately 1721 to 1742, was convinced that the continued expansion of London as a hub for international trade depended in no small measure on the speed with which goods could pass across the national border. He imagined London as a free port where little or no revenue was raised on incoming goods until they were marked for domestic consumption.[8] Coffee, tea and chocolate were to be the first major articles of trade affected: a statute of 1723 raised an excise of four shillings for every pound of these commodities destined for domestic consumption, levied at the point at which they were sold to London wholesalers.[9] Customs charges were substantially reduced, though a one shilling per pound duty was retained.

Walpole's excise depended on the innovative notion of bonded warehouses, within which the East India Company was authorized to store tea without paying the taxes imposed on its domestic consumption. Here it would remain under the watchful eye of officers of the Excise Board – the 'King's Lockers' – who monitored the delivery of tea and its periodic removal by tea wholesalers.[10] Following their acquisition of tea at the East India sale, dealers were required to record the net weight of their purchase with the collector of inland duties and pay the excise due. Only then could the tea be released into their ownership.[11] But the surveillance of tea sales envisaged by the Act extended well beyond the walls of the Company's tea warehouses. The excise officers were empowered to track the passage of the tea through the businesses of its wholesalers and retailers, to limit the capacity of illegal smuggled tea to be laundered as 'fairly traded' (such surveillance could be much more carefully exercised via excise officers operating across the distribution network, than by customs officers operating only at the port of entry).[12] Under section nine of the Act, each 'Druggist, Grocer, Chandler, Coffee house keeper, Chocolate house keeper' and any trader who was 'a seller of, or a Dealer in, Coffee, Tea, or Cocoa Nuts' was required to declare to the local excise department all the 'warehouses, store-houses, rooms, shops, cellars, vaults, and other places' where the commodities might be stored on their premises. The excise officers had the power to demand access to any of these 'entered places' during daylight hours, and to check that the establishment's records of tea movements matched those noted by their suppliers and customers.

Within London, and large areas of southern and central England, the Excise maintained a close watch on those through whose hands tea passed, from the officers of the East India Company, via the large dealers and wholesalers, to small grocers and 'sellers of teas' (both metropolitan and provincial). For tea dealers in the city, the regular visits of 'gaugers' – excise officers who measured the quantities of excised goods currently in stock – were part of the regular rhythm of the trade. Gaugers were directed in their work via detailed manuals of 'instructions' that they were required to carry on their person during the exercise of their duty, and which were updated and reissued whenever there was an important statutory development.[13] These specified the exact form officers should use in writing up their stock books, the abbreviations they should employ and the demeanour they should observe when conversing with traders. Outside the cities, officers on horseback bore responsibility for 'rides' on which they regularly surveyed a large number of businesses. Excisemen were required to keep precise records of the businesses they visited, updating stock books which were lodged at their local excise office. Here the records would be verified by supervisors against those returned by other officers; frauds could thus be detected that individual gaugers may have missed, and the excise officers themselves kept under observation.[14]

In Defiance of the Laws of Customs and Excise

In mid-April 1735, two officers from the Ipswich customs office – Oliver Newby and George Feilden – successfully intercepted some 450 pounds of contraband tea in the Suffolk countryside near Hadleigh. They knew very well that their prize was not secure until it had been conveyed back to their custom house some eight miles to the east. They may have had some expectation of the successful completion of their journey, having taken the precaution to procure the armed protection of five mounted soldiers: a sergeant and four infantrymen (or 'dragoons'). Not far into the journey, however, they were set upon by twenty men on horseback 'Arm'd with Blunderbusses, Firelocks and Pistolls'. One of the dragoons – John Hawson – described in a sworn testimony what happened next:

> That one of the said Number came up to this Deponant & fired
> a Firelock at him the Balls of which went through his Coat and
> that one of the Number . . . flung a Brass Blunderbuss at him
> which fell upon his head, at the same time another of the said
> Party came up to this Deponant and struck at him with the Butt
> end of his Firelock and that some time in the said affray this
> Deponants Horse fell down with him and severall of the said Party
> fell upon him and beat him . . . This Deponant verily believe[s]
> the Party aforementioned were Smuglers and that the said Party
> of Arm'd men took away the aforesaid Tea from this Deponant
> and carried it away with them.[15]

Hawson's breathless account is revealing of the vicious violent crime occasioned across the British countryside by the illegal trade in tea. It also demonstrates how little the smuggling gangs were intimidated by the revenue officers that they usually far outnumbered. This narrative of a state policing operation facing impossible odds in preventing the landing and distribution of untaxed tea is encountered time and again in the many hundreds of first-hand accounts of officers stationed in Britain's outports that are preserved in the records of the British Treasury. These cover the 70 years from around 1720 to 1790 that frame the illegal trade in tea.[16]

For the fevered anti-tea campaigner Jonas Hanway (see chapter Nine), the development of an illicit market for tea was a significant part of the vast body of evidence he had amassed to demonstrate its iniquity. The purchase of millions of pounds of contraband tea was an unpatriotic act, he claimed, in terms of its vicarious benefit to the trade of Denmark, Sweden, the Netherlands and – worse than any of these – France. 'What advantages we wantonly give to FRANCE in one shape or another,' he thundered:

> We enable FRANCE to extend her commerce; to breed up seamen;
> to build ships of war; to support the credit of her INDIA company,
> and perhaps to involve us soon in a very dangerous and expensive
> war. Thus we put a two-edged sword into her hand; and if prov-
> idence has not more mercy for us, than we have for ourselves, I
> am persuaded she will give us a blow, which we shall repent in
> sackcloth and ashes.[17]

Hanway's 'Essay on Tea' is introduced via a line engraving designed to represent this argument symbolically. Beneath a tree, overlooking a narrow beach, a small group of impoverished rural folk sit at a makeshift tea-table. Though their clothes hang in rags from their gaunt bodies, they have prioritized the purchase of tea and a rudimentary equipage, neglecting an infant crawling into the open fire on which they are boiling their kettle.

Frontispiece to essay on Tea.

Jonas Hanway, frontispiece to 'An Essay on Tea', *A Journal of Eight Days Journey from Portsmouth to Kingston Upon Thames* (London, 1756). This frontispiece illustrates Hanway's essay on the corrupting effects of tea drinking on the morals of the nation. A small group of dissipated individuals have established a simple tea-table near a beach. Their baby crawls unnoticed into the fire on which the water for the next pot of tea is being boiled. At the shoreline, a group of smugglers are unloading tea chests brought ashore from a small sailing ship anchored nearby. They pass a derelict public house, a forlorn reminder of happier times when English beer rather than Chinese tea satisfied the national palate.

The child's fate in this dysfunctional family is clearly emblematic of a wider unravelling of the moral fabric of the nation. Just offshore, the small ship of a smuggler rides at anchor, possibly pursued by a much larger vessel glimpsed on the horizon. A number of men have landed chests of tea, on which an approximation of Chinese lettering can just be made out. The national catastrophe of smuggled tea is evidenced by the derelict condition of a shoreline public house, purveyor of that most British of drinks: beer. Though the establishment's sign still hangs precariously from its wall-mounted bracket, in every other respect the building is in a state of advanced ruination: the door hangs off its hinges, the exterior rendering is cracked, the windows are bricked up, the roof is missing, the chimney fractured. If tea smuggling is allowed to continue, readers are asked to conclude, the edifice of the British nation itself will soon collapse.

Collet Mawhood, the 'druggist' encountered earlier in the East India sale room of 1719 purchasing a wide variety of teas, was called upon in 1746 to testify before a parliamentary committee 'Appointed to enquire into the Causes of the most Infamous Practices of Smuggling'.[18] For Mawhood, there was no doubting the 'cause' of tea smuggling. He reported that at the most recent East India sale 'the lowest Black Bohea Tea . . . was sold by the Candle at 3s. 4d. per Pound'.[19] A single pound of this tea would attract nearly two shillings in excise duty (the customs charge having already been included in the put-up price). A series of deductions for allowances such as the weight of the container (the 'super tare') and the amount of the commodity which would have been shaken to unusable dust in transit (the 'tret'), and a discount for prompt payment following the sale, 'brings the Price of this Tea to the Trader, to about 4 s. 8 d. the Pound'.[20] This contrasted – according to Mawhood – with the market in the Netherlands, where the same tea was available for two shillings per pound; in Sweden, he claimed, prices were still cheaper. Even accounting for the cost of transporting the tea, and assuming that perhaps one in five shipments was seized, Mawhood calculated that the cost price of illegal tea was over a shilling per pound lower than the legal equivalent – and this even after a significant duty reduction in the previous year. Mawhood's may have been a conservative estimate; others testifying to the committee claimed the price of a pound of Dutch bohea landed in Britain could be as low as two shillings and ninepence.[21]

By seeking to raise a large revenue on the domestic consumption of tea, eighteenth-century administrations had created a fertile ground for the establishment of an unofficial market operating below the systems of state surveillance. The organization of the trade in legal tea, and the collection of the apportioned revenue by officers of the customs and of the excise, was predicated on securing a single entry point: the port of London. In practice, of course, the island of Great Britain was particularly vulnerable to the landing of untaxed tea. As the countless archival accounts readily testify, few stretches of shoreline remained unaffected. The intricate and often sparsely populated coastal hinterlands of Scotland and northeast England were the principal target of smugglers originating from Sweden and Denmark, whereas traders carrying tea from the Netherlands and France – often passing through the Channel Islands of Guernsey and Alderney on the way – favoured the long Channel coastline from the Wash to the

Lizard. The west coast from Swansea in southern Wales to the Hebridean seaboard of Scotland was susceptible to tea smuggled via Ireland and the Isle of Man (until its revestment by the British Parliament under the Purchase Act of 1765).[22]

In 1733, the commissioners of customs provided the Treasury with a summary account of instances of tea and brandy smuggling which had been investigated and reported by their officers, as part of the evidence presented to a parliamentary committee 'appointed to inquire into the Frauds and Abuses in the Customs, to the Prejudice of Trade, and Diminution of the Revenue'.[23] The detail of these eyewitness accounts makes for compelling reading. Even at this relatively early moment in the emergence of tea running, it is apparent that customs and excise officers in coastal collections were significantly outmanned when it came to preventing smuggling or to impounding contraband goods that they had succeeded in locating. The enquiry of 1733 reported that 250 officers had been 'beaten abused, and wounded' in the previous decade, not to mention six 'who have been actually murdered in the Execution of their Duty'.[24] In December 1723, the officers stationed at the river port of Woodbridge in Suffolk were about to make a seizure of smuggled goods when they were attacked by 30 men on horseback, who beat them with whips and clubs. Eight years later, the Woodbridge officers reported another incident during which they were attacked by smugglers carrying pistols and 'great Whips'. Similarly, in April 1726, two officers at Wells on the north Norfolk coast – having made a seizure of tea and brandy – were set upon by men armed with clubs 'who knocked the Officers down and stamped on them and used the Officers in a very barbarous manner', before reclaiming their tea. Another company of smugglers, when their ship was boarded by the customs surveyor at Leigh on the Thames Estuary later in 1726, unceremoniously 'flung him over the side' before making arrangements for the landing of some 1,700 pounds of illegal tea.[25] Evidently, those who were charged with protecting His Majesty's revenue were often in fear of their lives, and were regularly the target of violent attack.

The reports often contain descriptions of the complicity of the residents of coastal towns and villages. Following the landing of smuggled goods by French ships at Boston in Lincolnshire in September 1729, the local officers reported 'that the Country people of any Substance living near the Shore were afraid of them and durst not give the Officers any Assistance for fear they should come a Shoar in the Night and Rob or burn their houses'. By contrast, the local residents near Beaumaris on the southeastern coast of Anglesey seem to have been happy to assist a gang of smugglers in May 1731: 'the officers . . . were pelted with Stones from the Shore by the Country people and were also fired upon by the Crew of a Wherry'. In September 1732, the officers of Southwold and Ipswich complained that – having pursued a gang of 40 smugglers as far as Thwaite in Suffolk – 'the Country people refused to assist . . . altho' they offered them a hansom Reward'. In the same month, it was reported that 50 local people lined the clifftops at Fowey in Cornwall to warn an incoming vessel of the presence of customs officers.[26]

Some of the most remarkable voices surviving in the historical evidence are testimonies provided to the 1746 committee by former smugglers claiming protection from prosecution under legislation of 1736.[27] According to Samuel Wilson, by then trading as an 'honourable' grocer in London, the form of local assistance described above was commonplace:

> Altho' the Danger of Seizures is greater at Sea, than at Land, yet the Smugglers commonly escape the Custom-House Sloops, by Means of Intelligence sent from the Inhabitants of the Coast, when those Sloops sail out of Port; and that the Generality of the People, on the Coasts, are better Friends to the Smugglers than to the Custom-House Officers.[28]

Robert Foster, 'surveyor of the searchers' at the London custom house, deposed that similar networks of intelligence confounded the activities of land-based officers: 'If People on the Road see a Custom-House Officer and Soldiers together, they suspect their Design and send Intelligence to the Smugglers, who thereupon hide their Goods, or take some other Road.'[29] Even when apprehended and brought to trial, local assistance often intervened on behalf of smugglers arraigned at country assizes: 'Juries are sometimes extreamly favourable to Smugglers,' complained George Metcalfe, solicitor to the customs, 'for that there are some Instances, in which, notwithstanding Smugglers have made no Defence, yet upon their Advocates imploring Mercy, the Juries have brought in Verdicts for the Defendants'.[30] It is clear that smuggling brought money and valuable employment to coastal communities; but the surviving evidence also suggests that smugglers were celebrated in rural districts – to use Eric Hobsbawm's term – as 'social bandits'.[31] The consumption of contraband tea can thus be understood as an explicit act of barefaced resistance to the surveillance and authority of the national government and of London's mercantile and state apparatus. Moreover, as James Walvin has argued, it can be located within the 'moral economy' of eighteenth-century rural life, in which customary practices were set against the intrusive intervention and surveillance of the state.[32]

The reports issued by the parliamentary committees of 1733 and 1746 contrast intriguingly. Whereas the trade in untaxed tobacco was the most widespread and most troubling aspect of smuggling considered by the earlier enquiry, the report of the second suggests that it had been supplanted by tea. The committee of 1746 heard from one former smuggler that 'Tea is by far the most considerable Commodity that is run . . . Running of most of the other Species of Goods depends upon, and are encouraged to be run merely from the Opportunity of Running them with Tea.'[33] Many witnesses, including Richard Sclater, former smugglers Abraham Walter and Shute Adams, and Mawhood himself, asserted that some 3 million pounds of tea were being run each year.[34] This figure is almost certainly too high: if accurate, it would mean that three of every four cups of tea drunk in Britain in this period held an infusion of smuggled leaves. Tea, a rapidly growing article of national consumption, nevertheless clearly supported an ever-growing and more profitable illicit trade. This in turn encouraged increasingly developed forms of smuggling organization and the establishment of more complex networks of distribution.

The role of London within those illicit networks evolved across the period. Reports from the early 1720s to the late '30s suggest that most smuggled tea – at least that landed on English coasts – was brought to London. The reasons for this were probably twofold. In the early decades of the century, patterns of tea consumption were most widely established in the metropolis. But London was also the national processing and distribution centre for East India Company tea; if excise controls could be circumvented and illegal tea laundered as legitimate, large profits were possible. Gabriel Tomkins – who had been transported for assaulting a customs officer in 1722 – gave evidence at the enquiry of 1733 in which he described how he and his associates, under cover of darkness, conveyed the tea which they landed on the Kent and Sussex coasts to safe houses a few miles from the city.[35] On subsequent nights they typically brought that tea, in amounts of one or two hundred pounds, into the metropolis for sale to grocers, druggists and wholesalers. Reports from the London custom house in the Treasury archives corroborate Tomkins's account, and evidence the routes into London via which illegal tea was brought. While some seizures were made to the west and southwest (including several in the vicinity of Richmond and Kingston), the southern – and particularly the eastern – approaches were much more vulnerable. The road from Essex across Bow Bridge and into the City via Aldgate was carefully watched. Various 'safe houses' such as those described by Tomkins were established in Whitechapel, Southwark, Stratford and other nearby towns and boroughs. Some appear to have been modified to provide a storage facility for smuggled goods; but, as with their colleagues in the country collections, officers often arrived too late to make seizures, as in the following description from March 1724:

> Severall horses came frequently to the Coach and Horses at Mile
> End with Tea, which house the Officers severall times Searcht

and found bags fresh emptied and likewise a Concealment in the house which would hold a large Quantity.[36]

By the time of the parliamentary committee of 1746, however, London had become a far less attractive entrepôt for illegal tea. The increased vigilance of revenue officers, and the ever tighter application of excise controls among the city's tea-selling businesses, were undoubtedly to some degree responsible for this increased caution. The committee heard from one former smuggler that when contraband tea was brought to London 'there is more Danger it's being seized, than when it is disposed of in the Country'.[37] Moreover, as tea drinking became a habit observed as much in the provinces as in the metropolis, the illegal tea trade was also able to establish distinct marketplaces of its own, with their own rhythms of supply and demand. Wilson testified that 'Tea is seldom now brought in great Quantities to London', being typically transported on horseback to market towns in inland Counties and sold to petty wholesalers in amounts of 1,000 pounds. In London, he claimed, the sale of illegal tea had been reduced to small-scale direct street selling:

> There are . . . a Number of Men called *Duffers*, who go on foot, and have Coats in which they can quilt a Quarter of a hundred Weight of Tea, and bring it to *London* in that Manner undiscovered; and that these *Duffers* supply the *Hawkers*, who carry it about the Town, and sell it to the Consumers.[38]

London nevertheless still represented an opportunity for the receivers of stolen tea to make a healthy profit. There is some evidence of complex frauds by which tea dealers would manage the passage of legal tea through their businesses in order to build up a credit on their account at the excise office. Illegal tea could then be introduced into their stocks unnoticed by the eye of the state.[39]

While there was little doubt that the fundamental cause of the illegal trade was the high rate of revenue charged on East India Company tea, this was exacerbated by its lack of proportionality. The incidence of the excise fell more heavily on the price of cheap bohea (at around 120 per cent in the period 1740–45) than it did on a premium tea such as hyson (around 30 per cent in the same period).[40] As early as 1733, London's tea dealers had organized themselves into a committee, meeting at the Swan Tavern in Exchange Alley, 'to consider upon proper Methods to apply to Parliament to prevent the clandestine Running of that Commodity'.[41] In March 1736, the group had presented a petition making the argument for the introduction of an *ad valorem* ('according to value') tax, calculated on the price for which tea was sold at the East India sale.[42] It was nevertheless to be another decade before their recommendations were taken seriously. In manuscript notes written during parliamentary debates just eleven days after the death of Robert Walpole (architect of the tea excise) in March 1745, his younger brother Horatio – the member for Norwich – ruefully accepted that the illegal tea market had barely suffered under the excise scheme:

> [Tea] is now not sold in shops only as it then was, but is vended by the smugglers themselves & their agents all over the Country, & by Higlers and Pedlars who are not under the Inspection of the Excise Officers.[43]

In the legislation subsequently passed, 'An Act for repealing the present Inland Duty . . . on Tea', an *ad valorem* rate was introduced to 'fall heaviest upon the Fine Teas, and consequently ease the inferior Sorts' (though a flat charge was retained at the lower rate of one shilling per pound).[44] Illegal tea trading had been driven underground by the tea excise; it had quickly evolved new practices less amenable to centralized detection and suppression. But it had also – as Horatio Walpole intimates – developed a network of agents which reached 'all over the country'. Indeed, it had proved to be much more successful in developing a nationwide demand for tea than the legal market associated with London.

Catlap for Ever

The statutory intervention of 1745 proved a simple relationship: the higher the taxes levied on the legal market, the faster the growth of the trade in smuggled tea. Given typical sales prices, the legislation of 1745 effectively halved the excise on the cheaper varieties of tea. The anecdotal opinion of those testifying at the enquiry of 1746 suggested that smuggling had been cut by a third. The East India Company soon found itself delivering tea out of its warehouses in greater quantities than ever before. Annual sales of bohea grew by over 300 per cent in the second half of the decade, while sales of green singlo increased at a rate that was only marginally lower.[45] Naval warfare also acted to the legal market's advantage, as the trade of the Company's European competitors was disrupted first by the War of the Austrian Succession, and then by the Seven Years War.[46] The end of these military campaigns in 1763 marked the resumption of the mercantile turf war of Britain's tea trade. By the mid-1760s, smugglers gathered in greater numbers, carried heavier weaponry and were prepared to exert more extreme violence.[47] Over a million pounds of tea per annum were thought to originate just from Sweden and Denmark, according to one estimate, while renewed concerns about the illicit traffic funnelled through the Channel

Islands were raised in 1763–4 by a number of south-coastal customs offices.[48] Even more troublingly, allegations began to circulate about the probity of certain offices, with suggestions that some agents – particularly in Scotland – were involved in a practice known as 'collusive seizure', whereby corrupt officials impounded tea from smugglers to be sold as 'prize tea', with a proportion of the profits from those sales being directed back to the smugglers.[49]

Total European imports of tea from Canton (that is, the combined investments of the individual national trading companies) rose from under 7 million pounds a year in the late 1750s to over 20 million pounds by 1770.[50] Much of this tea was destined for the British market. A temporary five-year reduction in tea duties from 1767–72 saw the annual quantities sold on the official London tea market increase by around 75 per cent,[51] but as the 1770s wore on, it was clear that legal tea sales had effectively flat-lined. Annual figures for 1772, 1776 and 1778 were close to those of fifteen years earlier. Sale prices were volatile, with the total value of annual sales regularly dropping to levels not seen since the early 1750s.[52] Any hopes of a recovery were dashed by an excise increase in 1780, which was followed by another fall in tea sales. Smugglers, meanwhile, made hay. The London excise office wrote to the Treasury in April 1772 to explain that

> Smuggling particularly in Tea and Brandy . . . has for some years past been greatly increasing [and] is now carried on by numerous and formidable Gangs to such a height that unless some more effectual assistance be given to our Officers they will be deterred from their duty . . . Smugglers assemble in Gangs of 50 or 60 or sometimes 100 horsemen, armed with Bludgeons, and loaded whips . . . Officers hav[e] been violently assaulted & wounded by these Gangs . . . Gangs have been so numerous that it was impossible for them to make any considerable seizure, and they have with difficulty escaped with their lives.[53]

The customs office in Edinburgh claimed that their representatives in Scottish ports had discerned the emergence of new practices in smugglers' behaviour, with the use of larger armed vessels, and extensive distribution networks that allowed smuggled tea to reach inland markets.[54] A Board of Excise report of 1783 estimated the smuggling fleet to comprise over 250 vessels of 20 tons or more; of these the largest were vessels of 350 tons with mounted carriage guns, carrying armed crews of up to 40 individuals (sometimes more). The Customs, by comparison, had a national total of 42 ships.[55]

By the early 1780s, it had become clear that tea was being consumed in all regions and among all socio-economic groups; but it was also clear that the East India Company, and therefore the national revenue, was seeing very little of the benefit of that growth. Given the enormous expense of the American War of Independence, such a failure to grasp an opportunity to service the national debt represented a fiscal disaster. Worse still, the direct beneficiaries of tea's colonization of Britain were the old rivals: France, Austria, the Netherlands, Sweden and Denmark. But it was the conclusion of the American War – a conflict popularly imagined to have commenced with a tea-related act of political and economic defiance – that provided the impetus for an economic solution to tea smuggling in Britain. As the conflict ended in colonial calamity, George III dismissed the coalition government led by his political opponents and installed as prime minister the 24-year-old William Pitt. Two thick folders of documents retained among Pitt's papers at the National Archives demonstrate that his political interest in the tea trade had begun as early as 1782.[56] He quickly established close working relationships with two key players in the legal trade: Francis Baring, who as one of the East India Company's directors had an immediate influence on the Company's decision-making; and Richard Twining, a prominent London tea merchant who had emerged in the late 1770s as a spokesperson for the London dealers.[57]

The only means by which smuggling could be eradicated, Pitt concluded, was to slash the duties so drastically that smugglers could no longer compete with the tea available legally in Britain. But the revenue lost as a result would have to be replaced, especially given the vast national debt for which Pitt's administration was now responsible. The tea revenue was therefore to be 'commuted to' (or 'exchanged for') an additional tax on windows – the concomitant introduction of a tax on candles of a halfpenny per pound led to the satirical view (encountered, as we have seen, in Dent's 'CATLAP FOR EVER') that the government was taxing light itself for the sake of the tea trade. In early June 1784, Pitt introduced new legislation in the House of Commons: the Commutation Bill. Riding high on his resounding general election victory in March, Pitt steered the bill through Parliament with expedition. Only one significant parliamentary debate was held, with opposition newspapers providing the vehicles for the most damaging denunciations.[58] Some of the bill's detractors focused on the questionable ethical grounds by which all of the country's households were to be taxed in order to fund the consumption of a non-essential foreign product. More frequently, critics expressed their lack of confidence in the East India Company's continued custodianship of the nation's tea supply, pointing to what they saw as a poor record in terms of the price and quality of the tea it supplied.[59] The bill nevertheless achieved its final reading in the House of Lords on 19 August, thus becoming law in time for the East India sale scheduled for September. All existing duties – which together amounted to around 119 per cent for cheap teas – were cancelled, and replaced with a single duty of 12.5 per cent. Under legislation of 1785, this was collected via both an import duty (set at 5 per cent) and an excise (set at 7.5 per cent).

The immediate impact on tea sales was remarkable. The gross weight of tea sold in 1784 nearly doubled that of 1783, even though the legislation had become law halfway through the year. The average poundage sold in the five years 1785–9 was nearly three times that of the five years 1779–83.[60] Smuggling evaporated within a year or two, with tea sellers around the country simply switching their supply from illicit rural networks to official routes which pointed back to the once-again powerful metropolis (the 60 per cent rise in the number of tea dealers registered with the Excise Board across the period 1784–93 tells its own story).[61] In return for safeguarding its tea trade, the Act also placed new legal responsibilities upon the East India Company:

> [They] shall thenceforward continue to make at the least four Sales in every Year, and, as near as conveniently may be, at equal Distances of Time, and shall put up at each Sales such Quantities of Tea as shall be judged sufficient to supply the Demand; and that at each and every such Sale, the Tea so put up shall be sold without Reserve to the highest Bidder . . . And that the said United Company shall from Time to Time send Orders for the Purchase of such Quantities of Tea . . . as, being added to the Stock in their Warehouses . . . shall amount to a sufficient Supply for the keeping a Stock at least equal to one Year's Consumption.[62]

A new statutory regime had effectively been created within which the state permitted the continuance of the Company's monopoly of the trade in tea. One shopkeeper commented that the legislation had brought about a 'perfect revolution in the tea trade'.[63] Sourcing tea in such quantities posed a real problem for the first few sales, but to make certain that the retail price of tea fell (a political necessity for Pitt, at least), it was necessary to ensure that supply met the new demand. In the immediate aftermath of the Commutation Act, the Company was forced to purchase tea from its European commercial rivals.[64] The hong merchants in China also had to adjust to the new state of affairs, by which the British East India Company became the dominant European participant in the Canton market over the course of the next twenty years.[65] Figures provided by the Company clerk Robert Wissett in 1801 indicate that while the Company rarely carried more than 40 per cent of the annual tea exported from Canton before 1784, its share in the 1790s was often over 90 per cent.[66] Neither the French nor the Dutch East India Companies survived the end of the century and though the Swedish Company continued for a short time to send up to three ships a year, it too soon gave up on the China trade, sending no ships to Canton after 1804. By the end of the century the British company's most powerful rivals in procuring tea cargoes were not European merchants at all but private American traders.

The new configuration forced the Company to recognize, and to meet, the demand for higher-quality teas. The result was an absolute reversal in the fortunes of legal sales of common bohea and the higher-grade congou (with its stronger, more robust infusion). For the 40 years before 1784, sales of bohea had averaged about 90 per cent of all the Company's black tea sales by weight.[67] Congou, by contrast, represented around 7 per cent of those sales across the same period. Both sets of figures had remained remarkably stable across the eighteenth century. In the 40 years after 1790, however, bohea represented just 13 per cent of black tea sales and congou 76 per cent. Congou was therefore far and away the most commonly drunk tea in the early nineteenth century. The sale price of the Company's congou soon dropped to a level not far above the pre-Commutation price of bohea: the higher-quality tea had thus become much more affordable. But it was also the case that smuggled tea had been predominantly congou for twenty years at least, with those taking tea outside London's influence being acquainted with a taste apparently more refined than their peers in the city. The post-1790 sales figures therefore demonstrate not only a pattern of national tea consumption which was more accurate than the Company's sales had hitherto indicated, but the fact that the drinkers of the Company's tea were belatedly emulating the superior tastes of the country at large. Green tea, in the meantime, declined from its pre-Commutation level of around a third of all sales, to a fifth – a level which it was to retain into the mid-nineteenth century.

Tea smuggling in eighteenth-century Britain represented, for the state and the Company alike, a troubling provincial antagonism to London's dominance of the supply and distribution of legally imported tea. The Commutation Act and the end of the illegal trade must accordingly be recognized as the reassertion of the city's power. Only the London trade was consulted during the framing of the bill, and it is clear that the legislation was primarily designed to advance the interests of its mercantile class.[68] Contemporary newspapers recognized it as a statute that was fundamentally pro-London in its effects.[69] Smuggling arguably had a greater impact on the nationwide uptake of tea in the period 1720–80 than the East India Company itself.[70] It was the dealers in contraband tea who made Scotland a nation of tea drinkers in the 1760s, and who were responsible for the establishment of distribution networks that ran through the coastal regions into the country's heartlands. It was smugglers who supplied tea to the provincial margins of Great Britain, establishing illicit routes to distribute tea imported from China through the European rivals to the

East India Company. It was they who were responsible for undermining the perception of tea drinking as a practice of the city's modish middling sorts. Above all, it was they who drove down the market prices for tea, and who thus brought the commodity within the reach of provincial working families.

NINE

The Democratization
of Tea Drinking

The fourth book of William Cowper's long poetic contemplation of
British life, *The Task* (1785), opens by describing the speaker's
pleasurable anticipation of a winter's evening spent in snug retirement.
His newspaper delivered by 'the herald of a noisy world' – who rides on
horseback with 'spatter'd boots, strapp'd waist, and frozen locks' – the poet
settles down to enjoy an uninterrupted hour or two of reading:

> Now stir the fire, and close the shutters fast,
> Let fall the curtains, wheel the sofa round,
> And while the bubbling and loud-hissing urn
> Throws up a steamy column, and the cups
> That cheer but not inebriate, wait on each,
> So let us welcome peaceful evening in.[1]

Complementing the warmth and comfort of the 'fire', 'shutters', 'curtains'
and 'sofa', the tea equipage completes this domestic scene, guaranteeing
the 'peaceful' sociability of a daily routine. The 'cups / That cheer but not
inebriate' have since become a commonplace image of eighteenth-century
tea drinking, the conceit firmly adopted by reformers who saw tea as a
sober alternative to the populace's predilection for spirits and strong ale.
But Cowper's drawing-room vignette is primarily one of self-conscious
and privileged leisure, a provincial version of Mr Spectator's metropolitan
tea-table of genteel philosophy and conversation, the site of the polite
family's critical engagement with the world beyond the hearth.

Although elsewhere it addresses the plight of the rural poor, *The
Task* does not obviously acknowledge that tea was no longer the preserve
of the better-off. Yet by the time the poem was published, this dried Chinese
leaf had transcended conventional boundaries of status and taste: no longer
was the question whether someone drank tea, but the quantity and quality
she (or he) partook. 'The consumption of Tea in this Kingdom is . . . not

William Redmore Bigg, *A Cottage Interior: An Old Woman Preparing Tea*, 1793, oil on canvas. Bigg's late eighteenth-century domestic interior illustrates the contemporary commonplace that tea was now consumed everywhere in Britain, 'from the palace to the cottage'. A woman sits clasping a pair of leather bellows as she waits for the cast-iron kettle on the fire to come to the boil. On the table to her right lies prepared a simple tea service (including a teapot, cup and saucer, caddy and sugar basin).

confin'd principally to the Rich & middle Classes of the People as heretofore', a paper prepared for the Commissioners of Excise had explained in the late 1770s; rather 'it has found an entrance into every Cottage'.[2] Indeed, the Commutation Act of 1784 was predicated upon just such an axiom. By 'commuting' state revenue from a high-percentage levy on (legal) domestic tea sales, to a window-based property charge, the government relied upon those who drank tea forming the same subset of people as those of fixed abode: in other words, more or less everyone.

With this principle in mind, documents prepared for William Pitt modelled the anticipated economic impact of the legislation on all classes of society. Researchers found that even family units whose dwelling places comprised 'Houses under 5 Windows consume about 3 oz. [of tea] per Week'. Extrapolating the projected 'Quantity of Tea which will probably be consumed in Great Britain on taking off the [excise] Duty', the Prime Minister's report calculated that those living in houses with 'under

7 Windows' (the poorest 40 per cent of families) would each require 10½ pounds of tea per annum (around 25 per cent of the total demand in England).[3] Pitt also sought information to reassure consumers that they had nothing to fear from the new window tax – not, at least, if one computed on the basis of those who were already paying their fair share of the existing excise. 'A Common Family at 10 lbs Bohea Consumption' would be as much as fourteen shillings and sixpence richer each year under the new arrangements; a 'middling Family' using twelve pounds of higher-quality tea could expect to save one pound and three shillings; even 'A Family of Distinction' annually consuming 48 pounds taxed at the highest rate would find itself one pound and four shillings to the good.[4]

Tea was one of the first international commodities to be subjected to mass consumption as part of Britain's pioneering engagement with nascent global modernity. By the late eighteenth century almost everyone in England (and much of the population in other parts of Great Britain and Ireland) drank tea of one kind or another. Households across the social scale included expenditure on the commodity in their weekly budgets. As such, tea was a universal experience of everyday life. But if this has now been an established social truth about Britain for over 200 years, in the 1780s it was a transformative paradigm, articulating something fundamentally new and distinct about the nation's habits. Moreover, the story of tea's ascendancy was by no means complete. For one thing, tea was far from saturating the market in volumes that would make it genuinely ubiquitous. It was typically taken just once a day with a main meal of breakfast or supper, rather than being consumed at all hours and upon all occasions. More significantly, tea's universality remained contested and controversial. Many eighteenth-century observers judged that in permeating the daily regimen of the labouring poor, tea had gone too far – that workers and paupers were imbibing a weak, foreign luxury unsuited to their physical needs and social station. The value of tea to Britain's economy and society continued to be vehemently (and sometimes viciously) debated, its heritage as an exotic luxury pitted against its newer guise as a national necessity.

Cottages and Factories

'Tea forms the morning's repast of almost every family in the kingdom', judged the East India Company clerk Robert Wissett in 1801.[5] Such claims for its popularity were not necessarily anything new. Thomas Short had considered the 'Infusion' to be 'universal' in 1730 (although he did except 'Persons . . . of the very lowest Rank'), while the Methodist preacher John Wesley's ad hoc interrogation of the liquid diet of 'the Abundance of People in *London*' during the mid-1740s was apparently met with the response that 'I drink scarce any Thing but a little Tea, Morning and Night.'[6]

In 1756, the merchant and philanthropist Jonas Hanway despaired that tea 'prevailed so universally', and indeed had done so 'for about twenty years'.[7] Nonetheless, the idea of tea's social universality preceded its actuality. As East India Company statistics illustrate, the flow of legal tea into Great Britain more than doubled in each twenty-year period of the eighteenth century. Only during the final two decades did the average annual quantity surpass the 12 million pounds determined by Pitt as necessary to furnish the entire population with a daily breakfast beverage.[8] Even if contraband had matched Company imports for some time prior to 1784, it was almost certainly not until the mid-century that such a level had been attained.[9] Throughout the first half of the nineteenth century, this upward trend in supply continued, although by now it effectively shadowed population increase. For around three-quarters of a century (1775–1850) in other words, tea consumption in Britain was both significantly widespread and relatively stable (if also modest in comparison with the per capita rates that were to follow after 1850).[10]

Why was it that the labouring classes in eighteenth-century Britain began to drink tea? What do we know about their practices and experiences in this respect? Direct testimony is inevitably limited, but patches of evidence can be quilted together.[11] It is clear from the work of economic historians that this dietary shift was not first and foremost a function of improved living standards. Although Britain's economy grew during this period of agrarian and industrial revolution, relative wages were basically stagnant (at least until the second quarter of the nineteenth century), while the conditions of the rural poor arguably worsened.[12] It is true that means of subsistence (keeping a cow, raising vegetables, home-brewing) were gradually jettisoned in favour of a burgeoning consumerism, but supply-side factors appear to have been the driving force. In the case of tea this meant rising imports, a fall in both retail price and excise duty (tea became far cheaper in relation to beer, for example), and improving technologies of business and transportation which distributed dried goods more effectively.[13] If tea had been actively appropriated by the elite and middling sorts as a marker of status and refinement, its adoption in cottages and factories was rather the effect of broader socio-economic re-organization. Sugared tea and white wheaten bread became the nutritional mainstays of the majority, supplanting traditional produce such as milk, cheese, ale and oatmeal. The workers whose daily regimen was transformed were not themselves the primary beneficiaries of changes that more obviously favoured businessmen profiting from local grocery, international commerce and intensive arable farming on enclosed land.

This is not to say that other factors were not in play. The members of the lower social orders who first acquired a taste for tea were by and large those in domestic service. Even during the first half of the eighteenth century, servants encountered the infusion through various means: as a contractual or occasional perquisite, as the leftovers from their employers' mealtimes and parties, as the purchase of a meagre salary in emulation of social superiors. Satires from the period regularly gesture in such directions. In Duncan Campbell's *A Poem upon Tea* (1735), a lady of quality learns in the course of (rhyming) conversation with her polite visitor that 'My *Suky Dainty* and *Bess Taste*, the Cook, / Will drink it sitting in the Chimney-nook. / I often catch them draining what I leave' (to which the lady rejoins, 'Poor honest Girls, they love it, I perceive').[14] With similar ironic sympathy, Jonathan Swift's *Directions to Servants* (1745) laments 'the Invention of small Chests and Trunks with Lock and Key, wherein [Ladies] keep the Tea and Sugar, without which it is impossible for a Waiting-maid to live'. Her direct access circumvented, the maid must 'buy brown Sugar' – literally and metaphorically unrefined – and then either 'pour Water upon the Leaves' already used for her mistress's tea (which therefore 'have lost all their Spirit and Taste'), or else procure her own supply 'in trust' from the 'Mistress of the Tea-shop'.[15] Mock astonishment meanwhile modulates the observation in John Shebbeare's *Letters on the English Nation* (1755) that 'even the common maid servants must have their tea twice a day, in all the parade of quality; they make it their bargain at first'.[16] Jonas Hanway concurred, berating the polite 'Mrs D.' that such 'bargain[s]' are 'true . . . of your servants in general, especially of the females, who DEMAND your SUBMISSION to this execrable custom, and you SUBMIT'.[17] The thrust of these squibs was upheld by government research in advance of the Commutation Act. Enquiries into a moderately wealthy English household revealed that the wet-nurse, waiting maid, cook, coachman and coachman's wife were all supplied with at least 2 ounces per week (or 'Tea twice each day'), and a smaller quantity allowed to 'a Girl to assist in the Nursery'. 'The present Foot boy does not drink Tea', the document remarks, though 'the former Boy did'.[18]

It is plausible then that tea's early purchase among the servants of the nobility and gentry – provincial as well as metropolitan – contributed to the social and geographical diffusion of the beverage. What is unquestionable is that by the 1790s, when two groundbreaking patrician surveys of working life published a wealth of data, tea was everywhere. David Davies's *The Case of the Labourers in Husbandry* itemizes domestic budgets for 122 parochial families across England, 112 (92 per cent) of which explicitly include weekly expenditure on tea (although tea is absent from the limited evidence gathered in Scotland and North Wales). The quantities involved are small, typically no more than 2 ounces (at around twopence per ounce), if just enough for a daily household cup. Grouped with sugar and butter, tea is virtually ever-present as a dietary staple, second only to flour in the poorest homes (although those with greater expendable income spent more on bacon).[19] Sir Frederic Eden's *The State of the Poor; or, An History of the Labouring Classes in England* (1797) reveals a similar picture. In Reading, Berkshire, 'Tea is generally used . . . twice a-day, by the Poor'; in Ashford, Kent, 'the Poor drink tea at all their meals'; in Swineshead, Lincolnshire, 'the Poor use much tea and water-pottage'; even in the 'wild country' of Underbarrow, Westmorland, 'tea has also found its way . . . and is used, more or less, in every cottage'.[20] Information gathered four decades later in December 1839 by the philanthropist Samuel Richard Bosanquet indicates congruent habits among the urban poor of London. A family living in Tavistock Mews with five children laid out one shilling per week on tea, just under 5 per cent of their modest £1 3s. 4d. expenditure. Elizabeth Sach, a widow of Little Russell Street with four young daughters, used 1s. 1d. from her 8s. 4½d. budget (just over one-eighth of the total) for 'tea and sugar'; and another widow (this time with five children), Elizabeth Whiting of Kenton Street, spent sixpence on 'tea and sugar' – over one-fifth of her 2s. 5d.[21] Despite the pitiable incomes of these families, tea was an inviolable item on their shopping lists, a marker of social participation that levered its drinkers just above the line of total penury.

By the early decades of the nineteenth century, the universality of tea was all but self-evident. 'Almost every one uses tea – that is, no one, scarcely, goes without tea at least once a day,' remarked the Borough tea dealer David Davies to a House of Commons select committee (which convened to review excise reforms) in 1834.[22] Indeed, the evidence presented reveals much about contemporary practices and perceptions of popular tea drinking. For a start, it is clear that the canny, scrimping constituents of the new mass market in tea exercised what discrimination was within their means. The cheesemonger John Chenery observed that 'Poor people think that two spoonsful of good congou tea will go further than three of [bohea]', and so were likely to buy smaller quantities of the more expensive but stronger variety.[23] Evidence from the wholesaler John Miller further explains that once the labouring classes 'have made [bohea] once or twice, they will boil the leaves, and find that they cannot get anything out of [it]'.[24] Congou was increasingly preferred because it tolerated repeated re-infusion.

The committee also heard about regional variations that stratified Britain's tea habit. John Reeves, a former East India Company Inspector of Teas at Canton, deposed that 'most of the agricultural districts require weak tea, and the manufacturing districts a strong tea'.[25] This view was deemed a matter of economics rather than taste by Miller. In the metropolis, he attested, 'the poorest class of people . . . will not have the bohea tea, they would sooner go without it, they detest the name of it'. This meant that supplies of this weaker variety were forced out to 'villages' where nothing else was available.[26] Miller's fellow wholesaler William Storrs Fry agreed that 'bohea' was now almost exclusively sold to itinerant hawkers, or to the provincial nobility and gentry for provisioning their servants, although

Davies countered that it continued to be drunk by 'the poorest and next to poorest' whether in 'London or the country'.[27] Certainly in the cities it appears that even relatively impecunious shoppers demonstrated some degree of discernment: the Strand retailer Edward Antrobus sold both 'Common [black] congou' and 'common [green] twankay' to the 'poorer classes', while Miller affirmed that a poor man tends to opt for 'Good congou tea and good twankay tea; that mixture is considerably used in manufacturing towns.'[28] Whether this 'mixture' was prepared by the grocer or his customers is unclear, but again geographical preferences were expressed. Thomas Binyon, a tea dealer from Manchester, adjudged that in his hometown the working classes 'consume equal parts' of green and black tea; 'but I have lived in the north of England, where they consume black altogether. In Birmingham they consume more green than black, and also in Nottingham.'[29]

The social and material experience of tea consumption among the poorest drinkers around the turn of the nineteenth century is generally a matter of speculation. It must have been the case that the relatively miniscule quantities used by the poor produced a fairly weak brew, one that was overpowered by the 'muscovado' or 'coarse' sugar which was typically added.[30] As Hanway asserted, 'WITHOUT sugar it is very unpleasant to the taste; and WITH it, the taste of sugar prevails so much over the taste of tea, as almost to destroy it' (elsewhere 'observing that most of the common people drink raw brown sugar').[31] This diminution would have been exacerbated by the repeated waters in which the leaves were infused, so that surely even the most robust congou or the bitterest twankay was entirely dissipated by the third or fourth hydration. Meanwhile, although the commentator George Sigmond opined in 1839 that the majority of British drinkers are 'fond of a strong beverage, and of a tea that can be tasted in spite of the sugar and milk' (gesturing towards the preparation that would be in favour by the early twentieth century), there is no indication that 'milk' was regularly procured by the labourers surveyed by Davies, Eden or Bosanquet.[32] There was indeed no dairy infrastructure yet sufficient to support the universal supplementation of tea in this fashion.[33]

Given the fuel required to raise water to boiling point, tea can only have been taken as part of the principal meal of most poor families, who would have cooked once (if at all) either to start or to end the working day. Although Wissett had indicated in 1801 that tea was a 'breakfast' regale, by the 1830s it was at least as commonly an afternoon or evening practice. A report of the Factory Enquiries Commission in 1834 indicated that a large number of mills in Derbyshire and Lancashire allowed workers between 15 and 30 minutes for 'tea', a break taken between lunch and closure as part of the time allocated to 'Relaxation for meals'. Some more enlightened employers even supplied hot water for free (although the benefit may also

Frederick Alvey (after J. C. Wilson), *What! d'ye think I am going to drink that ere common brown sugar?*, c. 1840–60, lithograph on paper. In this nineteenth-century London street scene, a customer engages the ageing female proprietor of an outdoor tea stall in an argument about the quality of her 'common brown sugar'. As well as satirizing both the habits and pretensions of the lower social orders, the image indicates that the public sale and consumption of tea was now widespread across the capital.

have been designed to increase the efficiency and decrease the duration of the tea break).[34] This was not the only way that a fortunate few avoided the trouble and expense of heating water. A cartoon of the mid-century by J. C. Wilson (reproduced in print by Frederick Alvey) depicts a makeshift tea stall erected on a cobbled street, at which an ageing female proprietor (arguing rancorously with a customer dissatisfied by the quality of her sugar) dispenses liquor from a large urn labelled 'Royal Albert Early

Breakfast Saloon'. Despite the unsympathetic inflections of the image, it seems that such businesses had become commonplace in English cities, purposely targeting relatively straitened consumers, and operated by those little wealthier than the patrons they served. Still, the experience of most was that the home hearth remained the likeliest and cheapest venue for brewing tea. Even the poorest Irish immigrants whom Friedrich Engels encountered in the industrial north of the 1840s equipped their squalid kitchens with a 'tea-kettle'. 'Where no tea is used,' Engels concluded, 'the bitterest poverty reigns'.[35]

An Idle Custom; an Absurd Expence

By the end of the eighteenth century, tea consumption was a near universal social practice in Britain. Commentators expressed diverse attitudes towards its infiltration of the lower orders, but they can be loosely grouped into a 'teaist' and an 'anti-teaist' camp, terms coined as early as 1720 to categorize proponents and opponents of the drink.[36] The anti-teaists' intense moral and economic anxiety initially led the charge, but during the first half of the nineteenth century they ceded ground to the teaists' more measured and sympathetic (and ultimately celebratory and bombastic) acceptance of the beverage's national significance. The herald of the anti-teaists was Jonas Hanway, who relentlessly censured tea and its adherents:

> There is a certain lane near RICHMOND, where BEGGARS are often seen in the summer drinking their tea. You may see it drank in cinder-carts; and what is not less absurd, sold out in cups to Haymakers. He who should be able to drive THREE FRENCHMEN before him, or she who might be a breeder of such a race of men, are to be seen SIPPING their tea! . . . What will be the end of such EFFEMINATE customs, extended to those persons, who must get their bread by the labors of the field! Look into all the cellars in LONDON, you will find men or women sipping their tea, in the morning or afternoon, and very often both morning AND afternoon: those will have TEA who have not BREAD.[37]

In Hanway's account, the tea drinking of the poor becomes 'an idle custom; an absurd expence'; a gross social impropriety that defrauds the nation of a vigorous labouring class and re-genders its soldiers as 'EFFEMINATE' cowards.[38] Above all, it is an act of self-immolation: enervating 'tea' supplants invigorating 'BREAD' in the diets of those upon whom Britain depends for both protection and production. 'I consider the drinking tea as LUXURY in the clearest sense of the word,' Hanway concludes, aligning it directly with that other *bête noire* of the moralizing middling sort during the 1750s, 'the use of GIN'.[39]

Hanway's vehement anti-tea dogma had its detractors (most notably Samuel Johnson and Oliver Goldsmith), but it was a position that many adopted.[40] One recurrent argument was that expenditure on tea dangerously diverted both alimentary and financial resources. As the poet turned husbandman Walter Harte inveighed, 'I have been well assured, by one of the most experienced practical judges of trade in *England, that as much superfluous money is expended on* TEA, SUGAR, &c. *as would maintain 4 millions more of subjects in* BREAD.'[41] A matrix of concerns is invoked here, connecting the physical well-being of labourers and their concomitant capacity for hard work with the numbers of their population, the scale of their economic output and the international flows of currency and commodities. Arthur Young, the period's most famous agricultural writer, expounded this theme in an early issue of his *Farmer's Letters*. Denouncing an allegedly overgenerous system of rural poor relief – which, he claimed, encouraged an unholy trinity of 'idleness, drunkenness, and tea-drinking' – Young affirmed that tea was detrimental to both individual and nation. Physiologically and mentally tea 'impairs' and 'debilitates' the labour force, Young bewails – albeit that his overriding concern is less the misery of widespread malnutrition than the threat to productivity and its macromanagement. Moreover, 'the trade we carry on for tea is totally *against* us in the balance.' From this perspective of mercantilist horror, the international market in tea 'is a branch of commerce by which we perpetually lose: thus burying our money in an unfathomable gulph, for a pernicious commodity that tends to our very ruin'.[42]

Young's apprehension of the 'pernicious' double bind in which tea pushes and pulls Britain towards the 'unfathomable gulph' of 'ruin' both validated Hanway's hysteria and established itself as a refrain of tea discourse during the following half-century. There were more level-headed articulations of anti-teaist concerns, such as Sir Frederic Eden's regret at how this 'deleterious beverage' devours the fuel and incomes of poor families across the land, but the haunting effects of tea and its spectres of indolence, voluptuousness and nervous exhaustion were in general the objects of severe reproach.[43] Targeting the self-indulgence and careless conversation of the tea-table, an anonymous *Essay on Modern Luxuries* (1777) decried its 'expence, the loss of time . . . spent in doing that which is worse, very much worse than doing nothing'. Tea imposes the languor of '*Indian* melancholy' where once were found 'the pleasing smiles, the dimpled damask cheek' of 'the artless, cheerful, innocent Country Girl', and 'the delight of the honest jolly Swain': 'a puny race of children are the wretched consequences of this pernicious liquor'. The author's proposed remedy is swift and ruthless: 'Let every poor family which drinks *Tea*, be erased from the Poor Books' (in order to deprive them of statutory financial relief), he determines, as if indigence were its own best cure.[44]

Tea's ultimate prophet of doom was the reformer, politician and essayist William Cobbett. In the very first monthly number of his campaigning periodical *Cottage Economy*, Cobbett labelled tea 'a weaker kind of laudanum' that 'corrupts boys as soon as they are able to move from home, and does little less for the girls to whom the gossip of the tea-table is no bad preparatory school for the brothel'. Tea's licensing of idling, 'gossip', profligacy – behaviours that are morally and economically toxic (the two are contiguous for Cobbett) – encapsulates all that *Cottage Economy* sought to countermand. 'Is it in the power of any man,' Cobbett exhorts rhetorically, 'to look back upon the last thirty years of his life, without cursing the day in which tea was introduced into England?' Against the events of such a 'day', he thunders, are leveraged 'a very considerable part of all the mortifications and sufferings of his life'.[45] Even temperance campaigners

S. W. Fores, *Genuine Tea Company*, 4 January 1825, hand-coloured etching on paper. At an urban tea stall, three men take pleasure in drinking tea. At the left of the group, a customer raises a large, steaming cup to his lips; the short figure in the centre has dipped a serving of bread into his tea; while the man on the right has 'saucered' his beverage, and now cools it further by blowing (oblivious to the howls of a dog onto which his scalding liquid drips). Impassive, the female stall-holder looks on. The title satirizes the uncouth manners of the clientele, while ironically recalling the name of Frederick Gye's upstart tea-retailing business in London.

against intoxicating liquors got in on the act. The Wesleyan preacher John Bowes challenged the faithful to 'abandon hurtful narcotics' of all kinds – including tea – so that 'Poor people would have more money to spare for bread, and both rich and poor would be able to give more to the fatherless and widow.'[46]

For at least three-quarters of a century, anti-teaist discourse confidently predicated its case upon revulsion at the bodily, social and national dereliction that tea was deemed to precipitate. Its adherents explicitly coupled the beverage with broader debates about 'luxury' that exercised moral philosophers and political economists. Indeed, tea often functioned synecdochically to articulate a writer's opprobrium. For 'J. N.', a surgeon writing in criticism of Simon Mason's *Good and Bad Effects of Tea Consider'd*, it was 'one of those evils which luxury has introduc'd amongst us'.[47] This was echoed in Hanway's equation of tea with gin, and his conviction that its maleficence was facilitated by the unseemly social restlessness of a

Edward Lacey, *It's Devilish Hot,* detail from *Devilish Familiar Salutations, c.* 1830–50, hand-coloured etching on paper. The humour in this image derives from the supposed intolerance to boiling-hot tea displayed by two infernal figures who are presumably acclimatized to the fires of Hell. A detail from a series of illustrations designed to send up the colloquial preference for 'Devilish familiar salutations', the cartoon trades upon a sense that the tastes and manners of the poorest tea drinkers are worthy of condemnation.

labouring class which strove to imitate the self-gratifying fashions of the wealthy. 'It is the CURSE of this nation, that the laborer and mechanic will APE the LORD,' he bemoaned, a function of 'the irresistible force of EXAMPLE'.[48] Such logic generates a severe irony: when financially stretched workers are led to emulate habits that are dissolute and fruitless, the consequence is downward (not upward) mobility for individuals, recession (not growth) for society. In other words, 'Luxury and Poverty are concomitant and reciprocal,' as the *Essay on Modern Luxuries* averred.[49] Moreover, the local cost in Britain was often unfavourably associated with the outsourcing of production and the adoption of foreign foodstuffs. 'China, Jamaica, the bake-house, the dairy, the poultry or fish-market, with the seasoning shop, must all combine now to furnish a chambermaid's breakfast!', complained Godfrey McCalman in 1787. The consequence was an impoverishment (built, as it happens, on unsustainable credit) that was figured as just as alien as tea from 'China' and sugar from 'Jamaica': 'The pulses of luxury and fashion, with an itch to be neighbour-like, nay, to press with forward vanity on superiours, are inundations, whose tides waft thousands beyond the latitude of a snug competency, to the cold and squalid coast of want.'[50]

One of the Principal Necessaries of Life

The anti-teaists regularly aligned themselves with anti-luxury (and frequently mercantilist) economic doctrine. Pitted against them were those attracted to more libertarian positions: Bernard Mandeville's controversial contention that economic growth cannot be optimized within a morally rigorous society, Adam Smith's recommendation that lubricating the global exchange of goods and money is more productive of national prosperity than is protectionism or the hoarding of treasure.[51] These propositions challenged – even threatened to collapse – the very distinction between a necessity (a commodity which fulfils a fundamental human need) and a luxury (a commodity that gratuitously exceeds the fulfilment of such needs, while simultaneously conveying pleasure to and signalling the refinement of its consumer).[52] The intellectual historian Christopher Berry demarcated the eighteenth century as the period during which luxury was subjected – philosophically and economically – to a process of 'de-moralizing' in Britain.[53] If the healthy circulation of capital is the vital blood of a nation, the argument ran, apparent luxuries can be reconfigured as economic (and thereafter social) necessities: in other words, as true public goods.

From this transformed perspective, the teaists interpreted the labouring poor's consumption of tea not as an indecent aping of the nobility, but rather as evidence of national advancement. Indeed, Robert Wissett described the phenomenal diffusion of tea in terms that emphasize its downward percolation: 'it may be literally said to have descended from the palace to the cottage, and from a fashionable and expensive luxury, has been converted into an essential comfort, if not an absolute necessary of life.'[54] Wissett perceived that complex processes of mass distribution had converted luxurious tea into something more 'essential', and therefore less morally questionable:

> I know there are those who think the use of Tea is injurious to the lower orders of the people, and that the portion of their small earnings, which they expend in its purchase, would be better employed in procuring more substantial food. Of such persons I would take the liberty of asking, Were Tea to be abolished, what could be substituted in the room of it?[55]

It is wrong, in other words, to see tea drinking as a reprehensible lifestyle choice of 'the lower orders of the people': the current market in groceries simply does not afford 'more substantial food' that can 'be substituted in the room of it'. In a piece that attacked the supposed collusion of the government and East India Company to keep prices (and therefore excise revenue) high, the economist John Ramsay McCulloch went even further than Wissett, declaring that 'Tea has become one of the principal necessaries of life.'[56]

McCulloch's position was an extreme one. As the imperialist Robert Montgomery Martin pointed out in a tract defending the East India Company's monopoly over the tea trade, 'if every warehouse in England were filled with tea during a famine, the leaf would not prolong animal existence forty-eight hours; consequently, it is not essential to the support of the labouring poor.'[57] Nonetheless, the cultural redesignation of tea as an 'essential comfort, if not an absolute luxury' signalled something remarkable about the domestic status of an Asian agricultural product in early nineteenth-century Britain. Clearly the sustained high volume of imports and the universal consumption of the beverage – despite statutory duties creeping back towards 100 per cent during the Napoleonic Wars – bespoke a profitable national trade. As the historian of commerce David Macpherson argued, 'On the first introduction of it, the high price certainly rendered it a *luxury*, attainable only by the most opulent classes: but afterwards, and especially since the reduction of the duty in the year 1784, tea has become an *economical substitute*, to the middle and lower classes of society, for malt liquor.' Rounding on those who unthinkingly demand that the poor revert to milk or ale for liquid sustenance, Macpherson elucidates a now-familiar paradox of globalization:

> we are so situated in our commercial and financial system, that tea, brought from the eastern extremity of the world, and sugar,

brought from the West Indies, and both loaded with the expenses of war freight and insurance, and charged with duties equal to, or exceeding, the whole value of the articles, compose a drink cheaper than beer, made of barley and hops growing in our own fields.[58]

As such, 'tea . . . from the eastern extremity of the world' feeds the poor, augments the Exchequer and frees up land in Britain for the farming of profitable perishable foods such as fresh beef. Whatever the actual conditions of labouring households, their taste for tea is necessarily understood in this context as macro-economic gain.

The new teaist orthodoxy was summarized by the former tea dealer William Smith in 1826. Succinctly dismissing hostility to luxuries as anachronistic, he implicitly dispensed with the problem of tea's status in that regard, for 'no article of extensive commerce can possibly exist – whether a mere luxury or a positive necessary – without enriching a nation in proportion to its extent.'[59] The more naturalized and universal tea drinking became, the more it was enlisted to symbolize the collective identity and enterprise of the United Kingdom (a new state created by Act of Parliament in 1800), particularly as they were constructed and transacted in the worlds of South and East Asia. Anticipating its own socially and politically engaged study of tea (by somewhat awkwardly re-imagining itself as a future possibility rather than an actually present text), George Sigmond's *Tea: Its Effects, Medicinal and Moral* proclaimed that:

> It would prove that our national importance has been intimately connected with [tea], and that much of our present greatness, and even the happiness of our social system springs from this unsuspected source. It would show us that our mighty empire in the East, that our maritime superiority, and that our progressive advancement in the arts and the sciences have materially depended upon it. Great, indeed, are the blessings which have been diffused amongst immense masses of mankind by the cultivation of a shrub, whose delicate leaf, passing through a variety of hands, forms an incentive to industry, contributes to health, to national riches, and to domestic happiness.[60]

In Sigmond's encomium, tea's bounty rolls full circle to enrich 'immense masses of mankind' at home and abroad. The harmonious concurrence of local demand with international supply – all facilitated via the technologies of 'our mighty empire', 'our maritime superiority' and 'our progressive advancement in the arts and the sciences' – ensures that 'national riches' and 'domestic happiness' become ideologically coterminous. Tea quite literally, in this formulation, confers 'greatness' upon Britain and its dominions.

What is lost in this stirring teaist vision of Britain is the wretchedness of those 'masses' who find themselves unable to furnish themselves with any accompaniment for their daily bread beyond this 'delicate leaf' (let alone the lives of those who labour distantly in its cultivation). No champion of tea himself, the clergyman David Davies used *The Case of the Labourers in Husbandry* to rebuke the hypocrisy of those who charged the very poorest with indulging extravagant tastes by purchasing cheap leaves and unrefined sugar:

> Still you exclaim, Tea is a luxury. If you mean fine hyson tea, sweetened with refined sugar, and softened with cream, I readily admit it to be so. But this is not the tea of the poor. Spring water, just coloured with a few leaves of the lowest-priced tea, and sweetened with the brownest sugar, is the luxury for which you reproach them. To this they have recourse from mere necessity: and were they now to be deprived of this, they would immediately be reduced to bread and water. Tea-drinking is not the cause, but the consequence, of the distresses of the poor.[61]

Tea may be an essential mainstay of national commerce, in other words, and a commonplace of the popular diet; but this is far from realizing a widespread diffusion of its 'blessings'. If the advent of tea's mass consumption in Britain marks a certain vital stage in the history of global capitalism, it is in part because it reminds us of capital's astonishing efficiency in monetizing the very population whose labour it remunerates at the lowest possible rates.

Understood in this context, the appropriate response to the 'Tea-drinking . . . of the poor' is not apoplexy but sympathy. Here perhaps was a position that synthesized the more polarized views of the teaists and anti-teaists. It was certainly with this in mind that Sir Henry Ellis, Commissioner of the Board of Control, claimed in 1834 to have framed a new scale of excise duties that contentiously taxed teas according to quality (from one shilling and sixpence on a pound of bohea, to three shillings on finer varieties such as souchong and hyson). 'The whole object I had in view was the interests of the lower orders, as far as they could be combined with the interests of the revenue,' he attested before the Select Committee convened to review the relevant Act of Parliament.[62] Meanwhile, in an essay of the 1850s first published in *Household Words* (a paternalistically philanthropic journal edited by Charles Dickens), Charles Knight went some way towards reconciling the optimism of Sigmond with the anger of Davies:

François David Soiron (after George Morland), *The Tea Garden*, c. 1790, hand-coloured engraving. The English painter George Morland specialized in genre pieces intended to be engraved for the print trade. This scene represents a well-to-do family of the middling sort at Ranelagh Gardens in London, enjoying a meal of tea in the open air, perhaps resting after an afternoon's promenade. Their delicate blue-and-white porcelain equipage includes a jug for milk or cream; to the rear of the group, a young gentleman refills the teapot from a kettle that has boiled on an unseen fire.

> Tea and coffee, then, are more especially essential to the poor.
> They supply a void which the pinched labourer cannot so readily
> fill up with weak and sour ale; they are substitutes for the country
> walk to the factory girl, or the seamstress in a garret. They are
> ministers to temperance; they are home comforts. Mrs Piozzi
> making tea for Dr Johnson till four o'clock in the morning, and
> listening contentedly to his wondrous talk, is a pleasant anecdote
> of the first century of tea; the artisan's wife, lingering over the last
> evening cup, while her husband reads his newspaper or his book,
> is something higher, which belongs to our own times.[63]

If Knight unduly sentimentalizes the 'home comforts' of the artisan and his wife 'lingering over the last evening cup', he is at least attuned to the 'pinched' misery of the 'labourer', and the extent to which once foreign and polite beverages have become 'essential', normative, everywhere. The 'factory girl' and 'seamstress' in no way luxuriate in their tea drinking, but it does at least imperfectly 'supply a void' within them. It also connects them – weakly, miserably perhaps, but also undeniably – in community with one another, and with Britons at large.

Sophistication, Fabrication, Substitution

The late eighteenth-century market for tea belonged to the seller. From statutorily controlled import routes – through the East India Company's supercargoes, ships and salerooms – to the opaque prices and practices connecting wholesalers and retailers nationwide, the quality and value of the teas brought to consumers were susceptible to endless manipulation and misrepresentation. If the Commutation Act dealt a fatal blow to European tea-smuggling networks, which had often landed goods superior to those readily available via official channels in Britain, it failed to address the widespread fraudulence that infected the supply chain at the lower end. Problems with adulterated and counterfeit teas had almost always been understood as endemic. As early as 1699, John Ovington had warned of the '*Sophistication*' of Chinese traders who 'prepare the *Leaves* with so much Art to make them still continue *green*, notwithstanding all the Length of Time they have been dried', and have even 'sometimes mixt some other Herbs of less value, to swell the Parcel' offered for sale.[64] At home, meanwhile, Parliament had targeted such deception throughout the period. In 1724, for example, 'An Act for more effectual preventing Frauds and Abuses in the Publick Revenues' had specifically established a fine of £100 (plus confiscation of the offending goods) for any 'Dealer in Tea' who 'shall alter, fabricate, or manufacture Tea with *Terra Japanica* ['Japan earth', an extract of *Acacia catechu*], or with any Drug or Drugs whatsoever, or cause or procure to be mixed with Tea any Leaves, other than Leaves of Tea'.[65] Notwithstanding such deterrents (and even without an overbearing tax burden), the expense and complexity of procuring the commodity from China – coupled with a resolutely dependable demand – effectively incentivized criminal risk-taking. As a consequence the purity of tea offered for retail in Britain would persist as a public anxiety throughout the nineteenth century.

Scientific disquisitions on the nature of tea, as well as manuals written for genteel consumers, frequently supplied tests for chemical adulteration. *The Tea Purchaser's Guide; or, The Lady and Gentleman's Tea Table and Useful Companion, in the Knowledge and Choice of Teas* (1785) recommended a try-before-you-buy policy, by rubbing the loose leaves between the fingers in order to check for tea that appears strangely 'greasy' or that 'sticks' to the skin. Fake tea is artificially produced from a range of unpalatable leaves in both China and Britain, the writer counsels. Bad stocks are visually titivated in Cantonese warehouses with colourful additives (particularly 'copperas' or iron sulphate, now known to cause constipation), while the 'musty brackishness' of sea-damaged chests is offset by 'an operation of fumigating, graying, drying, &c.' once the goods arrive in Britain. The more adventurous or determined tea drinker is advised how to detect sham leaves, for example by adding 'gall' to an infusion of green tea, which will then turn deep indigo or 'black' if iron sulphate is present.[66] While the drinker's satisfaction and well-being is the central consideration of such texts, by the nineteenth century there was acknowledgement within the trade that the synthetic colouration of tea was not simply an imposition of fraudulent foreign merchants but was also a response to demand. Giving evidence to the Select Committee on Tea Duties in 1834, John Reeves asserted that Chinese manufacturers 'openly' engage in 'the fabrication of black tea into green' (principally for the American market), at times even deploying 'Prussian blue' (a type of ferrocyanide) to achieve the effect of 'giving a bloom to green tea'.[67]

On the whole, however, practices of contamination were understood as a risk to public health, while those of inland fabrication were additionally perceived to defraud the nation of the excise duties paid at East India House on genuine tea. The state's confrontation of these issues in the early nineteenth century was reminiscent of attempts to outlaw adulteration that operated alongside the assault on smuggling some 50 years earlier.[68] A House of Commons report in 1783 had explained that in addition to the 5.75 million pounds of East India Company tea sold in Britain, and as much as 7.5 million pounds smuggled in via other European countries, the 'factitious tea which is annually manufactured from sloe, liquorice, and ash-tree leaves ... is computed at more than four millions of pounds'.[69] The post-Commutation intractability of this issue was repeatedly high-lighted, not least by a string of high-profile prosecutions in May 1818. Among multiple London grocers convicted of purveying 'Poisonous Tea!' (as a contemporary pamphlet sensationalized it), Edward Palmer of Red Lion Street in Whitechapel was fined £840 by the Court of Exchequer for 'having in his possession a quantity of sloe-leaves and white-thorn leaves, fabricated into an imitation of tea'.[70] George Sigmond recounted with grim irony that 'whilst the purchaser believed he was drinking a pleasant and nutritious beverage, he was swallowing the produce of the hedges round the metropolis, prepared in the most noxious manner'.[71] The History of the Tea Plant, commissioned (if not written) by the London tea dealer Frederick Gye in 1819, outlined an even more 'noxious' routine via which 'smouch' (fake bohea) was prepared using dried ash leaves. 'They are ... put upon a floor and trod upon till the leaves are small, then sifted and steeped in copperas with sheep's dung; after which, being dried on a floor, they are fit for use.'[72]

In the autumn of 1833, Britain was captivated by another tea scandal. The latest villain was Richard Heale of Mincing Lane, whose business lay a stone's throw from the East India Company's headquarters in the City of London. In 1832, Heale had been granted a patent for his 'Prepared British Leaf', a combination of 'sloe and white-thorn leaves, made up for home consumption'. While Heale expressly avoided describing his herbal compound as 'tea', the Board of Excise became increasingly suspicious about the scale of the manufacture, initially seizing around 10,000 pounds of the mixture from Heale's premises in mid-September.[73] A few days later, a hearing in front of the Lord Mayor at Mansion House was told that 'through the agency of one Mallard', suburban grocers not only bought the product in sizeable quantities, but were 'instructed' how 'to mix the British leaf with the real tea' in order to augment its bulk (one pound for every three of the genuine article, apparently). At only two shillings per pound for Heale's merchandise, the profits outstripped those that tea afforded (bohea auctioned in 1833 cost around five pence more per pound after duty). Evidence presented by Mr Farraday, 'a scientific man', explained the 'injurious' properties of the leaf, while a decoction of 'British Leaf' was sampled by the Lord Mayor and then passed around the courtroom at large, where it was judged 'exceedingly unpalatable' (although as a control, a cup of bohea was also found to be 'of most disagreeable flavour').[74] The case went against Heale, and as much as 1.25 million pounds of British Leaf was ordered to be incinerated. Five enormous pyres were constructed in the Excise Office Yard off Broad Street, and lit around nine o'clock on the morning of Thursday, 17 October; the fires continued burning past midnight. According to a contemporary newspaper report, 'The city for nearly half a mile round was scented by the smell arising from the burning piles of sloe and other leaves forming the British tea.'[75]

There can be little doubt that of the enormous volume of imitation tea unwittingly imported or deviously engineered in Britain – as much as 20–25 per cent of the total tea market, according to the Parliamentary Committee Report of 1783 – the majority found its way into the diets of the poorest drinkers. The execrable quality of British Leaf, combined with the fetid processes described by Gye, indicate that only the most gastronomically ignorant or financially constrained customers would allow themselves to be deceived repeatedly at the grubbier end of the retail trade. If ash leaves, iron sulphate and ovine faeces formed the labourer's cup of solace, there can be little wonder that it was enjoyed weak, its taste disguised as much as possible with strong brown sugar. Some commentators purported to be puzzled – for this and other reasons – by the populace's stubborn preference for a relatively costly, dubiously formed and distantly sourced commodity when the local landscape proffered a range of alternatives. Sage was a frequently favoured substitute, perhaps suggested by the rumours that the Chinese once accepted it from Dutch merchants as an article of barter for tea; although, as Godfrey McCalman was eager to point out, the possibilities were virtually endless. 'The poorer classes' should altogether abandon their taste for tea, he proposed, and instead make do with 'such things as providence and *nature* are pleased to put otherwise in their way, *viz*, milk, butter-milk, beer, mead, ale . . . also infusions of barley, oats, beans, pease, wheat, rice, rye'. Nor did his list of 'infusions' finish there:

> broth, thin soup with or without meal, beef-tea, barley-ptisan [tisane] coloured with milk, milk and water boiled with sugar, water with toast and a little spirits or wine, sweetened or buttered gruel, sassaphras, lemon, orange, apple and sloe teas, the cold or warm infusions of wormwood, chamomile, peppermint, thyme, sage, balm, ground-ivy, with a multitude of other simples, tedious to enumerate.[76]

Spotting an opportunity demarcated by McCalman and others, late eighteenth-century entrepreneurs created a range of succedaneums, anticipating the rise of what are now termed 'herbal teas'. These innovative compounds promised to allay concerns that persisted in relation both to the quality and cost of regular tea on sale in Britain, as well as to the healthfulness and social propriety of its consumption by certain (if not all) classes of people. Unlike the produce of clandestine adulteration, these surrogates made a virtue of not being tea; indeed, they often presented themselves as antidotes to tea's perceived ill effects. Nonetheless, from an early date their purveyors unashamedly capitalized on tea's market penetration through imitative branding. In 1725, Isaac Watts remarked that '*Tea*, which was the proper Name of one sort of *Indian* leaf, is now-a-days become a common Name for many Infusions of Herbs, or Plants, in *Water*: as *Sage-Tea*, *Alehoof-Tea* [made from ground ivy], *Lemon-Tea*, &c.'[77] An exotic term of relatively recent coinage, 'tea' was already sufficiently naturalized to function both literally and metaphorically, without undue ambiguity. Watts's semantic observation gestures towards one of tea's future foodways, in which herbs, fruits and spices (singly, and in innumerable combinations) all vie for infusion in our cups.

Many early herbal teas traded on the basis of local origins, or else asserted spurious connections with luminaries of the worlds of science and medicine. An advertisement for 'Sir Hans Sloane's British Tea' – 'a general restorative of the nervous system' – ran in *The Times* in 1784 (over 30 years after Sloane's death), alleging that the former Royal Physician had devised the recipe, 'recommending it, from the benefit his own naturally weak constitution had derived from the use of this preparation'.[78] Perhaps in imitation of 'Sloane's British Tea', a 'British Botanical Tea' was advertised the following decade, although more prominent by this stage was 'Dr Solander's Sanative English Tea', which had been available since at least 1787 (the

Swedish naturalist and antipodean explorer Daniel Solander died in 1782).[79] One publication endorsing Solander's Sanative English presented a series of 57 individually signed and dated patient testimonies, which authorized the outlandish properties attributed to this 'Mental Panacea'.[80] This strategy was also adopted during the early nineteenth century by the purveyors of 'Rev. J. Gamble's British Medicinal Tea' (also known as 'Herb Tea' and 'Salubrious Tea'), which was purportedly 'Patronized and Used by their Majesties and Nobility'.[81] Elsewhere, tea's very exoticism was harnessed in service of a surrogate. In the 1780s and '90s, for example, J. A. Cope profited handsomely from his prescription of 'Ginseng Tea' – an infusion of another Chinese vegetable – to hundreds of 'Nervous Persons'. Cope regularly published case studies of his latest successes in the London papers, as well as masquerading preposterously behind the persona of Count Belchingen (sometime physician to the Holy Roman Empress Maria Theresa of Austria, and a member of the order of the Knights Hospitaller).[82]

Rather different from these alternative therapies were non-teas designed in defiance of the excise. In the early 1820s, the firebrand orator Henry Hunt recommended his 'Radical Breakfast Powder', a concoction of British crops (rye, barley, peas) that were ground and roasted like coffee and designed to displace any beverage upon which tax was levied. The cause of Hunt's Powder was adopted by the seditious periodical *The Black Dwarf* in 1819–20, and re-emerged in the 1840s in service of the Chartist movement that sought political enfranchisement for the British working classes.[83] Hunt, and the proponents of Chartism who followed, designated tea a component of the state machinery; but at the same time they understood it to be an article now so widely consumed that it required supplanting in the imaginations and diets of the labouring poor if that machinery was to be withstood and overturned. Their simultaneous appropriation and rejection of tea (in the form of Radical Breakfast Powder) testifies to its utter absorption within national life, pointing paradoxically both to its status as a harbinger of the new globalization – with all of its pleasures and terrors – and to its increasingly valorized capacity to symbolize a widely shared and deep-rooted British identity.

Recalling Cowper's image of 'the cups that cheer', a writer in the *Edinburgh Review* for February 1816 detected something quasi-metaphysical about tea's relentless appropriation of a nation of drinkers:

> Its progress . . . has been something like the progress of truth; suspected at first, though very palatable to those who had courage to taste it; resisted as it encroached; abused as its popularity seemed to spread; and establishing its triumph at last, in cheering the whole land, from the palace to the cottage, only by the slow and resistless efforts of time, and its own virtues.[84]

In benign 'triumph', tea has colonized the entire social scale of Britain. That tea is valued for its 'popularity' even in the 'cottage' – provincial, straitened, backward – indicates the completeness of its 'cheering' subordination of British palates: tea had come to signify conservatism as well as modernity. Its victory is as inevitable as that of 'truth', binding it within a mythology of national 'progress'. Moreover, tea's entrance within homes throughout 'the whole land' was quite simply unprecedented: this was a decidedly foreign aliment, with no native precursor, that had barely been known a century earlier. Its nutritional value remained unimpeachably negligible, notionally the demarcation of a luxury foodstuff; yet it was a social and economic necessity, a mainstay of Britain's way of life. Over the century that followed, tea became ever more present, ever more affordable, ever more demotic, ever more British.

TEN

Tea in the Politics
of Empire

A ccording to popular accounts, the casting of 342 chests of tea into the sea at Griffins Wharf followed a cry of 'Boston Harbour a teapot tonight'.[1] The events are well known for their privileged place in the mything of the story of modern America.[2] It has become a historical convention to associate the events with the recognition of a series of common beliefs and shared interests between separate colonies that was ultimately to lead to the Declaration of Independence on 4 July 1776. Yet although the Boston Tea Party is closely associated with colonial resistance to British rule, the connections between Britain's great colonial disaster in the West and its commercial, mercantile, and imperial ambitions to the East are not widely recognized, still less understood in terms of the valuable trade in a Chinese leaf against which this transoceanic drama was played out. Britain's attempt to use tea as an agent of absolute economic, political and cultural command over its North American colonies failed on the ransacked decks of the *Dartmouth*, the *Eleanor* and the *Beaver* on 16 December 1773. But even to regard 'tea' as a symbol of British authority was – in many ways – to stretch a point; for while tea had become naturalized as part of the British way of life by the late eighteenth century, it was still procured only through the ongoing careful management of Britain's delicate trading relationship with the vast imperial power of Qing China, a territory which remained little known or understood in Britain even a century after regular tea imports began arriving on London's Legal Quays. As political and economic arguments against the East India Company's monopoly grew louder and more insistent at home, in Canton the Qing authorities were becoming increasingly alarmed at the outright dominance of the British trade. And as the Company discovered how the new powerfully addictive commodity available in its Indian plantations might finally provide an answer to a century-old problem – the identification of a product that could be traded for Chinese tea to ameliorate the vast imbalance of trade which saw silver coinage (or 'specie') draining from London to Canton – a contentious period in Sino–British trading relations began. By 1838 this was to lead to the tipping of 21,306 chests of opium, tea's alter ego, into the brackish waters of the Pearl River near Canton, at the order of Imperial Commissioner Lin Zexu.

The technologies of commercial imperialism that underpinned these developments were also at work in a series of agricultural experiments developed in the Indian territories administered by the East India Company. These trials pointed the way towards a future – as yet barely glimpsed – in which the tea trade would bypass China altogether. It had long been hoped that tea could be cultivated in territories subject to British control (see chapter Five). When the question seriously began to be asked whether India itself might offer the soil, climate and topography necessary for the cultivation of tea, an astonishing (re)discovery was made: a variety of tea (known to modern science as *Camellia sinensis* var. *assamica*) was already growing there. Indeed, in such profusion did the plant spread that there seemed few areas of the northeastern Assam province where these 'tea forests' (as British adventurers described them) were not to be found. Tea cultivation served a double imperial purpose. On the one hand, it justified the annexation of vast tracts of hilly Indian territory (authorized on the basis that the local people had apparently identified no immediate use for it) on which tens of thousands of new imperial subjects could be employed; on the other, it promised to reduce Britain's discomforting dependence on China for its tea supplies, thus addressing the vast imbalance of payments occasioned by the East India trade.

By the 1780s, tea had tightened its grip on British culture, habits and fashions; even (via the tea excise and customs charges) its fiscal security. Foreign policy towards North America in the 1770s, India in the 1830s and China in the 1840s demonstrates that tea – at the very height of its success in conquering national palates – became a lever upon which British imperial strategy itself was effected. By the early nineteenth century, tea was one central pillar of what was rapidly coalescing as an imperial project, an infusion which enabled – and justified – the brand of mercantile and military colonialism that delivered British territorial expansion.

The Destruction of the Tea at Boston

The contexts for the events of December 1773 reach back 50 years to Robert Walpole's introduction of the tea excise in 1723 (see chapter Eight). Cargoes stored in the East India Company's bonded warehouses had attracted the modest 'import duty' collected at the custom house, but only when it was clear that tea was destined for British consumers did the excise fall payable. The system was established in order to make it more straightforward for merchants to take advantage of opportunities for the onward sale of Company tea, a welcome influx of hard money into the national economy for those alarmed at the drainage of British 'specie' to China. In practice, little British tea was sold on the open market to European nations: they, like Britain itself, were keen to protect the interests of flag-carrying merchant monopolies. Not so the captive markets of Britain's overseas possessions. The North American colonies, in particular, represented a relatively untapped opportunity for mercantile profit, and (it was imagined) national revenue.

Recent work in the history of consumption has shown that, from the early 1720s, the prosperous towns of the eastern settlements of North America came to attach notions of status and fashion to consumer goods of British manufacture.[3] Tea was at the centre of this hunger for products of 'British' polite culture. A detail in the account of a visitor to New York in the late 1740s, keen to describe how a particular community procured its clean water, is particularly revealing:

> At a little distance there is a large spring of good water, which the inhabitants take for their tea and for the uses of the kitchen. Those, however, who are less delicate on this point, make use of the water from the wells in town, though it be very bad.[4]

Of all the 'uses of the kitchen' for which the water might be used, 'tea' is the only specific use mentioned. The quality of the tea that may be brewed, one might conclude, is one of the first considerations when adjudging 'good' water. It is at least an open question whether the 'delicacy' acknowledged is as much the refinement of the consumer's taste for tea, as it is her squeamishness about water quality. By mid-century, those among the middling sorts with opportunities for indulging in leisured pursuits spent time in dedicated 'tea gardens', familiar features of the distant landscape of London in this period. An advertisement of 1763 announced that tea is served at John Marshall's Spring Gardens from 3pm–6pm, at which 'the best of green tea &c Hot French Rolls will be provided'.[5] By the 1770s, a valuable trans-Atlantic trade supported the popular consumption of British products in North America. Annual tea re-exports from London appear typically to have fluctuated between 10 and 15 per cent of total East India Company imports;[6] much of this was destined for the American colonies. In addition to this 'approved' tea, it is clear that large quantities were shipped off the grid into the eastern sea ports of North America in the period 1720–84, and that many American merchants made their living by shipping contraband tea.

Tea was not carried to New York by the East India Company, but rather by private trading firms who made purchases at the London East India sale. Although this tea was exempted from Walpole's excise, retail prices for all varieties on colonial markets reflected not only the fact that the leaves had been sold to the highest bidder at the London sale, but also the additional costs of freight, insurance and labour involved in their re-transportation across the Atlantic. Notwithstanding these swollen costs, the British government – facing a crippling national debt accrued during the military campaigns of the 1750s and '60s – was keen to bring to an end a situation in which His Majesty's subjects in North America were consuming British goods effectively duty-free.[7] A series of ill-judged taxation measures – passed and repealed in quick succession by short-lived Whig administrations – sought to raise taxes directly in America.[8] The first warning signs followed the Stamp Act of 1765, which required that legally binding documents be produced on embossed, dutied paper manufactured in London.[9] The Act occasioned rioting on the streets of Boston and New York, and threats to organize boycotts of British goods from a group formally establishing itself as the 'Sons of Liberty'. Though the measure was repealed in early 1766, a number of statutes of 1767 effectively created a colonial excise regime covering a wide range of consumer goods. These taxes popularly became known – and denigrated – as the 'Townshend Duties', after the chancellor of the exchequer who proposed them, but who then died before their political repercussions became clear.

The Townshend Duties were designed ostensibly to ensure that Britain's overseas possessions paid their own way: the revenue raised was to cover the cost of colonial administration, the salaries of the governors, military personnel, judges and their associated retinues. At the core of the new taxation regime was 'An Act for granting certain Duties in the British Colonies and Plantations in America', which covered a wide range of goods including glass, lead, printers' pigments and paper.[10] Among these articles of trade a single line specified the flat duty paid on a solitary perishable item of consumption: 'For every Pound Weight Avoirdupois of Tea, three Pence'. In the colonies, previously shelved plans to organize consumer boycotts of British goods were hastily revived and pursued with renewed fervour, but though the protests initially had the support of key merchants in Boston and New York, once again they quickly began to disintegrate. Meanwhile, another new administration in London (under Lord North) repealed most of the Townshend Duties in March 1770. One duty was retained in order to establish a clear precedent for taxing consumption in America: the excise on tea.[11] This, gambled the British government, was the one British product that American consumers could not do without, and for which they would be prepared to sacrifice their principles.

At first the gamble seemed to have paid off handsomely. Protest diminished. British imports resumed. The Townshend Duty on tea was paid. It took a further ill-judged piece of legislation to set in play a chain of events that would lead to genuinely revolutionary activity: 'an Act to allow a Drawback of the Duties of Customs on the Exportation of Tea to any of his Majesty's Colonies or Plantations in America . . . and to . . . grant

Licences to the East India Company to export Tea Duty-free', popularly known as the Tea Act of 1773.[12] At section 4, the Act detailed that the Treasury may grant specific licences allowing the Company to 'export Tea, on their own Account, to the British plantations in America, or to Foreign Parts, without exposing such Tea to Sale here [in Britain]'. This answered a longstanding complaint among American consumers: that an additional middle man, the re-exporter, was introduced in the colonial trade, which made the retail price of tea in America even higher when compared with Britain. This policy would reduce the cost of a pound of bohea by much more than the threepence of the Townshend Duty, serving the additional benefit of rendering unviable the business of American tea smugglers.[13] But the fatal spark was the decision to use the Tea Act as a way of solving another problem for the British establishment: how to deal with the daunting quantities of surplus tea mouldering (it was said) in the warehouses of the East India Company. The solution seemed so elegant. Grant the Company licences, under the Act, to export large cargoes of this low-grade tea directly to American harbours. Require the colonial customs houses to oversee the landing of the cargoes, to be purchased and then distributed by appointed local consignees. The retail price in colonial shops would fall, profits would be directed to Leadenhall Street, and the Townshend Duty would be remitted to the British Treasury.

The proposal's architects did not reckon on the political activism of groups that had already been founded in response to the Stamp Act and the Townshend Duties, and which had already acquired some skill at advertising and enforcing consumer boycotts. Tea, singled out by North as the sole carrier of imperial taxation, now became a lightning rod for wider discourses of dispute in colonial North America, whether commercial, ideological or political. News about the shipping of East India Company tea long preceded its arrival, and the inhabitants of New York, Charleston, Pennsylvania and Boston waited to see which harbour would receive the first ships. The *Dartmouth* was sighted at the entrance to Boston Harbor on 28 November. It was soon joined by the *Eleanor* and the *Beaver*. Their arrival precipitated an intense fourway stand-off between local shopkeepers, merchants and private citizens determined to prevent the importation of British goods; the offices of British colonial administration (the governor, and the custom house) and the tea consignees, who were bound by colonial policy and legal contract to receive the shipment; the captains of the vessels themselves, obliged legally to land the cargoes; and the naval personnel stationed in the harbour, charged with protecting British interests. The protestors were determined to prevent the landing of the cargo (and its formal 'receipt' by the Custom House), on the basis that until this occurred the Townshend Duty would not fall due. The ships' captains felt that they had no authority to leave, and would be

Sarony and Major, *The Destruction of the Tea at Boston Harbour*, c. 1846, lithograph. A widely reproduced mid-nineteenth-century coloured lithograph commemorating what had, by this time, become known as the 'Boston Tea Party' (though 'The Destruction of the Tea at Boston Harbour' repeats an earlier commonplace term for these events). Crowds cheer at the harbourside as men, disguised – in accordance with popular accounts – as 'Mohawk Indians', throw tea chests into the harbour. In the middle distance, the events are repeated on a second ship.

held in breach of their contracts if they returned to London with the tea. What happened next is, of course, well known.[14] There can be little doubt that the boarding of the ships by a group of protesters on 16 December, some reportedly 'under the disguise of Mohawk Indians', and the dumping of the tea (some claim 'in silence') into the harbour, was a rebellious act of collective resistance to the imposition of a distant imperial authority.[15] Moreover, it is clear that the protestors' decision to 'make tea' in Boston harbour was a deliberate inversion of a symbolically British cultural performance.[16] But it is also the case that the decision was ultimately a practical one: the only obvious way out of a stalemate that had paralysed all parties.[17]

John Adams, noting the events of 16 December in his diary a day later, immediately recognized their significance for the future history of the American colonies. This 'Destruction of the Tea', he observed, 'is so bold, so daring, so firm, intrepid and inflexible, and it must have so important Consequences, and so lasting, that I cant but consider it as an Epocha in History'.[18] History proved him right – but for decades, the events of that night rather faded from public memory. In his revisionist account of the way in which the American Revolution came to be remembered and memorialized, Alfred Young has demonstrated that the term 'Boston

Tea Party' – which first appeared in print only in 1834 – was part of a wider movement to re-establish local connections with the independence struggle. This cultural re-appropriation continues to this day. The recent popular political support accorded to the right-wing 'Tea Party' reminds us of the continuing resonance of tea in the American popular imagination, with the impositions of a politically distant overlord.[19]

Undoubtedly a Wholesome Tea

In the attempts by the British government to collect revenue in North America from tea sales, the practices of a distant 'fashionable' metropolis – performed admiringly in colonial consumer behaviour – became associated instead with the mercantile colonialism of an aggressive imperial state. But the structural problems in the East India trade that had precipitated the disastrous Tea Act were to persist. In the decade 1780–90, the Company typically received a return of 5 per cent on its investment in tea.[20] By 1800, the Company was importing five times as much tea as it had in 1773; it was, after all, now obliged by the Commutation Act to retain stocks sufficient to meet consumer demand. But sale prices of that tea between 1800 and 1820 declined to such an extent that the Company barely trod water in terms of the year-on-year value of its sales, notwithstanding continued volume growth.[21] The downward pressure on the overall value of the market suggests the degree to which the Company's directors had lost the control that they had once enjoyed over the domestic tea trade.

In *Tsiology* (1826), retired tea dealer William Smith memorialized 150 years of the Sino–British trade in terms that suggested how (unproblematically to its supporters) tea enabled British imperial expansion:

> The increase of the Tea trade and the rapidity with which the East India Company has obtained territories . . . is unparalleled in the history of any age. An establishment at its commencement purely commercial . . . now possesses dominion over an extent of 300,000 square miles, containing above forty millions of inhabitants, and producing a yearly revenue of fourteen millions. Such are the wonderful effects of commercial enterprise![22]

Smith's tone, however, is strangely nostalgic. He, like other observers, was able to read in the tea leaves that the trade was on the cusp of great change. At the 1811 renewal of its charter for twenty years (1814–34), the Company had lost its monopoly on the East India trade with the sole exception of the trade in tea. The Company was vulnerable to accusations that it represented a trading model based on monopolistic tendencies that had become increasingly outmoded following the influence of the more liberal approach advocated by Adam Smith in *The Wealth of Nations* (1776), especially as it was developed in terms of international trade by David Ricardo in *On the Principles of Political Economy and Taxation* (1817).[23] In 1831, as many expected, Parliament refused to grant a further charter renewal beyond 1834. The long process of winding down the Company's trading business began.

The routes plied by the tea trade were also to change in ways that *Tsiology*'s author could scarcely have imagined. In 1823, a Scottish army officer and adventurer named Robert Bruce discovered tea thriving in the

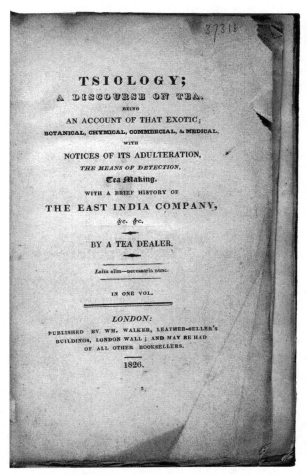

[William Smith], title page from *Tsiology; a Discourse on Tea. Being an Account of That Exotic* (London, 1826). An encyclopaedic account of the British fascination with tea, whose anonymous 'tea dealer' author is often identified as William Smith, a former partner of tea wholesalers Smith and Kemble. Though much of the book's contents is derived from earlier publications, its detailed account of the organization of the early nineteenth-century London tea business stands as a unique record of a system that was about to disappear, as trading models based on an open marketplace replaced the closed-door approach that had prevailed.

wild in the Assam province of India. He died within a year; and for a while, news of his discovery seems to have been regarded as an intriguing story rather than an established fact. Certainly when the Governor-General of India – W. C. Bentinck (1774–1839) – described on 24 January 1834 'the great advantage which India would derive from the successful introduction of the tea plant', tea's native growth in Indian soil appears to have been little known, perhaps little believed, by the colonial establishment.[24] Bentinck recommended the establishment of a Tea Committee charged with the task of covertly procuring cuttings from China, and cultivating them in India with the assistance of 'Chinese agency'. The secret had eluded the Dutch (who had been trying to cultivate tea in Java for decades) and the Portuguese (who had set up a small community of Chinese tea planters in the environs of Rio de Janeiro with the purposes of creating a tea plantation).[25] While the plants themselves appeared to thrive, the tea produced from their harvest proved bitterly disappointing. It was assumed, therefore, that the tea plant must be susceptible to minute changes in its growing conditions: the temperature, the humidity, the altitude, the direction of prevailing winds, the properties of the soil.

The opportunities represented by relocating tea cultivation and manufacture to land under British control were not lost on those expressing support for such an endeavour. Bentinck presented to the committee a proposal dated February 1834 by 'a very intelligent gentleman of the name of Walker':

> The commercial relations of this country with China have lately assumed a character of uncertainty, by no means corresponding to the importance of the trade, or consistent with the dignity, of the British empire. This unsatisfactory state of affairs has originated from a combination of causes . . . The jealous policy of the Chinese Government in her intercourse with all nations; the apprehension which she has always entertained of our formidable empire in the East Indies; the ignorance, price, and prejudice of the Government; a consciousness of her own strength in some points, and her weakness in others; the rapacity and corruption of her officers, and occasionally the misconduct of our own people.[26]

Moving between the discourse of agriculture and trade, and that of brinkmanship and armed conflict, the 'very intelligent gentleman' goes on to describe the unreasonable and demeaning restrictions placed upon the British in Canton notwithstanding the recent 'brilliant and rapid progress of our arms', and expresses confidence that 'the forces of China would be almost powerless against European tactics'.[27] It is unacceptable, he concludes indignantly, that a commodity which 'has become a luxury to all' in Britain should have no more secure 'guarantee' than 'that at present furnished by the mere toleration of the Chinese government'. Their monopoly of tea production 'will be easy for us to destroy'. The British consumer would be relieved of the embarrassment of being 'indebted' to China; moreover, 'when the skill and science of the Europeans, aided by thermometers, &c, shall once be applied to the cultivation and preparation of tea in favourable situations, the Chinese tea will soon be excelled in quality and flavour'.[28] Even the respected East India Company botanist Nathaniel Wallich (1786–1854), offering a detailed analysis of the viability of growing Chinese tea, argued that given the anticipated success of the experiment 'we shall not long continue dependant on the will and caprice of a despotic nation for the supply of one of the greatest comforts and luxuries of civilized life.'[29]

China – secretive, remote and unknowable to the minds of European merchants and diplomats – represented an unnerving political and ethical challenge to Britain's growing imperial self-importance. Bringing tea cultivation and production within the aegis of European agrarian economics, with an increasing emphasis on intensive farming and mechanized agriculture, could release British merchants and consumers from this troubling sense of subservience. For Bentinck's tea committee, events quickly took an unexpected turn. By January 1836, it had been made aware of the work of Charles Bruce (1793–1871), the brother of Robert. Since the early 1830s, Charles had been the commander of a division of gunboats stationed in Sudiya in the northeast of Assam province; he was also a keen explorer, and had evidently invested considerable energy in charting the region and becoming acquainted with the local inhabitants. Most importantly, Bruce had a unique area of expertise: an intimate knowledge of the location of a number of 'tea forests', where uncultivated Assam tea plants flourished in a wide variety of soil conditions.[30] Even better, Bruce's knowledge of the customs and languages of the people of nearby villages made him a powerful advocate for the colonial government's ambitions for forest clearance, and formal tea cultivation. He was quickly relieved of his army duties, and appointed the Tea Committee's superintendent of the tea plantations.

The Tea Committee's excitement about Bruce's discoveries is clear from an exchange of letters included in the House of Commons Parliamentary Papers. Wallich was dispatched from Calcutta to meet with Bruce in Upper Assam. 'No scheme of this nature', he wrote eagerly, 'was ever entered upon with such a progressive accumulation of favourable and confirmatory circumstances'.[31] The high-risk plan to smuggle tea plants from southeastern China for cultivation in India was – at least for the time being – abandoned, and Bruce was encouraged to take forwards the development of regularized tea plantations in Assam. He provided a further welcome piece of intelligence, that it 'ever has been a custom among the Assam Rajahs never to tax or take any rent from any one that would take the trouble to cultivate hills'. If the British Government were to establish tea plantations, then the local Rajah 'could not in equity ask one rupee for it, or any other hill that may hereafter be discovered with tea on it'.[32] Reports of the first infusions of 'Assam souchong' occur in letters of late September 1837; Wallich reported to the government that the sample 'affords a most promising indication of the success which may be reasonably anticipated will attend the endeavours now employed to cultivate and produce profitable and merchantable tea in Upper Assam'.[33]

The first chests of Assam tea were auctioned with considerable enthusiasm in London in January 1839 (though the East India Company's directors cautioned that this was occasioned 'by the great excitement and competition created by the novelty and curiosity of the sale').[34] The success of the venture led to the establishment of a new international trading entity – the Assam Company – to exploit the commercial potential of Indian tea.[35] By the 1850s, the landscape of northeastern India was being transformed by the techniques of Empire, as the indigenous forestation was cleared, a monoculture established and models of indentured servitude imposed upon the local inhabitants. Travellers of the mid-century were optimistic about these developments. Although the botanist Robert Fortune, who published in 1852 an account of his travels in the tea-producing areas of China and India, visited many of the larger-scale tea plantations under cultivation in Assam, he seems nevertheless to have assumed that – as with the Chinese growers – Indian farmers would enjoy some kind of ownership (perhaps psychological, rather than proprietorial) and personal investment in the tea they cultivated. Julie Fromer has described how Fortune understood tea as not only beneficial to the imperial authorities who sought a dependable source of the commodity that had become a necessity of British life, but also to the 'natives of India' who would thus be civilized by the opportunity to participate in polite British practices of tea drinking. As Fortune put it:

> The poor *paharie*, or hill peasant, at present has scarcely the common necessaries of life, and certainly none of its luxuries . . . If part of these lands produced tea, he would then have a healthy beverage to drink, besides a commodity which would be of great value in the market. Being of small bulk compared with its value, the expense of carriage would be trifling, and he would have the means of making himself and his family more comfortable and more happy.[36]

Fortune, Fromer concludes, is confident that the cultivation of tea would in time effect a remarkable change in the status of the labouring poor of India: they would be transformed into 'middle-class citizens of the British Empire'.[37]

The Tea War

The economic, agricultural, political and imperial terrain of British India guaranteed the ultimate success of the great Assam tea experiment. Even so, in the late 1830s – notwithstanding the cessation of the East India Company's trading activities and the appearance of the first ocean-going paddle steamers in the South China Sea[38] – it must have been difficult to imagine that the diplomatic theatre of the tea trade, formalized since 1757 by a decree of the Qianlong Emperor, would ever change: the careful negotiation at Macau; the awkward navigation of the Pearl River; the hiring of compradors and linguists at Whampoa; the engaging of hong merchants in Canton; the dalliance with the hoppo and his officers; indeed, the entirety of the complex, exotic, unnerving contexts of trading with China.

Notwithstanding its strict terms, this 'Canton System' – as it had become known – provided consistency and stability for all parties in the European China trade. The vast increase in the number and size of the ships, however, together with the challenges facing the tea trade in Britain, inevitably had consequences in terms of the East India Company's retinue

William Daniell, *A View of the European Factories at Canton*, c. 1800, oil on canvas. Daniell's painting captures the Canton waterfront at the turn of the nineteenth century. To the right foreground, an oceangoing Chinese junk is attended by innumerable shallow sampans, while on the left a number of smaller junk-rigged ships can be seen. In the background the factories associated with the trades of various nations can be identified by the flags flying above. These include the Netherlands, Britain, Sweden, France, the Holy Roman Empire and the United States.

in China. In 1704, four English ships – the *Eaton*, the *Kent*, the *Sidney* and the *Stretham* – traded at Canton; each weighed around 350 tons. In the two seasons of 1799–1801, by contrast, a total of 54 British ships anchored in the Pearl River delta, each averaging a little over 1,100 tons.[39] Trade was now managed not by individual Company officials travelling with each vessel, but by a semi-permanent 'Select Committee' of supercargoes which moved between the English factory at Canton and rented accommodation in Macau as the season determined. The supercargoes were joined from 1790 by a new permanent Company appointment – the Inspector of Teas – created in order to guarantee the provenance and quality of exported tea.[40] Via the careful management of local and regional administrators, the Canton system had absorbed this growth while maintaining the arm's-length character of Sino–European trade; yet its collapse would arrive far sooner than Indian tea. Moreover the immediate contexts were not, in any straightforward sense, those of the tea trade itself.

By 1763, in the aftermath of the Battle of Plassey, the East India Company acquired the opium monopoly previously controlled by the Nawab of Bengal.[41] Aware of the ready market for the drug in China, the Company explored how a regular opium trade might be established. The appeal is obvious: the vast imbalance of trade that saw British bullion reserves draining to China could be largely redressed. But even setting aside the moral and ethical concerns that such a trade might occasion, the mercantile and political stakes were high. The Qing authorities had long been alert to the threat presented by Indian opium; the earliest imperial edict banning imports of this addictive drug dated from 1729. If the Chinese authorities in Peking were to learn that the East India Company was involved in, or directly sponsored, the trade in opium, it was reasonable to conclude that Canton would be closed to British trade and the tea supply halted. Notwithstanding the efforts of the trade, the volume of opium sold in China – with the tacit collusion of the local authorities – rose fourfold between 1770 and 1800, typically averaging around 4,000 chests every year. By selling opium on the open market in India to the private merchants (from the late 1780s consolidated as trading firms or 'agency houses') which plied the 'country trade' with China, the Company concealed its involvement in the narcotics trade from the attention of the imperial authorities.[42] Though levels of opium trading remained broadly steady until around 1830, they rose rapidly through the early 1830s, reaching 30,000 chests per annum by 1836. By this stage, the British tea trade was effectively underwritten by the value of the opium trade. Nevertheless, very little of the hard money released via opium sales left China – rather, a complex system of credit facilitated the exchange of opium for tea. This might follow several routes, but typically opium traders (usually merchants from the agency houses) paid the silver coinage raised through sales of the drug directly into the East India Company's exchequer at Canton, in return for bills of exchange redeemable in Calcutta or London (which they might cash, or use as credit to buy more opium). The East India Company would then use the funds in its Canton treasury to purchase tea from the hong merchants.[43]

With the ending of the East India Company's trading rights in 1833, many of the leading agency houses (such as Jardine Matheson and Dent) emerged as the principal British trading companies in China. By this time, opium trading at Canton had become an open secret. The deregulation of the trade made it more difficult for British officials to maintain any kind of meaningful surveillance or control over the behaviour of its merchants (a responsibility which passed from the Company's Committee of Super-cargoes to the newly created office of Chief Superintendent of British Trade in China). At the same time, the British financiers who funded the agency houses, flushed with success in their demands for a free East India trade at home, were increasingly impatient for similar freedoms in China.[44] As tensions grew on both sides, a pretext for armed hostilities emerged. In late 1838, the Daoguang Emperor appointed the governor-general of Hupei and Hunan – Lin Zexu – as imperial commissioner in Canton, with the specific remit to end the British trade in opium. Lin's arrival in March 1839 was followed by swift action to curb the trade: the sale of opium was banned, with all ships wishing to trade at Canton required to seal a 'no-opium bond' (which, if contravened, was punishable by the death of the merchants and the confiscation of the ship's cargo). Lin demanded that all existing stocks held by foreign merchants were to be surrendered, and he underscored his determination by dispatching thousands of Chinese troops to lay siege to the Canton factories housing hundreds of British and American merchants. The stand-off was only resolved when the British superintendent – Charles Elliot – ordered the merchants to surrender some 20,000 chests, rashly promising that the British government would reimburse them for their lost goods.[45] Over the course of six weeks ending in mid-May 1839, Lin directed the destruction of an estimated 2.6 million pounds of opium, which was dissolved in the Pearl River delta near Humen town at Boca Tigris, close to the deep-water anchorages to the south of Whampoa Island typically used by merchant ships.

Before the first reports of these events were published in Britain in 1839 and 1840, there had been little wider acknowledgement of the con-nection between the tea trade and the opium trade. Most tea drinkers in Britain were blissfully unaware of the secret steeped alike within each cup of bohea, congou, hyson, souchong and twankay.[46] While tea had broadly succeeded in persuading its devoted public of its gentle, nourishing, healthful properties, opium was quickly demonized as a baneful narcotic. In 1836, John Davis, who had recently returned from a brief appointment as joint superintendent of British trade in Canton, had observed in his

The Destruction of Opium by Official Lin, c. 1840, watercolour on paper. This painting, by an unknown Chinese artist, depicts the destruction of vast quantities of opium in the waters of the Pearl River at Boca Tigris. Labourers (or, perhaps, soldiers) are depicted hacking open the packages containing the refined drug, allowing them to be dissolved in the water, while imperial commissioner Lin Zexu directs proceedings from the shore. Other senior local officials look on from a pavilion nearby.

wide-ranging *The Chinese: A General Description of the Empire of China and its Inhabitants* that

> Opium has of late formed about *one-half* of the total value of British imports . . . and that tea has constituted something less than the same proportion of our exports . . . The pernicious drug, sold to the Chinese, has exceeded in market-value the wholesome leaf that has been purchased from them.[47]

A reviewer of Davis's treatise in the *Quarterly Review* for July 1836 noted with some incredulity that 'It is a curious circumstance that we grow the poppy in our Indian territories to poison the people of China, in return for a wholesome beverage which they prepare, almost exclusively, for us.'[48] Moreover, the production of opium was detrimental to the Assam tea experiment, argued Charles Bruce in 1839. In his view, the 'dreadful plague' of opium had consumed the Indian tea-plantation workers; 'few but those who have resided long in this unhappy land know the dreadful and immoral effects which the use of opium produces.'[49] In the same year, London clergyman Algernon Thelwall (eldest son of the 1790s radical John Thelwall) opined that the opium trade was responsible for the 'murder' of nearly 100,000 Chinese people every year.[50]

Inside a Chinese 'Hong', c. 1800, watercolour and ink on paper. A Chinese painting depicting the inside of a Cantonese merchant hong. The scene is dominated by an enormous pair of balances, suspended from a wooden tripod. To the left, a European and Chinese merchant are engaged in conversation. On each side of the building, labourers standing in shallow containers roll tea leaves with their feet. The process is observed and recorded by a group of three clerks seated around a table at the right.

Youqua, *Wampoa*, c. 1850, oil on canvas. Youqua's depiction of the deep water anchorage at Whampoa Island (Huangpu) records the heyday of the international tea trade's focus on Canton. In the immediate foreground, the European cemetery on Danes Island (Changzhou) can be glimpsed. Ships from the United States, Britain and France anchor in the channel, while an early paddle-steamer passes behind the island to the right. The Whampoa pagoda, which survives today, rises from a headland beyond. Canton itself is out of sight; it was reached via the channel passing out of the frame on the left hand side.

Over the summer of 1839, British and American merchants in Canton grew weary of a stalemate that had frozen all trading. By the autumn Lord Palmerston's Whig government, incensed by the destruction of the cargoes of British merchants and by the factory siege, and encouraged by the renewed petitions of merchants desperate for free trading rights in China (the most influential of whom was William Jardine), decided to act.[51] Palmerston dispatched an expeditionary force which arrived in Macau in the summer of 1840, quickly blockading Canton and occupying the port of Chusan: the first Anglo–Chinese War – popularly known as the Opium War – had begun. By the summer of 1841 the British effectively controlled Chusan, Ningpo, Amoy and Canton. On the ground fighting was much fiercer, though the conflict was still hopelessly one-sided. British forces moved rapidly up the Yangtze river, taking Shanghai along the way. As Nanking was about to fall, leaving the route to Peking itself open, the Qing government decided to negotiate a treaty.

The Treaty of Nanking, agreed in the late summer of 1842, contained a number of overarching principles that were of immense significance for Britain's deregulated East India trade.[52] Five ports were opened to British trade: Canton, Amoy, Foochow, Ningpo and Shanghai. There was to be open correspondence between British and Chinese officials of equal rank, the monopoly on trade enjoyed by the hong merchants would be abolished, and the island of Hong Kong was to be ceded to Britain. As hostilities ceased, so a new deregulated China trade began, with Canton still very much at its centre. A painting dating from this period, attributed to Chinese artist Youqua, depicts Whampoa as a bustling merchant port with no fewer than fifteen visiting East Indiamen (including one paddle-steamer), together with a number of junk-rigged Chinese ships. The flags flown from the visitors' masts evidence their countries of origin: America, France and – of course – Britain, though these ships now belong to a variety of private trading concerns rather than the East India Company, already passing from memory. In its depiction of the port's energy and vibrancy, the painting offers a remarkable contrast with the seventeenth-century view of Dutch ships at Canton offered in a painting attributed to Johannes Vinckboons (c. 1663). These ships are not interlopers in an unknown, mysterious land; rather, they are engaged in a profitable mercantile exchange from which both parties benefit. After all, a tea trade without China – even in the mid-nineteenth century – was inconceivable to most observers.

The Anglo-Chinese conflict of 1840–42 was indeed an 'opium war' – it had undeniably been caused by the British desire to secure financial gain though the trade in a drug which its political and business leaders knew to be addictive and baneful to health. The private merchants who lobbied the Palmerston government and who – in part – engineered the conflict itself wanted more than anything else to trade freely in opium. But it was also a 'tea war': even as late as the 1860s, Britain continued to depend on the opium trade to fund its purchase of tea, the 'necessary luxury' of its people.[53] The provisions of the Nanking Treaty – particularly those referring to the recognition of British rank, and the opening of the ports – had been key goals of East India tea merchants since the early eighteenth century. The tea trade was also more than ever a necessity for the state revenue: it has been calculated that revenue from the tea excise met nearly two-thirds of the annual cost of the civil establishment in Britain in the 1830s, including the Crown.[54] For the state, then, the war was also about protecting a vital revenue stream. It allowed the perpetuation of a system of money laundering by which the profits of the opium trade were superficially cleansed – ethically, morally, politically – through the sanative leaves of Chinese tea.

George Cruikshank, *The T Trade in Hot Water! or, a pretty Kettle of Fish!!! – Dedicated to T. Canister & T. Spoon Esquires.*, 14 November 1818, hand-coloured etching on paper. Cruikshank's topical satire indicates the consternation generated in the established tea-trade by Frederick Gye's London Genuine Tea Company. Gye exploited fears concerning the poor quality and high cost of tea retailed to consumers. In this cartoon an oriental figure lights the 'Chinese Gunpowder' of 'Genuine Tea' – using a taper labelled 'Pro Bono Publico' ('for the public good') – which boils a kettle containing Gye's bickering and unhappy competitors. These tradesmen are decanted into a willow-pattern teapot, the tree upon which bears signs to two prisons, Newgate and the King's Bench. On Gye's 'London Tea House' a herald proclaims 'No Adulteration'.

ELEVEN

The National Drink of Victorian Britain

'Bring me a cup of Tea and *The Times!*' commanded the eighteen-year- old Queen Victoria upon acceding to the throne in June 1837 – or so it is claimed.[1] This apocryphal story's nineteenth-century provenance and whiff of plausibility indicate much about tea's status and meanings in Victorian Britain. If Catherine of Braganza's seventeenth-century habit was thought to confirm both that queen's fashionable oriental taste and tea's elite exclusivity, this later rumour demonstrates tea's historically transformed capacity to signify a different queen's desire to identify with her subjects, through direct participation in the rituals of middle-class domesticity. Nothing could be more ordinary, nothing more admirable in the young Victoria than this measured response to a situation in which private grief merged with public duty: the inward comfort of tea, the external perspective of the news. And nothing could be more British. By the outset of the new monarch's reign, tea's constant availability and social universality were unquestioned facts of life in Britain: tea had been naturalized as a thoroughly British commodity.

During the period of Victoria's reign, tea did not merely remain everybody's drink: it became everybody's drink, all of the time. According to an anonymous statistician from Lewis & Company, an importer and wholesaler based in London's Crutched Friars, the annual per capita consumption of tea in Britain rose more than threefold between the 1830s and the 1880s (from 1.48 pounds in 1836 to 5.0 pounds in 1885).[2] This steady, significant increase was in stark contrast to the first third of the century, when increasing tea supplies were wholly absorbed within population growth. Indeed, by around 1880 tea drinking attained a level commensurate with that calculated for the early twenty-first century.[3] Capturing this step change in everyday material habits, contemporary perceptions of tea figured it not just as a universal social routine, but as a ubiquitous marker of national character. From the 1820s onwards, the conceit of 'this tea-drinking nation' entered public circulation as an epithet epitomizing how tea enlaced individual Britons within a shared sense of identity, marking them as civilized, pacific, sober and industrious. Addressing the Society of Arts on 13 February 1861, the pioneering dietician Edward Smith (1819–1874) argued that 'the characteristic of the food of an Englishman has heretofore been roast-beef and beer; but, without interfering with the pre-eminence of those substances, we may certainly now add the further characteristic of tea.'[4] A couple of years later, the Birmingham grocer (and father of the founder of Typhoo Tea) John Sumner (1824–1907) declared that 'the great Anglo-Saxon race are essentially a tea-drinking people', as if this relationship with an Asian leaf was a self-evident and indelible biological necessity rather than an elaborate historical phenomenon.[5] This cultural imaginary of tea was widespread, engrained, multifaceted: a product of persistent negotiations across the range of economic, intellectual, social, geographical and political environments within which the empire of tea was unflaggingly at work.

Breaking the Market

The Commutation Act had reinforced the East India Company's hegemony over Britain's tea trade, consolidating a single point of national wholesale at quarterly London auctions that were held behind closed doors and attended only by licensed tea brokers. By the 1820s this system was widely comprehended as inadequate and archaic. Upstart tea merchants such as John Nicholson breached the sacrosanct confidentiality with which Company sales were privileged, by publishing openly the details of each and every 'Break' (or lot) that was put up, thereby empowering grocers and customers to apprise themselves of the once-secret qualities, quantities and values of tea shipped that season from China.[6] This unprecedented transparency prefigured the final victory for free traders, when the East India Company's long monopoly was finally revoked.[7] The Government of India Act (1833) terminated the Company's commercial functions while appropriating its bureaucratic and ideological apparatus to support the ongoing colonial administration of British India (the Company and its Indian assets would be fully nationalized in 1858).

If the frenzy of speculation that followed deregulation was not without its drawbacks, nationwide demand was now sufficiently unshakeable to flourish in the hands of private commerce. Nonetheless, the new tea start-ups were not assisted by Parliament's simultaneous reform of the excise duty, which reverted from an *ad valorem* tax that had crept back to around 100 per cent (since the all-time low of the 1780s), to a specific rate that reached two shillings and twopence per pound of tea in 1840. This drove up the cost of the cheapest teas for the poorest consumers – adding 200 per cent or more to the wholesale price of approximately one shilling

– and inhibited the potential for market expansion. In time these adverse conditions generated swells of opposition that rode both popular commercial demand and polite moral anxiety (especially that resurfacing around the easy accessibility of inexpensive gin). Such pressures eventually persuaded the Chancellor of the Exchequer, William Gladstone, to make good on a promise he had shelved during the Crimean War by lowering duties to one shilling per pound in 1863, and then sixpence in 1865.[8]

In the two decades that followed Gladstone's reforms, annual imports of tea retained for home consumption (as opposed to those that were re-exported) almost doubled (from 99,367,000 pounds to 182,000,000 pounds). Perhaps more significantly, the wholesale 'Price of Sound Common Congou' fell to around sixpence per pound.[9] The net effect was that by 1881 the basic price of black tea to retailers hovered close to one shilling per pound, a threefold reduction over the course of 40 years. In addition to domestic manoeuvres, vital external factors were in play: a revolution in shipping (from the clippers of the mid-century that raced annually to land the first teas of the season, to long-distance steamers that capitalized on the opening of the Suez Canal in 1869); a further revision in the relationship with China following the Second Opium War (or 'Arrow War') of 1856–60; the maturing of British tea gardens in colonial India.[10] All of this meant that a remarkable conjunction of means (political, economic, infrastructural, military, imperial) was now actively instrumented in service of Britain's tea habit, and in search of Britain's tea profits.

Even before the advent of free trade, entrepreneurial spirits had been provoking irritation in the traditional networks that channelled the supply of tea in Britain. Foremost among them was Edward Eagleton, whose warehouse stood at the sign of the Grasshopper on Bishopsgate-street-within. In the late eighteenth century, Eagleton was a disruptive innovator, defiantly subverting the prevailing business norms of the British tea industry. He promoted his business aggressively beyond the capital through regular advertisements in provincial newspapers. He slashed his prices in order to achieve high-volume sales at the lowest profit margins. He refused to blend the teas he bought from the East India Company, instead selling them 'genuine as imported'. And he implemented branded packaging – 'in fine paper, with my name and catalogue printed, and the price marked on each parcel' – to reassure retail customers of the authenticity of his goods.[11] In the context of clandestine auctions and opaque wholesale practices, such methods were deeply unsettling for the established trade.

Eagleton inspired an imitator and emulator in the maverick merchant Frederick Gye (1781–1869), a lottery-winning printer who threw himself into tea in 1818 despite his inexperience. Exploiting contemporary fears about counterfeit and adulterated stocks, Gye launched the London

Genuine Tea Company on 5 November (a date deeply associated with the defence of British liberties), which promised visitors to its 'Principal Warehouse' an open view in person of the unblended teas, where 'purchasers may have the satisfaction of seeing them weighed (if preferred) from the original packages, as they arrive from China'. Customers across Britain could order whole chests of tea, which Gye undertook to have 'forwarded in the original packages, delivered direct from the East India Warehouses'. Smaller quantities would come 'packed in lead cases', enclosed in a depiction of the London Genuine Tea Company's 'principal Establishment, in Ludgate-hill, and sealed with the Company's Seal'.[12] Within a year the Company boasted tremendous success, having 'Nearly Five Hundred Country Agents ... already appointed' across Britain by August 1819, and claiming average daily sales of a staggering 2,500 pounds during the following September and October (around 3 per cent of the national market).[13] Like Eagleton, Gye's approach was both mimicked – a handbill promoting Sparrow's 'Original London Genuine Tea Warehouses' bore more than a passing resemblance to Gye's own wrappers – and excoriated. A 'Committee' of 21 rival dealers constituted itself expressly to undermine this unwelcome intrusion within a cosily restricted market, engaging in a public relations spat with Gye that culminated in George Cruikshank's satirical etching *The T Trade in Hot Water! or, a pretty Kettle of Fish!!!* of 1818. Cruikshank imagines a coterie of tea dealers heated to a rolling boil in an enormous kettle on Ludgate Hill that is fired by the 'Chinese Gunpowder' of 'Genuine Tea'. An onlooker signals the engraver's sympathies, remarking 'My eye! How the *scum bubbles* up to the top!!'[14]

Eagleton and Gye had seen the future of the domestic retail trade: a public attracted by distinctive national brands, happily reassured by promises of directness and purity, and ready to embrace the convenience of pre-packaged goods that delivered a consistently predictable consumer experience. In the mid-nineteenth century, John Horniman (who began vending tea on the Isle of Wight in 1826) developed a model that comprehended and capitalized upon this context, accomplishing enduring success where Eagleton and Gye knew only fits and starts. Horniman built a national network of agents, whom he licensed to sell tea in a customer-friendly range of packages (from 2 ounces to 1 pound in weight) that were mechanically filled at his Wormwood Street headquarters.[15] In *Tea: Its Mystery and History* (1878), an elaborate advertising puff by Samuel Phillips Day (his dedication 'to the Lovers of Pure Tea' is an unmistakable reference to Horniman's strapline), readers are taken inside this 'Tea Establishment'. The visit begins on the 'Blending Floors' where Horniman's selection of leaves was composited, before moving in sequence to the 'Testing Room' for tasting and quality assurance, the 'Weighing Floors' for packing meticulously measured smaller quantities in tinfoil and larger ones in tins, and

Horniman's Tea Company, *Horniman's Pure Black Tea,* c. 1890, printed advertisement. Horniman's advertising regularly championed the Chinese origins, pure and uniform qualities, and competitive price of its tea. In this late nineteenth-century advert, intended to replicate the dimensions of a quarter-pound 'Packet' (the smallest offered at retail), the oriental aesthetic of the packaging and porcelain cup are appropriated to underwrite the 'great STRENGTH and CHEAPNESS' of 'Horniman's Pure BLACK Tea'.

the 'Labelling Room', where the sealed packages were branded with the firm's insignia. This virtual tour came courtesy of an 'Extract from Mr Lo Fong Loh's Journal', the words of a travelling student who had visited the premises with 'H. E. Li Fung Pao (Director of the Chinese Educational Mission)', both of them hailing 'from the Tea districts of China'.[16] The scale and efficiency of the operation, underwritten by Loh's approval for the product's integrity and purity (Horniman's was the first British tea he found 'like to that I have been accustomed to use when at home'), is deliberately staged to ensnare drinkers who stubbornly trust the idiosyncratic practices and uncertain procurement of local grocers and specialist merchants.[17] Although traditional wholesalers such as Lewis & Company sought to encourage individual retailers to adapt to the peculiarities of water supply and customer taste, equipping them with extensive tasting notes designed to assist the mixing of 'your own speciality' blend, the gradual acquiescence of the Victorian tea market to Horniman's and its regional powerhouse competitors (Lipton, Mazawattee, Brooke Bond, Ridgways, the Co-operative Wholesale Society) unquestionably presaged the domination of British tea sales in the twentieth century by increasingly hefty corporations.[18]

The charges of contamination and adulteration which had riddled Britain's tea trade since the eighteenth century comprised a facet of the market that Gye, Horniman and others laboured both to exploit and to overturn. Indeed, Horniman's proudly emblazoned across its posters and packaging the endorsement of Arthur Hill Hassall, a committed sanitary campaigner and author of *Food and its Adulterations* (1855). Anatomizing Victorian fears about food safety in a brave new industrial world, Hassall collated in this substantial volume an extensive series of reports that formed the basis of testimony he had presented as chief scientific witness to a parliamentary select committee. Hassall itemized three categories of adulterants in the case of tea (as for other principal foodstuffs). Firstly came those for 'adding *weight and bulk*', such as 'Exhausted Tea Leaves' and 'Leaves other than those of Tea'. Then there were those for 'imparting *colour* and for concealing other adulterations', like 'Indigo, Prussian Blue, Turmeric, Chinese Yellow, Red Lead, Umber, Red and Yellow Ochre'. Finally Hassall itemized additives intended 'to impart *smell, flavour, pungency*, and other properties', including 'Catechu, Gum, Sulphate of Iron, Le Veno Beno, Chinese Botanical Powder'. The detailed report on 'Tea, and its Adulterations' includes precise descriptions of each miscreant substance,

"At the DOCKS, where HORNIMAN's TEAS are in Bond, I took samples from original chests of Black and Green Tea, which I analyzed and found perfectly PURE and free from the usual artificial facing, the quality being equally satisfactory."

Signed, ARTHUR HILL HASSALL, M.D.

Author of 'Food Adulterations Detected.'

LONDON, February 19th, 1874.

Horniman's Tea Company, endorsement poster by Arthur Hill Hassall, *c.* 1874, printed advertisement. Arthur Hill Hassall, a prominent sanitary campaigner in the mid-nineteenth century, produced the period's most influential and damning expositions of criminal abuses in the food industry. His explicit endorsement of Horniman's was a coup for a company that promoted its 'pure' teas as a reliable antidote to the nefarious practices of adulteration with 'facing' chemicals such as Prussian blue, or substituting tea leaves with those from ash trees or plumbago shrubs. The bold Victorian poster font printed sparsely on white paper emphasizes the value Horniman's placed on Hassall's support.

a series of chemical analyses and detection tests, and attentive botanical and microscopic engravings of both tea and its less than savoury substitutes.[19]

Over half of Hassall's material focused on 'Green Tea', despite the fact that it accounted for just one-seventh of total UK tea imports by 1855. Persistent public concern about the 'facing' of green tea with compounds designed to appeal to the eye (but not the palate) perhaps help to account for levels remaining static during the mid-century while those for black teas rocketed.[20] Hiding behind the oriental soubriquet Ti Ping Koon, the writer of *Death in the Tea Pot* (1874) – a sensationalist pamphlet bearing a cover illustration that merges a porcelain teapot with a chinoiserie skull – singled out 'Green Tea' coloured with ferrocyanic 'Prussian Blue' for special condemnation.[21] ('Green Tea' is even diagnosed as precipitating a gentle clergyman's demonic possession and eventual suicide – owing to its destructive agitation of the brain – in a gothic tale of that name by Sheridan Le Fanu.[22]) More generally, Koon contends, 'the public are slowly being poisoned by the daily use of an infusion' including 'the Tea known as "black"', which 'has so depreciated in quality that any man with a thirty years' knowledge of Tea . . . will tell you that "fine" Tea is extinct'.[23] The fault, it is determined, lies with a combination of fraudulent Chinese middlemen in Hong Kong, accommodatingly inattentive European merchants and almost wilfully ignorant domestic consumers. For one author, at least, the advantages of free trade and the advent of the mass market had debased – rather than invigorated – the British experience of tea.

A Tea-drinking Nation

Tea functioned in Victorian Britain as a powerful signifier of national identity, a shared taste that united all people – metaphorically if not actually – across a series of social divides. As regular consumers of a commodity that was fundamental to Britain's commercial (and later imperial) prosperity, tea drinkers both contributed to and literally embodied national wealth through the indulgence of their daily habit. The tea-table, once a gossipy and scandalous resort for tattling women and effeminate men, was reimagined as a nurturing heterosocial (mixed-sex) refuge at the heart of middle-class domesticity.[24] Whereas 'anti-teaist' eighteenth-century social reformers had condemned the labouring poor's appetite for the beverage, little trace of such moral indignation now endured. Instead tea was perceived – and with approbation – to suffuse the social structure as 'the only real luxury which is common to rich and poor alike', as Samuel Phillips Day attested.[25] For Day, the 'cup of tea' was an endlessly repeated and refracted practice of Britishness that was at once sober, healthful and gratifying:

The artist at his easel, the author at his desk, the statesman fresh from an exhaustive oration, the actor from the stage after fulfilling an arduous rôle, the orator from the platform, the preacher from the pulpit, the toiling mechanic, the wearied labourer, the poor governess, the tired laundress, the humble cottage housewife, the votary of pleasure even, on escaping from the scene of revelry, nay, the Queen on her throne, have, one and all, to acknowledge and express gratitude for the grateful and invigorating infusion.[26]

No longer an exotic and enervating novelty to be treated with suspicion, this 'infusion' could now be credited – in the words of the Scottish journalist Leitch Ritchie – as an agent of universal 'moral reform and social improvement'. It was, Ritchie declared, a most 'civilising juice'.[27]

If such an optimistic diagnosis associated tea squarely with broader ideological interests in nineteenth-century Britain, it was also invested with a scientific rationale. For Ritchie it was tea's nature as a 'stimulant' that was 'civilising'. As his countryman and contemporary James F. W. Johnston explained in *The Chemistry of Common Life* (1855), 'it exhilarates without sensibly intoxicating'. Johnston, an enthusiastic popularizer of chemical knowledge, itemized three main physiopsychic principles of tea with a modern perspicuity that had been largely absent from earlier accounts: its 'volatile oil', which conveys a 'narcotic influence'; the 'theine', which 'soothes the body and enlivens the mind'; and 'tannin', tea's astringent (and costive) property.[28] All three still remain a focus for dieticians.[29] The essential oil L-Theanine – especially prevalent in green tea, and imparting its distinctive *umami* (pleasant savoury) taste – is thought by some authorities to enhance mental concentration and reduce anxiety. Theine, discovered by the French chemist Oudry in 1827, was identified in 1838 with caffeine (originally isolated in 1819 by Friedlieb Ferdinand Runge), a crystalline alkaloid and highly addictive drug. As its earliest European devotees detected, tea makes a human feel more awake and alert: this is principally because caffeine suppresses the brain's reception of the sleep-inducing chemical adenosine.[30] Tea's comparatively small quantities of tannins are now known to be antioxidant (although they can also inhibit the absorption of vegetable irons).

Johnston's work was both praised and revised by Edward Smith, in a medical dissection of William Cowper's poetic maxim concerning 'the cups that cheer but not inebriate'. Smith explained that the 'cheerfulness' which users derive from tea is physiological at root, arising from the enhanced frequency and depth of respiration that it chemically provokes. Small, frequent doses produce the most pronounced results, Smith observed, noting that in all of his experimental subjects 'the cheerfulness which we have already quoted was uniformly and delightfully present'.[31] Psychotropic, habit-forming, cheering: Victorian tea – with its capacity to socialize and to civilize – was a perfect adjunct to national desires for progress and pre-eminence, orderliness and sobriety.

The revitalizing hit supplied by repeated, modest measures of tea helps to account for why Victorian Britons insatiably increased their intake as prices dropped and supply rose. The types and qualities of tea available during the mid-century would have been largely recognisable to shoppers 100 years earlier, not least via the persistence of adapted Chinese names (bohea, congou, souchong, twankay), although green tea was now sold principally to mix with black ('the usual proportion is four spoonfuls of black to one of green', Mrs Beeton recommended in 1861).[32] Nonetheless, the growing quantity on the market clearly had a substantial effect upon the material practices and social experience of preparing and taking tea. In terms of the equipage, the dainty teapot was increasingly supplanted by the sizeable copper tea urn (silver in the wealthiest families), an eighteenth-century innovation that was now widespread in domestic contexts. Urns were designed to insulate a significant volume of the infusion that could be dispensed on demand from a pressure-driven tap towards the base of each unit, located crucially above the level where the leaves settled. A more homely equivalent, the tea-cosy – a woollen cover designed to enclose a teapot – was popularized by the 1860s, again enabling drinkers to preserve the warmth of large amounts of tea over an extended period.[33] Connoisseurs worried about the gastronomic and even medical consequences of this over-stewed beverage, which exacerbated a more general disposition to serve an 'extract . . . of a fine, rich, thick, muddy colour, something between Thames water at London Bridge, and Barclay and Perkins' Entire' (a brand of dark ale).[34] The 'hideous normal taste' of such tea could only be 'concealed' via the routine addition of sugar and (where affordable) milk.[35] Nonetheless, a drink of just this character was now a regular refresher of labour, not only via the institution of factory tea breaks (already underway during the first half of the century: see chapter Nine), but also as a sober substitute for the beer customarily distributed to agricultural labourers.[36]

At the other end of the social scale, 'the five o'clock Tea' took root in 'the houses of the aristocracy'.[37] The 'afternoon tea of modern times' appealed to the tea aesthete Gordon Stables, who instructed (in 1883) that 'there ought to be an air of refinement in the room in which it is partaken . . . The tea equipage should be neat and well chosen, and the tea itself the finest and best procurable for love or money.'[38] Nonetheless, it was the social function of this new tea event that was foremost. As *Manners of Modern Society* (a contemporary manual of etiquette) advised in 1872, 'people do not assemble at these five o'clock teas to eat and drink, but merely to see and talk to each other, and take a cup of tea the while as a refreshment.'[39] Documentary research by Jane Pettigrew indicates that as

Sir John Everett Millais, *Afternoon Tea (The Gossips)*, 1889, oil on canvas. The painting depicts three children engrossed in the rituals of a tea-party picnic. Millais disconcertingly overlays childhood innocence with a sense of the more complex personal and social preoccupations of the adult women whose world these girls unconsciously imitate. A miniature willow-pattern tea service and plates of ripe summer fruits complete the scene.

early as 1841 a coterie of high-status women surrounding Anna Maria, Duchess of Bedford (a favourite of Queen Victoria), was regularly invited to her room and regaled with afternoon tea brewed in 'her grace's own private tea kettle'.[40] Clearly this was an occasion for elite networking and social exchange, albeit predicated upon the pastoral spectacle of a noble-woman preparing and serving a meal. *Manners of Modern Society* later explained that 'as "little teas" are thoroughly social gatherings, servants should be excluded if possible' (although evidence from the early twentieth century notes that Queen Mary, consort of George v, made tea only after the equipage had been wheeled in on a pair of trolleys by two footmen).[41] In Sir John Everett Millais's *Afternoon Tea* (also known as *The Gossips*, 1889), the three young subjects are both sentimentalized and sexualized as they sit absorbed not only by one another's conversation, but by their own performances of social nicety and attentiveness. Certainly the tea-charged willow-pattern crockery and disturbingly ripe summer fruits are imagined as the superficial excuse – rather than the actual purpose – for gathering.

The fashion for afternoon tea spread slowly among families of quality in the 1850s and '60s before extending across the upper middle classes during the final third of the century.[42] Unlike the so-called 'high tea' of working Britain – the principal evening meal for the majority of households – this 'modern' social gathering was self-consciously an intermediary (not to mention somewhat extravagant) moment of replenishment and exchange between luncheon and dinner. Among those of more constrained means who desired to imitate such practices lay the imagined readership of Agnes Maitland's *Afternoon Tea Book* (1887). Maitland catered for 'the many households where afternoon tea is a daily institution of considerable importance, and where, nevertheless, it is not always convenient to send to a confectioner for the little delicacies required'.[43] Respecting both the need for economy and the thirst for elegance, Maitland set down recipes for an elaborate range of cakes, sandwiches and ices that were well beyond the reach of the working classes. Nonetheless, her implication is clear: in the middle stations of life 'afternoon tea' focused as much upon nourishment as it did upon networking.

Middle-class Society Tea

Domestic felicity and stability – identified above all with the economy and piety of the middle class – were central to Victorian ideations of identity, whether individual, national or imperial. As a uniting focus of the family home, tea insinuated itself structurally within this vision. The literary historian Julie Fromer has demonstrated that tea scenes in nineteenth-century novels stage dramas of social and sexual identity, of domesticity and empire. In George Eliot's *Middlemarch* (1871–2), for example, Rosamond Lydgate's vain preoccupation with the details of dress and the possibility of amorous intrigue disrupts the dutiful administration of her husband's tea. This contrasts with the simple moral goodness of Mary Garth, who instinctively offers the beverage to a disappointed lover, and whose mother later upsets the family tea service at a moment of domestic crisis. At the outset of Henry James's *The Portrait of a Lady* (1880–81), meanwhile, the 'peculiarly English picture' of an afternoon tea party is unsettled by the author's observation that only men (decidedly not 'the regular votaries of the ceremony') are present, signalling the novel's anatomization of the challenges to and reinforcement of traditional femininity in a world that is both bound by convention and excited by modernity.[44] Although Fromer perspicuously reads this material in relation to a broader contemporary discourse of tea, it is also the case that there are cultural artefacts from the period that focus more intently on the beverage. Georgic poetry, children's books, song scores, comic satires and radical polemic were all deployed in ways that explored tea's role at the heart of Victorian life, not least within ongoing debates concerning family, gender and class.

'Temperance' conjures one encapsulation of tea's overarching significance for the middle classes of mid-Victorian Britain. Tea's remarkable facility to operate as a non-toxic, non-intoxicating, non-perishable daily beverage – inspiring pleasure that crosses social boundaries – singled it out as both a bedrock of affluence and a panacea for dissolution. Charles Barwell Coles's *Tea: A Poem* (1865) explores these themes in a thousand lines or so of serious blank verse.[45] Opening in georgic commendation of Britons' commercially fuelled determination 'To raise, instruct, and civilize the world' (l. 81), Coles identifies tea – in direct contrast with wine – as a 'Friend to the rich and poor' (l. 99). Over the passage of time and space, tea's benign 'qualities / And tyrant habit have enthrall'd the race / Of free-born Britons in a magic bond' (ll. 204–6). Like Britain's expansionist territorial ambitions, it would seem, the empire of tea's 'conquest is legitimate, obtain'd / By virtues yielding nutriment and health' (ll. 209–10). Such portentous sentiments are but a prelude to the dramatic social vignettes that unfold across the remaining 800 lines of the poem. Above all, Coles privileges two tales of intemperance reformed. First comes the story of Eugenio, a handsome gin addict rescued from the mire of drunken despair when Mira, a chaste schoolmistress, administers a 'cup . . . / Of tea with slice of lemon [that] appear'd / The fabled nectar of the gods' (ll. 692–4). Thenceforth Eugenio commits himself to a new life as a temperance evangelist who will 'sing the delight of a good cup of Tea'.[46] Even more saccharine is the final narrative, in which a philanthropic gentleman is moved by the penury of two sick and starving children to revivify their alcoholic parents. As the 'balmy cup' (l. 873) supplants gin in their diet, tea redeems this desperate couple, who are rewarded by their benefactor with funds to emigrate to the promise of honest labour in Australia. Again and again in Coles's poem, tea civilizes and rehabilitates via its physiological effects and social meanings. By focusing on the fragility of childhood innocence, and the susceptibility of domestic bliss to the agonies of debauchery, Coles illustrates tea's appeal to all members of a household, its emblematic capacity to unite them in heart, body and mind.

As 'tea' became more and more of a family meal – often taken in the nursery, without the paterfamilias in attendance – so its social thematics increasingly incorporated infantile discipline and entertainment.[47] *Questions for our Sunday Tea-table* (1863) preferred Bible quizzes for the intellectual amusement and theological instruction of middle-class families, while in *Evenings at the Tea-table* (1871) the fictional Mrs Gower presides as a party of children recount and critique a series of moralizing and sentimental narratives. Such books imply that their titular site has a steady and self-evident cultural meaning.[48] The Victorian tea-table is a safe, domestic, feminized space for friendly interaction – between men and women, adults and children – which values improving conversation, and the gentle renegotiation of problematic ideas and attitudes. Other children's texts concentrated on the commercial mediation of tea itself. *The History of a Cup of Tea in Rhymes and Pictures* (1860) took juvenile readers on a journey from the Chinese plantation, through the manufactory (where it cannot resist a dig at the local merchant's 'dishonest tricks') to the dockside. Finally the illustrations' oriental aesthetic gives way to a comfortable British interior where 'A Family Cup of Tea' is in progress:

> Hurrah! at length we see it here,
>   Upon our own Tea Table placed;
> And soon our spirits it will cheer,
>   From out the Urn that it has graced.[49]

A later children's poem, *A Tale of Tea, by a Teapot* (1884), instruments a similar strategy (although Indian tea gardens now appear alongside Chinese estates), while emphasizing at greater length the complete social diffusion of the beverage in Britain. On the final page, moreover, tea's remarkable utility is seen to extend beyond its primary function. The maidservant in a middle-class household strews damp tea-leaves on the dining-room floor in order to attract and more effectively sweep up dust.[50] Tea has 'virtue to the last', the poem explains: keeping Britain together, keeping Britain working, keeping Britain clean.[51]

Nineteenth-century tea culture recurrently validates the beverage's civic feminization of its drinkers. Robert Rhodes Reed's *The Song of the Tea-pot* (1855) is a hymn to the 'most intimate friends of all classes', imagining a heterosocial idyll in which the gentle but sophisticated tastes of 'kind ladies' soften the worldly coldness of '*mankind*' (whose homosocial gatherings at their 'clubs' revolve around 'French-fashion'd coffee'). A subtle if constrained feminism emerges, which exploits the commonplace assertion that women are the best 'judges of Tea' by extrapolating the benefits of their homely provision for both individual men and society at large:

> Philosophers, Statesmen, the truth may conceal,
> But their grandest ideas grace the ev'ning meal;
> Ev'n Poets, Divines, Men of Bus'ness, find
> That infusion of tea giveth strength to the mind.
> Perhaps the grand secret is this *only then*
> *The Ladies can hold conversation with men!*

The Song of the Tea-pot reminds (or rather instructs) its audience that behind every strong man is a steadfast woman, who daily shares his 'ev'ning meal', explores his 'grandest ideas' before they are exposed to wider scrutiny, and enjoys with him the 'strength' of 'mind' that an 'infusion of tea' imparts.

The title-page illustration elaborates further, conjuring a scene in the heavens in which men and women of the upper and middle classes attend a tea party. Cupid pours the tea, while at the centre of the frame a young man is seated next to his lover (his eyes are on her, hers are cast down). Tea has brought them together, tea enables their 'conversation', tea will sustain their future together for both private and social good.[52]

For all that *The Song of the Tea-pot* lightly eulogizes feminine acuity and government at the tea-table, the text promulgates a conservative, gendered social politics. Such views were not unusual in the discourse of tea. A poem by Edward Edmondson performs an elaborate vote of 'thanks to

Title page from Robert Rhodes Reed (lyric) and Carlo Minasi (music), *The Song of the Tea-pot* (London, [1855]). An oversized silver teapot hangs from the proscenium arch of a Victorian Music Hall (or is it the chancel arch of a church?), beneath which three *putti* drink tea together. The tea plant has been trained like a vine up the left-hand side of the archway; to the right, an angelic figure pulls back the curtain. The scene beyond, emanating from the steam of the *putti*'s tea-urn, is at once heavenly and mundane. At a middle-class tea party, serviced by a fourth *putto* in the guise of Cupid, men and women mingle both socially and (it is hinted) romantically.

the ladies' for the faithful administration of 'warm tea' to their menfolk. *A Poem on a Cup of Warm Tea* (1865) is structured in two distinct sections, opening in praise of tea as a sociable, healthful, temperate beverage before proceeding to recommend judicious, affectionate and companionate marriage. This is without doubt an arrangement in which the woman's management of her household, children and fireside is crucial to the husband's efficiency and felicity:

> One foot on the cradle, the baby she's rocking,
> With worsted and needle she's mending a stocking;
> When the husband returns quite weary with toiling,
> The toast is just ready, and the water is boiling.[53]

Others pushed even further this direct association between the qualification of virtuous and submissive domestic femininity (in a wife) and the ready provision of nourishing, nurturing tea (for her man). In Alexander T. Teetgen's dialogue *A Mistress and her Servant* (1870) – designed as an advertising brochure for the Tea Warehouse on Bishopsgate-street-within – the lady of a suburban house discusses the public affairs of the day with Mr Love-a-cup (the husband of her laundress, and an ageing dock worker). When conversation turns to the vexed question of 'women's rights', the pair concur in their disapproval of 'this foolish rage for turning women into men'. 'THE MOST SENSIBLE WOMEN OF ENGLAND DON'T WANT IT!', Love-a-cup insists; indeed, the only 'women's rights' he is minded to defend are their entitlements to 'a nice sweetheart, a good husband, a lovely family, and a happy home'.[54] The instinctive sexism of this pamphlet presumably reflects the attitudes which the proprietors of the Tea Warehouse imputed to their (principally) female customers, although it is perhaps also designed to appeal to the male householders who ultimately financed tea's consumption.

By contrast, some writers were prepared to unsettle tea's connotations as a harmonizing agent at the heart of the home. The Victorian tea-table's layered history and present ubiquity offered a familiar social setting that could be reconfigured as a site of satire and a conduit for political debate, vestiges of its eighteenth-century forebear. Two short dramas from the mid-century – *A Storm in a Tea Cup* (1855) and *A Cup of Tea* (1869) – deployed the ritualistic administration of tea at a marital breakfast table to cast an implausible veneer of polite affection across the troubled relationships upon which their comedy depends.[55] Sexual humour also energizes *The Husbands' Tea Party* (1875), which congregates at the house of Peter Hyson, a middle-class tea dealer. Alongside his guest Narcissus Newcome (a confectioner), Hyson is mercilessly teased by an alliance of Benjamin Burly Brass (a brazier and fellow guest) and John Dodgin (a greengrocer, and the 'Day Waiter' who has come to Hyson's house in order to service the assembly). Their crime is an unmanly readiness to acknowledge and concede ground to the tastes and whims of their wives; and while Newcome continues to insist that 'Peace and sunshine illuminate my domestic circle', Hyson is persuaded to resolve that 'I'll not any longer be content with absolute petticoat government'.[56] Yet as Mrs Hyson returns home (off-stage) to break up the party, Peter's nerve fails him, and he hurriedly ushers his friends out of the back door. The tea party itself is not a satirical target (indeed, the stout Brass is as happy as the waifish Newcome to drink the stuff), but tea's propensity to soften the boundaries between men and women – so lauded by *The Song of the Tea-pot* – here teeters into a dangerous tendency to effeminize and subvert the social order.

Markers of class were also in the sights of music-hall tea satires. Two songs from the end of the nineteenth century send up the middle-class afternoon tea as a hollow transaction characterized by gastronomic disaster and stilted sociability. 'Sitting Down to Tea' (1891) allows the forced politeness of social interaction to triumph absurdly against a comically dismal bill of fare. Nothing is as it should be: the butter is 'margarine, / Which has turned a trifle green', the 'jam's with mildew furred', the 'sugar's full of sand', and 'the pickled salmon, too, / Has been soused in Irish stew'. Yet the real humour lies in the comic injunctions – barbed with sincerity – to maintain an illusion of enjoyment and respectability in such predicaments. 'Sweetly smile without a word', 'Don't in scorn your nose turn up', 'Any fuss you mustn't make': such are the commands of etiquette presaging the refrain 'When with company you're sitting down to tea'.[57] In 'Middle Class Society Tea' (1894), meanwhile, social punctilios disguise the guests' dislike not for the food, but for one another. Unnerved from the outset by an agitated hostess, and upset by her 'rude little beast' of a son Tommy, the visitors nonetheless smile outwardly and satisfy their stomachs before trudging home to complain that '"We'll never go *there* any more" / '"Twas a shockingly dull affair"'. Their hypocritically 'pleasant' host, meanwhile, disparages the 'fathead crowd' that has gorged at his table. Not surprisingly, the singer concludes (although not without a hint of snobbery):

> Oh! the Middle Class Society Tea
> May be fun for some, but it is'nt for me.
> You meet such a very mixed Companee
> At a Middle Class Society Tea.[58]

If tea constructed opportunities for 'mixed' interaction, it was clearly a 'Companee' that some would rather avoid. As these satires demonstrate, tea's symbolic capacity could be exploited to expose cracks (as well as to paper over them) in the dependable public stolidity and virtuous private sentimentality of the Victorian middle class.

Submerged beneath the surface of so much Victorian tea literature lurk anxieties and uncertainties about the stability of class structures, the integrity of domestic life, and what unites one person with (or distinguishes one from) another. Tea's ubiquitous purchase upon the everyday diets of ordinary people – above all its colonization of the slightly suffocating environment of the family home – enabled it to encapsulate the unspoken rules governing social identities, roles and interactions. Rarely do texts from the period invite a straightforward interrogation of this ideological power of tea, but the prologue to a new feminist periodical did just that. *Kettledrum* – contemporary slang for an afternoon tea party, but also self-consciously signifying a noisy instrument – was launched in January 1869. Its editor Josephine Butler (1828–1906) opened by ironically promising to confine her magazine to 'Tea-table talk and tea-table interests'. As Butler's argument proceeds, however, it transpires that the 'Woman's Kingdom' of the 'tea-table' is dynamically connected with global networks of capital and labour, and with dominant constructions of status and gender. The tea leaves and equipage are outputs of international agriculture, manufacture and commerce, Butler reminds her readers. As such they implicate consumers in unpalatable compromises concerning the trade in opium between India and China, the exploitation of African Caribbean workers on sugar plantations, the conditions and education of those employed in domestic industries, the raising and expenditure of the national revenue. Meanwhile, by assembling a mixed and lively company of guests – male and female, young and old – the tea-table 'kettledrum' establishes an environment in which ideas and opinions about such issues can be aired critically, productively and freely. The limits of discussion in fact melt away: 'there is no topic of interest which may not be touched upon in the course of our tea-table gossip'. If the tea-table is 'the empire which all concede' to women, it need not be a realm of submissive acquiescence to the status quo. Understood radically (through Butler's eyes), tea – as commodity, practice and event – instantiates the much later feminist rallying cry that the personal is political.[59]

The Tea of the Future

Britain's relationship with tea underwent a radical transformation in the final third of the nineteenth century. In the mid-1850s, commercial shipments began to arrive from plantations in India that were owned by British investors and managed by British agriculturists. While the quantities of 'Assam' tea were small at the outset, they surpassed those from China within 35 years. Alongside imports from Ceylon (Sri Lanka), they would temporarily wipe out Chinese exports to Britain in the early twentieth century.[60] A beverage that for 200 years had been experienced (in Pepys's words) as 'a China drink' – the guise in which it had infiltrated the national consciousness – was suddenly something rather different. No longer a drain on the national treasury (or, as it had become, a potentially troubling opportunity to profit from a distant market in narcotics), tea was now a commodity internal to the economy of empire. Yet Indian tea's rapid takeover of the British market was not inevitable. Even in the early 1880s, industry observers seemed reluctant to anticipate the revolution that was at hand. The compiler of the Indian *Tea Cyclopædia* (1881) would go no further than to concede that 'We have a giant to contend with in China, and while we do not believe that India will ever become a "Jack the Giant Killer," she may grow into a giant of equal proportion, if she is only wise in time, and is content with real, if slow, progress.'[61] Like many pragmatists, the writer feared that the fragile condition of India's tea infrastructure (which had seemed near to collapse in the mid-1860s following a burst of speculative 'tea mania') was at risk from the challenges of a flooded marketplace, within which Chinese competitors were better placed to deal with low prices.[62]

One recurring trope of tea discourse from the brief period when British imports from China and India seemed destined to remain relatively equal was to represent the characteristics of their respective teas as inherently complementary. For the writer of *Tea and Tea Blending*, the 'great strength' of Indian teas supplies 'a valuable quality which would not allow them to be ignored'; if 'their harshness made them unacceptable to the public by themselves', they could be expediently 'mixed with China teas'. Indian teas are a boon for domestic blenders, he opines, because production is explicitly directed towards isolating and nurturing single traits that are best appreciated when artfully combined in a mixture: 'dark colour', 'delicately fine aroma', 'intense pungency'.[63] In *The Happy Blend; or, How John Bull was Suited to a T.* (1885), a comic narrative that parallels this argument, the titular hero and epitome of old England discovers that while Chinese tea is 'rather thin' and Indian tea 'too biting to the throat to be pleasant', the cup bestowed upon him by the spirit of the 'HAPPY BLEND' is knocked back with 'gusto' and 'is indeed Tea'.[64]

Others were more bullishly imperialist in outlook. For Captain Hathorn, whose *Handbook of Darjeeling* (1863) was designed to recommend the benefits of colonizing that region, tea cultivation gave renewed purpose and enhanced security to Britain's Indian adventure:

> Our position in India would be materially strengthened by the colonization of these hills by numbers of European farmers, who, with families springing up around them, in a healthy climate,

would soon furnish a yeomanry that would set at defiance the hostile attempts of our semi-barbarian neighbours.[65]

Hathorn's pragmatic recommendation was heeded by Lieutenant-Colonel Edward Money, a tea planter in northeastern India who would later pose a stark question for British readers of *The Tea Controversy* in 1884: 'TEA is a national beverage. Two parts of the world are rivals for its production. Which produces the better article?'[66] In his carefully itemized five-point case for India, Money grants primary significance not to the product so much as to the producer. 'The Indian is grown and manufactured on large estates under the superintendence of educated Englishmen, and skill and

Illustrations from *The Happy Blend; or, How John Bull was Suited to a T.* (London, [1885]). In his search for the best-tasting and most economical cup of tea, John Bull encounters four allegorical personages proffering different solutions. Clockwise from bottom left are a turbaned Indian (his tea too 'biting'), a pig-tailed Chinaman (his tea 'rather thin'), a 'cunning looking man' (whose 'Bogus Tea' comes with endless free gifts), and the oddly Luciferian 'Happy Blend' (whose beverage, Bull judges, 'is indeed Tea'). These figures illustrate a generic advertising pamphlet, which includes a blank space for retailers to insert business directions to shops where readers could purchase speciality blended teas, presumably combining Chinese and Indian leaves.

capital are combined to produce the best possible article.' China tea, by contrast, is produced by poorer artisans 'in the rudest way'. It follows from this contention (in Money's second point) that Indian methods are also superior, generating 'a clean article' which benefits from mechanized processes; whereas 'in China it is hand-made . . . by nearly nude men bending over the tables on which the leaf is rolled. They perspire freely: the result need not be minutely described!' The unavoidable impurity of Chinese leaves is sadly aggravated by fraudulent adulteration (point three). Moreover, 'Indian [tea] is naturally stronger than the Chinese' (due to both varietal difference and climatic conditions), meaning that it 'goes further' (points four and five).[67]

According to the reassuring logic of Money's imperial ideology, the British acquisition and quasi-military settlement of Indian territory has introduced unprecedented social organization, agricultural expertise and industrial technology to the region. This coming of civilization to India enables 'educated Englishmen' who superintend 'large estates' to apprehend and exploit the natural potential of local vegetation in a manner simply unthinkable by indigenous peoples. Meanwhile, small-scale Chinese plantations have been surpassed by European ingenuity, a triumph that is morally valorized by markedly divergent attitudes towards business ethics. Underneath Money's systematic exposition lies a confident assumption that the natural order of cultivated teas and human races are providentially and inevitably being synchronized in British India.

If Money's optimistic treatise is reasonably composed in its derogation of Chinese teas, ultimately (if erroneously) conceding that India's best hope is to achieve market parity with China, there were contemporaries readier to demonize the competition. Gordon Stables's *Tea: The Drink of Pleasure and of Health* (1883) opens by rewriting received wisdom concerning tea's origins, exercising a spurious Darwinian deduction that while the plant is native to India it must have been carried to China from elsewhere in Asia. Declaring his preference for the taste of 'the Indian teas', which 'are more racy, penetrating, and possess more backbone' – terms that echo his understanding of the racial differences between Britons and Chinese – he was in no doubt that 'Indian Tea [is] the Tea of the Future'.[68] Stables keyed into voguish degeneration theories, articulating his view that human races, like natural organisms, flourish and then diminish; and 'the Chinese, one of the most ancient races on the face of the earth . . . seems to be in its dotage'. Its people's effeminate physiognomy and contaminated tea is material evidence of this deterioration, whereas British 'tea-drinking . . . has certainly not lowered us as a nation. Our march is steadily onwards, and "Progress" and "Enlightenment" are the words inscribed on our banners.'[69] The rapid reversal in the global tea industry – where once Chinese growers taught English farmers in India, 'we can now teach them' – is nature's way

'One of Lipton's Tea Gardens, Ceylon', printed advertisement in *The Graphic*, 18 December 1896. This newsprint advertisement markets Lipton's teas aimed at a range of budgets (from one shilling to one shilling and sevenpence per pound). The Scottish grocer Thomas Lipton travelled to Ceylon (Sri Lanka) in 1890, where he successfully negotiated ownership of 'tea-gardens' that could cheaply and exclusively supply his British retail business. This image claims that the imperial capital and expertise of the planter, coupled with the colonial landscape and labour of the subcontinent, create tea that is the 'finest the World can produce' – fit for royal appointment 'to Her Majesty the Queen', and outstripping the traditional manufactures of China.

of demonstrating (happily for Britain) the justice and necessity of 'our' commercial ascendancy.[70]

In competing with China's export market, Britain's Indian tea trade benefited from a number of infrastructural advantages: a shorter geographical distance, an integrated legal framework, a shared cultural and bureaucratic history. Alongside these practical considerations, the racist myths articulated by writers like Money and Stables underwrote the decisions of British wholesalers, retailers and consumers to switch their allegiances. In 1887, when John Lane Densham was seeking to re-energize the family tea firm, he coined an Indian-sounding name to register as a trademark: 'Mazawattee' synthesizes the Hindi *mazaa* ('pleasure' or 'fun') and the Sinhalese *vatta* ('garden'), while crucially retaining a phonic echo of the English 'tea'.[71] Three years later, the Scottish grocery magnate Thomas Lipton travelled to Ceylon, where he invested in land and machinery that would enable him to bring his product 'direct from the tea garden to the teapot'.[72] The tea of empire was accruing unstoppable momentum.

Indian production transformed not just tea's cultural status, but the actual experiences of British consumers. The growing public penchant for black teas had been in evidence long before those from Assam entered the fray, but this intervention does appear to have been terminal. While the 'racy' robustness of Indian tea resulted partly from varietal difference, there is no doubt that the ingenious mechanized processes introduced by British industrialists on the subcontinent were vital for maximizing this natural distinction. As Money boasted, on many plantations, machines had replaced the traditional artisanal methods initially imported from across the Himalayas, and this technology both effectively standardized and unexpectedly altered the taste and appearance of Britain's tea. *Tea and Tea Blending* explained (albeit at second hand) how the withering of fresh leaves, once achieved gently over several hours by means of the sun or charcoal stoves, was now completed in five minutes using a 'cyclone withering and drying machine'. A 'green withered and cutting machine' replaced manpower to 'cut the leaves into the requisite size of square', while a 'link and lever rolling machine' could approximate the bruising effects of rolling by hand via a ribbed drum (compressed by the 'powerful application of the lever principle') that held up to 80 pounds of tea at once. Drying was again rapidly accomplished in a 'chamber exposed to hot air' that dispensed with direct charcoal heating, instead sealing the leaves in zinc-bottomed drawers. Finally, a 'unique circular motion sifting machine' separated the tea by size into four basic grades. Their names – variations on the themes of pekoe, souchong and congou – were the only vestiges of Chinese tea culture to persist.[73]

This radical mechanization of tea manufacturing – an antecedent of the twentieth-century's crush-tear-curl method – increased the extent and efficiency of oxidization that leaves underwent, thus enhancing the distinctive notes of black tea. It was also designed to bring more processed vegetation to market, preserving the 'Fannings' and 'Dust' that in other contexts might be deemed industrial waste. These residual products supplied the bulk for cheaper teas, imparting a dark 'liquor' that consumers were persuaded to associate with quality and strength. When John Sumner junior (1856–1934) assumed responsibility for his family business in Birmingham, his new 'Typhoo Tipps' were predominantly derived not from hand-rolled leaf-buds but from fannings, the coarse by-product of a more refined commodity. As Stables had thundered – albeit without a trace of irony – 'Indian tea' really was the 'Tea of the Future'. That future would incorporate a system of industrialized food production that creams off the finest cuts for those who can pay, and represents as premium aliments its recycled detritus for others appropriated beneath the 'banners' of a '"Progress" and "Enlightenment"' that they barely know.

Above all, Indian plantations made tea truly British. Finally the tea industry assumed patterns and structures that stemmed from – rather than operating in parallel dissonance to – Britain's own commercial history.

'Planter's Bungalow', frontispiece from Edward Bamber, *Tea* (London, 1868). The image is historically startling for its transposition of the tea-plantation from a Chinese to an Indian landscape (signalled most obviously by the presence of an elephant). Writing from personal experience of Darjeeling, Bamber portrayed the world of the planter's jungle bungalow as one of adventure, courage and loneliness. In this image tea bushes under cultivation constitute the middle ground of the scene; the building to the left rear is perhaps used to process the tea leaves.

Tea retained its intricately negotiated associations with healthfulness, sociability, domesticity and temperance; but its modified taste and enticing darkness subtly erased any lingering sense that this cultural heritage had once been translated from China. As the boundaries of nationhood gave way to the expansiveness of empire, so Victoria's subjects at home and overseas were linked by material relations of production and consumption, and by ideal fictions of national identity and international community. In a strange, desperately literary conclusion to *Tea* (1868), a tract by the early Indian pioneer Edward Bamber, the reader is invited on a trek through the Darjeeling jungle, where 'Man meets man as man' and the 'Planter' is 'the only European among all those dark skins'. Bamber's closing words challenge us to keep 'in imagination' this hostile environment where 'the planter prepares the Tea, which you infuse on your tables, within four stone walls, and comfort around'. 'There is', we are reminded, 'a contrast'. Yet if anything, Bamber draws attention to continuities of taste, purpose and fortune that connect the colonial 'planter' and domestic consumer, and which thereby serve to collapse – as much as to reinforce – the geographical distance and cultural foreignness between plantation and tea-table.[74]

Less than a decade after Bamber's excursus, when Albert Edward, Prince of Wales, visited his future dominions in South Asia, the emperor-in-waiting was presented with a 'Silver Swami Tea Service' by the Gaekwad Maharaja of Baroda.[75] This vassalic tribute, 'consisting of 12 teacups, saucers, and teaspoons, a teapot, sugar bowl with sugar tongs, milk jug, and three salvers', had been crafted by Indian smiths working for P. Orr and Sons of Madras (Chennai). Like the tea it was notionally designed to serve, the silver equipage was a product that united an utterly exotic natural resource with colonial knowhow, British tableware decorated with outlandish heathen 'Swami' deities. A beautiful, costly and unprecedented gift, the service returned to Europe with the prince and was exhibited at London's signature royal museums in South Kensington and then Bethnal Green. Later it moved to the Paris Exposition, where it prompted a rush for Indian silver, before showing in Edinburgh, Glasgow, Aberdeen and York.[76] Not only was there now British tea for Britons everywhere, all of the time, but the orientalism of its presentation and performance had been naturalized, dislocated by a strange familiarity from the threatening possibility of actual difference.

In *Tea: The Drink of Pleasure and of Health*, Gordon Stables expresses an adamant confidence not just in British tea culture, but in its geo-historical pre-eminence. It is unfair to accuse the author – a writer of boys' adventure stories and an early caravanning enthusiast – of being anything more than a man of his time (even if not all men of his time so uncritically championed the 'English . . . love of fair play').[77] Amid his book's unsettling chauvinism, Stables inserts a seeming homage to the *Chajing* of Lu Yu, although if conscious, the compliment is presumably meant as much as a valediction as a paean to the Chinese way of tea. Stables describes in

P. Orr & Sons (Calcutta), five-piece tea service, *c.* 1876, silver, gilded silver, ivory. Albert, Prince of Wales (later Edward VII), completed an imperial tour of British India in 1875–6. The Gaekwad Maharaja of Baroda presented him with an exquisite tea service, wrought from Indian silver and manufactured by P. Orr and Sons in Madras (Chennai). As this similar surviving equipage demonstrates, the tools of a British afternoon tea are visually re-imagined through their encounter with the traditional iconography of 'Swami' deities.

sensuous detail both how to select tea leaves and how to prepare one's body and environment for drinking, before itemizing the modern British tea equipage in terms that evoke Lu Yu's register, words that had been resonating for more than a millennium. It is a simpler, shorter list than Lu's – limited to tea-kettle, water, fire, teapot or urn, and cosy – but it shares his aesthetic pedantry concerning the integrity, attractiveness and cleanliness of these everyday materials.[78] As Stables's book demonstrates, tea was no longer merely engrained within the national identity of Victorian Britain: it was part of its very fabric. Tea was a fundamental component of what it meant to be British at the end of the nineteenth century; while Britishness was becoming foundational to the global experience of tea.

Jean Metzinger, *Tea Time (Woman with a Teaspoon)*, 1911, oil on cardboard. Metzinger's painting, described as 'The Mona Lisa of Cubism' when it was first exhibited, depicts a woman in the act of drinking tea. She is caught in the moment of lifting a teaspoon, her teacup on the table before her. In the Cubist method's fracturing of time and space, the teacup is observed at once in profile and from above.

TWELVE

Twentieth-century Tea

ctober 1936, the London Commercial Sale Rooms at Mincing Lane: the auctioneer calls the lot. 'Assam Broken Pekoe: how much for this?' Almost immediately a host of competing voices call out rising prices: 'One and three – Half – Three and a half – Four' (bids being allowed to advance in farthings). From the rostrum, the auctioneer brings the lot to an end, announcing 'All done at Four-three'. Bringing his gavel down, he calls the abbreviated record 'Four-three Crosby', meaning tea has sold for the price of one shilling, four pence and three farthings per pound, purchased by Crosby, a firm of tea brokers.[1] The tea on offer here was grown in plantations in Assam in northern India; 'Broken Pekoe' was the second most sought after grade, made from a slightly larger and less tender leaf than the top ordinary grade of 'Broken Orange Pekoe'. A guide for grocers advised that this grade had 'rather less colour in the cup' than the finest, but was 'useful as a filler in a blend'.[2] The London Public Tea Auction at Mincing Lane, the 'Street of Tea', was a highly specialized market, and in the first half of the twentieth century, the most significant in the world.

In the twentieth century, tea's empire grew to encompass the whole globe. Tea expanded its zones of production by finding new customers and establishing new cultures of consumption. Major innovations in mechanized methods of production and cultivation were mirrored in new public forms of consumption in tea-shops, canteens and cafeterias, and in more efficient forms of preparation, including the tea-bag and instant tea from the automat. In this expansion, what can be hard to fathom is the degree to which tea in the twentieth century had become an almost wholly British drink, not only in gustatory and cultural consumption, but also in cultivation, manufacture and marketing. The scale of British domination of the tea business in the mid-twentieth century is hard to overestimate. There were important tea companies with long histories in Europe, such as A. C. Perch's Thehandel in Copenhagen, and the van Nelle and Douwe Egbert firms in Amsterdam; and in America, companies such as Red Rose Tea,

247

Salada and Bigelow. But these companies were no match for the globally dominant British firms of the twentieth century, especially Brooke Bond, Liptons, Lyons and Tetley. By the early twentieth century, the global production and trade in tea was dominated by 'British' tea, cultivated by British companies on British-owned plantations, backed by British finance in British colonies and dominions. This global trade was organized and regulated by the tea market in London, where the great majority of the world's tea was graded, blended and sold. Furthermore, the people of Britain consumed more tea per head of population than any other nation.

But although the global market for tea underwent significant growth in size and reach, the British taste for tea, in the first half of the twentieth century, became less varied and curious. Tea had become, overwhelmingly, just tea: primarily a black Indian or Ceylonese product, blended to produce a consistently strong, bitter beverage that stained the water quickly, with high colour. The wide variety of teas once prominent in the trade sank from view, available only from high-end speciality retailers, coded as a form of elite or esoteric knowledge. Tea from the major firms was, in effect, an industrial product, manufactured at a central unit and distributed by a complex chain of service.

For most of the twentieth century, the tea trade was organized along the lines established in the later nineteenth century. Retail teas sold to British consumers, and those in North America, northern Europe, Australia and New Zealand, were identified by brand names, often named after the grocer who had first sold the blend. The biggest brands at the turn of the century were Brooke Bond, Typhoo, Liptons and Lyons. Tea was imported from the different producer territories in distinct parcels that differed widely according to their place of origin, their manufacture and even from season to season. Yet each brand worked hard to ensure that its tea was the same from year to year and from cup to cup. The role of the tea blender accordingly became central to the tea trade: by adjusting the proportion of each kind or parcel of tea, the blender exercised great skill in producing a beverage that recreated a control specimen in terms of flavour, colour and price. A package of generic branded tea might in principle contain any tea from anywhere. So while tea manufacture – that age-old, and by this period largely mechanized, process of withering, rolling, fermenting, drying and grading – occurred in the colonial tea-producing regions, the tea trade itself was focussed in the metropole, in the complex space delineated by Mincing Lane, comprising the tasting room, tea auction and blending room.

Between 1900 and 1970, Mincing Lane dealt with between 60–80 per cent of tea sold in Britain, with the remainder made up of tea purchased directly in producer countries, either by public auction or private treaty. The wholesale industry provided constant employment for the tea tasters, men with discerning palates who controlled the creation and consistency of the blends. Their tasting sessions were marathon affairs in which the taster and his pot-boy would sample, in a few hours, hundreds of small cups of tea, recording their impressions and valuations as they went.[3] Behind the 'shabby doors' of Mincing Lane, one writer commented in 1934, the fate of the world's tea crop was decided by the tasters, 'with their almost eternally steaming kettles', who 'taste and value the cargoes which it is their duty to sell on commission'.

> On long wooden benches are rows of white china pots in which samples of tea are made and allowed to infuse for four minutes before the taster with his tireless palate begins the unending round ... When the samples are ready for tasting they are poured into cups and the leaves are turned into the pot lids, as further evidence of their qualities ... The tea taster goes round, sips the teas, rolls them voluptuously on his tongue and spits them out again. He can often tell you in which garden they have been grown, and, to a farthing, what price they will command at auction later in the day.[4]

On the decisions of the tea tasters' delicate palates depended the flavour of the nation's favourite blends.

The London Public Tea Auction at Mincing Lane was established in 1834 after the dismantling of the East India Company monopoly. In the early twentieth century, when this market was as famous as the Stock Exchange in Old Broad Street, the auction itself was held in the London Commercial Sale Rooms, a white tiled room high up in Mincing Lane, until 1937, when it moved across the road to Plantation House. The tea was sold by open outcry in a specially built salesroom, with the brokers arranged on steeply tiered, curved banks of seating. Although in principle anyone might attend the auction, bids were restricted to full members of the Tea Brokers' Association of London, which had been formed in 1899. This regulated both who might sell and buy tea. Selling brokers inspected and sampled tea, establishing type and grades, and organized the auction. Buying brokers either worked directly for the large tea companies, or as 'market men' instructed by smaller buyers: the tea auction was distinctive for allowing the winning bid on a 'break' to set the price for other bidders on the same consignment (tea firms had no need of large consignments of some kinds of tea for their particular blends). The tea sold at Mincing Lane was dispatched from bonded warehouses to the various tea firms, where it was blended and packed for distribution by the tea dealers and grocers.[5]

In 1920, writing in *The Economic Consequences of the Peace*, the economist John Maynard Keynes imagined tea at the centre of the modern mercantile world.

The inhabitant of London could order by telephone, sipping his morning tea in bed, the various products of the whole earth, in such quantity as he might see fit, and reasonably expect their early delivery upon his doorstep; he could at the same moment and by the same means adventure his wealth in the natural resources and new enterprises of any quarter of the world, and share, without exertion or even trouble, in their prospective fruits and advantages; or he could decide to couple the security of his fortunes with the good faith of the townspeople of any substantial municipality in any continent that fancy or information might recommend.[6]

Keynes understood tea as one of the staple commodities of global commerce, a product central to the British economy, yet also as an international trade subject to forces well beyond it. When he established the London and Cambridge Economic Service in 1923 to develop and analyse new forms of statistical information about the economy, he considered tea as an important constituent of British trade. In his report on 'Stocks of Staple Commodities' of 1923, Keynes estimated that 'about three-quarters of the total world production [of tea] passes through this country . . . in particular no less than 88 per cent of the 1921 crop in India, Ceylon, and the East Indies, which countries provide nearly the whole of the tea in which there is a world market, were shipped to the United Kingdom for distribution.'[7] In 1923, tea on the global market was predominantly from British colonies in South Asia: 46 per cent from India (Assam, Darjeeling) and 24 per cent from Ceylon (Sri Lanka). The biggest competitor was tea from the Netherlands colonies in Java and Sumatra (12 per cent). Only 10 per cent was sourced from China, with small quantities from Japan and Formosa (Taiwan). The newest producer zone was Nyasaland in Africa (now Malawi), which contributed very small quantities (0.1 per cent). As Keynes was aware, the quantity reported for China, Japan and Formosa was only that exported, and ignored a considerable domestic consumption. The 1924 report by Keynes also commented on consumption, using further information from 'Messrs Harrison and Crosfield', a tea firm based in London. They estimated that the average consumption of tea in the United Kingdom had gone up from 300 million pounds per annum in 1913 to 410 million pounds in 1923 (including the Irish Free State). In 1923, this represented more than 53 per cent of the total world consumption of 732 million pounds – and 8.7 pounds per person per year.[8]

Modernist Tea-time

Cultural evidence suggests that by the beginning of the twentieth century, tea had become closely imbricated in the everyday, almost unseen through its common familiarity. The French painter Jean Metzinger's *Tea Time* (1911), now in the Philadelphia Museum of Art, depicts a woman in the act of drinking tea: caught in the moment of lifting a teaspoon, her teacup on the table before her. When this painting was first shown at the Salon d'Automne in Paris in 1911, the art critic André Salmon described it as 'the *Mona Lisa* of Cubism' because of her enigmatic expression and comely beauty.[9] Although some aspects of what is depicted are obscure, the scene remains quite legible through the geometric fragmentation of the Cubist method: the teacup, for example, is observed at once in profile and also from above. The fractured planes of the painting suggest different moments captured successively and displayed simultaneously on one picture plane. The art historians Mark Antliff and Patricia Dee Leighten describe Metzinger's method here as capturing a series of distinct moments: 'Metzinger's model is both in the act of tasting and touching. Her left hand grasps the cup and saucer . . . and her right hand delicately suspends the spoon between cup and mouth.'[10] Her attitude suggests she is an artist's model taking a break: she is drinking tea because she is not posing. In Metzinger's image, tea provides a momentary break in everyday life: here, a woman is depicted in the essentially unimportant action of drinking tea. The domestic ordinariness of tea is what makes the pose appropriate for Metzinger's Cubist treatment.

Modernist novels also depict tea absorbed within the ordinary flow of daily life. D. H. Lawrence's novel *Sons and Lovers* (1913) develops a concise guide to the various social formations of tea in early twentieth-century Britain. A fictionalized account of his own upbringing, the novel is set among the working-class culture of a mining community in the North of England, and proceeds from Lawrence's idea of introducing 'a woman of character and refinement' into the 'lower-class' world of the colliery town.[11] Lawrence makes tea a telling signal of this status inconsistency when he depicts distinctly different ways of representing what 'tea' means, each iteration coded with different values and connotations. Tea, it seems, can be both a hot beverage and a meal taken in the evening (which might include, but need not, that hot beverage). The first tea performance, in chapter Two, depicts Walter Morel, the miner, preparing a tea drink during his idiosyncratic breakfast ritual. Walter comes downstairs in the darkened house, early in the morning: his first act is to revive the fire to boil water for tea in a kettle left filled on the hob. When the tea is prepared, he drinks it by himself:

> He toasted his bacon on a fork and caught the drops of fat on
> his bread; then he put the rasher on his thick slice of bread, and

cut off chunks with a clasp-knife, poured his tea into his saucer, and was happy.[12]

His habit of sipping tea from the saucer was common in the early twentieth century, although always considered a breach of etiquette by the polite. 'Saucering' tea helps cool the hot beverage for consumption, but, as Morel's happiness suggests, also has a profound gusto-aesthetic pleasure. Tea in this scene is symptomatic of Morel's self-conscious working-class life: its consumption is a part of his unvarnished plebeian world.

Later in the same chapter, a different kind of tea ritual is practised by Walter's wife, Gertrude Morel, when she entertains the neurasthenic Congregational clergyman Mr Heaton before her husband returns from the pit. On such occasions, the narrator explains, 'she laid the cloth early, got out her best cups, with a little green rim', serving him tea while she prepared the family's meal and they discuss his next sermon. Here 'tea' is an occasion for a form of polite heterosexual sociability, signalled by her best china and the pious topic of conversation. When Morel returns from the pit, he drinks tea in a way calculated as a riposte to the clergyman's politeness: 'He poured out a saucerful of tea, blew it, and sucked it up through his great black moustache, sighing afterwards.' Although strictly counter to polite precepts, Morel's gustatory enthusiasm is imbued in the novel with a kind of plebeian nobility. Later in the chapter, the family, including the children, eat a meal they also call 'tea'. With the 'tea-things on the table', William reads aloud from a children's Sunday-school magazine (*The Child's Own*) – though this occasion is ruined by their father's bad mood, who 'ate and drank more noisily than he had need'.[13] Tea, then, allows the curiously bifurcated world of the Morels, not quite working-class, not quite middle-class, to be dissected and explored.

The tea ritual also resonates in the novel's treatment of Paul Morel as he emerges through the novel as an artist, a man of imagination, sensitivity and high culture. When Paul brings Clara, the woman he is courting, home to meet his parents, it is tea that clarifies the emotional dynamic:

At tea Clara felt the refinement and sang-froid of the household. Mrs. Morel was perfectly at her ease. The pouring out the tea and attending to the people went on unconsciously, without interrupting her in her talk. There was a lot of room at the oval table; the china of dark blue willow-pattern looked pretty on the glossy cloth. There was a little bowl of small, yellow chrysanthemums. Clara felt she completed the circle, and it was a pleasure to her. But she was rather afraid of the self-possession of the Morels, father and all. She took their tone; there was a feeling of balance. It was a cool, clear atmosphere, where everyone was himself, and in harmony. Clara enjoyed it, but there was a fear deep at the bottom of her.[14]

Tea here is a social litmus test that clarifies Clara's fit with the family, legible to the participants and the reader alike, without being stated explicitly. The tea event engages the characters in a performance – of politeness, sociability and sincerity – that establishes quickly and clearly whether she is an acceptable match. The role of tea as a social arbiter of status does not need to be explained by Lawrence's narrator: the encounter over tea facilitates a social ritual of infinite variety but telling readability.

The tea ceremony was purposefully constructed as an important signal of British social life and customs. The English journalist Muriel Harris tried to explain this to an American audience in an essay published in *The North American Review* in 1922. In her estimation, the British had won the First World War on the back of tea and its values of civility and politeness. Tea, she thought, had an uncommon ability to connect the great and good to the common people. 'The solvent that is tea accommodated a million inter-relationships where friction was possible.' Explaining this, Harris claimed that afternoon tea 'makes a halfway house between English formality and English expansion'.

> Strangers are often at pains to reconcile the English stiffness and coldness with the expansiveness of the English house and its manner of hospitality. In one sense, the Englishman's house is his castle, strongly barred against intruders, extremely jealous of its privacy, resentful of any attempt to penetrate its fastnesses. In another, it is an open door, welcoming, free, hospitable. You have to be given the freedom of the castle and it is yours. Without this freedom, you are a mere outsider. The English tea is at once a preliminary to this freedom and a relaxation from the forms of life. There is no set service, no special time within an hour or so. It comes after the day's efforts and provides the little stimulus which overcomes fatigue. The shining silver reflecting the leaping fire, the sound of the kettle, the warm scent of the flowers, the low book-box or stand, full perhaps of brand new books, all these elements which have grown up around the tea function, provide a quiet, expansive atmosphere in which both friend and family can feel themselves most perfectly at home.[15]

This vision of polite domesticity and ritual ceremony drew the attention of numerous artists. Hilda Fearon's *The Tea Party* (1916) and Ethel Sands's *Tea with Sickert* (1911–12) both balance the visual splendour of the tea-things with the sociable encounter of tea-time: the figures, so much less

Hilda Fearon, *The Tea Party*, 1916, oil on canvas. Tea's enduring association with domesticity and the family continued in the 20th century. A nanny sits with two children in the garden, at a cloth-covered table laid for tea. The enormous shiny urn dominates the scene, next to a tray with teapot, milk jug and sugar bowl, and two giant white cups and saucers.

important than the tea-things, have been subsumed into tea-time (recalling Harris's social solvent). The American essayist Agnes Repplier concluded that 'the tea-hour in England combines the permanence of an institution with the agreeable formlessness of an incidental occurrence.' She argued that tea crossed status boundaries through its relation to sociability: 'As an institution it is kindly, as an incident it is stimulating . . . Tea is friendly to the rich, and serves the hospitable instincts of the poor . . . Tea is their social offering, their comfortable incentive to gossip.'[16]

Tea-shop Modernity

The tea trade had been transformed in the late nineteenth century by the emergence of a new kind of tea retailer, the 'tea-shop', dedicated to the sale of the prepared hot drink and light meals, rather than the dry commodity. These tea-shops made two related innovations over previous forms of commercial food service: they adopted tea as their governing metaphor and they offered an urban space that was hospitable to women of the middle orders of society. In this way, the sociable space of the tea-shop in the early twentieth century was as innovative and transgressive as the coffee-house had been in the late seventeenth century. Tea lends these places an important set of cultural assumptions – polite, leisured, ordinary, convivial and, most important, a female-friendly sociability – but in fact the tea they offered had relatively little to do with their business. There was no menu detailing esoteric varieties and higher grades of tea: it was good, but ordinary, vended alongside coffee and other drinks, as well as light refreshments and casual meals. The definition of tea-shop in the *Oxford English Dictionary* gets this irony right: a tea-shop is 'a café where tea is served'.

Many tea-rooms were small-scale affairs, run by an owner-proprietor with help from one or two relatively unskilled staff. Books offering practical advice to those interested in establishing a tea-room business give a sense of their priorities: an example was Helen Jerome's *Running a Tea-room and Catering for Profit,* published by Pitman in 1936.[17] The guidebooks argued that owners needed little or no experience in the tea or catering trades, and that the business could be established for a small

Walter Bayes, *Tea Shop in the High Street, Colchester; Recording Britain, c.* 1940, pen and ink and watercolour on paper. Painted in 1940 for the 'Recording Britain' scheme, organized by the Ministry of Information to record everyday life in Britain during the Second World War, Bayes's watercolour depicts two mixed groups and a lone woman drinking tea in the polite but bourgeois interior of an ordinary high street tea-shop in Colchester.

capital outlay. Owners were told to aim for a 'Cheerful Room with Cosy Service', as one writer suggested.[18] Business advice books considered such businesses primarily as a spatial interaction of aesthetics and labour ('There is usually one waitress to each 15 customers . . . Chintz curtains and table-cloths are cheap and cheery').[19] Tea-shops were primarily open during the day, were focused on a simple hot food service, and took almost no interest at all (at least in the advice books) in tea itself: no mention of where to source it, how to prepare it or the different kinds available. 'The *general* impression made on a customer is very important . . . A bright, clean, and *cheerful* atmosphere is in itself a powerful appetite-creator, and to maintain such a state of affairs should be your particular care.'[20] Tea-shops, typified by a homely form of 'Tudorbethan' architecture, pink rose wallpaper and lace curtains, came to be seen as characteristic of a certain kind of fusty English village life: such businesses were parodied by John Betjeman in *Ghastly Good Taste* (1933) as 'Olde Teae Shoppes'.[21] Although tea is prominently signalled in the names of these places, knowledge of, or discourse on, tea and its varieties is almost entirely absent.

The commercial tea-shop market was dominated by the several large chains in the early twentieth century. In 1887, a long-established catering firm, the Aerated Bread Company, set up a 'tea-shop' in London to retail its baked goods to urban customers, served alongside tea and other beverages. This was mass catering, designed to provide a cheaper and more accessible form of food and beverage service than that obtainable in expensive and high-status restaurants. It offered, in a polite space decorated to a good standard, a profitable business selling 'such insignificant comestibles as a glass of milk and bun, or a cup of tea and a buttered scone'.[22] The unstated point here was that tea-shops offered a new space of commercial urban sociability in competition with the pub and the restaurant. Until tea-shops became common, *The Observer* newspaper concluded in 1912, 'it was practically impossible to obtain tea, coffee, cocoa and other light refreshments except at public houses', where they were served alongside 'intoxicating liquors'. In consequence, 'The cheerful and cleanly tea shop rapidly grew in popular favour.'[23] Within a decade, there were more than 50 A.B.C. tea-shops. Rival companies were stung into competition: tea-trading companies such as J. Lyons and Liptons opened a series of tea-shops, as did other dairy and catering firms: the British Tea Table Company, Ye Mecca, Cabins.

The large chains, especially the A.B.C. and Lyons tea-shops, were concentrated in cities. In London they were prominent in the City and the West End, where they catered for customers that contemporaries thought were new and distinctive. At one end, their clientele was leisured and polite, such as the theatregoers and shoppers who thronged the city's new department stores. At another end it was oriented towards the City's white-collar workers, offering cheap lunches to the new echelons of clerks, secretaries and typists in the City's banks and merchant firms. What was especially noticeable about the new tea-shops' consumers was that they included women: inoculated from the impolite context of the pub, these places were equally hospitable to both sexes. Indeed, contemporary commentators celebrated the tea-shops as giving women in the common stations of life, for the first time, a refuge in the city. As such, tea-shops have been analysed and celebrated as making an important contribution to the emancipation of women in the early twentieth century, alongside such innovative cultural formations as 'New Women', suffragettes, bicycling and cigarettes. Erika Rappaport argues that the tea-shop, the department store and the theatre allowed women to participate in the public sphere in the period by forging them a new role as public consumers, an identity constructed for them by advertisements, newspaper editorials, social criticism, legislation and street protests.[24]

To most contemporaries, the most striking aspect of the new tea-shop chains was their extravagant scale and luxury fittings. Despite the ordinary, even homely, fare they offered, Lyons and A.B.C. lavished their tea-shops with decidedly grand interiors. The American writer Theodore Dreiser, visiting a Lyons near Piccadilly in London in 1914, commented on the incongruity between the middle-class clientele and the elite decor. He recalled

being struck with the size and importance of it even though it was intensely middle class. It was a great chamber, decorated after the fashion of a palace ball-room, with immense chandeliers of prismed glass hanging from the ceiling, and a balcony furnished in cream and gold where other tables were set, and where a large stringed orchestra played continuously during the lunch and dinner. An enormous crowd of very commonplace people were there – clerks, minor officials, clergymen, small shop-keepers – and the bill of fare was composed of many homely dishes such as beef-and-kidney pie, suet pudding, and the like – combined with others bearing high sounding French names.[25]

Dreiser's unease at the apparent mismatch between elegant surroundings and common clientele overlooks the massive scale of these tea-shops. The Coventry Street Lyons Corner House, built in 1909, originally seated 2,000 customers, but a later addition raised this to a capacity of 4,500.[26]

Most Lyons tea-shops were less grand, even though they brought a measure of elite style to the high streets of Britain. These tea-shops were hygienic, modern and reassuringly similar to each other, making use of mirrors and marble to indicate high status. These institutions operated a single nationwide pricing structure, so a cup of tea and a muffin were the same price everywhere. Being both repeatable and ubiquitous made the Lyons experience a forerunner of the Starbucks model of branded coffee-house chain in the present period. The uniformed waitresses, known as 'Nippies', wore regulation black dresses with white caps, collars and aprons. The Nippy was an important part of the spectacle of popular luxury offered by the Lyon's tea-shops, at once a commercial standardized worker and an avatar of the servant class of the wealthy and the nobility. Modernist writers, Scott McCracken suggests, found in the figure of the Nippy a telling status ambiguity, as she simultaneously aroused 'feelings of attraction and repulsion in the male viewer'. For many Modernist writers, the teashop was a site of 'sexual spectacle': Katherine Mansfield, Jean Rhys, Dorothy Richardson and Virginia Woolf all use the tea-shop as a paradigmatic space of the urban public, which, as McCracken says, 'was as much a zone of conflict and contestation as it was of refreshment and social encounter'.[27]

The scale of the new tea-shop chains brought its own challenges. As McCracken has observed, the real business of Lyons was the new forms of organization it brought to supply and distribution in the catering trades. A commentator in *The Times* argued in 1912 that 'Tea-shops when properly managed are a very remunerative enterprise. The secret of their success lies largely in effective organization, in the fact that they prepare most of the food they sell, and in gauging the probable demand for per-ishable eateries.'[28] The industrial scale of these businesses was met by an industrialization of its practices. McCracken concludes: 'In its enthusiasm for new manufacturing techniques and processes, Lyons developed a kind of Fordism of food: in the 1930s Lyons boasted that it sold 750,000 muffins and crumpets a week.'[29] It is perhaps not entirely surprising to learn that in 1947 Lyons automated some of their processes by developing the world's first computer for commercial purposes, LEO (Lyons Electronic Office) 1, to process inventory, orders and payments.[30]

Tea Goes to War

Tea played an important role in the cultural imagination of British identity, both erasing and consolidating its exotic and imperial origins. This asso-ciation made tea especially amenable to British propaganda in war time. Tea was one of the goods promoted by the Empire Marketing Board in the 1930s, in an advertising campaign which sought to establish a consumer preference, reinforced by tariffs, for tea from the dominions (India, Ceylon and the tiny production of East Africa), over tea from the Netherlands East Indies, China, Japan, and Formosa (Taiwan). John Grierson's award-winning documentary film *A Song for Ceylon* (1934) showed how tea was central to the culture and economy of both metropolis and empire.[31] Tea had become a 'totemic foodstuff' that offered a simplified synecdoche of

British values of politeness, equality and sociability. Cinema used 'tea's symbolic power to help define British characteristics and present an image of Britain to itself'. In Alfred Hitchcock's *The Lady Vanishes* (1938), tea drinking is used to mark the difference between British and 'foreign' passengers on a train journey through a fictional European country. Those passengers that take tea are recognized as British, by viewers and by themselves, and so combine to assist the British spy, Miss Froy, evade capture.[32]

On the outbreak of war in 1939, it was clear that tea and the tea trade were going to play an important role – one of the 'sinews of war'. A commentator concluded: 'Normal advertising and other publicity work came to a stop and a campaign of tea in the service of the War effort began.'[33] As the BBC journalist Richard Dimbleby later claimed, tea was an important weapon in the British fighting machine, both on the home front and in the armed forces. 'Tea has played a major part in the war', he claimed in 1947, 'as the comforter of the weary, the supporter of the weak, and the protector of the cold'. Early in the war, the Empire Tea Bureau organized a 'Tea Car' service: a mobile canteen mounted in the back of a van or truck, which served tea for the military wherever they were found, whether on the Home Front, at Dunkirk or during the Blitz. Dimbleby reported that the 'tea van' was 'one of the most popular vehicles' wherever it was encountered, 'swaying on its way to a camp, hospital, or aerodrome, delivering hundreds of cups of tea to troops who had not expected it'.[34] The 'mobile tea kitchens', numbering more than 1,500 by 1942, and funded and staffed by charities, carried 'food and hot tea to civilians bombed from their homes, to air raid wardens standing watch, to firefighters battling against incendiaries, and to men in the three armed services'.[35] Factory workers in the ordnance industries were provided with tea by a new organization, the Tea Bureau (Catering Services), which brought them tea on a trolley service to their workstations. It was not good tea, but, as the children's author and mobile-canteen volunteer Noel Streatfeild said, 'to the best of our ability we supplied good, hot, strong tea, as sweet as the sugar allowance would permit. It was not always easy.'[36] Although the tea was variable in quality, the mobile canteen established an important new sociable zone for tea consumption: around the canteen window, under the awning, by day and night, gathered a notably egalitarian and inclusive group, comprising men and women, who drank tea, socialized and found solace.

In April 1940, the new minister of food, Frederick Marquis, Lord Woolton, announced that the government was to take control of the tea trade under emergency plans that had been developed in 1937. All current stocks of tea, held in bond, were requisitioned and the ministry took over the task of contracting with producers in India, Ceylon and East Africa, taking all the tea available, at a price based on the average received by growers in 1936–8. In the United Kingdom, tea was rationed, with prices pegged

Ministry of Information Photo Division, *Blitz Canteen: Women of the Women's Voluntary Service Run a Mobile Canteen in London, England, 1941*, black-and-white photograph. Tea cars from the Women's Voluntary Service served tea to service personnel and the public across London during the Blitz. Here two young women volunteers, the socialites Patience 'Boo' Brand and Rachel Bingham, serve tea to men of the Royal Engineers, who have been building bridges across bomb craters in main thoroughfares.

at those ruling on 1 July 1940. The government was greatly concerned about how to manage the rationing of the 'national beverage' – potentially a very unpopular move.[37] Each consumer was limited to 2 ounces of tea a week, a reduction of one-third from the official computation of regular consumption (2.9 ounces a week). Organizations and companies wanting to supply tea to their workers or the services were eligible for an extra allowance. To buy tea at the regulated price, consumers had to use a coupon in their ration books: retailers presented the coupons collected from purchasers to their local food office. Unlike in the Great War, when one national brand was established (known as 'Pool Tea' in the trade), each tea firm packaged their own brands and sold them through their own distribution channels. Despite the enormously complicated supply chain, now directed through the Ministry of Food, the trade successfully endeavoured to ensure that 'tea was always on the retailer's shelves' when a 'ration book was presented at the counter'.[38] By 1942, supplies of tea from China and the Far East were cut entirely by Japanese occupation, leaving India, Ceylon and East Africa almost the sole producers for the world market. Taking emergency powers, the nascent United Nations mandated the British government, through the Ministry of Food, to take control of the global tea trade and ensure equitable supplies to all Allied and neutral nations.[39] During the war worldwide production declined, falling to around 730 million pounds in 1943, below what it had been in 1905.[40] Nonetheless, when war ended in 1945, the global tea trade had been literally monopolized by British firms. This may have been, for the British trade, peak tea.

The British Way of Tea in the Mid-twentieth Century

A good sense of the British 'way of tea' in the mid-twentieth century is caught in an essay by George Orwell, published in the *Evening Standard* on 12 January 1946, against the backdrop of severe food shortages across Europe. Orwell's essay 'A Nice Cup of Tea' was one of a popular Saturday series in the newspaper on British popular culture: one considered the perfect pub, while another was an early and brave defence of traditional British food and dishes. Orwell's essay on tea is of a piece with these, a mildly patriotic encomium to an under-appreciated aspect of British culture, at a time when it was changing rapidly under the heavy strains of the economic disaster of victory. Orwell begins by eulogizing the importance of tea – 'one of the mainstays of civilisation' – but frets that it is both not fully understood, and its use is subject to 'violent dispute'. His own eleven-point recipe for the perfect cup of tea, he admits, is subjective, and would not garner anything like universal agreement. Orwell's recipe aimed to wring as many hot and strong cups of tea out of a 2-ounce ration as could be expected. He advised that consumers should use 'Indian or Ceylonese tea', which he thought had more 'stimulation in it' than 'China tea' ('That comforting phrase "a nice cup of tea"', he said, 'invariably means Indian tea'). He specified that tea should be made 'in small quantities' and 'in a teapot' rather than an urn; and the pot 'should be warmed beforehand' by being placed on the hob. The tea should be strong: 'For a pot holding a quart . . . six heaped teaspoons would be about right.' He advised against any strainers, muslin bags or 'other devices to imprison the tea' (he is groping anachronistically for 'tea-bags' here): 'the tea should be put straight into the pot.' It was also important, he thought, to take the teapot to the kettle, as the water should actually be boiling at the moment of impact with the leaves. After making the tea, 'one should stir it, or better, give the pot a good shake, afterwards allowing the leaves to settle.' To drink the tea, Orwell advised a 'good breakfast cup – that is, the cylindrical type of cup, not the flat, shallow type', which allowed the tea to cool too quickly. Tea, he said, should be served with milk, not cream; and the tea should be poured into the cup first. This, he acknowledged, was one of the most controversial points of his rules: 'in every family in Britain there are probably two schools of thought on the subject.' Lastly, tea 'should be drunk *without sugar*'. He asked:

> how can you call yourself a true tea-lover if you destroy the
> flavour of your tea by putting sugar in it? . . . Tea is meant to be
> bitter, just as beer is meant to be bitter. If you sweeten it, you are
> no longer tasting the tea, you are merely tasting the sugar; you
> could make a very similar drink by dissolving sugar in plain hot
> water.[41]

Orwell's rules not only describe a way of tea making, but an attitude to
its consumption. He does not imagine his cup of tea as a sociable occasion,
nor does he propose any kind of artificially staged ritual. For him, tea can
be reduced to a stimulating beverage, to be consumed hot, dark, bitter and
lactified. The prescriptions he outlined in 1946 continue to have much force,
and to be widely debated, in the British tea preparation. The milk-in-first
debate rumbles on, for example, as does the question of whether to heat
the teapot, the wisdom of adding sugar and the matter of how fresh and
how hot the water should be.[42] Since this time, engineers have determined
a British Standards Institution technical specification for tea making (BS
6008:1980), which has been complemented by official, albeit light-hearted
advice about how to make a 'perfect cup of tea' issued by the Royal Society
of Chemistry.[43] The unresolved questions of British tea making, of course,
apply primarily to the scenario in which loose tea is prepared in a teapot.
Orwell was not to know in 1946 that over the next few decades this was
about to become increasingly unusual.

Rationing tea came to an end in October 1952. The supply of tea to
the global market by producer countries had recovered from its war-
imposed shortage. In Britain, the allowance had for some time been
increased to what was assumed to be its 'natural' level of 3 ounces a week,
at or above demand. In preparation, the tea-trade free-market auctions
at Mincing Lane restarted in August 1952, and at the first sale, the price
fell below the control level. So while many important commodities
remained on the ration, tea was taken off on 3 October 1952. The Times
newspaper commented:

> Whatever may be the limitations of British taste, tea undoubtedly
> comes first as the national drink. The thought of what the world
> must have been like before tea came in was, long ago, dismissed
> as unthinkable. The Minister of Food may be congratulated on
> having been able to free so popular a prisoner from the gaol of
> rationing.[44]

At the end of the war, at the end of rationing, tea's position in British
culture was at its apogee. Tea was seemingly unassailable: not 'a' but 'the'
national drink.

Yet the post-war fortunes of tea have not been as kind as this suggests. Tea had a good war, but in the subsequent decades it has had to fight hard to keep pace with rival drinks and rival trades. Britons still consume more tea than any other beverage, but tea is not culturally 'hot'. In 1956, tea consumption in Britain reached a new height of 2.88 ounces per head per week, but then began a long and sustained decline of almost 60 per cent by the end of the century, to 1.2 ounces. In the cultural imagination, tea suffered in comparison with coffee (with its modern coffee bars and frothy espresso-based drinks) and, after the 1970s, with carbonated soft drinks. Tea remained domestic, homely, ordinary – but also dull and forgettable. Even the tea auction at Mincing Lane was in decline, as the auctions staged in producer regions gained in prominence. The final London tea auction took place in June 1998.[45]

Modern Efficiency: The Rise of the Tea-bag

The idea of selling tea in portion-sized small bags was devised in the United States in the early twentieth century. Early examples used textile sachets, known as tea balls, that could be placed in a teapot or urn. Numerous entrepreneurial American tea importers claimed to have been instigators of this innovation. In 1903, for example, two women took out a patent for a fabric 'small pocket with terminal flap . . . especially adapted for holding tea leaves', suitable to make a single cup of tea in a cup.[46] Other tea companies claimed to have been selling similar items from around the same period: one tea man, Thomas Sullivan, maintained that the tea-bag evolved in 1908 from the sample sachets of tea he had made up in silk bags.[47] The rationale in each case was convenience and efficiency: in this sense, the tea-bag is an indicator of modernity and of the American century. The tea-bag appealed to the manufacturer because it was more frugal, making cheap tea go further. Tea-bags could compete in price with loose-leaf tea, despite the extra cost embedded in the manufacture of the sachet: one pound of tea made about 200 cups as loose-leaf, but more than 300 in tea-bags.[48] By 1947, 35 per cent of tea sold in the United States was retailed in tea-bags.[49]

It was not until 1953 that the first British company, Tetley, began selling similar tea bags. Tetley was an old grocery firm, founded in 1837, specializing in the Indian trade. Their early tea bags, packed in individual paper envelopes, were recognized as an American intervention. A verse satire in the *Manchester Guardian* in 1953 complained:

Of tea alone Great Britain brags;
Americans have not a clue.
Americans make tea with bags.[50]

Despite the frosty reception, the American invention prospered. A packet of 'De Luxe Quality Tetley Tea Bags' was expensive – a box containing 48 bags cost 7s. 11d.– and contained, they claimed somewhat hyperbolically, 'the finest high grown tea, and only the tenderest tips of that', 'made the connoisseur way'.[51] Their advice about the method was simple: 'drop the tea bag into a warmed pot, pour out tea pure, clear and flavourful, with never a leaf in sight.'[52] Early adopters had to be reminded not to open the bag itself and pour out the tea leaves. Other British tea firms followed: Twinings developed a tea-bag for the American market in 1956, for example. But Tetley led the growth: tea-bags comprised 0.75 per cent of overall tea sales in 1960, 6 per cent in 1967 and 16 per cent in 1972. All the tea companies were forced to respond, launching tea-bag versions of best-selling tea brands such as Brooke Bond, PG Tips and Typhoo in the 1960s.[53] By 2013, tea bags accounted for 91 per cent of the tea drunk in Britain.[54]

The tea-bag changed the sociability of tea. Making tea in a teapot imagined a slow service, steeping the leaves for three to six minutes, with the infusion available for a number of people. While the teapot was communal and sociable, the tea-bag was essentially a lonely singleton: one bag per mug. Tea-bags made it more convenient for a drinker to make tea quickly, but in so doing, the almost ineluctable connection between tea and sociability was revised. Tea-bags also changed the tea itself, making use of the lowest-quality grades of tea, known as fannings and dust. These grades comprise very small particles of tea leaf, originally produced only as a by-product of the manufacturing process of higher-grade leaf teas. 'Dust grade' is literally tea waste, while 'fannings' are the second smallest tea grade, sifted or winnowed out of the higher grades. However, as impecunious tea drinkers have long known, dusts and fannings produce strong, dark tea liquor. Tea-bags allowed companies to use these cheaper grades to make a strong and flavoursome tea without muddying the liquor.

Changing technology in the tea industry helped produce more tea of these low and strong grades suitable to tea-bags. In 1931, Sir William Mckercher, of Amgoorie Tea Estate in Assam, developed a more efficient and quicker method of manufacturing tea. Now known as the crush-tear-curl system, his process radically shortened and entirely mechanized the tea manufacturing process, turning the essentially handmade artisanal production of tea into one organized by the work-time discipline of factory labour. The machinery continuously processes the tea through a series of contra-rotating toothed rollers, so that the leaves are cut, torn and curled, producing a relatively fine-grained and completely oxidized black preparation.[55] This method, industry apologists enthuse, produces a 'quick infusing tea' that can 'penetrate the paper barrier' of the tea-bag.[56] Faster and cheaper than the classical methods of tea manufacture, crush-tear-curl involves little direct human labour: furthermore it results in a reliable tea,

Salada tea-bag, 1975. Tea-bags were pioneered by various American companies at the beginning of the twentieth century, but became popular in the post-war period. To the consumer
they offered convenience and efficiency, while to the manufacturer they allowed cheaper
and lower grades of tea a wider use. By 2013, tea bags accounted for 91 per cent of the tea drunk
in Britain.

with a strong liquor, consistent flavour and mild bitterness. Crush-tear-
curl has become the dominant method of tea production, especially in
South Asia and Africa, where 90–95 per cent of production follows the
method.

In the post-war period, tea fitted itself for the modern world by
becoming more convenient and more efficient. The tea-bag transformed
tea making from a semi-ritualized preparation process requiring specialist
equipage and skill into a quick, dependable and quotidian event. Tea, too,
has changed, produced by factory methods to maximize economic efficiency
and produce a consistently dark and highly flavoured liquor. Becoming
modern made tea more accessible and more reliable. Consumers could
now purchase a branded product that would produce the same taste day
after day, year after year.

New self-service tea machine, *c.* 1945. Twentieth-century dreams of automatic tea imagined a technologically enhanced experience, combining speed and efficiency with the relaxation and leisure implied in tea drinking.

Epilogue: Global Tea

In the last half century, tea has become increasingly popular around the world, and increasingly the subject of global multinational business systems. As tea manufacture becomes ever more industrialized, the British 'way of tea' delineated by Orwell has become progressively less common, even endangered. Although traditionalists may decry this, tea's late modern foodways have witnessed a plethora of new ceremonies, observed in the brief encounter between a mug and a tea-bag, in the automatic drama of coin-operated instant tea being squirted into a paper cup, in the wrist-twisting action used to open a ready-to-drink iced tea served in a plastic bottle. Each of these everyday performances is stamped with the ghostly memory of more elaborate rituals from previous generations. But this history of tea has been largely forgotten, a loss of memory that conceals its enduring qualities of exoticism and luxury.

Corporatized and ubiquitous, tea is now normal, quotidian, regular, unexceptional. Ironically, this makes tea a remarkably successful commodity. The International Tea Committee, an industry lobby group, estimates that up to 3 billion cups of tea are consumed every day around the world. A very big business, tea engenders keen competition. In 2013, the market intelligence agency Euromonitor calculated from trade sources and national statistics that the global marketplace for hot drinks was worth just over U.S.$138 billion. Of this, tea was estimated at a little over U.S.$40 billion, representing volume sales of 2.4 million tonnes. Although this makes tea barely more than half the value and size of the worldwide coffee trade (U.S.$80 billion, 4.8 million tonnes), converting these figures into liquid servings demonstrates that tea is actually imbibed in greater quantities. Euromonitor estimates 'brewed volume' in 2013 at 290 billion litres of tea, compared to 162 billion litres of coffee.[1] Tea wins the battle for the throat, though it loses that for the wallet, because much less tea than coffee is needed to make a cup. Given that the standard metric portion is 250ml, this amounts to 1.16 trillion cups of tea brewed globally per annum: an average of 165 per person. The UK Tea Association attributes 955 cups per year to each person in Britain.

Tea as a product and a culture represents an important early example of globalization. The leaf repeatedly remade itself and its customers through its journey from China to Europe in the seventeenth and eighteenth centuries. The East India Company is sometimes described as one of the first multinational corporations.[2] Indeed, the Western encounter with tea – appropriating, commodifying and incorporating it within daily habits – is a formative case study for understanding how modern capitalism invented and refined its strategies for monetizing life and accumulating profits. That story continues today, with tea at its heart.

The commercial contexts of tea have been transformed in late consumer capitalism by the rise of the multinational corporation. Over the past half-century, most of the independent tea firms noticed over the course of this book have been subsumed within global enterprises. Typically, historical brand names are preserved and exploited to enhance value, concealing less welcome processes of efficiency and rationalization. An early example of corporate takeover was the acquisition of Twinings Crosfield (founded as Tom's Coffee-house in 1706) by Associated British Foods in 1964, where it was joined later by another venerable tea firm, Jacksons of Piccadilly (founded in 1815). At Associated British Foods, these firms became part of a multinational food processor with a large presence in sugar and baker's yeast, sitting alongside successful consumer labels including Ovaltine and Primark. Twinings remains a thriving and profitable brand. Its marketing emphasizes the firm's enduring history, using a logo that subtly updates one adopted in 1787. It operates a retail shop/museum on the Strand in London, near the location where the company first traded. There is even a blend called '1706', a most un-eighteenth-century mixture of tea from Africa, India and Sri Lanka. This obsession with heritage, which extends to Twinings's customary 'signature blends', is contraindicated by the modernity of their offering, now predominantly sold in tea-bags, and joined by a large range of herbal and fruit-flavoured tisanes and ready-to-drink iced teas.

The international corporate trajectory of many tea brands reiterates the leaf's persistent transcontinental morphing. British tea has gone global. Typhoo Tea, created by a Birmingham grocer in 1903, was merged in 1968 with Cadbury Schweppes, and subsequently was subject to a management buy-out in 1984. In 1990, it was acquired by an investment vehicle of a private equity company; while in 2005, Typhoo was sold (along with its re-launched Ridgways brand) to the Apeejay Surrendra Group of India. This company has a long history as an Indian tea producer, which has diversified into shipping, hotels, real estate and logistics. A similar narrative can be followed in the case of Tetley, founded in 1837. It was acquired by Allied Breweries in 1961, and was merged in 1978 into their Lyons tea firm to form the Lyons Tetley beverage division. This was divested in 1995, when Tetley was also subject to a management buy-out. In 2000, Tetley was acquired by the Tata Group of India, a major multinational conglomerate with interests that range from steel and cars to hotels, telecoms and food products. Tata Tea, headquartered in Kolkata, is currently the second largest tea producer in the world: the Tetley brand remains the most successful in the United Kingdom. Long associated with Britain's Indian empire, both Typhoo and Tetley have now been acquired by Indian multinational corporations. The empire, it seems, has eaten itself, as a former colonial enterprise engorges its metropolitan master.

All tea firms and multinationals, however, are dwarfed in the twenty-first century by the Anglo-Dutch leviathan Unilever. This corporation is the world's leading tea company, comfortably ahead of all its major rivals. Its brands – including Lipton, Brooke Bond and PG Tips – were each founded in the nineteenth or early twentieth centuries by specialist tea firms. Brooke Bond, established in a tea-shop in Lancashire in 1869, developed the PG Tips brand in 1930 ('PG' stands for 'pre-gest', signalling the brand's physiological value as an aperitif preparatory to digestion; 'tips' indicates the privileged part of the tea plant ostensibly used in production). In 1968, Brooke Bond merged with Liebig, the maker of Oxo cubes, which in turn was acquired by Unilever in 1984. Lipton went through a similar process of corporate acquisition: founded in 1890, its North American arm was bought by Unilever in 1938, followed in 1972 by its UK tea business. Lipton Yellow Label tea, although not distributed in the UK, is the world's number one tea brand in terms of sales. The tea itself is primarily grown in Kenya at the Kericho tea gardens. Alongside Lipton Yellow Label, Unilever sells tea under the PG Tips brand (UK), Lyons (Ireland), Bushells (Australia), Choysa (New Zealand), Red Rose (Canada), Sariwangi (Indonesia), Saga (Poland) and Scottish Blend (Scotland). Tea is irrefutably big business.

And what of China, the first major source of tea for the world market? At the beginning of the twentieth century, tea cultivation in China remained a locally organized and customary village enterprise, largely confined to traditional areas, where it was produced by the peasantry on smallholdings using methods that had remained unchanged for centuries. The trade suffered in the twentieth century, along with agriculture in China in general, so that the quantity of tea available for export declined in the 1920s and '30s to less than half its level two decades earlier. Indeed, exports fell so low that China's role in the global market for tea diminished to almost nothing. After the revolution of 1949, tea agriculture was reorganized on collective principles (during the Great Leap Forward).

The disaster of collectivization, which caused a widespread rural famine, also saw a rapid decline in output, with the area under cultivation falling significantly. But Mao Zedong, during a tour of inspection in Anhui province in 1958, declared that tea production should be encouraged, proclaiming that 'In future many more tea fields should be opened up on mountain slopes.'[3] During the Cultural Revolution, the tea industry was the subject of policies designed to increase productivity, with cadres of students and peasants instructed to plant tea on designated hillsides. Between 1965 and 1976, the land dedicated to tea farms increased nearly 300 per cent, and output more than doubled. Although tea production grew slowly in the 1980s and '90s, it has expanded rapidly in this century. China is once again the biggest cultivator of tea in the world, producing 1.64 million tonnes in 2011, or about 38 per cent of global production. Sales have risen concomitantly (from U.S.$2.8 billion in 1998 to U.S.$14.7 billion in 2013), driven especially by domestic consumption, reflecting the increasing sophistication and wealth of the Chinese market.[4] The proportion available for export, meanwhile, has declined in recent years; in a period when the global tea trade has swollen significantly, China has played a relatively marginal role.[5] The Chinese tea industry has generally resisted the corporatization witnessed elsewhere. With the market fragmented by a very large number of producers, the leading hot tea brand in China is Unilever's Lipton's Yellow Label, despite its relatively small share of sales.[6]

In search of enhanced sales and more consumers, the tea industry has innovated in recent decades, not least via developments in iced tea and herbal tea. Iced tea emerged in the southern United States in the mid-nineteenth century. Early recipes proposed that tea leaves and sugar should be steeped for several hours before straining the beverage to serve it chilled or over ice. The result is a bittersweet drink that is particularly refreshing in hot weather.[7] The Tea Association of America estimated in 2013 that 'approximately 85% of tea consumed in America is iced', a proportion matched in no other country.[8] Today, much American iced tea comes in a factory-prepared, ready-to-drink form: predominantly water, flavoured with a tiny quantity of low-grade tea, augmented by cheap additives and sweetened variously with sugar, corn syrup or synthetic substitutes. Since it generates considerably more profit than loose-leaf tea, almost all the major tea corporations have launched iced tea lines. Lipton-branded iced tea, a joint venture with PepsiCo, has been marketed in cans since 1991, and is a product line now sold in over 110 territories; Unilever iced teas also include Brisk and Pure Leaf. Moreover, such ready-to-drink iced teas retail at a premium in comparison to branded soft drinks, meaning that other multinationals have had to respond. Coca-Cola, for example, has three iced tea brands: Honest Tea (premium), Gold Peak (mid-range) and Fuze (popular/value). Ready-to-drink iced tea

Is modern tea miserable? In 1946 George Orwell's recipe for the perfect cup of tea was detailed in eleven stages. But in recent decades, over 90 per cent of all hot tea in Britain is made with a tea-bag, often directly in the mug in which it will be consumed. Modern tea preparation has been reduced from an elaborate and comforting ritual to a quick and unceremonious encounter between a mug and a tea-bag, assisted by hot water and milk.

accounts for almost all the growth in the tea market across the world, both in volume and in value.[9]

Another innovating market with even deeper roots is herbal tea. Hot herbal beverages – also called tisanes – are traditional in many cultures, and often promoted for their medicinal qualities. Tisanes infuse fragrant herbs and flowers in hot water before the liquor is drained off for consumption. As herbal tea contains no *Camellia sinensis*, purists do not consider it tea, but it is clear that tea's foodways are being exploited to market and to normalize an analogous product. In the late twentieth century, the widespread adoption of the tea-bag transformed herbal 'tea' into a massive consumer product. Tea-bagging herbal tisanes greatly extended their variety and ease of use – so much so that it might be said that the tea-bag invented modern herbal tea. Just as fannings and other low-grade, hyper-processed manufacturing outputs supply *Camellia sinensis* in conventional tea-bags, so the sachet system monetizes poor-quality herbal dust to supplant fresh leaves and artisanal preparations. The tea-bag has also allowed tea companies to combine fruit and other flavours with tea itself, generating a bewildering panoply of possibilities. In the twenty-first century, long established tea brands such as Lipton and Twining's are among the major industry players to diversify product lines in order to chase the profits of non-tea teas.

As tea has become modern, it has become quotidian and immiserated. Tea has been reduced to a dependable but superficial experience in which the beverage is of average quality at best. The hot drinks industry has worked hard to discipline tea into a branded consumption experience: corporate tea is a consistently dark and strongly flavoured liquor, its dully unvarying flavour profile repeated time after time. This recipe has been overwhelmingly successful for producers. But it has also been an overwhelming disaster for tea itself, which has had to sacrifice much in order to remain so popular.

Furthermore, although tea companies are profitable, they operate in mature markets with little room for growth. The tea industry is beginning to recognize this conundrum. Its analysis indicates that to make more money, it needs to educate consumers, to reconnect them with wider and deeper practices of tea drinking and with knowledge about tea's history.[10] Insiders point to a lesson from the world of coffee, where companies led by Starbucks have promoted a 'gourmet' experience that commands premium prices. Howard Shultz, the CEO of Starbucks, has described how he adopted a deliberate strategy to make what he calls the 'romance of coffee' – an invocation of its heritage and cultural complexity – central to the customer's encounter with a Starbucks store.[11] Not surprisingly, Starbucks has developed a boutique tea model. Although its first tea brand, Tazo, gained no traction, in 2012 it purchased an Atlanta company called Teavana, which had been founded with the intention of learning from the fine wine and gourmet coffee sectors. Teavana offers a range of expensive teas alongside herbal and fruit-flavoured tisanes, which are sold in brightly coloured tins at speciality retail outlets in upscale shopping malls. By 2014, there were over 330 of these stores in the USA and Mexico, selling prepared hot tea as well as leaf tea and items of modern tea equipage.

If the consumer experience of tea has been troublingly cheapened, the deepest immiseration is that of tea's producers. Not the board members serving transnational conglomerates, of course, but rather the labourers who intensively harvest the crop across South Asia, East Africa and elsewhere. For all the technologizing invention of the last 150 years, tea leaves are still universally handpicked: gruelling, repetitive, physical labour that requires deftness, speed and stamina. A report in 2008 by SOMO, the Netherlands-based Centre for Research on Multinational Corporations, revealed how structural to the tea industry's quest to deliver ever greater affordability to consumers (and not just those in the West) are a raft of miseries for tea pickers: poor working conditions, low wages, limited collectivization, exposure to toxic pesticides, untreated injuries from falling on the slopes and from carrying heavy loads, ethnic discrimination and sexual harassment, instances of child labour.[12] According to Gethin Chamberlain, writing in *The Observer* in 2013, Assam tea pickers earn around twelve pence per hour at rates fixed regionally by unsympathetic and unwavering pay-bargaining units, a situation that effectively forces rural teenage women into the hands of human traffickers for sale into domestic and sexual slavery in urban districts.[13]

Barbara Crowther of the Fairtrade Foundation argued in 2013 that 'poverty level wages on [tea] plantations have become the acceptable cost of our relentless search for the best bargains' as Western consumers (although in the drive for shareholder value, some of the blame must also be apportioned to the owners of production).[14] Wholesale tea auction prices have fallen in real terms by around 50 per cent since the 1980s, while retail prices have remained stable: the big-brand profit in corporate tea is realized downstream from cultivation, in blending, packing and marketing.[15] The challenges facing those seeking to exercise corporate social responsibility are further exacerbated by the ecological compromises enforced by any monoculture: since the nineteenth century, rainforests have been levelled in India to grow tea. Publicly, not least to allay the mild anxieties of tea drinkers in Europe and North America, multinational brands have increasingly claimed to source tea that is ethically produced in a sustainable and environmentally friendly manner. Tea 2030, for example, has drawn together world-leading corporations, who have thereby committed themselves 'to forging a sustainable future for tea'; stakeholders include Tata Global Beverages, Unilever and Yorkshire Tea, as well as the Ethical Tea Partnership and the Rainforest Alliance.[16] Although we are instinctively wary of this trope of late consumer capitalism, by which multinationals seek to cloak their profit motive in ethical subterfuge, it is difficult on the surface not to commend the value of at least some Fairtrade enterprises such as Lujeri Tea Estates, which resources Malawian smallholders with training, seedlings and fertilizers.[17]

In conclusion, we offer three different stories about the current state of tea and its cultures of consumption in Britain. The first is set in Prufrock on Leather Lane, London, an exemplary third-wave coffee-house in which one of the authors wrote some of this book. Here, alongside the flat whites and single-estate pour-over coffees, there is a brief tea list, comprising a short range of high-quality unbranded Chinese single-origin 'rare' teas, including a green, an oolong and a pu'er. The tea is precisely brewed – with water temperature exactly calibrated for each variety – and steeped for three minutes, then served in a porcelain cup, with the tea leaves alongside in a stainless-steel strainer basket. The tea service is completed by an invitation to return the same leaves for a second or third infusion. That this gourmet tea service can exist alongside coffee is one signal that high-grade speciality tea might have a future in the West – although the resurgence of interest in fine tea remains a tiny fraction of the market. A host of small high-end tea companies has emerged, such as Jing, Postcard Tea, the Canton Tea Company and the Rare Tea Company. The rationale of these small businesses is to grow and serve the market for rare and fine teas, which are produced according to traditional methods, in small quantities, and retail for high prices in both Asia and the West. Henrietta Lovell, who founded the Rare Tea Company in 2004, has said that her purpose is re-education: 'I want people to appreciate good tea the way they appreciate good wine . . . People understand wine and don't mind paying a bit more for something beautifully crafted and delicious. If people felt the same way about tea, people on tea farms would thrive. If I can make people appreciate tea, it will change the world.'[18] These outfits offer customers access to a premium 'gourmet tea' experience, reinforced by marketing strategies that try to inform and re-educate both the head and throat through websites, blogs, tastings, sample selections and speciality tea-shops. Such small acts of resistance to corporate tea perhaps offer one alternative to its immiseration.

The second story, meanwhile, is set in London at the family home of another of this book's authors. Here a regular blend of Sri Lankan, East African and Indian leaves, contained in paper tea-bags (of the un-bleached, Fairtrade variety) is prepared typically in mugs, exceptionally in a teapot, most mornings of the week. It is as much a part of the ritual of waking up and preparing for the day as getting dressed and eating breakfast. This metropolitan home is thereby connected with millions of others across the United Kingdom and the world. But it is not only a drink of the early morning. Tea is equally the companion of DIY labours on weekend afternoons, of early evening family reunions and of the eerie quiet after midnight in winter, when the writer feels the chill in a house where the central heating system has powered down. Sometimes that tea is adulterated not only with milk, but with sugar, too, so that it can perform its time-honoured role as a restorative. The elements of a basic tea equipage – kettle, teapot, milk bottle, sugar bowl, mugs – are brought together, both at times of intense grief and at moments associated with the most profound joy: when bad news is received; when disappointment interrupts the quiet routines of life; when ecstasy's calmness reigns in the minutes after a child is born.

The third author has a confession to make. He is British. And another: he is addicted to tea. Not, of course, to the fine-grade, high-quality tea that is enjoying a modest resurgence. The occasional joy discovered in such elevated iterations of the beverage is one of untutored wonder, devoid of nuance, surprised by strangeness. No, the colonizing tea that is his first waking thought and true breakfast is the strong, dark, bitter tea of Britain. Almost undrinkable without anaesthetizing milk, this tea is curiously irresistible once admixed. Sourced from a major supermarket, its loose-leaf, 'Fairtrade' attributes are vestigial reminders of the actual nature and human labour upon which his habit depends, momentarily stemming the tide of forgetting in which we are forever enjoined to immerse ourselves (although such recollection is immediately displaced by the categorization of the black crumpled specks in the caddy as 'leaves', or the notion that a tiny monetary premium makes a real difference to Malawian small-holders). Such quotidian tea drinking is not, however, a principally critical practice: rather it has become instinct, soothingly reliable, meeting a profoundly unnecessary need. Neither is the taste of this lactified herbal infusion necessarily enjoyable – its qualities are barely noticed unless the preparation has erred (over-stewed leaves, rancid milk, unwanted sugar) – nor does it precipitate a discernible rush in body, mind or spirit. Yet tea's effects – mild and intangible – have become fundamental to routines of private and social being. To be so clasped by tea evidences its remark-able suitability as a ubiquitous commodity of our late modern consumer capitalism – the paradigms of which, after all, it has partly constructed. Achieving near-permanent market saturation, it enriches the few, envelops the many. Dispiritingly, beautifully, tea leads its drinkers into global flows, where we locate and dislocate, fashion and undo ourselves. Above all, tea binds together those whom it captivates: most intimately at home; more diffusely in the workplace; more disparately still – and yet no less significantly – across the city, nation and planet where we live.

REFERENCES

Introduction

1 Stephen Blankaart, *A Physical Dictionary* (London, 1702), p. 304.
2 *Mercurius Publicus*, 12–19 March 1663.
3 'The Tea Trade', *The New Annual Register, or General Repository of History, Politics, and Literature, for the Year 1824* (London, 1825), p. 515.
4 Jonathan Swift, 'A Compleat Collection of Genteel and Ingenious Conversation', in *Prose Works of Jonathan Swift*, ed. Herbert Davis (Oxford, 1957), vol. IV, p. 139.
5 Eliza Haywood, *The Female Spectator*, 5th edn, 4 vols (London, 1755), vol. II, p. 82.

ONE: Early European Encounters with Tea

1 David Porter, *Ideographia: The Chinese Cipher in Early Modern Europe* (Stanford, CA, 2001); Robert Markley, *The Far East and the English Imagination, 1600–1730* (Cambridge, 2006).
2 Lu Yu, *The Classic of Tea: Origins and Rituals*, trans. Francis Ross Carpenter (Hopewell, NJ, 1974), p. 115.
3 Victor H. Mair and Erling Hoh, *The True History of Tea* (London, 2009), p. 27; see also Lihui Yang, Demin An and Jessica Anderson-Turner, *Handbook of Chinese Mythology* (Santa Barbara, CA, 2005), p. 195.
4 Mair and Hoh, *The True History of Tea*, p. 30; *The Songs of the South: An Ancient Chinese Anthology of Poems by Qu Yuan and other Poets*, ed. and trans. David Hawkes (Harmondsworth, 1985), pp. 269–70.
5 Huang Hsing-Tsung, *Fermentation and Food Science*, Science and Civilisation in China, 6 (part 5) (Cambridge, 2000), pp. 507–19.
6 Samuel Ball, *An Account of the Cultivation and Manufacture of Tea in China* (London, 1848), pp. 3–6; see also William H. Ukers, *All about Tea*, 2 vols (New York, 1935), vol. I, pp. 15–22.
7 Lu Yu, *The Classic of Tea*, p. 116.
8 Ibid., pp. 62–9; see also Huang, *Fermentation and Food Science*, pp. 521–2.
9 Lu Yu, *The Classic of Tea*, pp. 77–99; see also Huang, *Fermentation and Food Science*, pp. 556–7.
10 Lu Yu, *The Classic of Tea*, p. 74.
11 Mair and Hoh, *The True History of Tea*, pp. 62–3.
12 Lu Yu, *The Classic of Tea*, p. 111.
13 Ibid., p. 116; see also Huang, *Fermentation and Food Science*, p. 557.
14 Mair and Hoh, *The True History of Tea*, pp. 40–44, 84–94.
15 Ibid., pp. 58–9.

16 Ibid., pp. 55, 64–5.

17 Ibid., pp. 71–83.

18 Lu Yu, *The Classic of Tea*, p. 116.

19 Huang, *Fermentation and Food Science*, p. 523.

20 Ibid., p. 529.

21 Ibid., pp. 538–41.

22 Michael Cooper, 'The Early Europeans and Tea', in *Tea in Japan: Essays on the History of Chanoyu*, ed. Paul Varley and Kumakura Isao (Honolulu, HI, 1989), pp. 101–33 (pp. 101–4).

23 Giovanni Battista Ramusio, *Secondo Volvme delle Navigationi et Viaggi* (Venice, 1559), fol. 15v (our translations).

24 Gaspar da Cruz, *Tractado em quese co[m] tam muito por esteso as cousas da China* (Évora, 1570).

25 Ibid., sig. [e viii]v.

26 Samuel Purchas, *Purchas his Pilgrimes*, 4 vols (London, 1625), vol. III, p. 180.

27 Jonathan D. Spence, *The Memory Palace of Matteo Ricci* (London, 1985), pp. 132–61.

28 *The China that Was: China as Discovered by the Jesuits at the Close of the Sixteenth Century*, trans. by Louis J. Gallagher (Milwaukee, WI, 1942), pp. 26–7; for the original see Nicolas Trigault, *De Christiana Expeditione apud Sinas* (Augsburg, 1615), p. 16. See also Trigault, *De Christiana Expeditione*, p. 69 (Gallagher, *The China that Was*, p. 105); and Huang, *Fermentation and Food Science*, pp. 507–12.

29 *Iohn Huighen van Linschoten: His Discours of Voyages into ye Easte & West Indies* (London, 1598), p. 46; for the original see Jan Huyghen van Linschoten, *Itinerario, Voyage ofte Schipvaert van Jan Huygen van Linschoten* (Amsterdam, 1596), pp. 35–6. See also Mair and Hoh, *The True History of Tea*, pp. 93–109.

30 Alessandro Valignano, *Historia del Principio y Progresso de la Compañia de Jésus en las Indias Orientales, 1542–1564*, quoted in *They Came to Japan: An Anthology of European Reports on Japan, 1543–1640*, ed. Michael Cooper (Ann Arbor, MI, 1965), p. 261.

31 Richard Wickham to William Eaton, 27 June 1615, Hirado (draft): London, British Library, India Office Records G/12/15, p. 16. See also *The English Factory in Japan, 1613–1623*, ed. Anthony Farrington, 2 vols (London, 1991), vol. I, pp. 295–6; Anthony Farrington, 'The Japan Letter Book of Richard Wickham, 1614–1617', in *India Office Library and Records: Report for the Year 1979* (London, 1979), pp. 35–45.

32 Heren XVII to Anthony van Diemen, 2 January 1637, Amsterdam: quoted in G. Schlegel, 'First Introduction of Tea into Holland', *T'oung Pao*, Second Series, 1 (1900), pp. 468–72 (p. 469).

33 Schlegel, 'First Introduction of Tea into Holland', p. 468.

34 Alexandre de Rhodes, *Divers Voyages et Missions du Pere Alexandre de Rhodes en la Chine* (Paris, 1654), pp. 62–3 (our translation); see also *Sommaire des Divers Voyages, et Missions Apostoliques, du R. P. Alexandre de Rhodes* (Paris, 1653), pp. 25–9.

35 *Ambassade des Hollandois à la Chine*, trans. Melchisédech Thévenot (Paris, 1666), sig. a iiir (our translation).

36 'De l'Usage du Tay, qui est fort ordinaire en la Chine' ('On the use of tea, which is commonplace in China'), in de Rhodes, *Divers Voyages*, pp. 62–7 (our translations).

37 Cooper, 'The Early Europeans and Tea', pp. 105–11.

38 Henriette Rahusen-de Bruyn Kops, 'Not Such an "Unpromising Beginning": The First Dutch Trade Embassy to China, 1655–1657', *Modern Asian Studies*, 36 (2002), pp. 535–78; Markley, *The Far East and the English Imagination*, pp. 110–29. See also John E. Wills, *Pepper, Guns, and Parleys: The Dutch East India Company and China, 1662–1681* (Cambridge, MA, 1974).

39 Johan Nieuhof, *Het Gezantschap der Neêrlandtsche Oost-Indische Compagnie, aan den Grooten Tartarischen Cham, den Tegenwoordigen Keizer van China* (Amsterdam, 1665); trans. into English as *An Embassy from the East-India Company of the United Provinces, to the Grand Tartar Cham Emperour of China*, trans. John Ogilby (London, 1669).

40 Nieuhof, *Embassy*, pp. 41, 61, 79–80, 126–7, 142–3.

41 Ibid., p. 127.

42 Ibid., p. 41.

43 Ibid., pp. 248–9.

44 Ibid., p. 134.

45 *Mercurius Politicus*, 23 September 1658; Thomas Garway, *An Exact Description of the Growth, Quality, and Vertues of the Leaf Tee, alias Tay* ([London], [*c.* 1664]). See also *Tea and the Tea-table in Eighteenth-century England*, ed. Markman Ellis, Richard Coulton, Matthew Mauger and Ben Dew, 4 vols (London, 2010), vol. II, pp. 1–3.

46 Garway, *Exact Description*.

47 Lu Yu, *The Classic of Tea*, p. 59.

48 Translator's side-note in *The History of that Great and Renowned Monarchy of China* (London, 1655); for the original see Alvaraez Semedo, *Relatione della Grande Monarchia della Cina* (Rome, 1643), pp. 27–8.

49 Jacques Specx et al to Heren XVII, 15 Dec 1629, Batavia: quoted in W. Ph. Coolhaas, ed., *Generale Missiven van Gouverneurs-Generaal en Raden aan Heren XVII: Deel I, 1610–1638* ('s-Gravenhage, 1960), p. 276.

TWO: Establishing the Taste for Tea in Britain

1 Samuel Hartlib, *Ephemerides*, No. 254, 4 August 1654, *The Hartlib Papers*, 2nd edn (Sheffield, 2002), HP 29/4/29A-B; Hartlib, 'Observ. 59' concerning 'Herba Theê Indiæ Orientali', HP 42/4/5A–6B; Nicolaes Tulp, 'Caput LIX. Herba Theé', *Observationes medicæ. Editio nova* (Amsterdam, 1652).

2 Hartlib, *Ephemerides* [Dec] 1657, HP 29/6/23A. Contractions expanded.

3 Purchasing Power Calculator, measuringworth.com (accessed 20 June 2014).

4 John Beale to Hartlib(?) 3 November 1657, HP 52/15A.

5 *Ephemerides* [Dec] 1757, HP 29/6/23A.

6 *An Exact Description of the Growth, Quality, and Vertues of the Leaf Tee, alias Tay* ([London], [*c.* 1664]).

7 Tulp, *Observationes medicæ*, pp. 400–403.

8 Nicolaes Tulp, *Medical Observations*, trans. Boris Ginsburgs, in *Codex Thea* (Philadelphia, 2011), at www.melange-tea.com/codex_thea/Source:Tulp/2011 (accessed 29 September 2012).

9 Pies added an account of tea to a work on the natural history of the East Indies by Jacob de Bondt (1591–1631). Willem Pies, ed., *De Indiae utriusque re naturali et medica libri quatuordecim* (Amsterdam, 1658); Jakob de Bondt, *An Account of the Diseases, Natural History, and Medicines of the East Indies* (London, 1769), p. 153.

10 *Endlesse Queries: or, An End to Queries, Laid down in 36 Merry Mad Queries for the Peoples Information* (London [13 June 1659]), pp. 3–4.

11 Rudi Mathee, 'Exotic Substances: The Introduction and Global Spread of Tobacco, Coffee, Cocoa, Tea, and Distilled Liquor, Sixteenth to Eighteenth Centuries', in *Drugs and Narcotics in History*, ed. Roy Porter and Mikulás Teich (Cambridge, 1995), pp. 24–51 (45).

12 *The Diary of Samuel Pepys*, trans. and ed. Robert Latham and William Matthews, 11 vols (London, 1970–83), vol. I, 25 September, p. 253.

13 Ibid., vol. VI, 13 December 1665, p. 328.

14 Ibid., vol. VIII, 28 June 1667, p. 302.

15 *The Closet of the Eminently learned Sir Kenelme Digbie Kt. Opened* (London, 1669), pp. 155–6.

16 *Mercurius Publicus*, No. 11, 12–19 March, 1662/3, p. 177.

17 East India Company, Court Minutes, 22 August 1664, London, British Library, India Office Records B/26, fol. 415r.

18 George Birdwood, *Report on the Old Records of the India Office* (London, 1891), p. 221–2; Hosea Ballou Morse, *The Chronicles of the East India Company Trading to China, 1635–1834*, 5 vols (Oxford, 1926–9), vol. I, p. 9.

19 East India Company Correspondence, London, British Library, India Office Records E/3/47, fol. 53v; see also Morse, *The Chronicles of the East India Company*, vol. I, pp. 62–3.

20 Morse, *The Chronicles of the East India Company*, vol. I, pp. 64–5.

21 Agnes and Elisabeth Strickland, *Lives of the Queens of England, from the Norman Conquest; with Anecdotes of Their Courts*, 12 vols (London, 1840–48), vol. IV, p. 230.

22 William H. Ukers, *All About Tea* (New York, 1935), p. 44.

23 Jonas Hanway, 'An Essay on Tea', in *A Journal of Eight Days Journey from Portsmouth to Kingston upon Thames* (London, 1756). For Johnson's review: *The Literary Magazine*, I/7 (1756), pp. 335–42; II/8 (1757), pp. 161–7.

24 I am grateful to Michael P. Parker and Timothy Raylor, editors of the forthcoming *The Poems of Edmund Waller* (Oxford University Press), for sharing their conclusions on this matter in advance of publication.

25 Edmund Waller, 'Of Tea, Commended by Her Majesty', *The Second Part of Mr. Waller's Poems Containing . . . Whatever of His is Yet Unprinted* (London, 1690), p. 61. See also *The Poems of Edmund Waller*, ed. G. Thorn Drury (London, 1893), p. 222.

26 Hartlib, *Ephemerides*, [Dec] 1757, HP 29/6/23A.

27 Gladys Scott Thomson, *Life in a Noble Household, 1641–1700* (London, 1937), pp. 169–70.

28 James Tyrrell to Locke, [c. 10 June 1682], *The Correspondence of John Locke*, ed. E. S. De Beer, 8 vols (Oxford, 1976–89), vol. II, Letter 715, pp. 523–5.

29 Kristof Glamann, *Dutch-Asiatic Trade: 1620–1740*, 2nd edn ('s-Gravenhage, 1981), p. xvii. See also Simon Schama, *The Embarrassment of Riches: An Interpretation of Dutch Culture in the Golden Age* (London, 1987), pp. 171–3.

30 Cornelis Bontekoe, *Tractat van het excellenste kruyd thee* (1678), ed. F.M.G. de Feyfer, in *Opuscula selecta neerlandicorum de arte medica* (Amsterdam, 1907–55), vol. XIV (1937), pp. 114–465.

31 Christoph Schweikardt, 'More than Just a Propagandist for Tea: Religious Argument and Advice on a Healthy Life in the Work of the Dutch Physician Cornelis Bontekoe (1647–1685)', *Medical History*, XLVII/3 (2003), pp. 357–68 (p. 363). See also Harold John Cook, *Matters of Exchange: Commerce, Medicine, and Science in the Dutch Golden Age* (New Haven, CT, and London, 2007), pp. 293–7.

32 Bontekoe, *Tractat van het excellenste kruyd thee*, pp. 447, 459, 443.

33 Francis Lodwick, *On Language, Theology, and Utopia*, ed. Felicity Henderson and William Poole (Oxford, 2011), p. 414.

34 Cornelis Bontekoe and Steven Blankaart, *Gebruik en Mis-bruik van de Thee* (Den Haag and Amsterdam, 1686)

35 Annet Mooij, *Doctors of Amsterdam: Patient Care, Medical Training and Research (1650–2000)*, trans. Beverley Jackson (Amsterdam, 2002), p. 67.

36 R. S. Woolhouse, *Locke: A Biography* (Cambridge, 2007), p. 198.

37 Locke to Philippus van Limborch, 22 September/2 October 1686, *Correspondence*, vol. III, Letter 865, p. 36.

38 Locke to van Limborch, 14/24 November [1686], *Correspondence*, vol. II, Letter 840, pp. 763–4.

39 Kenneth Eastham Dewhurst, *John Locke, 1632–1704, Physician and Philosopher: A Medical Biography. With an Edition of the Medical Notes in his Journals* (London, 1963), pp. xii, 331

40 Entry for Monday, 30 October 1684, Bodleian Library MS Locke f. 8, p. 206, quoted in Peter Anstey and Stephen Harris, 'Locke and Botany', *Studies in History and Philosophy of Biological and Biomedical Sciences*, 37 (2006), pp. 151–71 (p. 167).

41 Locke to Sir John Somers, Baron Somers, 28 January 1698, *Correspondence*, Letter 2384, VI, 308.

42 Locke to Thomas Herbert, Earl of Pembroke, 28 November/8 December 1684, *Correspondence*, Letter 797, vol. II, 665.

43 Locke to Somers, 28 January 1698, *Correspondence*, vol. VI, Letter 2384, p. 308n.

44 Locke to Pembroke, 28 November/8 December 1684, *Correspondence*, vol. II, Letter 797, p. 665.

45 Locke to van Limborch, 14/24 November [1686], *Correspondence*, vol. II, Letter 840, pp. 763–4.

46 Bodliean Library, MS. Locke c. 31, ff. 80–82.

47 Locke to van Limborch, 14/24 November [1686], *Correspondence*, vol. III, Letter 877, pp. 68–73 (68–9).

48 Bontekoe, *Tractat van het excellenste kruyd thee*, pp. 453–4.

49 Dewhurst, *Locke*, p. 241.

50 Ibid., p. 241.

51 Kenelme Digbie noted a similar recipe for 'Tea with Eggs', recorded by Edmund Waller from a Jesuit from China, in 1664 (*The Closet of the Eminently learned Sir Kenelme Digbie Kt. Opened* (London, 1669), pp. 155–6).

52 Locke to van Limborch, 20 September 1689, trans. De Beer, *Correspondence*, vol. III, Letter 1182, p. 690.

53 Van Limborch to Locke, 30 September 1689, trans. De Beer, *Correspondence*, vol. III, Letter 1184, p. 695

54 Locke to van Limborch, 13 December 1689, trans. De Beer, *Correspondence*, vol. III, Letter 1213, p. 755.

55 *London Gazette*, 8 August 1689.

56 Paul D'Aranda to Locke, 14/24 July 1690, *Correspondence*, vol. IV, Letter 1306, pp. 106–7; Dr Pieter Guenellon to Locke, 3/13 August 1697, *Correspondence*, vol. VI, Letter 2292, pp. 170–71.

57 John Locke, *Of the Conduct of the Understanding*, 5th edn, ed. Thomas Fowler (Oxford, 1901), p. 100.

58 Locke's notes on China are Bodleian MSS Locke c. 27. See Ann Talbot, 'The Great Ocean of Knowledge': *The Influence of Travel Literature on the Work of John Locke* (Leiden, 2010), pp. 179–99 (p. 190).

59 *Krachten vande thee; nae't oversetten der Chinesche sprake: ende heeft dese nae-volgende deughden* (no place, undated [1686?]) Koninklijke Bibliotheque, 's-Gravenhage. KW 511 B 42.

60 *The Diary of John Evelyn*, ed. E. S. De Beer (Oxford, 1955), vol. IV, p. 84.

61 Robert Hooke, 'Qualities of the herb called Tea or Chee. Transcribed from a Paper of Tho: Povey Esq. Oct 20 1686', Collection of scientific papers and letters, British Library, Sloane MS 1039, f. 139r.

62 John Ovington, *An Essay upon the Nature and Qualities of Tea* (London, 1699), p. 2.

THREE: The Tea Trade with China

1   Paul Van Dyke, *The Canton Trade: Life and Enterprise on the China Coast, 1770–1845* (Hong Kong, 2005), pp. 35–50.
2   Ibid., p. 31.
3   Despatches to the East, London, British Library, India Office Records E/4/12, fols 18v–21r.
4   Charles Lockyer, *An Account of the Trade in India* (London, 1711).
5   For the original Charter, see Philip Lawson, *The East India Company: A History* (London, 1993), p. 4. The definition is reiterated by parliamentary statute as late as 1825 (see 6 Geo. 4, c. 107, s. 115).
6   Philip Lawson, *The East India Company: A History* (London, 1993), pp. 43–4. See also Keay, *The Honourable Company: A History of the East India Company* (London, 1991), p. 202; Lawson, *The East India Company*, p. 51.
7   Lawson, *The East India Company*, p. 44. See also Keay, *The Honourable Company*, p. 177; K. N. Chaudhuri, *The Trading World of Asia and the English East India Company* (Cambridge, 1978), pp. 81–2.
8   Chaudhuri, *The Trading World of Asia*, pp. 434–6; Lawson, *The East India Company*, p. 55.
9   See discussion in Lawson, *The East India Company*, p. 58.
10 See Keay, *The Honourable Company*, pp. 211–13; Chaudhuri, *The Trading World of Asia*, p. 436.
11 Chaudhuri, *The Trading World of Asia*, pp. 508–9.
12 Directors of the English Company to President Catchpole and Council in China, 27 June 1700, quoted in Peter Pratt, *Materials for a History of the Rise and Progress of the Trade to China*, India Office Records G/12/6, p. 833.
13 Chaudhuri, *The Trading World of Asia*, p. 387.
14 Ibid., p. 538. For the difficulties associated with ascertaining statistics for 1690–1709, see p. 465.
15 Company Correspondence, India Office Records E/3/47, fol. 53v.
16 Court Minutes, India Office Records B/39, pp. 196, 274.
17 Despatches to the East, India Office Records E/3/92, fol. 180v.
18 Commerce Journals, India Office Records L/AG/1/6/4, p. 118.
19 Despatches to the East, India Office Records E/3/92, fol. 264v.
20 Commerce Journals, India Office Records L/AG/1/6/4, pp. 235, 292.
21 Despatches to the East, India Office Records E/3/93, fol. 63v.
22 Commerce Journals, India Office Records L/AG/1/6/4, p. 407.
23 Quoted in Pratt, *Materials*, India Office Records G/12/6, p. 825, contraction expanded.
24 Despatches to the East, India Office Records E/3/93, fol. 262v.
25 Rowan Hackman, *Ships of the East India Company* (Gravesend, 2001), p. 196.
26 Except where otherwise acknowledged, details concerning the *Stretham*'s passage are taken from the ship's manuscript journal (India Office Records L/MAR/B/311A).
27 Anthony Farrington, *Catalogue of East India Company Ships' Journals and Logs, 1600–1834* (London, 1999), p. 621
28 Andrew S. Cook, 'Establishing the Sea Routes to India and China: Stages in the Development of Hydrographical Knowledge', in *The Worlds of the East India Company*, ed. H. V. Bowen et al. (Woodbridge, 2002), pp. 119–36.
29 'Notices derived from the Consultation of the Supercargoes of the United Company's Ship Streatham on voyage to China', India Office Records G/12/7, p. 975.
30 [Journal of the *Stretham*], India Office Records L/MAR/B/311A [p. 40].

31 Anthony Farrington, *A Biographical Index of East India Company Maritime Service Officers, 1600–1834* (London, 1999), p. 273.

32 'Diary and Consultation Book of William Fazerkerley Esq, Chief, Richard Morton, Edmond Godfrey . . . appointed a Councill for Mannaging the affairs of The Hon.ble United Company of Merchants of England Trading to the East Indies in China for the year 1723', India Office Records G/12/24, pp. 101–2.

33 *Records of Fort St George: Despatches to England, 1701–02 to 1710–11* (Madras, 1925), p. 10.

34 'The Consultations and Diary Books of Thomas Pitt Esq President and Governour &c. Councill their Proceedings and Transactions in the Affairs of the Right Honble United Trade to the East Indies in the Presidency of the Coast of Choromandel &c', 11 February 1704, Fort St George, India Office Records G/19/13, p. 138.

35 Pratt, *Materials*, India Office Records G/12/7, p. 977; Lockyer, *An Account of the Trade in India*, pp. 98–9.

36 Pratt, *Materials*, India Office Records G/12/7, p. 977.

37 Fort St George Factory, India Office Records G/19/13, fol. 162.

38 *Fort St George: Despatches*, p. 16.

39 James Cuninghame to the 'Supracargoes and Captains in the Service of the Honourable Company Trading to the East Indies', 8 May 1705, London, British Library, Sloane MSS 3321, fols 117r–118r. See also Danny Wong Tze-Ken, 'The Destruction of the English East India Company Factory on Condore Island, 1702–1705', *Modern Asian Studies*, 46 (2012), pp. 1097–115.

40 Lockyer, *An Account of the Trade in India*, p. 98.

41 Keay, *The Honourable Company*, p. 205; Hosea Ballou Morse, *The Chronicles of the East India Company Trading to China, 1635–1834*, 5 vols (Oxford, 1926–9), vol. I (1926), pp. 46–9, 52–5.

42 Morse, *The Chronicles of the East India Company Trading to China*, I, pp. 109–21. For archival records concerning the failed attempt to establish a Liampo trading post at nearby Chusan, see India Office Records G/12/14. For a brief overview see Keay, *The Honourable Company*, pp. 209–11.

43 Keay, *The Honourable Company*, pp. 206–9; Morse, *The Chronicles of the East India Company Trading to China*, vol. I, pp. 78–98.

44 Letter Book, E/3/94 f. 28.

45 Lockyer, *An Account of the Trade in India*, p. 99.

46 Van Dyke, *The Canton Trade*, pp. 10, 16. See also Weng Eang Cheong, *Hong Merchants of Canton: Chinese Merchants in Sino-Western Trade, 1684–1798* (Richmond, Surrey, 1997), pp. 28–9.

47 'Notices . . . of the United Company's Ship Streatham', India Office Records G/12/7, p. 978.

48 Van Dyke, *Canton Trade*, pp. 39–40.

49 Details of the *Sidney*'s voyage are taken from the journal of Thomas Cason, Second Mate, India Office Records L/MAR/B/715B.

50 'Diary of Capt. Edd Harrison, Messrs Ed. Herris & John Cooke, Supra Cargoes of the United Company's Ship Kent', India Office Records G/12/7, p. 1026.

51 Cheong, *Hong Merchants of Canton*, p. 12.

52 Lockyer, *An Account of the Trade in India*, p. 101. For more on these three merchants, see Cheong, *Hong Merchants of Canton*, pp. 34–7.

53 Van Dyke, *Canton Trade*, p. 11.

54 Despatches to the East, India Office Records E/3/95, fols 18v–21r.

55 Lockyer, *An Account of the Trade in India*, pp. 116–17.

56 Ibid., p. 117.

57 'Diary of . . . the United Company's Ship Kent', India Office Records G/12/7, p. 1060.

58 Commerce Journals, India Office Records L/AG/1/6/6, p. 25.

59 *Daily Courant*, 3 October 1705.
60 'Consultations and Diurnal Transactions . . . for the Year 1724 in China', India Office Records G/12/25, fol. 8r.
61 India Office Records, G/12/24, pp. 69–71.
62 'Consultations and Diurnal . . . for the Year 1722 in China', India Office Records G/12/21, fols 20v and 22r.
63 'Diary and Consultation Book containing the Transactions and Mannagement of Affairs relating to the disposal & Investing the Cargoes . . . Ann. 1720 & 1721', G/12/22, fol. 2r.
64 India Office Records G/12/22, fol. 3r.
65 'Diary and Consultation Book . . . for the year 1723', India Office Records G/12/24, pp. 80–81. For more on Suqua, see Cheong, *Hong Merchants of Canton*, pp. 37–40.
66 'Diary . . . 1723', pp. 87–8.

FOUR: The Elevation of Tea

1 John Ovington, *A Voyage to Suratt, in the Year, 1689. Giving a Large Account of that City and its Inhabitants, and of the English Factory there* (London, 1696), p. 218.
2 Ibid., pp. 306, 307–8.
3 Ibid., pp. 308–9.
4 Ibid., p. 309.
5 John Ovington, *An Essay upon the Nature and Qualities of Tea. Wherein are shown, I. The soil and climate where it grows. II. The various kinds of it. III. The rules for chusing what is best. IV. The means of preserving it. V. The several virtues for which it is fam'd* (London, 1699).
6 Ovington, *Essay upon Tea*, Henry E. Huntington Library and Art Gallery, San Marino, California. Shelfmark: 297111.
7 Ibid., sig. A2.
8 Thomas Southerne, *The Wives Excuse; or, Cuckolds Make Themselves: A Comedy* (London, 1692), Act IV, Scene I, pp. 37–8.
9 *Collection for Improvement of Husbandry and Trade*, 13 December 1695; *London Gazette*, 22 August 1700; *Post Man and the Historical Account*, 15 April 1707.
10 *British Mercury*, Wednesday, 1 October 1712; *London Evening Post*, 19 December 1738.
11 Johann Pechlin, *Theophilus Bibaculus, sive de Potu Theae Dialogus* (Frankfurt, 1684), p. 80.
12 Nahum Tate, 'To Mr. J. Ovington, on his Voyage to Suratt', in Ovington, *Voyage to Suratt* (1696), unpaginated (pp. [ix–xii]).
13 Nahum Tate, *Panacea: A Poem Upon Tea: in Two Canto's* (London, 1700), p. 4.
14 Ibid., p. 16.
15 Ibid., p. [ix].
16 Louis-Daniel Le Comte, *Memoirs and Observations . . . Made in a Late Journey through the Empire of China* (London, 1697).
17 Tate, *Panacea*, p. 13.
18 Ibid., pp. 18, 20, 29, 34.
19 Peter Anthony Motteux, *A Poem upon Tea* (London, 1712), p. 15.
20 Peter Anthony Motteux, *A Poem in Praise of Tea* (no place, undated), ESTCT70455. This version of the poem, a folio with no title-page, exists in one copy in the British Library (BL:11633.h.10): conjecturally dated to 1701 (range 1699–1705).
21 *The Tea-kettle: A Poem. Humbly inscrib'd to Miss H————lt* (Dublin, 1730).

22 Alexander Pope, 'The Rape of the Lock' (1714), ed. Geoffrey Tillotson, in *The Twickenham Edition of the Poems of Alexander Pope*, 6 vols (London, 1954), vol. II, pp. 79–212.

23 Joseph Addison, *The Spectator*, no. 10 (12 March 1711), in *The Spectator*, ed. Donald F. Bond, 5 vols (Oxford, 1965), vol. I, p. 44.

24 Sociable reading of *The Spectator* at the tea-table is noted in numbers 92, 140, 158, 212, 216, 246, 276, 300, 323, 395, 488, 536, 606.

25 Steele, *The Spectator*, No. 4 (5 March 1711), vol. I, p. 22.

26 Thomas Killigrew (1657–1719), *Chit-chat: A Comedy* (London, [1719]).

27 Samuel Johnson, 'Review of *A Journal of Eight Days' Journey* by Jonas Hanway', *Literary Magazine*, II/13 (1757).

28 Thomas Brown, 'On Tea Tables and Visiting Days', in *Essays Serious and Comical* (London, 1707), p. 39.

29 Colley Cibber, *The Lady's Last Stake; or, The Wife's Resentment: A Comedy* (London, 1708), p. 9.

30 *Tea, a Poem: In Three Cantos* (London, 1743), pp. 29–30.

31 *Weekly Journal and Saturday Post*, 14 May 1720 (Issue 76), reprinted in *A Collection of Miscellany Letters: Selected out of Mist's Weekly Journal*, 5 vols (London, 1722–7), vol. I (1722), Letter 75, pp. 225–7.

FIVE: The Natural Philosophy of Tea

1 Gaspard Bauhin, ΠΙΝΑΞ [Pinax] *theatri botanici* (Basel, 1623), p. 147 (translation ours).

2 Louis-Daniel Le Comte, *Memoirs and Observations . . . Made in a Late Journey through the Empire of China* (London, 1697), pp. 229r; for the original see *Nouveaux Mémoires sur l'état présent de la Chine*, 2 vols (Paris, 1696).

3 Ibid., p. 229v.

4 Ibid., p. 228r.

5 John Ovington, *An Essay upon the Nature and Qualities of Tea* (London, 1699), pp. 9–14.

6 James Petiver to James Cuninghame, [8 January 1698?], London (draft): British Library, Sloane 3333, fols 113r–116v (fols 113r–113v) (italics supplied, contractions expanded).

7 C. E. Jarvis and P. H. Oswald, 'The Collecting Activities of James Cuninghame FRS on the Voyage of the *Tuscan* to China (Amoy) between 1697 and 1699', *Notes and Records of the Royal Society* (in press: forthcoming).

8 James Cuninghame, 'Plants of China etc' (1698–9): British Library, Sloane 2376, fols 63r, 69r (translation ours).

9 'Drawings of Chinese Plants': British Library, Additional MS 5292; James Cuninghame, 'Catalogus Plantarum, quarum Icones in Chinâ delineate sunt' ('A Catalogue of Plants, of which Images were Illustrated in China'): Sloane 2376, fols 82–110; London, Royal Society, 'Journal Book of the Royal Society, 1696–1702', JBO/10, p. 146. See also Jane Kilpatrick, *Gifts from the Garden of China: The Introduction of Traditional Chinese Garden Plants to Britain, 1698–1862* (London, 2007), pp. 34–48.

10 'Com[m]ission & Instructions given by the Court of Directors of the English Company Trading to the East Indies To . . . The Councill for the Affaires of the said Company in China', 23 November 1699 (copy): British Library, India Office Records E/3/94, fols 58r–62v.

11 India Office Records E/3/94, fol. 59v; Court of Directors (New Company) to Allen Catchpole, 25 November 1701, London (copy): British Library, India Office Records E/3/94, fols 180v–184r (183r).

12 India Office Records E/3/94, fol. 59r.

13 [Peter Pratt], 'Materials for a History of a Series of Attempts first by the English and afterwards by the United East-India Company to Acquire & Establish a Trade at the Port of Chusan in China' ([1830]): British Library, India Office Records, G/12/14.

14 James Cuninghame to James Petiver, 20 December 1700, Chusan: British Library, Sloane 3321, fol. 65r-v.

15 James Petiver to James Cuninghame (draft), 16 July 1701, London: British Library, Sloane 3334, fols 78r-79v (fol. 78r).

16 'A Large Draught of the North Part of China. Shewing all the Passages and Chanells into the Harbour of Chusan', in John Thornton, *The English Pilot: The Third Book* (London, 1703). See also James Cuninghame to Hans Sloane, 22 November 1701, Chusan: British Library, Sloane 4025, fols 92-3; 'Chusan Diary': British Library, India Office Records G/12/16, fol. 268v; '[A Chart of Part of the North Coast of China, Showing the Passages and Channels into the Harbour of Chusan]' (manuscript): British Library, Cartographic Items 62865(5).

17 Cuninghame to Sloane, 22 November 1701, fol. 92v; see also James Cuninghame to James Petiver, 22 November 1701, Chusan: British Library, Sloane 3321, fol. 89r.

18 James Cuninghame, 'Part of Two Letters to the Publisher from Mr James Cunningham, FRS and Physician to the English at Chusan in China', *Philosophical Transactions*, 23 (1702-3), 1201-9.

19 Cuninghame to Sloane, 22 November 1701, fol. 92v.

20 James Petiver, 'A Description of some Coralls, and other Curious Submarines . . . ; as also an Account of some Plants from Chusan and Island on the Coast of China; Collected by Mr James Cuninghame, Chyrurgeon & FRS', *Philosophical Transactions*, 23 (1702-3), 1419-29.

21 James Petiver, *Gazophylacii naturæ et artis decas tertia* ([London, 1704?]), pp. 33-4; James Petiver, *Catalogus classicus et topicus* (London, 1709), tab. XXI; see also [Pratt], 'Chusan', p. 18.

22 Markman Ellis, Richard Coulton, Matthew Mauger and Ben Dew, eds, *Tea and the Tea-table in Eighteenth-century England*, 4 vols (London, 2010), vol. II, pp. 17-18, 87-9.

23 Detlef Haberland, *Engelbert Kaempfer, 1651-1716: A Biography*, trans. Peter Hogg (London, 1996), pp. 150-51.

24 Engelbert Kaempfer, 'The Natural History of the Japanese Tea', in *The History of Japan*, trans. J. G. Scheuchzer, 2 vols (London, 1727), vol. II, 1-20 (appendix) (p. 12). For the original see Engelbert Kaempfer, *Amœnitatum exoticarum politico-physico-medicarum* (Lemgo, 1712), pp. 605-31.

25 Kaempfer, 'Japanese Tea', pp. 7-9, 15.

26 John Hill, *Exotic Botany Illustrated* (London, 1759), pp. 21-2.

27 Hill, *Exotic Botany Illustrated*, p. 22; *Potus Theae* (Upsala, 1765), p. 2.

28 John Ellis to Carl Linnaeus, 19 August 1768, London, in *A Selection of the Correspondence of Linnæus, and Other Naturalists*, ed. James Edward Smith, 2 vols (London, 1821), vol. I, pp. 229-35 (232); John Ellis, *Directions for Bringing over Seeds and Plants from the East-Indies and other Distant Countries* (London, 1770), p. 28.

29 John Coakley Lettsom, *The Natural History of the Tea-tree, with Observations on the Medical Qualities of Tea, and Effects of Tea-drinking* (London, 1772), p. 7.

30 J. C. Loudon, *Arboretum et fruticetum britannicum; or, The Trees and Shrubs of Britain*, 8 vols (London, 1838), vol. I, pp. 392-5.

31 Robert Fortune, *Three Years' Wanderings in the Northern Provinces of China* (London, 1847), pp. 197-200, and *A Journey to the Tea Countries of China*

(London, 1852), pp. 272–4; Samuel Ball, *An Account of the Cultivation and Manufacture of Tea in China* (London, 1848), pp. 307–32.

32 Ramusio, *Navigationi et Viaggi*, fol. 15v (our translation).

33 Robert Lovell, *ΠΑΜΒΟΤΑΝΟΛΟΓΙΑ [Pambotanologia] . . . or, A Compleat Herball* (Oxford, 1659), p. 458; and Garway, *Exact Description*.

34 Simon Paulli, *A Treatise on Tobacco, Tea, Coffee, and Chocolate*, trans. Robert James (London, 1746), esp. pp. 58, 169–70; for the original see Simon Paulli, *Commentarius de abusu tabaci americanorum veteri, et herbæ thee asiaticorum in Europa Novo* (Strasbourg, 1665).

35 Thomas Short, *A Dissertation upon Tea* (London, 1730), pp. 19–20.

36 Ibid., p. 3.

37 Ibid., p. 57.

38 Ibid., p. 4.

39 Thomas Short, *Discourses on Tea, Sugar, Milk, Made-wines, Spirits, Punch, Tobacco, &c.* (London, 1750).

40 Thomas Percival, *Essays Medical and Experimental* (London, 1767), p. 129.

41 Ibid., pp. 125–6.

42 Simon Mason, *The Good and Bad Effects of Tea Consider'd* (London, 1745), pp. 21, 42.

43 S. A. Tissot, *An Essay on Diseases Incident to Literary and Sedentary Persons*, ed. J. Kirkpatrick, 2nd edn (London, 1768), pp. 141, 143.

44 Tissot, *Essay*, pp. 146, 149, 150.

45 Penelope Hunting, 'Dr John Coakley Lettsom, Plant-collector of Camberwell', *Garden History*, 34 (2006), 221–35; see also *Tea and the Tea-table*, vol. II, pp. 137–9.

46 *Dissertatio inauguralis medica, sistens observations ad vires theae pertinentes, etc.* ('Inaugural dissertation in medicine, establishing pertinent observations to men concerning tea'; Leiden, 1769).

47 Lettsom, *Natural History*, pp. 39–49.

48 Ibid., pp. 45–62.

49 James Boswell, *Boswell's London Journal, 1762–1763*, ed. Frederick Albert Pottle and Peter Ackroyd (New Haven, CT, 2004), p. 189.

50 Lettsom, *Natural History*, pp. 44, 52, 49.

51 Londa Schiebinger, *Plants and Empire: Colonial Bioprospecting in the Atlantic World* (Cambridge, MA, 2004), p. 7.

52 John Ellis to Carl Linnaeus, 24 October 1758, London, in *Correspondence of Linnæus*, vol. I, p. 107.

53 Fa-ti Fan, *British Naturalists in Qing China: Science, Empire, and Cultural Encounter* (Cambridge, MA, 2004), pp. 36–8.

54 Linnaeus to Ellis, 8 December 1758, Uppsala, in *Correspondence of Linnaeus*, vol. I, pp. 109–10. Letters from Linnaeus to Ellis were written in Latin and translated by Smith.

55 Ellis to Linnaeus, [December 1760], London, in *Correspondence of Linnaeus*, vol. I, pp. 138–9.

56 Linnaeus to Ellis, 3 April 1761, Uppsala, in *Correspondence of Linnaeus*, vol. I, p. 141.

57 Ellis to Linnaeus, 2 June 1761, London, in *Correspondence of Linnaeus*, vol. I, p. 147.

58 Richard Drayton, *Nature's Government: Science, Imperial Britain, and the 'Improvement' of the World* (New Haven, CT, 2000), p. 59; Fan, *British Naturalists in Qing China*, pp. 89–90.

59 Linnaeus, 'Om Thée och Thée-drickandet' ('On Tea and Tea-drinking', 1746), quoted and trans. in Lisbet Koerner, *Linnaeus: Nature and Nation* (Cambridge, MA, 1999), p. 137.

60 Linnaeus to Gustav Ekeberg, 18 August 1763, Uppsala, quoted and translated in Koerner, *Linnaeus*, p. 138.

61 Linnaeus to Ellis, 15 August 1765, Uppsala, in *Correspondence of Linnaeus*, vol. I, p. 169.

62 See for example Ellis to Linnaeus, 29 October 1765, London, in *Correspondence of Linnaeus*, vol. I, p. 181.

63 Ellis to Linnaeus, 19 August 1768, London, in *Correspondence of Linnaeus*, vol. I, p. 232.

64 Ellis to Linnaeus, 27 November 1769, London, in *Correspondence of Linnaeus*, vol. I, p. 242.

65 Ellis to Linnaeus, 19 November 1771, London, in *Correspondence of Linnaeus*, vol. I, p. 273.

66 Lucia Tongiori Tomasi, *An Oak Spring Herbaria* (Upperville, VA, 2009), pp. 136–7.

67 *Gazetteer and Daily Advertiser*, 24 May 1774.

68 *Daily Advertiser*, 2 November 1772.

69 Lettsom, *Natural History*, p. vi.

70 *London Evening Post*, 22–4 October 1771.

71 Fan, *British Naturalists in Qing China*, p. 90.

72 'Tea and Herbal Infusions', Tregothnan online shop, at http://tregothnan.co.uk (accessed 5 May 2014).

73 John Ellis to William Tryon (Governor of New York), 4 February 1772, London (draft): London, Linnean Society, John Ellis Notebook 2, fols 109v–110r.

SIX: The Market for Tea in Britain

1 Trial of Elizabeth Blake, 16 January 1760, *Old Bailey Proceedings Online* (t17600116–23), www.oldbaileyonline.org (accessed 21 February 2013).

2 Nick Robins, *The Corporation that Changed the World: How the East India Company Shaped the Modern Multinational* (London, 2006), p. 19.

3 Trial of Francis Skinner and John Barden, 15 October 1729, *Old Bailey Proceedings Online* (t17291015–73)

4 R. C. Jarvis, 'The Metamorphosis of the Port of London', *London Journal*, 3 (1977), pp. 55–72 (p. 58). See also *The Cambridge Social History of Britain, 1750–1950*, ed. F.M.L. Thompson, 3 vols (Cambridge, 1990), vol. I, p. 475.

5 William J. Ashworth, *Customs and Excise: Trade, Production, and Consumption in England, 1640–1845* (Oxford, 2003), pp. 133–53.

6 Trial of William Martin, 15 May 1746, *Old Bailey Proceedings Online* (t17460515–25).

7 Margaret Makepeace, *The East India Company's London Workers: Management of the Warehouse Labourers, 1800–1858* (Woodbridge, 2010), p. 18.

8 Court Minutes, 12 March 1734, London, British Library, India Office Records B/63, p. 281. See also Makepeace, *The East India Company's London Workers*, pp. 18–19.

9 'The Memorial of the Court of Directors of the United Company of Merchants of England Trading to the East Indies', London, The National Archive, Treasury Papers T/1/336/5.

10 Makepeace, *The East India Company's London Workers*, p. 19.

11 'Particulars and Conditions of Sale of the Magnificent and Important Freehold Warehouses situate in Cutler Street, New Street, and Devonshire Square, Bishopsgate . . . known as the Honourable the East India Company's Bengal, Private Trade, and Tea Warehouses . . . To be Sold by auction in the Old Sale Room in the East-India House, on Friday, the 11th day of March 1836' (Home Miscellaneous, India Office Records H/763A, p. 30).

12 'General Plan of Part of the City of London shewing in what Situation the Buildings are Erected', Home Miscellaneous, India Office Records H/763A, pp. 7–8.

13 See Makepeace, *The East India Company's London Workers*, p. 40.

14 'Estimate of the Excise & Custom of Tea for 5 years from the 5th July 1762 to the 5th July 1767' (British Library MSS Eur G37/83/5 fol. 20v); Makepeace, *The East India Company's London Workers*, p. 24. See also Hoh-Cheung Mui and Lorna H. Mui, *The Management of Monopoly: A Study of the English East India Company's Conduct of its Tea Trade, 1784–1833* (Vancouver, 1984), p. 32.

15 Makepeace, *The East India Company's London Workers*, pp. 101–4.

16 For example, the trials of James Barnes, 10 April 1793, and Thomas Yeamen, 14 January 1795, *Old Bailey Proceedings Online* (t17930410–15 and t17950114–5).

17 Court Minutes, 18 May 1737, India Office Records B/64, p. 334. For the emergence of the industrial emphasis on time-keeping, see E. P. Thompson's 'Time, Work-discipline, and Industrial Capitalism', *Past and Present*, 38 (1967), pp. 56–97.

18 Trial of John Quincey, 6 May 1761, *Old Bailey Proceedings Online* (t17610506–7).

19 Trial of Daniel Serjant, 11 September 1793, *Old Bailey Proceedings Online* (t17930911–94).

20 Trial of George Bristow, 16 September 1795, *Old Bailey Proceedings Online* (t17950916–20).

21 Hoh-Cheung Mui and Lorna H. Mui, 'The Commutation Act and the Tea Trade in Britain, 1784–1793', *The Economic History Review*, n.s., 16 (1963), pp. 234–53 (p. 240).

22 Trial of Richard Martin, 8 June 1791, *Old Bailey Proceedings Online* (t17910608–12).

23 'Brokers Marks & Characters', Davison Newman papers, London, London Metropolitan Archives, CLC/B/066/MS08631, unfoliated documents.

24 Hoh-Cheung Mui and Lorna H. Mui, 'Smuggling and the British Tea Trade before 1784', *American Historical Review*, 74 (1968), pp. 44–73 (p. 52).

25 Thomas Short, *Discourses on Tea, Sugar, Milk, Made-wines, Spirits, Punch, Tobacco, &c., with Plain and Useful Rules for Gouty People* (London, 1750), p. 27.

26 *The Diary of Samuel Pepys* (3 September 1662), ed. Robert Latham and William Matthews, 11 vols (London, 1995), vol. III, pp. 185–6.

27 See Jon Mee, '"Mutual Intercourse" and "Licentious Discussion" in *The Microcosm of London*', *London Journal*, 37 (2012), pp. 196–214.

28 [William Smith], *Tsiology; a Discourse on Tea, being an Account of that Exotic; Botanical, Chymical, Commercial, & Medical, with notices of its Adulteration, the Means of Detection, Tea Making, with a brief History of The East India Company* (London, 1826), p. 108.

29 For example, the *Daily Post* for 20 January 1722 records the completion of the sale which had begun in September 1721.

30 Makepeace, *The East India Company's London Workers*, p. 11.

31 Samuel Proctor, *The East-India Sale, September the First, 1719* (London, 1719).

32 'Amount of the East India Company's Sale of Goods from the 5th September 1764 to the 17th August 1768 inclusive', British Library MSS Eur G37/83/5, fol. 26c.

33 See Charles Lockyer, *An Account of the Trade in India* (London, 1711).

34 John Coakley Lettsom, *The Natural History of the Tea-tree* (London, 1772), p. 25; Richard Twining, *Observations on the Tea and Window Act, and on the Tea Trade*, 2nd edn (London, 1785), p. 40.

35 Mui and Mui, *The Management of Monopoly*, pp. 4–9.

36 *The History of Miss Betsy Thoughtless*, 4 vols (London, 1751), vol. II, p. 283.

37 Trial of George Bristow, 16 September 1795, *Old Bailey Proceedings Online* (t17950916–20).

38 Mui and Mui, *The Management of Monopoly*, p. 8.

39 Samuel Johnson, *A Dictionary of the English Language, in which the Words are Deduced from their Originals*, 2 vols (London, 1755), vol. I, 263.

40 Pehr Osbeck, *A Voyage to China and the East Indies*, 2 vols (London, 1771), vol. I, p. 248.

41 Thomas Short, *A Dissertation upon Tea, explaining its Nature and Properties by Many New Experiments* (London, 1730), p. 13.

42 *Sold by Samuel Walter, druggist, at the Queen Elizabeth's Head* (London, [1701]).

43 *Post Man and the Historical Account*, 2–4 May 1704.

44 *Post Man and the Historical Account*, 24–7 June 1704.

45 *Daily Courant*, 18 August 1707; *Post Man and the Historical Account*, 11–13 January 1705.

46 *Daily Courant*, 13 July 1709; *Daily Courant*, 3 May 1708.

47 Humphrey Broadbent, *The Domestick Coffee-man, shewing the True Way of Preparing and Making of Chocolate, Coffee and Tea* (London, 1722), p. 13.

48 This is also how Mawhood defines his business in his 1755 will (Last Will and Testament of Collet Mawhood, 10 April 1755 (proven 7 February 1758), London, The National Archives Prob/11/835).

49 Sidney W. Mintz, *Sweetness and Power: The Place of Sugar in Modern History* (London, 1986), pp. 108–17. For the consumption figures, see p. 67.

50 Nancy Cox and Claire Walsh, '"Their shops are Dens, the buyer is their prey": Shop Design and Sale Techniques', in *The Complete Tradesman: A Study of Retailing, 1550–1820* (Aldershot, 2000), pp. 76–115.

51 Ibid., pp. 91–3.

52 Trials detailed within *Old Bailey Proceedings Online*: Edward Thackerill, 25 October 1758 (t17581025–5); Benjamin Watkins, 11 December 1765 (t17651211–60).

53 Trials detailed within *Old Bailey Proceedings Online*: Peter Burn, 10 May 1780 (t17800510–15); John Hudson and William Blankflower, 29 April 1747 (t17470429–30); James Stansbury, 27 February 1745 (t17450227–12).

54 'Trade Card of D. Hernon, Grocer', London, British Museum, Heal Collection 68.140.

55 Maxine Berg and Helen Clifford, 'Selling Consumption in the Eighteenth Century: Advertising and the Trade Card in Britain and France', *Cultural and Social History*, 4 (2007), pp. 145–70, pp. 165–7. See also Cox and Walsh, '"Their shops are Dens, the buyer is their prey"', pp. 107–15, and Troy Bickham, 'Eating the Empire: Intersections of Food, Cookery and Imperialism in Eighteenth-century Britain', *Past and Present*, 198 (2008), pp. 71–109 (pp. 81–94).

56 See trade card of Richard Knight, 'Tea Dealer and Grocer', London, Museum of London A13891.

57 Ambrose Heal, *London Tradesmen's Cards of the XVIII Century: An Account of their Origin and Use* (London, 1925), p. 3.

58 'Parkinson from Twining's, tea dealer & grocer', Farmington, CT, Lewis Walpole Library 66 733 AL325 Folio.

59 'Raitts Tea Warehouse, at the Green Canister', Lewis Walpole Library 66 726 T675 Quarto.

60 Trade cards forming part of the British Museum, Banks Collection: William Chance (Banks, 68.32), John Dawson (Banks, 68.39).

61 See Bickham, 'Eating the Empire', p. 88.

62 John Heigham Gresham, Banks Collection (Banks, 68.56); Jane Taylor, Heal Collection (Heal, 37.47); John Harling, Heal Collection (Heal, 68.134).

63 Bickham, 'Eating the Empire', p. 88.

64 James Randall, Banks Collection (Banks, 68.104); William Barber, versions in both Banks and Heal Collections (Banks, 68.7 [though catalogued at D,2.2364]); Heal, 68.16).

65 Trade card of John Reece, Banks Collection (Banks, 68.106 [though catalogued at D,2.2367]).
66 Trade card of George Harris, Banks Collection (Banks, 68.60 [catalogued at D,2.2380]). See also Bickham, 'Eating the Empire', p. 90.

SEVEN: The British Way of Tea

1 I am grateful to David Beasley of the Goldsmiths' Hall for advice about dating these items.
2 Kate Retford, *The Art of Domestic Life: Family Portraiture in Eighteenth-century England* (New Haven, CT, and London, 2006).
3 Marcia Pointon, *Strategies for Showing: Women, Possession, and Representation in English Visual Culture, 1665–1800* (Oxford, 1997), p. 28.
4 Paul H. Varley and Isao Kumakura, *Tea in Japan: Essays on the History of Chanoyu* (Honolulu, 1989).
5 *London Chronicle or Universal Evening Post*, 21 March 1765.
6 *A Treatise on the Inherent Qualities of the Tea-herb: Being an Account of the Natural Virtues of the Bohea, Green, and Imperial Teas* (London, 1750), p. 6.
7 Lynette Hunter, 'Women and Domestic Medicine: Lady Experimenters, 1570–1620', in *Women, Science and Medicine, 1500–1700: Mothers and Sisters of the Royal Society*, ed. Lynette Hunter and Sarah Hutton (Stroud, Gloucestershire, 1997), pp. 89–107.
8 Nahum Tate, *Panacea: A Poem Upon Tea: in Two Canto's* (London, 1700), p. 44.
9 Ibid.
10 Catherine Beth Lippert, *Eighteenth-century English Porcelain in the Collection of the Indianapolis Museum of Art* (Indianapolis, IN, 1987), pp. 59, 214.
11 The distinction between front and back stage functions is derived from Erving Goffman (*The Presentation of Self in Everyday Life* (Garden City, NY, 1959)), and was taken up by Lorna Weatherill (*Consumer Behaviour and Material Culture in Britain, 1660–1760* (London, 1996)) in a similar manner.
12 Robert Dodsley, 'The Footman. An Epistle to my Friend Mr Wright', in *A Muse in Livery; or, The Footman's Miscellany* (London, 1732), pp. 17–21.
13 Duncan Campbell, *A Poem upon Tea: Wherein its Antiquity, its several Virtues and Influences are Set Forth* (London, 1735), p. 17.
14 Ibid., pp. 10, 11.
15 *Tea, a Poem: In Three Cantos* (London, 1743).
16 Ambrose Philips, *The Tea-pot; or, the Lady's Transformation: A New Poem* [Dublin?, 1725?], in *The Poems of Ambrose Philips*, ed. M. G. Segar (Oxford, 1937), pp. 164–5.
17 *Tea: A Poem; Or, Ladies into China-Cups; a Metamorphosis* (London, 1729).
18 Alexander Pope, 'The Rape of the Lock' [1714], in *The Twickenham Edition of the Poems of Alexander Pope*, vol. II: *The Rape of the Lock and other Poems*, ed. Geoffrey Tillotson, 2nd revd edn (London and New Haven, CT, 1954), Canto II, ll. 105–6; Canto III, ll. 158–61.
19 See Elizabeth Kowaleski-Wallace, *Consuming Subjects: Women, Shopping, and Business in the Eighteenth Century* (New York, 1997), pp. 52–4. See also Moira Vincentelli, *Women and Ceramics: Gendered Vessels* (Manchester, 2000).
20 Benjamin Franklin, *Poor Richard: The Almanacks for the Years 1733–1758*, ed. Norman Rockwell (New York, 1976), p. 187.
21 Thomas Tickell, *Kensington Garden* (London, 1722), pp. 23–4.
22 Juliet Claxton, 'The Countess of Arundel's Dutch Pranketing Room', *Journal of the History of Collections*, XXII/2 (2010), pp. 187–96.

23 Arthur Lane, 'Queen Mary II's Porcelain Collection at Hampton Court',
    Transactions of the Oriental Ceramic Society, 25 (1949–50), pp. 21–31; Peter
    Thornton, *Seventeenth-century Interior Decoration in England, France and Holland*
    (New Haven, CT, and London, 1978), pp. 249–50.
24 Stacey Sloboda, 'Fashioning Bluestocking Conversation: Elizabeth Montagu's
    Chinese Room', in *Architectural Space in Eighteenth-century Europe: Constructing
    Identities and Interiors*, ed. Meredith S. Martin and Denise Amy Baxter
    (Burlington, VT, 2010), pp. 129–48.
25 Elizabeth Montagu to Edward Montagu, Tunbridge, 8 September 1751,
    Huntington Library, San Marino, CA, MO2241.
26 Marie-Anne du Boccage, *Letters concerning England, Holland and Italy*, 2 vols
    (London, 1770), vol. I, pp. 7–8.
27 Geoffrey Godden, *Oriental Export Market Porcelain and its Influence on European
    Wares* (London, 1979), pp. 15–42.
28 Despatches to the East, India Office Records E/3/94, fols 230r–235r.
29 Godden, *Oriental Export Market Porcelain*, p. 42.
30 Elinor Gordon, *Chinese Export Porcelain: An Historical Survey* (New York, 1975),
    p. 75.
31 Aubrey Toppin, 'The China Trade and Some London Chinamen', *Transactions of
    the English Ceramic Circle*, 3 (1935), pp. 37–56.
32 Steele, *The Spectator*, no. 552 (3 December 1712), vol. IV, p. 478.
33 Robert Finlay, 'The Pilgrim Art: The Culture of Porcelain in World History',
    Journal of World History, IX/2 (Fall 1998), pp. 141–87 (pp. 166–7).
34 Robert Finlay, *The Pilgrim Art: Cultures of Porcelain in World History* (Berkeley,
    CA, 2010), p. 16.
35 Geoffrey Godden, *Godden's New Guide to English Porcelain* (London, 2004),
    pp. 71–5.
36 *London Daily Advertiser*, 8 February 1753.
37 Mark Elliott, *Emperor Qianlong: Son of Heaven, Man of the World* (New York,
    2009), pp. 107–25.
38 *Public Advertiser*, 14 July 1770.
39 Jean Joseph Marie Amiot, 'Vers sur le Thé', in *Éloge de la ville de Moukden, et de
    ses environs; poëme, composé par Kien-Long, Empereur de la Chine, & de la
    Tartarie* (Paris, 1770), pp. 329–37.
40 *Public Advertiser*, Monday, 9 March 1772, p. 2; Sir William Chambers, *A
    Dissertation on Oriental Gardening*, 2nd edn (London, 1773), pp. 118–21.
41 *Kien Long: A Chinese Imperial Eclogue. Translated from a Curious Oriental
    Manuscript* (London, 1775).
42 Peter Pindar, 'Ode to Coffee: In the Manner of Kien Long', in *The Works of Peter
    Pindar, Esq.*, (London, 1809).

EIGHT: Smuggling and Taxation

1 [William Dent], *Catlap for Ever; or, the Smuggler's Downfal* (London, 1784), The
   British Museum 1868,0808.5356. See also Frederick George Stephens and Mary
   Dorothy George, *Catalogue of Political and Personal Satires in the British Museum*,
   12 vols (London, 1870–1954), vol. VI (1938), pp. 158–9.
2 [Francis Grose], *A Classical Dictionary of the Vulgar Tongue* (London, 1785),
   pp. 41 and 179.
3 Definition of smuggling provided in the title of 19 Geo. II, c. 34.
4 'A Grant of Certain Impositions upon Beer, Ale and other Liquors, for the increase
   of his Majesty's Revenue during his Life', 12 Car II, c. 23. See also Robert Wissett,

A View of the Rise, Progress and Present State of the Tea Trade in Europe ([London], 1801), sig. B4r–C1v.

5 22 & 23 Car. II, c. 5.

6 1. Wil. & Mar., Sess. 2, c. 6; 4 & 5 Wil. & Mar., c. 5, section 13; 6 & 7 Wil. III, c. 7; 9 & 10 Wil. III, c. 14; 12 & 13 Wil. III, c. 11; 3 & 4 Ann., c. 4; 6 Ann., c. 22; 7 Ann., c. 7; 10 Ann., c. 26; 3 Geo. I, c. 7.

7 William J. Ashworth, *Customs and Excise: Trade, Production, and Consumption in England, 1640–1845* (Oxford, 2003).

8 Dorothy Marshall, *Eighteenth Century England* (London, 1962), p. 164; Paul Langford, *The Excise Crisis: Society and Politics in the Age of Walpole* (Oxford, 1975), pp. 31–3; Peter Linebaugh, *The London Hanged: Crime and Civil Society in the Eighteenth Century*, 2nd edn (London, 2006), p. 178; J. V. Beckett, 'The Levying of Taxation in Seventeenth- and Eighteenth-century England', *English Historical Review*, 100 (1985), pp. 285–308 (p. 303); Ashworth, *Customs and Excise*, pp. 69, 76.

9 10 Geo. I, c. 10. See also Langford, *The Excise Crisis*, p. 32.

10 Hoh-Cheung Mui and Lorna H. Mui, *The Management of Monopoly: A Study of the English East India Company's Conduct of its Tea Trade, 1784–1833* (Vancouver, 1984), p. 32.

11 Mui and Mui, '"Trends in Eighteenth-century Smuggling" Reconsidered', *Economic History Review*, new series 28 (1975), pp. 28–43 (p. 33).

12 Langford, *The Excise Crisis*, pp. 26–8.

13 For example, *Instructions to be Observed by the Officers Employ'd in the Duty on Coffee, Tea, and Chocolate, in London* (London, 1724), reproduced in the collection *Tea and the Tea-table in Eighteenth-century England*, ed. Markman Ellis, Richard Coulton, Matthew Mauger and Ben Dew, 4 vols (London, 2010), vol. III, pp. 7–15. See also Miles Ogborn, *Spaces of Modernity: London's Geographies, 1680–1780* (New York, 1998), p. 194.

14 Ashworth, *Customs and Excise*, pp. 118–19.

15 London, National Archives, Treasury Papers T 1–495, pp. 311–12.

16 Mui and Mui, '"Trends"', p. 29.

17 [Jonas Hanway], *A Journal of Eight Days Journey from Portsmouth to Kingston upon Thames . . . To which is added, An Essay on Tea, Considered as Pernicious to Health, Obstructing Industry, and Impoverishing the Nation* (London, 1756), p. 310.

18 The two reports are most readily accessible in *Smuggling Laid Open, in all its Extensive and Destructive Branches; with Proposals for the effectual Remedy of that most Iniquitous Practice* (London, 1763).

19 'First Report from the Committee appointed to enquire into the Causes of the most Infamous Practice of Smuggling', ibid., pp. 1–60 (pp. 15–16).

20 Mui and Mui, '"Trends"', pp. 34–6; The discount for prompt payment was ended in 1784; tret itself was discontinued in 1800 (p. 36).

21 'First Report', p. 29.

22 Louis Dermigny, *La Chine et l'Occident, le commerce à Canton au XVIII siècle, 1719–1833*, 4 vols (Paris, 1964), vol. II, pp. 659–68; Ashworth, *Customs and Excise*, p. 177; Mui and Mui, 'Smuggling and the British Tea Trade before 1784', *American Historical Review*, 74 (1968), pp. 44–73 (p. 50). For the Isle of Man see Ashworth, *Customs and Excise*, pp. 197–200.

23 'An Account of the particular Instances of Frauds which have come to the knowledge of the Commiss:rs of the Customs relating to Tea and Brandy in London and the Out Ports with the Proceedings which have been had thereupon', Treasury Papers T 64/149.

24 'The Report of the Committee Appointed to inquire into the Frauds and Abuses in the Customs', *House of Commons Parliamentary Papers* (London, 1733), p. 610.

25 For these cases, see 'An Account', pp. 20, 24 and 25.

26 Ibid., pp. 34, 41, and 47.

27 9 Geo. II, c. 35. See Frank McLynn, *Crime and Punishment in Eighteenth Century England* (London, 1989), p. 184.

28 'First Report', pp. 18–19.

29 'Further Report from the Committee appointed to Enquire into the Causes of Smuggling', in *Smuggling Laid Open*, pp. 61–149 (p. 65).

30 'Further Report', p. 64.

31 Eric J. Hobsbawm, *Primitive Rebels: Studies in Archaic Forms of Social Movement in the 19th and 20th Centuries* (Manchester, 1959). The concept was extended in *Bandits* (Harmondsworth, 1972).

32 Walvin, *Fruits of Empire: Exotic Produce and British Taste, 1660–1800* (London, 1997), p. 19. The notion of a 'moral economy' is drawn from the work of E. P. Thompson in *Customs in Common* (London, 1991). See also John Stevenson, *Popular Disturbances in England, 1700–1870* (London, 1979).

33 'First Report', p. 45.

34 See 'First Report' as follows: Sclater, p. 11; Walter, pp. 23–4; Adams, p. 25; Mawhood, p. 13. Others suggested £4 million (p. 31) or £2 million (p. 48).

35 *The Report of the Committee*, pp. 610–11.

36 'An Account', p. 15.

37 'First Report', p. 24.

38 Ibid., p. 19.

39 Testimony of Samuel Wilson, 'First Report', pp. 39–40.

40 'Returns showing the Number of Pounds Weight of Tea sold by the East India Company, for Home Consumption, in each Year from 1740 down to the Termination of the Company's Sales', *House of Commons Parliamentary Papers* (London, 1845), pp. 2–5. See also Mui and Mui, '"Trends"', pp. 30–31.

41 *Daily Journal*, 27, 29, 30 and 31 January 1733.

42 *The Case of the Dealers in Tea* ([London, 1736]).

43 Horatio Walpole, 'Some Thoughts on Running Tea' [dated 29 March 1745] (British Library Add MSS 74051), fols 123–5 (fol. 124).

44 18 Geo. II, c. 26; 'A True State of the Smuggling, &c. Of Tea, with an Effectual Method for Preventing It' (British Library Add MSS 74051), fol. 121.

45 Drawn from 'Returns . . . of Tea sold by the East India Company', 1845.

46 Dermigny, *La Chine et l'Occident*, vol. II, p. 448.

47 Mui and Mui, 'Smuggling', pp. 56–7.

48 'Summary of Volume of Tea Smuggled into Britain from Sweden and Denmark', Treasury Papers T 1/425/199–200. For reports concerning the Channel Islands see T 1/429/11–19, T 1/431/56–59 and T 1/433/101–103. See also Dermigny, *La Chine et l'Occident*, vol. II, p. 662.

49 Officers of the Leith Custom House to the London Customs surveyors, 9 July 1762 (Treasury Papers T 1/426/339–342).

50 Figures from Mui and Mui, 'Smuggling', p. 53; and Wissett, 'Total Quantities of Tea exported from *Canton* to *Europe* and *America*', in *A View of the Rise . . . of the Tea Trade in Europe*, sig. ii3v.

51 Ashworth, *Customs and Excise*, pp. 178–9.

52 Drawn from 'Returns . . . of Tea sold by the East India Company', 1845.

53 'Excise Memorial relative to Smuggling', Treasury Papers T 1/489/147–148.

54 Mui and Mui, *Management of Monopoly*, p. 13. For smuggled tea in Scotland see Mui and Mui, 'Smuggling', pp. 56–8; Ashworth, *Customs and Excise*, pp. 179–81.

55 Ashworth, *Customs and Excise*, pp. 186–9.

56 National Archives, Chatham Papers PRO 30/8/293 and PRO 30/8/294.

57 Mui and Mui, 'William Pitt and the Enforcement of the Commutation Act, 1784–1788', *English Historical Review*, 76 (1961), pp. 447–65. See also Lucy S. Sutherland, *The East India Company in Eighteenth Century Politics* (Oxford, 1952).

58 Mui and Mui, 'William Pitt', pp. 450–51.

59 *Tea and the Tea-Table*, IV, pp. x–xiii and 301–2.

60 Drawn from 'Returns ... of Tea sold by the East India Company', 1845.

61 Hoh-Cheung Mui and Lorna H. Mui, *Shops and Shopkeeping in Eighteenth Century England* (London, 1989), pp. 161–4.

62 From section 5 of the Commutation Act (24 Geo. III, sess. 2, c. 38).

63 Mui and Mui, *Shops and Shopkeeping*, p. 255. See also Mui and Mui, *Management of Monopoly*, p. xi.

64 Mui and Mui, 'William Pitt', p. 460.

65 Mui and Mui, *Management of Monopoly*, pp. 95–7.

66 Wissett, 'An Account of the Quantities of Tea Exported from China in English and Foreign Ships, from the Year 1768', in *A View of the Rise ... of the Tea Trade in Europe*, sig. i3r–ii2r.

67 Calculations are based on the data contained in 'Returns ... of Tea sold by the East India Company', 1845.

68 See Mui and Mui, 'The Commutation Act and the Tea Trade in Britain, 1784–1793', *Economic History Review*, new series, 16 (1963), pp. 234–53 (p. 252).

69 Mui and Mui, 'Commutation Act and the Tea Trade', p. 244.

70 Mui and Mui, *Shops and Shopkeeping*, p. 251; Walvin, *Fruits of Empire*, pp. 18–19.

NINE: The Democratization of Tea Drinking

1 William Cowper, 'The Task: A Poem', IV. 5–6, 36–41, in *The Poems of William Cowper*, ed. John D. Baird and Charles Ryskamp, 3 vols (Oxford, 1980–95), vol. II (1995), pp. 187–8.

2 London, National Archives, Treasury Papers, T 1/542, fol. 229r.

3 National Archives, Chatham Papers, PRO 30/8/294, fol. 176r.

4 National Archives, Chatham Papers, PRO 30/8/294, fol. 168r.

5 [Robert Wissett], *A View of the Rise, Progress and Present State of the Tea Trade in Europe* ([London, c. 1801]), sig. C4v.

6 Short, *Dissertation*, p. 3; John Wesley, *A Letter to a Friend, Concerning Tea*, 2nd edn (Bristol, 1749), p. 4.

7 [Jonas Hanway], *A Journal of Eight Days Journey from Portsmouth to Kingston upon Thames ... To which is added, An Essay on Tea, Considered as Pernicious to Health, Obstructing Industry, and Impoverishing the Nation* (London, 1756), p. 272.

8 'Returns showing the Number of Pounds Weight of Tea sold by the East India Company, for Home Consumption, in each Year from 1740 down to the Termination of the Company's Sales', *House of Commons Parliamentary Papers* (London, 1845), pp. 2–5.

9 Hoh-Cheung Mui and Lorna H. Mui, '"Trends in Eighteenth-century Smuggling" Reconsidered', *Economic History Review*, 2nd series, 28 (1975), pp. 28–43.

10 W. Scott Tebb, *Tea and the Effects of Tea Drinking* (London, [1905]).

11 John Burnett, *Plenty and Want: A Social History of Diet in England from 1815 to the Present Day* (London, 1966), pp. 1–50; John Burnett, *Liquid Pleasures: A Social History of Drinks in Modern Britain* (London, 1999), pp. 49–69.

12 Peter H. Lindert and Jeffrey G. Williamson, 'English Workers' Living Standards during the Industrial Revolution: A New Look', *Economic History Review*, 2nd series, 36 (1983), pp. 1–25; Joel Mokyr, 'Is There Still Life in the Pessimist Case?

Consumption during the Industrial Revolution, 1790–1850', *Journal of Economic History*, 48 (1988), pp. 69–92; Charles Feinstein, 'Pessimism Perpetuated: Real Wages and the Standard of Living in Britain during and after the Industrial Revolution', *Journal of Economic History*, 58 (1998), pp. 625–58; Maxine Berg, 'Consumption in Eighteenth- and Early Nineteenth-century Britain', in *The Cambridge Economic History of Modern Britain*, ed. Roderick Floud and Paul Johnson, 3 vols (Cambridge, 2004), vol. I, pp. 357–86.

13 Carole Shammas, 'The Eighteenth Century English Diet and Economic Change', *Explorations in Economic History*, 21 (1984), pp. 254–69.

14 Duncan Campbell, *A Poem upon Tea* (London, 1735), p. 13.

15 Jonathan Swift, *Directions to Servants* (London, 1745), pp. 81–2.

16 [John Shebbeare], *Letters on the English Nation*, 2 vols (London, 1755), vol. II, p. 38.

17 [Hanway,] *A Journal of Eight Days Journey*, p. 243.

18 National Archives, Chatham Papers, PRO 30/8/293, fol. 26r.

19 David Davies, *The Case of the Labourers in Husbandry Stated and Considered, in Three Parts* (London, 1795), pp. 136–87.

20 Sir Frederic Eden, *The State of the Poor: or, An History of the Labouring Classes in England*, 3 vols (London, 1797), vol. II, pp. 14, 280, 404; vol. III, p. 779.

21 S. R. Bosanquet, *The Rights of the Poor and Christian Almsgiving Vindicated* (London, 1841), pp. 91–102.

22 *Report from the Select Committee on The Tea Duties: with Minutes of Evidence* ([London], 1834), p. 77. This David Davies is not the clergyman author of *The Case of the Labourers in Husbandry* (1795).

23 *1834 Select Committee*, p. 40.

24 Ibid., p. 42.

25 Ibid., p. 11.

26 Ibid., p. 44.

27 Ibid., pp. 50–57, 76.

28 Ibid., pp. 33, 38.

29 Ibid., p. 62.

30 Ibid., p. 79.

31 [Hanway,] *A Journal of Eight Days Journey*, pp. 229, 269.

32 George Gabriel Sigmond, *Tea: Its Effects, Medicinal and Moral* (London, 1839), p. 62.

33 Burnett, *Liquid Pleasures*, pp. 29–48.

34 Factory Enquiries Commission, *Supplementary Report of the Central Board of His Majesty's Commissioners . . . as to the Employment of the Children in Factories, and as to the Propriety and Means of Curtailing the Hours of their Labour*, 2 vols (London, 1834), vol. I, pp. 255–68.

35 Friedrich Engels, *The Condition of the Working Class in England* [1892], ed. Victor Kiernan (Harmondsworth, 1987), pp. 107, 125.

36 'Letters For and Against Tea-drinking', from Nathaniel Mist's *Weekly Journal*, in *Tea and the Tea-table*, ed. Markman Ellis, Richard Coulton, Matthew Mauger and Ben Dew, 4 vols (London, 2010), vol. I, pp. 49–59.

37 [Hanway,] *A Journal of Eight Days Journey*, pp. 244–5.

38 Ibid., p. 223.

39 Ibid., p. 274.

40 *Tea and the Tea-table*, vol. III, pp. 59–61.

41 [Walter Harte], *Essays on Husbandry*, 2 vols (London, 1764), vol. I, p. 166.

42 [Arthur Young], *The Farmer's Letters to the People of England* (London, 1767), pp. 171–2.

43 Eden, *The State of the Poor*, vol. I, pp. 535, 548.

44 *An Essay on Tea, Sugar, White Bread and Butter, Country Alehouses, Strong Beer and Geneva, and other Modern Luxuries* (Salisbury, 1777), pp. 14–27.

45 *Cobbett's Cottage Economy*, 1 August 1821, pp. 13, 20; see also Leonora Nattrass, *William Cobbett: The Politics of Style* (Cambridge, 1995), pp. 153–6.

46 John Bowes, *Temperance, as it is Opposed to Strong Drinks, Tobacco and Snuff, Tea and Coffee* (Aberdeen, [1836?]), p. 12. See also James Henry, *A Letter to the Members of the Temperance Society showing that the Use of Tea and Coffee cannot be Safely Substituted for that of Spirituous Liquors* (Dublin, 1830), pp. 15–16, 20.

47 J. N. Surgeon, *Remarks on Mr Mason's Treatise upon Tea* (London, 1745), p. 16.

48 [Hanway,] *A Journal of Eight Days Journey*, p. 244.

49 *Modern Luxuries*, p. 20.

50 Godfrey McCalman, *A Natural, Commercial and Medicinal Treatise on Tea* (Glasgow, 1787), pp. 119–20.

51 Christopher Berry, *The Idea of Luxury: A Conceptual and Historical Investigation* (Cambridge, 1994), pp. 126–76.

52 Ibid., pp. 3–13.

53 Ibid., pp. 101–25.

54 Wissett, *A View of the Rise, Progress and Present State of the Tea Trade*, sig. [C4r].

55 Ibid., sig. [C4v].

56 John Ramsay McCulloch, 'Observations on the Trade with China', *Edinburgh Review; or Critical Journal*, 39 (1823–4), pp. 458–67 (p. 463).

57 R. Montgomery Martin, *The Past and Present State of the Tea Trade of England, and of the Continents of Europe and America* (London, 1832), p. 80.

58 David Macpherson, *The History of the European Commerce with India* (London, 1812), p. 132.

59 [William Smith], *Tsiology; A Discourse on Tea* (London, 1826), p. 105; for attribution see Hoh-Cheung Mui and Lorna H. Mui, *Shops and Shopkeeping in Eighteenth Century England* (London, 1989), p. 353.

60 Sigmond, *Tea*, pp. 2–3.

61 Davies, *Labourers*, p. 39.

62 *1834 Select Committee*, p. 67.

63 Charles Knight, 'Dear and Cheap', in *Once Upon a Time*, 2 vols (London, 1854), vol. II, pp. 180–208 (p. 192).

64 Ovington, *Essay*, pp. 8, 15.

65 11 Geo. I, c. 30 (1724), 'CAP. XXX. An Act for more effectual preventing Frauds and Abuses in the Publick Revenues'.

66 *The Tea Purchaser's Guide; or, The Lady and Gentleman's Tea Table and Useful Companion* (London, 1785), pp. 32–8.

67 *1834 Select Committee*, pp. 8–9.

68 11 Geo. I, c. 30, 'An Act for more effectual preventing Frauds and Abuses in the Publick Revenues' (1724); 4 Geo. II, c. 14, 'An Act to prevent Frauds in the Revenue of Excise, with respect to Starch, Coffee, Tea and Chocolate' (1730); 17 Geo. III, c. 29, 'An Act for the more effectual Prevention of the manufacturing of Ash, Elder, Sloe, and other Leaves, in Imitation of Tea, and to prevent Frauds in the Revenue of Excise in respect to Tea' (1776).

69 *First Report from the Committee, Appointed to Enquire into the Illicit Practices used in Defrauding the Revenue (24th December, 1783)* (London, 1784), p. 15.

70 *Poisonous Tea! The Trial of Edward Palmer, Grocer* (London, 1818); *Morning Post*, 18 May 1818.

71 Sigmond, *Tea*, p. 54.

72 [Frederick Gye?], *The History of the Tea Plant* (London, [1819]), p. 48; see also 'The Tea and the Sloe', *Literary Journal, and General Miscellany of Politics, Science, Arts, Morals, and Manners*, 1 (1818), p. 201.

73 *Morning Chronicle*, 18 September 1833.

74 *Morning Chronicle*, 26 September 1833.

75 *Morning Post*, 18 October 1833.

76 McCalman, *A Natural, Commercial and Medicinal Treatise on Tea*, pp. 118–19.

77 Isaac Watts, *Logick; or, The Right Use of Reason in the Enquiry after Truth* (London, 1725), p. 87.

78 *The Times*, 4 August 1784.

79 *Morning Herald*, 5 June 1794, *Felix Farley's Bristol Journal*, 20 October 1787.

80 *Dr Solander's Sanative English Tea* ([London], [1795]); H. Smith, 'An Essay on Foreign Teas', in *An Essay on the Nerves, Illustrating their Efficient, Formal, Material, and Final Causes* (London, [1795]).

81 *Patronized and Used by their Majesties and Nobility. Rev. J. Gamble's British Medicinal Tea* ([London], [1801?]).

82 Count Belchilgen and J. A. Cope, *An Essay on the Virtues and Properties of the Ginseng Tea* (London, 1786); see also *Tea and the Tea-table*, vol. II, pp. 181–3.

83 *The Black Dwarf, a London Weekly Publication*, 20 October 1819, 27 October 1819, 1 December 1819, 22 December 1819, 12 January 1820, 19 January 1820, 2 February 1820, 13 December 1820, 7 March 1821.

84 'The Culloden Papers' (review), *Edinburgh Review; or, Critical Journal*, 26 (1816), pp. 109–35 (p. 117).

TEN: Tea in the Politics of Empire

1 Alfred Young, *The Shoemaker and the Tea Party: Memory and the American Revolution* (Boston, MA, 1999), pp. xv, 87, 102.

2 Ibid., p. 87.

3 T. H. Breen, *The Marketplace of Revolution: How Consumer Politics Shaped American Independence* (Oxford, 2004); and by the same author, '"Baubles of Britain": The American and Consumer Revolutions of the Eighteenth Century', *Past and Present*, 119 (1988), pp. 73–104.

4 Quoted in Esther Singleton, *Social New York under the Georges, 1714–1776* (New York, 1902), pp. 22–4.

5 Andrew F. Smith, *New York City: A Food Biography* (Lanham, MD, 2014), pp. 119–20.

6 Robert Wissett, 'Tea Imported and Exported, made up from the Custom-house Books', in *A View of the Rise, Progress and Present State of the Tea Trade in Europe* (London, 1801), sig. ii3r–4r.

7 From 1755–1764, National Debt rose from £72,289,673 to £129,586,789 (T. L. Purvis, 'The Seven Years' War and its Political Legacy', in *A Companion to the American Revolution*, ed. J. P. Greene and J. R. Pole (Oxford, 2004), p. 115.

8 Breen, *The Marketplace of Revolution*, p. 218, and '"Baubles"', p. 89.

9 Breen, *Marketplace of Revolution*, pp. 218–22, and '"Baubles"', pp. 89–97. See also Edmund S. Morgan and Helen M. Morgan, *The Stamp Act Crisis: Prologue to Revolution* (Chapel Hill, NC, 1953); and Merritt Jensen, *Founding of a Nation: A History of the American Revolution* (Oxford, 1968), particularly chapters 10–12.

10 7 Geo. III, c. 46.

11 Robert Tucker and David Hendrickson, *The Fall of the First British Empire: Origins of the War of American Independence* (Baltimore, MD, 1982), pp. 278–9. See also Benjamin Laberee, *The Boston Tea Party* (New York, 1964), pp. 70–73.

12 13 Geo III, c. 44.

13 Breen, *The Marketplace of Revolution*, p. 300.

14 Laberee, *The Boston Tea Party*, particularly pp. 126–45.

15 James Murray, *An Impartial History of the War in America*, 2 vols (Newcastle-upon-Tyne, 1782), vol. I, p. 397. On the use of disguises, see D. A. Grinde Jr and B. E. Johnson, *Exemplar of Liberty: Native America and the Evolution of Democracy* (Los Angeles, CA, 1991).

16 Young, *The Shoemaker and the Tea Party*, p. 102.

17 An eyewitness account of the events of that day was published as a special issue of the *Pennsylvania Journal* on 24 December 1773, entitled *Christmas-box for the Customers of the Pennsylvania Journal* (reprinted in the collection *Tea and the Tea-table in Eighteenth-century England*, ed. Markman Ellis, Richard Coulton, Matthew Mauger and Ben Dew, 4 vols (London, 2010), vol. IV, pp. 47–50).

18 L. H. Butterfield et al., eds, *Diary and Autobiography of John Adams*, 4 vols (Cambridge, MA, 1961), vol. II, pp. 85–7.

19 Early coverage reflected on these links; for example, David Servatius, 'Anti-tax-and-spend Group Throws "Tea Party" at the Capitol', *Deseret News*, 7 March 2009, www.deseretnews.com. The symbolic use of tea in political demonstration predates the Tea Party movement: 'Demonstrators Hurl Tea Bags in Bid against Rising Taxes', *Victoria Advocate*, 23 July 1991, p. 6.

20 Frederic Wakeman Jr, 'The Canton Trade and the Opium War', in *The Cambridge History of China*, 15 vols (Cambridge, 1978–), vol. X: *Late Qing, 1800–1911* (1978), ed. John K. Fairbank, pp. 163–212 (pp. 166–7).

21 'Returns Showing the Number of Pounds Weight of Tea sold by the East India Company, for Home Consumption, in each Year from 1740 down to the Termination of the Company's Sales', *House of Commons Parliamentary Papers* (London, 1845), pp. 2–5.

22 [William Smith], *Tsiology; a Discourse on Tea* (London, 1826). For attribution of authorship, see Hoh-Cheung Mui and Lorna H. Mui, *Shops and Shopkeeping in Eighteenth-century England* (London, 1989), p. 353.

23 For a range of views see [Smith], *Tsiology*, p. 224; John Ramsay McCulloch, *Effects of the East India Company's Monopoly on the Price of Tea* (London, 1824); McCulloch, *Observations on the Influence of the East India Company's Monopoly on the Price and Supply of Tea* (London, 1831); James Silk Buckingham, *History of the Public Proceedings on the Question of the East India Monopoly, during the Past Year* (London, 1830).

24 W. C. Bentinck, 'Minute by the Governor-General' (24 January 1834), in 'Return to an Order of the Honourable House of Commons . . . for Copy of Papers Received from India relating to the Measures Adopted for Introducing the Cultivation of the Tea Plant within the British Possessions in India', *House of Commons Parliamentary Papers* (London, 1839), pp. 5–6. Subsequent references to this collection will be in the form *Papers Received from India*.

25 Nathaniel Wallich, 'Observations on the Cultivation of the Tea Plant, for Commercial Purposes, in the Mountainous parts of Hindostan', in *Papers Received from India*, pp. 12–15 (p. 14).

26 Walker, 'Proposition to the Honourable the Directors of the East India Company to Cultivate Tea upon the Nepaul Hills, and such other parts of the Territories of the East India Company as may be Suitable to its Growth', in *Papers Received from India*, pp. 6–12 (p. 6).

27 Ibid., pp. 6–7.

28 Ibid., pp. 7–12.

29 Wallich, 'Observations on the Cultivation of the Tea Plant', p. 15.

30 C. A. Bruce, Superintendent of Tea, to Captain F. Jenkins, Agent to Governor-General, Gowahatty, 20 December 1836, in *Papers Received from India*, p. 91.

31 N. Wallich, Esq., MD, to J. W. Grant, Esq., 3 March 1836 (in *Papers Received from India*, p. 61).

32 C. A. Bruce, Esq., Commanding Gun Boats, to Lieutenant J. Miller, Commanding at Suddeya, 14 April 1836, in *Papers Received from India*, pp. 71–72.

33 N. Wallich, Esq., MD, Secretary to the Tea Committee, to W. H. Macnaghten, Esq., Secretary to Government of India, 5 September 1837, in *Papers Received from India*, pp. 92–3.

34 Quoted in W. Nassau Lees, *Tea Cultivation, Cotton, and other Agricultural Experiments in India: A Review* (London, 1863), pp. 26–7. For details of the sale, see Denys Forrest, *Tea for the British: the Social and Economic History of a Famous Trade* (London, 1973), pp. 110–12.

35 Roy Moxham, *Tea: Addiction, Exploitation, and Empire* (London, 2003), pp. 101–4.

36 Robert Fortune, *A Journey to the Tea Countries of China; including Sung-Lo and the Bohea Hills; with a Short Notice of the East India Company's Tea Plantations in the Himalaya Mountains* (London, 1852), p. 395.

37 Julie E. Fromer, *A Necessary Luxury: Tea in Victorian England* (Athens, GA, 2008), p. 65.

38 Hunt Janin, *The India–China Opium Trade in the Nineteenth Century* (Jefferson, NC, 1999), p. 170.

39 Paul Van Dyke, *The Canton Trade: Life and Enterprise on the China Coast, 1700–1845* (Hong Kong, 2005), p. 105.

40 Testimony of John Reeves in the *Report from the Select Committee on the Tea Duties* (House of Commons, 1834), pp. 1–2.

41 Brian Inglis, *The Opium War* (London, 1976), pp. 18–22.

42 For agency houses, see Wakeman, 'The Canton Trade and the Opium War', p. 167.

43 Jack Gray, *Rebellions and Revolutions: China from the 1800s to 2000*, 2nd edn (Oxford, 2002), p. 28; Wakeman, 'The Canton Trade and the Opium War', p. 168.

44 Wakeman, 'The Canton Trade and the Opium War', pp. 173–4.

45 See ibid., pp. 185–8; Inglis, *The Opium War*, pp. 116–21.

46 See Inglis, *The Opium War*, pp. 126–7.

47 John Francis Davis, *The Chinese: A General Description of the Empire of China and its Inhabitants*, 2 vols (London, 1836), vol. II, pp. 435–6.

48 *Quarterly Review*, 112 (June 1836), pp. 489–521 (p. 518).

49 Charles Bruce, 'Report on the Manufacture of Tea, and on the Extent and Produce of the Tea-Plantations in Assam', *Edinburgh New Philosophical Journal*, 27 (April 1839), pp. 126–61 (p. 157).

50 Algernon Thelwall, *The Iniquities of the Opium Trade with China* (London, 1839), p. 40.

51 See Inglis, *The Opium War*, pp. 124–6.

52 Wakeman, 'The Canton Trade and the Opium War', pp. 211–12; June Grasso et al., *Modernization and Revolution in China* (New York, 1997), pp. 39–40; Inglis, *The Opium War*, pp. 164–5.

53 John Fairbank, 'The Creation of the Treaty System', in *The Cambridge History of China*, vol. X: *Late Qing, 1800–1911*, pp. 213–63 (p. 223).

54 For more on the value of tea to the British treasury in this period, see Inglis, *The Opium War*, p. 198.

ELEVEN: The National Drink of Victorian Britain

1 Samuel Phillips Day, *Tea: Its Mystery and History* (London, 1878), p. 68.

2 [Anon.], 'Tea Statistics', in *Tea and Tea Blending* (London, 1886), pp. 36–7.

3 W. Scott Tebb, *Tea and the Effects of Tea Drinking* (London, [1905]), p. 7. See also John Burnett, *Liquid Pleasures: A Social History of Drinks in Modern*

Britain (London, 1999), p. 57; and Roberto A. Ferdman, 'Where the World's Biggest Tea Drinkers Are', *Quartz*, 20 January 2014, http://qz.com/168690 (accessed 1 April 2014).

4 Edward Smith, 'On the Uses of Tea in the Healthy System', *Journal of the Society of Arts*, 9 (1861), pp. 185–97 (p. 186).

5 John Sumner, *A Popular Treatise on Tea: Its Qualities and Effects* (Birmingham, 1863), p. iii.

6 [William Smith], *Tsiology: A Discourse on Tea* (London, 1826), pp. 107–25; see also Markman Ellis, Richard Coulton, Matthew Mauger and Ben Dew, eds, *Tea and the Tea-table in Eighteenth-century England*, 4 vols (London, 2010), vol. III, pp. 167–8; and Moffat's *Sale List of the East India Company's December Tea Sale, 1827* (London, 1827).

7 John Crawfurd, *Chinese Monopoly Examined* (London, 1830); R. Montgomery Martin, *The Past and Present State of the Tea Trade of England* (London, 1832). See also Hoh-cheung Mui and Lorna H. Mui, *The Management of Monopoly: A Study of the English East India Company's Conduct of its Tea Trade, 1784–1833* (Vancouver, 1984).

8 Burnett, *Liquid*, pp. 58–9.

9 *Tea Blending*, pp. 34–7.

10 David R. MacGregor, 'The Tea Clippers, 1849–1869', in *British Ships in China Seas: 1700 to the Present Day*, ed. Richard Harding, Adrian Jarvis and Alston Kennedy (Liverpool, 2004), pp. 217–24; Malcolm Cooper, 'From *Agamemnon* to *Priam*: British Liner Shipping in the China Seas, 1865–1965', in *British Ships*, pp. 225–38; Immanuel C. Y. Hsü, *The Rise of Modern China*, 6th edn (Oxford, 2000), pp. 205–19; John K. Fairbank, 'The Creation of the Treaty System', in *The Cambridge History of China*, ed. John K. Fairbank and Denis Twitchett, 15 vols (Cambridge, 1978-), vol. X: *Late Qing, 1800–1911* (1978), pp. 213–63 (pp. 243–61). See also below, and chapter Ten.

11 *Morning Herald*, 4 November 1786; *E. Johnson's British Gazette and Sunday Monitor*, 16 May 1784. See also *Bath Chronicle*, 3 June 1784; *Felix Farley's Bristol Journal*, 13 January 1787; *Lloyd's Evening Post*, 4–6 September 1799; Mui and Mui, *Shops*, pp. 268–72.

12 *Morning Post*, 30 October 1818.

13 *Trewman's Exeter Flying Post or Plymouth and Cornish Advertiser*, 12 August 1819; *Morning Chronicle*, 6 November 1819.

14 *Morning Post*, 7 November 1818, 17 November 1818, 19 November 1818.

15 See for example *The Essex Standard, and General Advertiser for the Eastern Counties*, 6 February 1857.

16 See also Steven A. Leibo, 'The Sino-European Educational Missions, 1875–1886', *Asian Profile*, 16 (1998), pp. 443–51.

17 Day, *Tea*, pp. xii–xvi.

18 *Tea Blending*, pp. 97–117. See also Jane Pettigrew, *A Social History of Tea* (London, 2001), p. 93; Burnett, *Liquid*, pp. 62–4, 67–8; and Ken Teague, *Mr Horniman and the Tea Trade* (London, 1993).

19 Arthur Hill Hassall, *Food and its Adulterations* (London, 1855), pp. iv–v, 268–320.

20 *Tea Blending*, pp. 34–5.

21 Ti Ping Koon, *Death in the Tea Pot* (London, 1874), pp. 11–13.

22 J. Sheridan Le Fanu, 'Green Tea', in *In a Glass Darkly*, 3 vols (London, 1872), vol. I, pp. 1–95.

23 Koon, *Death in the Tea Pot*, pp. 3, 8.

24 Julie E. Fromer, *A Necessary Luxury: Tea in Victorian England* (Athens, OH, 2008), especially pp. 26–115.

25 Day, *Tea*, p. 71.

26 Ibid., p. 63. See also *The Private Life of the Queen, by a Member of the Royal Household* (New York, 1901), pp. 276–7, 280–81.

27 Leitch Ritchie, 'The Social Influence of Tea', *Chambers Edinburgh Journal*, 29 January 1848, p. 65.

28 James F. W. Johnston, *The Chemistry of Common Life*, 2 vols (Edinburgh, 1855), pp. 169–76. See also John Woods, *A Brief History of Tea, with a Glance at the Flowery Land* (Richmond, [1853]), p. 8; and George Vivian Poore, *Coffee and Tea* (London, 1883), pp. 3–11.

29 John H. Weisburger and James Comer, 'Tea', in *The Cambridge World History of Food*, ed. Kenneth F. Kiple and Kriemhild Coneè Ornelas (Cambridge, 2000), pp. 712–20 (pp. 718–19); 'Physiological and Pharmacological Effects of *Camellia sinensis* (Tea): [Proceedings of the] First International Symposium', ed. John H. Weisburger, *Preventive Medicine*, 21 (1992), pp. 329–91, 503–53.

30 Alan Weinberg Bennett and Bonnie K. Bealer, *The World of Caffeine: The Science and Culture of the World's Most Popular Drug* (London, 2001), pp. xvii–xxi.

31 Smith, 'On the Uses of Tea in the Healthy System', p. 188.

32 Isabella Beeton, *The Book of Household Management*, 2 vols (London, 1861), p. 880.

33 John Tyndall, *Heat: A Mode of Motion*, 3rd edn (London, 1868), p. 274.

34 *Tea Blending*, p. 105; Koon, *Death in the Tea Pot*, p. 10.

35 Koon, *Death in the Tea Pot*, p. 9.

36 T. Bland Garland, 'Tea v. Beer in the Harvest Field', in John Abbey, *Intemperance: Its Bearing upon Agriculture*, 3rd edn (London, 1882), pp. 19–20.

37 Day, *Tea*, p. 68.

38 Gordon Stables, *Tea, the Drink of Pleasure and of Health* (London, [1883]), p. 77.

39 [Eliza Cheadle], *Manners of Modern Society: Being a Book of Etiquette* (London, [1872]), p. 158.

40 Letter from Fanny Kemble, Belvoir Castle (Northumberland), 27 March 1842, quoted in Pettigrew, *A Social History of Tea*, p. 102.

41 [Cheadle], p. 158; Charles Oliver, *Dinner at Buckingham Palace*, ed. Paul Fishman and Fiorella Busoni (London, 2003), p. 20.

42 Pettigrew, *A Social History of Tea*, pp. 102–5.

43 Agnes C. Maitland, *The Afternoon Tea Book* (London, 1887), p. vii.

44 Fromer, *A Necessary Luxury*, pp. 198–210, 263–75.

45 Charles Barwell Coles, *Tea: A Poem* (London, 1865).

46 Ibid., p. 44.

47 Arnold Palmer, *Movable Feasts: Changes in English Eating-habits*, ed. David Pocock (Oxford, 1984), pp. 101–3.

48 [Anon.], *Questions for our Sunday Tea-table* (Liverpool, 1863); [Anon.], *Evenings at the Tea-table* (London, 1871).

49 *The History of a Cup of Tea in Rhymes and Pictures* (London, 1860), pp. 8, 11.

50 *A Tale of Tea, by a Teapot* (London, [1884]), pp. [11–16].

51 See also *The Cat's Tea-party*, Aunt Mavor's Picture Books for Little Readers (First Series), 13 (London, [1854]); Richard André, *The Animated Tea Service* (London, [1882]).

52 Robert Rhodes Reed (lyric) and Carlo Minasi (music), *The Song of the Tea-pot* (London, [1855]).

53 Edward Edmondson, *A Poem on a Cup of Warm Tea, for a Vote of Thanks* (Leeds, [1865]), p. [4].

54 Alexander T. Teetgen, *A Mistress and her Servant (from Daily Life)* (London, [1870]), pp. 12–13.

55 Bayle Bernard, *A Storm in a Tea Cup: A Comedy, in One Act* (Leipsic, OH, 1856); *A Cup of Tea: A Comedietta in One Act*, Lacy's Acting Edition, 83 (London, [1869]).

56 James Taylor Staton, *The Husbands' Tea Party* (Manchester, 1875), p. 15.
57 C. D. Hickman (lyric) and J. Ellis (composer), *Sitting Down to Tea* (London, [1891]).
58 Leslie Harris, *Middle Class Society Tea* (London, [1894]).
59 *Kettledrum: A Magazine of Art, Literature, & Social Improvement* (London, 1869), pp. 1–2.
60 [Anon.], 'Tea Statistics', in *Tea and Tea Blending by a Member of the Firm of Lewis & Co.*, 4th edn (London, 1894), pp. 60–61; see also Tebb, *Tea and the Effects of Tea Drinking*.
61 *The Tea Cyclopædia* (Calcutta, 1881), p. 324.
62 J. G. Hathorn, *A Handbook of Darjeeling; with Brief Notes on the Culture and Manufacture of Tea* (Calcutta, 1863), p. 121.
63 *Tea Blending*, p. 98.
64 *The Happy Blend; or, How John Bull was suited to a T.* (London, [1885]).
65 Hathorn, *Darjeeling*, p. 121.
66 Edward Money, *The Tea Controversy (a Momentous Indian Question)*, 2nd edn (London, 1884), p. 1.
67 Money, *Controversy*, pp. 8–11.
68 Stables, *Tea, the Drink of Pleasure and of Health*, pp. 15, 24.
69 Ibid., pp. 47–8.
70 Ibid., p. 17.
71 Pettigrew, *A Social History of Tea*, p. 96.
72 Bob Crampsey, *The King's Grocer: The Life of Sir Thomas Lipton* (Glasgow, 1995), pp. 45–52.
73 *Tea Blending*, pp. 74–7. See also Edward Money, *The Cultivation and Manufacture of Tea*, 4th edn (London, 1883), pp. 222–71.
74 E. F. Bamber, *Tea* (London, 1868), pp. 38, 40. See also E. F. Bamber, *An Account of the Cultivation and Manufacture of Tea in India, from Personal Observation* (Calcutta, 1866).
75 F. W. Emery, *Hindoo Mythology Popularly Treated: being an Epitomized Description of . . . the Silver Swami Tea Service, Presented . . . to HRH the Prince of Wales* (Madras, 1875).
76 Vidya Dehejia, 'Whose Taste? Colonial Design, International Exhibitions, and Indian Silver', in Dehejia et al., *Delight in Design: Indian Silver for the Raj* (Ocean Township, NJ, 2008), pp. 8–37 (p. 13).
77 Stables, *Tea, the Drink of Pleasure and of Health*, p. 35.
78 Ibid., pp. 98–101.

TWELVE: Twentieth-century Tea

1 'Tea auction 1936', *London Sound Survey*, www.soundsurvey.org.uk/index.php/survey/radio_recordings/1930s/1416 (accessed 23 November 2013).
2 *Tea and Tea Blending: A Guide for the Young Grocer* (London, 1952), pp. 5–6.
3 Cuthbert Maughan, *Markets of London: A Description of the Way in which Business is Transacted in the Principal Markets and in many Commodities* (London, 1931), pp. 97–102.
4 Philip Jordan, 'The Romance of Tea', *Fortnightly Review*, 135 (February 1934), pp. 220–29.
5 David A. S. Cairns, *The Monopolies and Restrictive Practices Commission. Report on the Supply of Tea* (London, 1956–7); *National Board for Prices and Incomes. Report no. 154. Tea Prices* [Cmnd. 4456] (London, 1970–71), Maughan, *Markets of London*, pp. 100–101.

6 John Maynard Keynes, *The Economic Consequences of the Peace* (1920), in *The Collected Writings of John Maynard Keynes*, ed. Donald Moggridge (London, 1989), vol. II, p. 11.

7 'Stocks of Staple Commodities', *London and Cambridge Economic Service, Special Memorandum No. 1* (April 1923).

8 'Stocks of Staple Commodities', *London and Cambridge Economic Service, Special Memorandum No. 6* (June 1924).

9 André Salmon, *L'Art Vivant* (Paris, 1920), p. 135.

10 Mark Antliff and Patricia Leighten, *Cubism and Culture* (London, 2001), p. 79.

11 D. H. Lawrence to Edward Garnett, 19 November 1912, No. 516, *The Letters of D. H. Lawrence*, ed. James T. Boulton, in *Works* (Cambridge, 1979), vol. I, p. 476.

12 D. H. Lawrence, *Sons and Lovers*, ed. Helen Baron and Carl Baron, in *Works* (Cambridge, 1992), pp. 37–8.

13 Ibid., pp. 45, 47, 56.

14 Ibid., p. 367.

15 Muriel Harris, 'The English Tea', *North American Review*, 215 (1 January 1922), pp. 229–36.

16 Agnes Repplier, *To Think of Tea!* (London, 1933), pp. 235–6.

17 Helen Jerome, *Running a Tea-room and Catering for Profit* (London, 1936).

18 'The Cheerful Room with Cosy Service', *Luncheon and Tea-room Journal*, I/1 (May 1934), pp. 3–4.

19 Pierre Dubois, *How to Run a Small Hotel or Guest House, etc. With a Chapter on Running a Tea Room* (London, 1945), p. 71.

20 'The Importance of "Atmosphere"', *Luncheon and Tea-room Journal*, II/11 (March 1935), pp. 70–71.

21 John Betjeman, *Ghastly Good Taste: Or, A Depressing Story of the Rise and Fall of English Architecture* (London, 1970), p. 108.

22 'Catering Companies', *The Times*, 19 October 1912, p. 16.

23 '"A.B.C." Jubilee To-morrow: Tea Shops and Temperance', *The Observer*, 27 October 1912, p. 15.

24 Erika Diane Rappaport, *Shopping for Pleasure: Women in the Making of London's West End* (Princeton, NJ, 2000).

25 Theodore Dreiser, 'Some More About London', in *A Traveller at Forty, etc.* (London, 1914), pp. 80–81.

26 Peter Bird, *The First Food Empire: A History of J. Lyons & Co.* (London, 2000), p. 99.

27 Scott McCracken, *Masculinities, Modernist Fiction and the Urban Public Sphere* (Manchester, 2007), pp. 128, 96.

28 'Catering Companies', *The Times*, 19 October 1912, p. 16.

29 McCracken, *Masculinities*, p. 97.

30 Georgina Ferry, *A Computer Called LEO: Lyons Tea Shops and the World's First Office Computer* (Hammersmith, 2003).

31 *A Song for Ceylon*, dir. Basil Wright, prod. John Grierson, Empire Marketing Board, 1934, 40 mins, B&W, www.colonialfilm.org.uk.

32 Richard Farmer, *The Food Companions: Cinema and Consumption in Wartime Britain, 1939–45* (Manchester, 2011), pp. 186–7.

33 R. D. Morrison, *Tea: Memorandum relating to the Tea Industry and the Tea Trade of the World* (London, December 1943), p. 57.

34 Richard Dimbleby, 'That Weapon – Tea', in *Tea on Service* (London, 1947), pp. 25, 30.

35 'Tea is Important Sinew of War', *Tea and Coffee Trade Journal*, LXXXII/1 (January 1942), pp. 30–32.

36 Noel Streatfeild, 'Tea on a Mobile', in *Tea on Service*, p. 53.

37 Robert Mackay, *Half the Battle: Civilian Morale in Britain during the Second World War* (Manchester, 2002); Ina Zweiniger-Bargielowska, *Austerity in Britain: Rationing, Controls, and Consumption, 1939–1955* (Oxford, 2000). On rationing: Angus Calder, *The People's War: Britain, 1939–45* (London, 1969), pp. 380–87.

38 'The Backroom Story', in *Tea on Service*, pp. 92–3; Morrison, *Tea*, pp. 57–60.

39 'Tea Allocation Agreement Planned to Stabilize the World Tea Market', *Tea and Coffee Trade Journal*, LXXXII/8 (August 1942), p. 10.

40 Vernon Dale Wickizer, *Coffee, Tea and Cocoa: An Economic and Political Analysis* (Stanford, CA, 1951), p. 207.

41 George Orwell, 'A Nice Cup of Tea', in *Smothered Under Journalism*, vol. XVIII: *1946*, in *The Complete Works of George Orwell*, ed. Peter Davison (London, 1998), no. 2857, pp. 33–5.

42 Fiona McClymont, 'The Knack: How to Make a Cup of Tea, by Sam Twining', *The Independent*, 1 August 1998.

43 British Standards Institution, 'Tea: Preparation of Liquor for Use in Sensory Tests', BS 6008:1980; Royal Society of Chemistry, 'How to Make a Perfect Cup of Tea' (2003), www.rsc.org (accessed 13 November 2013).

44 'Tea Off Ration from Sunday', *The Times*, 3 October 1952, pp. 6–7.

45 'End of the Road for City Tea Auctions', *The Times*, 29 June 1998, p. 45.

46 R.G. Lawson and M. McLaren, 'Tea-leaf Holder', United States Patent Office, patent 723287, issued 24 March 1903.

47 'Tempest in Tea', *Klipinger Magazine*, I/12 (December 1947), pp. 43–4 (p. 43).

48 Wickizer, *Coffee, Tea, and Cocoa*, p. 403.

49 'Tempest in Tea', p. 43.

50 Mercutio, 'A Nice Cup of Tea', *Manchester Guardian*, 23 May 1953.

51 *The Times*, 29 March 1958, p. 1.

52 *The Times*, 12 April 1958, p. 1.

53 John Price, 'The Quiet Revolution of Tea Bags', *The Times*, 17 November 1967, p. 20; 'Tea Bags Stir Up Competition', *The Times*, 1 November 1972, p. 19.

54 *Key Note Market Assessment: Hot Beverages*, ed. Robert Hucker (London, 2013), pp. 34, 54.

55 Nick Hall, *The Tea Industry* (Burlington, VT, 2000), pp. 25–32.

56 David Walker quoted in Wendy Komancheck, 'From the Field to the Cup', *Tea & Coffee Trade Journal*, CLXXXI/11 (November 2009), pp. 36–42; online www.teaandcoffee.net (accessed 7 April 2014).

Epilogue: Global Tea

1 'Hot Drinks in 2013: Creating an Experience, Finding the Value', *Euromonitor*, July 2013, p. 2; 'Unilever Group in Hot Drinks (World)', *Euromonitor*, June 2014, p. 2.

2 Andrew Wood and Susan M. Roberts, *Economic Geography: Places, Networks and Flows* (London, 2011), p. 76.

3 Quoted in Keith Forster, 'The Strange Tale of China's Tea Industry during the Cultural Revolution', *China Heritage Quarterly*, 29 (2012), www. chinaheritagequarterly.org (accessed 14 April 2014).

4 *Tea Production in China: IBIS World Industry Report No. 1539* (Melbourne, June 2013).

5 Dan Etherington and Keith Forster, *Green Gold: The Political Economy of China's Post-1949 Tea Industry* (Hong Kong, 1993)

6 Tom Miller, 'Why Foreigners are Beating China's Tea-makers on Their Home Turf', *Financial Times*, 15 September 2009: http://blogs.ft.com.

7   Marion Cabell Tyree, *Housekeeping In Old Virginia: Containing Contributions From Two Hundred and Fifty of Virginia's Noted Housewives, Distinguished for Their Skill In the Culinary Art and Other Branches of Domestic Economy* (Louisville, KY, 1878), p. 64.

8   Tea Association of America, New York, 'Tea Fact Sheet – 2013', www.teausa.com (accessed 14 April 2014)

9   '2013 Beverage Report, Part 5: Iced Tea', *CSP Daily News*, 12 March 2013, www.cspnet.com (accessed 12 March 2014).

10 'Drinking Cultures of the World: Globalization Creates Opportunities', *Euromonitor*, March 2010.

11 Howard Schultz, *Pour Your Heart Into It: How Starbucks Built a Company One Cup at a Time* (New York, 1997), p. 37.

12 Sanne van der Wal, *Sustainability Issues in the Tea Sector: A Comparative Analysis of Six Leading Producing Countries* (Amsterdam, 2008), pp. 7–11.

13 Gethin Chamberlain, 'How Poverty Wages for Tea Pickers Fuel India's Trade in Child Slavery', *The Observer*, 20 July 2013.

14 Barbara Crowther, 'Fairtrade: The Real Cost of Cheap Tea', *Guardian Professional* www.theguardian.com (accessed 16 May 2014).

15 Van der Wal, *Sustainability Issues in the Tea Sector*, pp. 41–2.

16 'Tea 2030', *Forum for the Future*, www.forumforthefuture.org (accessed 16 May 2014).

17 Lujeri Tea, www.lujeritea.com (accessed 16 May 2014).

18 Hester Lacey, 'The Inventory: Henrietta Lovell', *Financial Times*, 29 November 2013.

Bibliography

Ashworth, William J., *Customs and Excise: Trade, Production, and Consumption in England, 1640–1845* (Oxford, 2003)

Ball, Samuel, *An Account of the Cultivation and Manufacture of Tea in China* (London, 1848)

Bamber, E. F., *An Account of the Cultivation and Manufacture of Tea in India, from Personal Observation* (Calcutta, 1866)

——, *Tea* (London, 1868)

Bennett, Alan Weinberg, and Bonnie K. Bealer, *The World of Caffeine: The Science and Culture of the World's Most Popular Drug* (London, 2001)

Berg, Maxine, 'Consumption in Eighteenth- and Early Nineteenth-century Britain', in *The Cambridge Economic History of Modern Britain*, vol. I: *Industrialisation, 1700–1860*, ed. Roderick Floud and Paul Johnson (Cambridge, 2004), pp. 357–86

——, and Helen Clifford, 'Selling Consumption in the Eighteenth Century: Advertising and the Trade Card in Britain and France', *Cultural and Social History*, IV (2007), pp. 145–70

Bickham, Troy, 'Eating the Empire: Intersections of Food, Cookery and Imperialism in Eighteenth-century Britain', *Past and Present*, CXCVIII (2008), 71–109

Bird, Peter, *The First Food Empire: A History of J. Lyons & Co.* (London, 2000)

Boulton, William Biggs, *The Amusements of Old London: Being a Survey of the Sports and Pastimes, Tea gardens and Parks, Playhouses and other Diversions . . . from the 17th to the Beginning of the 19th century* (London, 1901)

Bowen, Huw V., 'Tea, Tribute and the East India Company, c. 1750–c. 1775', in *Hanoverian Britain and Empire: Essays in Memory of Philip Lawson*, ed. Stephen Taylor, Richard Connors and Clyve Jones (Woodbridge, 1998), pp. 158–76

——, *Revenue and Reform: The Indian Problem in British Politics, 1757–1773* (Cambridge, 1991)

——, Margarette Lincoln and Nigel Rigby, eds, *The Worlds of the East India Company* (Rochester, NY, 2003)

Bowes, John, *Temperance, as it is Opposed to Strong Drinks, Tobacco and Snuff, Tea and Coffee.* (Aberdeen, [1836?])

Boxer, Charles Ralph, *Dutch Merchants and Mariners in Asia, 1602–1795* (London, 1988)

Bramah, Edward, *Tea and Coffee: A Modern View of Three Hundred Years of Tradition* (London, 1972)

Breen, T. H., *The Marketplace of Revolution: How Consumer Politics Shaped American Independence* (Oxford, 2004)

Brenner, Robert, *Merchants and Revolution: Commercial Change, Political Conflict, and London's Overseas Traders, 1550–1653* (Princeton, NJ, 1993)

Brewer, John, and Roy Porter, eds, *Consumption and the World of Goods* (London, 1993)

British Standards Institution, 'Tea: Preparation of Liquor for Use in Sensory Tests', BS 6008 (1980)

Broadbent, Humphrey, *The Domestick Coffee-man, Shewing the True Way of Preparing and Making of Chocolate, Coffee and Tea* (London, 1722)

Brown, Peter B., *In Praise of Hot Liquors: the Study of Chocolate, Coffee and Tea-drinking, 1600–1850* (York, 1995)

Burnett, John, *Liquid Pleasures: A Social History of Drinks in Modern Britain* (London, 1999)

——, *Plenty and Want: A Social History of Diet in England from 1815 to the Present Day* (London, 1966)

Cairns, David A. S., *The Monopolies and Restrictive Practices Commission: Report on the Supply of Tea* (London, 1956–7)

Campbell, Duncan, *A Poem upon Tea: Wherein its Antiquity, its several Virtues and Influences are set forth* (London, 1735)

Carnell, Rachel, 'The Very Scandal of her Tea Table: Eliza Haywood's Response to the Whig Public Sphere', in *Presenting Gender: Changing Sex in Early-modern Culture*, ed. Chris Mounsey (Lewisburg, PA, 2001), pp. 255–73

Carruthers, Bruce G., *City of Capital: Politics and Markets in the English Financial Revolution* (Princeton, NJ, 1996)

The Case of the Dealers in Tea (London, 1736)

Chang, Elizabeth Hope, *Britain's Chinese Eye: Literature, Empire, and Aesthetics in Nineteenth-century Britain* (Stanford, CA, 2010)

Chatterjee, Piya, *A Time for Tea: Women, Labor, and Post/Colonial Politics on an Indian Plantation* (Durham, NC, 2001)

Chaudhuri, K. N., *The English East India Company: The Study of an Early Joint-stock Company, 1600–1640* (London, 1965)

——, *The Trading World of Asia and the English East India Company, 1660–1760* (Cambridge, 1978)

Cheong, Weng Eang, *Hong Merchants of Canton: Chinese Merchants in Sino-Western Trade, 1684–1798* (Richmond, 1997)

Ching, Julia, and Willard G. Oxtoby, eds, *Discovering China: European Interpretations in the Enlightenment* (Rochester, NY, and Woodbridge, 1992)

Claxton, Juliet, 'The Countess of Arundel's Dutch Pranketing Room', *Journal of the History of Collection*, XXII/2 (2010), pp. 187–96

Cole, R. B., 'Form versus Function: A Study of Some Early Worcester Tea Wares', *Journal of the Northern Ceramic Society*, XX (2003/4), pp. 59–64

Cole, W. A., 'The Arithmetic of Eighteenth-century Smuggling: Rejoinder', *Economic History Review*, XXVIII (1975), pp. 44–9

Cook, Harold John, *Matters of Exchange: Commerce, Medicine, and Science in the Dutch Golden Age* (New Haven, CT, and London, 2007)

Cooper, Michael, 'The Early Europeans and Tea', in *Tea in Japan: Essays on the History of Chanoyu*, ed. Paul Varley and Kumakura Isao (Honolulu, HI, 1989)

Crampsey, Bob, *The King's Grocer: The Life of Sir Thomas Lipton* (Glasgow, 1995)

Day, Samuel Phillips, *Tea: Its Mystery and History* (London, 1878)

Dikötter, Frank, Lars Laaman and Zhou Xun, *Narcotic Culture: A History of Drugs in China* (London, 2004)

Drake, F. S., *Tea Leaves: Being a Collection of Letters and Documents Relating to the Shipment of Tea to the American Colonies in 1773, by the East India Tea Company* (Boston, 1884)

Dubois, Pierre, *How to Run a Small Hotel or Guest House, etc: With a Chapter on Running a Tea Room* (London, 1945)

Ellis, Markman, Richard Coulton, Matthew Mauger and Ben Dew, eds, *Tea and the Tea-table in Eighteenth-century England*, 4 vols (London, 2010)

——, *The Coffee-house: A Cultural History* (London, 2004)

Emmerson, Robin, *British Teapots & Tea Drinking, 1700–1850: Illustrated from the Twining Teapot Gallery, Norwich Castle Museum* (London, 1992)

Etherington, Dan, and Keith Forster, *Green Gold: The Political Economy of China's Post-1949 Tea Industry* (Hong Kong, 1993)

Evans, John C., *Tea in China: The History of China's National Drink* (New York and London, 1992)

Fan, Fa-ti, *British Naturalists in Qing China: Science, Empire, and Cultural Encounter* (Cambridge, MA, 2004)

Farrington, Anthony, *The English Factory in Japan, 1613–1623* (London, 1991)

——, *Trading Places: The East India Company and Asia, 1600–1834* (London, 2002)

Feld, Steven, 'The Tea Ceremony: A Symbolic Analysis', in *Empire of the Senses: The Sensual Culture Reader*, ed. David Howes (Oxford and New York, 2005)

Ferry, Georgina, *A Computer Called LEO: Lyons Tea Shops and the World's First Office Computer* (Hammersmith, 2003)

Finlay, Robert, 'The Pilgrim Art: The Culture of Porcelain in World History', *Journal of World History*, IX/2 (1998), pp. 141–87

——, *The Pilgrim Art: Cultures of Porcelain in World History* (Berkeley, CA, 2010)

Forrest, Denys, *Tea for the British: The Social and Economic History of a Famous Trade* (London, 1973)

Forster, Keith, 'The Strange Tale of China's Tea Industry during the Cultural Revolution', *China Heritage Quarterly*, XXIX (March 2012)

Fortune, Robert, *A Journey to the Tea Countries of China: Including Sung-Lo and the Bohea Hills with a Short Notice of the East India Company's Tea Plantations in the Himalaya Mountains* (London, 1852)

Fortune, Robert, *Three Years' Wanderings in the Northern Provinces of China* (London, 1847)

Frank, Caroline, *Objectifying China, Imagining America: Chinese Commodities in Early America* (Chicago, IL, 2011)

Fromer, Julie, '"Deeply Indebted to the Tea Plant": Representations of English National Identity in Victorian Histories of Tea', *Victorian Literature and Culture*, XXXVI (2008), pp. 531–47

——, *A Necessary Luxury: Tea in Victorian England* (Athens, OH, 2008)

Frost, Thomas, 'The Tea-gardens of the 18th Century', in *Bygone Middlesex*, ed. W. Andrews (London, 1899), pp. 164–74

Furber, Holden, *Rival Empires of Trade in the Orient, 1600–1800* (Minneapolis, MN, 1976)

Gardella, Robert, *Harvesting Mountains: Fujian and the China Tea Trade, 1757–1937* (Berkeley, CA, and London, 1994)

[Garway, Thomas], *An Exact Description of the Growth, Quality, and Vertues of the Leaf Tee, alias Tay* (London, 1664)

Glamann, Kristof, *Dutch-Asiatic Trade: 1620–1740*, 2nd edn (The Hague, 1981)

Godden, Geoffrey, *Godden's New Guide to English Porcelain* (London, 2004)

——, *Oriental Export Market Porcelain and its Influence on European Wares* (London, 1979)

Goodman, Jordan, 'Excitantia or how Enlightenment Europe took to Soft Drugs', in *Consuming Habits: Deconstructing Drugs in History and Anthropology*, ed. Jordan Goodman (London, 1995), pp. 126–47

Greenberg, Michael, *British Trade and the Opening of China, 1800–42* (Cambridge, 1951)

Griffiths, John Charles, *Tea: The Drink that Changed the World* (London, 2007)

Griffiths, Percival Joseph, *The History of the Indian Tea Industry* (London, 1967)

Gye, Frederick, *The History of the Tea Plant* (London, [1819])

Hall, Nick, *The Tea Industry* (Burlington, MA, 2000)

Hanway, Jonas, *A Journal of Eight Days Journey from Portsmouth to Kingston upon Thames . . . To which is added, An Essay on Tea* (London, 1756)

Harler, Campbell Ronald, *The Culture and Marketing of Tea* (London, 1933)

Harris, Muriel, 'The English Tea', *North American Review*, CCXV (1 January 1922), pp. 229–36

Harvey, Karen, 'Barbarity in a Teacup? Punch, Domesticity and Gender in the Eighteenth Century', *Journal of Design History*, XXI/3 (2008), pp. 205–21

Hathorn, J. G., *A Handbook of Darjeeling: With Brief Notes on the Culture and Manufacture of Tea* (Calcutta, 1863)

Heckethorn, C. W., 'Old London Taverns and Tea Gardens', *Gentleman's Magazine*, CCLXXXVII (September 1899), pp. 223–46

Heiss, Mary Lou, *The Story of Tea: A Cultural History and Drinking Guide* (Berkeley, CA, 2007)

Henry, James, *A Letter to the Members of the Temperance Society showing that the Use of Tea and Coffee cannot be Safely Substituted for that of Spirituous Liquors* (Dublin, 1830)

Hillemann, Ulrike, *Asian Empire and British Knowledge: China and the Networks of British Imperial Expansion* (Basingstoke, 2009)

Hsia, Adrian, *The Vision of China in the English Literature of the Seventeenth and Eighteenth Centuries* (Hong Kong, 1998)

Huang, H. T., *Science and Civilisation in China*, vol. VI: *Biology and Biological Technology, Part 5: Fermentations and Food Science* (Cambridge, 2000)

Instructions to be Observed by the Officers Employ'd in the Duty on Coffee, Tea, and Chocolate, in London (London, 1724)

Israel, Jonathan I., *Dutch Primacy in World Trade, 1585–1740* (Oxford, 1989)

Janin, Hunt, *The India-China Opium Trade in the Nineteenth Century* (Jefferson, NC, 1999)

Jerome, Helen, *Running a Tea-room and Catering for Profit* (London, 1936)

Jordan, Philip, 'The Romance of Tea', *Fortnightly Review*, CXXXV (February 1934), pp. 220–29

Jörg, C.J.A., *Porcelain and the Dutch China Trade*, trans. Patricia Wardle (The Hague, 1982)

Keay, John, *The Honourable Company: A History of the English East India Company* (London, 1991)

Kennedy, Rachel, *Between Bath and China: Trade and Culture in the West Country, 1680 to 1840* (Bath, 1999)

Kitson, Peter, *Forging Romantic China: Sino-British Cultural Exchange, 1760–1840* (Cambridge, 2013)

Kowaleski-Wallace, Elizabeth, 'Tea, Gender, and Domesticity in Eighteenth-century England', *Studies in Eighteenth-century Culture*, XXIII (1994), pp. 131–45

——, *Consuming Subjects: Women, Shopping, and Business in the Eighteenth Century* (New York, 1997)

Laberee, Benjamin, *The Boston Tea Party* (New York, 1964)

Lach, Donald F., and Edwin J. Van Kley, *Asia in the Making of Europe*, vol. III: *The Century of Advance* (Chicago, 1998)

Lane, Arthur, 'Queen Mary II's Porcelain Collection at Hampton Court', *Transactions of the Oriental Ceramic Society*, XXV (1949–50), pp. 21–31

Lawson, Philip, *The East India Company: A History* (London, 1993)

Lees, W. Nassau, *Tea Cultivation, Cotton, and other Agricultural Experiments in India: A Review* (London, 1863)

Lettsom, John Coakley, *The Natural History of the Tea-tree, with Observations on the Medical Qualities of Tea, and Effects of Tea-drinking* (London, 1772)

Liu, Tong, *Chinese Tea* (Cambridge, 2012)

Liu, Yong, *The Dutch East India Company's Tea Trade with China, 1757–1781* (Leiden and Boston, MA, 2007)

McCalman, Godfrey, *A Natural, Commercial and Medicinal Treatise on Tea* (Glasgow, 1787)

McCracken, Scott, *Masculinities, Modernist Fiction and the Urban Public Sphere* (Manchester, 2007)

McCulloch, John Ramsay, *Effects of the East India Company's Monopoly on the Price of Tea* (London, 1824)

——, *Observations on the Influence of the East India Company's Monopoly on the Price and Supply of Tea* (London, 1831)

Macfarlane, Alan, *Green Gold: The Empire of Tea* (London, 2003)

McKendrick, Neil, John Brewer and J. H. Plumb, *The Birth of a Consumer Society: The Commercialization of Eighteenth-century England* (London, 1983)

Mair, Victor H., and Erling Hoh, *The True History of Tea* (London, 2009)

Maitland, Agnes C., *The Afternoon Tea Book* (London, 1887)

Markley, Robert, *The Far East and the English Imagination, 1600–1730* (Cambridge, 2006)

Martin, R. Montgomery, *The Past and Present State of the Tea Trade of England, and of the Continents of Europe and America* (London, 1832)

Mason, Simon, *The Good and Bad Effects of Tea Consider'd* (London, 1745)

Mathee, Rudi, 'Exotic Substances: The Introduction and Global Spread of Tobacco, Coffee, Cocoa, Tea, and Distilled Liquor, Sixteenth to Eighteenth Centuries', in *Drugs and Narcotics in History*, ed. Roy Porter and Mikulás Teich (Cambridge, 1995), pp. 24–51

Maughan, Cuthbert, *Markets of London: A Description of the Way in which Business is Transacted in the Principal Markets and in Many Commodities* (London, 1931)

Merritt, Jane T., 'Tea Trade, Consumption, and the Republican Paradox in Prerevolutionary Philadelphia', *Pennsylvania Magazine of History and Biography*, CXXVIII/2 (2004), pp. 117–48

Mintz, Sidney W., *Sweetness and Power: The Place of Sugar in Modern History* (London, 1986)

Money, Edward, *The Tea Controversy (A Momentous Indian Question)*, 2nd edn (London, 1884)

Morrison, R. D., *Tea: Memorandum Relating to the Tea Industry and the Tea Trade of the World* (London, 1943)

Morse, Hosea Ballou, *The Chronicles of the East India Company Trading to China 1635–1834*, 5 vols (Oxford, 1926–9)

Motteux, Peter Anthony, *A Poem upon Tea* (London, 1712)

Moxham, Roy, *Tea: Addiction, Exploitation, and Empire* (London, 2003)

Mui, Hoh-Cheung, and Lorna H. Mui, 'Smuggling and the British Tea Trade Before 1784', *American Historical Review*, LXXIV/1 (1968), pp. 44–73

——, 'The Commutation Act and the Tea Trade in Britain, 1784–1793', *Economic History Review*, XVI/2 (1963), pp. 234–53

——, 'Trends in Eighteenth-century Smuggling Reconsidered', *Economic History Review*, 2nd series, XXVIII (1975), pp. 28–43

——, 'William Pitt and the Enforcement of the Commutation Act, 1784–1788', *English Historical Review*, LXXVI (1961), pp. 447–65

——, *Shops and Shopkeeping in Eighteenth-century England* (London, 1989)

——, *The Management of Monopoly: A Study of the English East India Company's Conduct of its Tea Trade, 1784–1833* (Vancouver, 1984)

Mui, Lorna H., 'Andrew Melrose, Tea Dealer and Grocer of Edinburgh, 1812–1833', *Business History*, IX (1967), pp. 31–45

Nelson, Claire, 'Tea-table Miscellanies: The Development of Scotland's Song Culture, 1720–1800', *Early Music*, XXVIII/4 (2000), pp. 596–620

O'Connell, Helen, '"A Raking Pot of Tea": Consumption and Excess in Ireland', *Literature and History*, XXI/2 (2012), pp. 32–47

Orwell, George, 'A Nice Cup of Tea', in *Smothered under Journalism*, vol. XVIII: *1946*, in *The Complete Works of George Orwell*, ed. Peter Davison (London, 1998), no. 2857, pp. 33–5

Ovington, John, *An Essay upon the Nature and Qualities of Tea* (London, 1699)

Parmentier, J., *Tea Time in Flanders: The Maritime Trade between the Southern Netherlands and China in the 18th Century* (Bruges-Zeebrugge, 1996)

Pettigrew, Jane, *A Social History of Tea* (London, 2001)

——, *Design for Tea: Tea Wares from the Dragon Court to Afternoon Tea* (Stroud, 2003)

Pocock, John Greville Agard, *Barbarism and Religion*, vol. IV: *Barbarians, Savages and Empires* (Cambridge, 2005)

Porter, David, 'A Peculiar but Uninteresting Nation: China and the Discourse of Commerce in Eighteenth-century England', *Eighteenth-century Studies*, XXXIII/2 (Winter 2000), pp. 181–99

——, 'Writing China: Legitimacy and Representation, 1606–1773', *Comparative Literature Studies*, XXXIII (1996), pp. 98–122

——, *Ideographia: The Chinese Cipher in Early Modern Europe* (Stanford, CA, 2001)

——, *The Chinese Taste in Eighteenth-century England* (Cambridge, 2010)

Rahusen-de Bruyn Kops, Henriette, 'Not Such an "Unpromising Beginning": The First Dutch Trade Embassy to China, 1655–1657', *Modern Asian Studies*, XXXVI (2002), pp. 535–78

Rappaport, Erika Diane, *Shopping for Pleasure: Women in the Making of London's West End* (Princeton, NJ, 2000)

Repplier, Agnes, *To Think of Tea!* (London, 1933)

Robins, Nick, *The Corporation that Changed the World: How the East India Company Shaped the Modern Multinational* (London, 2006)

Royal Society of Chemistry, 'How to Make a Perfect Cup of Tea', undated press release (London, 2003)

Schama, Simon, *The Embarrassment of Riches: An Interpretation of Dutch Culture in the Golden Age* (London, 1987)

Schiebinger, Londa, *Plants and Empire: Colonial Bioprospecting in the Atlantic World* (Cambridge, MA, 2004)

Schivelbusch, Wolfgang, *Tastes of Paradise: A Social History of Spices, Stimulants, and Intoxicants*, trans. David Jacobson (New York, 1992)

Schlegel, George, 'First Introduction of Tea into Holland', *T'oung Pao*, second series, I/5 (1900), pp. 468–72

Scott, J. M., *The Tea Story* (London, 1964)

Sen, Sudipta, *Empire of Free Trade: The East India Company and the Making of the Colonial Marketplace* (Philadelphia, PA, 1998)

Shammas, Carole, 'The Eighteenth-century English Diet and Economic Change', *Explorations in Economic History*, XXI (1984), pp. 254–69

Shapin, Steven, *Changing Tastes: How Foods Tasted in the Early Modern Period and How They Taste Now*, The Hans Rausing Lecture 2011, 14 (Uppsala, 2011)

Sherman, Sandra, 'Impotence and Capital: The Debate over Imported Beverages in the Seventeenth and Eighteenth Centuries', in *1650–1850: Ideas, Aesthetics, and Inquiries in the Early Modern Era*, ed. Kevin L. Cope and Anna Battigelli (New York, 2003), vol. IX

Short, Thomas, *A Dissertation upon Tea* (London, 1730)

——, *Discourses on Tea, Sugar, Milk, Made-wines, Spirits, Punch, Tobacco, &c., with Plain and Useful Rules for Gouty People* (London, 1750)

Sigmond, George Gabriel, *Tea: Its Effects, Medicinal and Moral* (London, 1839)

Sloboda, Stacey, 'Fashioning Bluestocking Conversation: Elizabeth Montagu's Chinese Room', in *Architectural Space in Eighteenth-century Europe: Constructing Identities and Interiors*, ed. Meredith S. Martin and Denise Amy Baxter (Burlington, VT, 2010), pp. 129–48

Smith, William, *Tsiology: A Discourse on Tea* (London, 1826)

Smith, Woodruff, 'Complications of the Commonplace: Tea, Sugar, and Imperialism', *Journal of Interdisciplinary History*, XXIII/2 (1992), pp. 259–78

——, 'From Coffee-house to Parlour: The Consumption of Coffee, Tea, and Sugar in North-western Europe in the Seventeenth and Eighteenth Centuries', in *Consuming Habits: Deconstructing Drugs in History and Anthropology*, ed. Jordan Goodman (London, 1995), pp. 148–63

Stables, Gordon, *Tea: The Drink of Pleasure and of Health* (London, 1883)

Steensgaard, Niels, 'The Growth and Composition of the Long-distance Trade of English and the Dutch Republic before 1750', in *Rise of Merchant Empires: Long Distance Trade in the Early-modern World, 1350–1750*, ed. James Tracey (Cambridge, 1990), pp. 102–52

——, *The Asian Trade Revolution of the Seventeenth Century: The East India Companies and the Decline of the Caravan Trade* (Chicago, 1975)

Sumner, John, *A Popular Treatise on Tea: Its Qualities and Effects* (Birmingham, 1863)

Surak, Kristin, *Making Tea, Making Japan: Cultural Nationalism in Practice* (Stanford, CA, 2012)

Surgeon, J. N., *Remarks on Mr Mason's Treatise upon Tea* (London, 1745)

Tate, Nahum, *Panacea: A Poem Upon Tea in Two Canto's* (London, 1700)

Tea Bureau, *Tea and Tea Blending: A Guide for the Young Grocer* (London, 1952)

The Tea Cyclopædia (Calcutta, 1881)

Tea on Service (London, 1947)

The Tea Purchaser's Guide; or, The Lady and Gentleman's Tea Table and Useful Companion (London, 1785)

Tea: A Poem in Three Cantos (London, 1743)

Tea: A Poem; or, Ladies into China-cups; a Metamorphosis (London, 1729)

Teague, Ken, *Mr Horniman and the Tea Trade: A Permanent Display in the South Hall Gallery of the Horniman Museum* (London, 1993)

Tebb, W. Scott, *Tea and the Effects of Tea Drinking* (London, [1905])

Thomas, Peter David Garner, *Tea Party to Independence: The Third Phase of the American Revolution, 1773–1776* (Oxford, 1991)

Thomson, Gladys Scott, *Life in a Noble Household, 1641–1700* (London, 1937)

Toppin, Aubrey, 'The China Trade and Some London Chinamen', *Transactions of the English Ceramic Circle*, XXX (1935), pp. 37–56

A Treatise on the Inherent Qualities of the Tea-herb: Being an Account of the Natural virtues of the Bohea, Green, and Imperial Teas (London, 1750)

Twining, Richard, *Observations on the Tea and Window Act, and on the Tea Trade*, 2nd edn (London, 1785)

Twining, S. H., *The House of Twining, 1706–1956: Being a Short History of the Firm of R. Twining and Co. Ltd. Tea and Coffee Merchants* (London, 1956)

Ukers, William H., *All About Coffee* (New York, 1922)

——, *All About Tea* (New York, 1935)

Van der Wal, Sanne, *Sustainability Issues in the Tea Sector: A Comparative Analysis of Six Leading Producing Countries* (Amsterdam, 2008)

Van Dyke, Paul, *The Canton Trade: Life and Enterprise on the China Coast, 1700–1845* (Hong Kong, 2005)

Varey, Simon, 'Three Necessary Drugs', in *1650–1850: Ideas, Aesthetics, and Inquiries in the Early Modern Era*, ed. Kevin Cope (New York, 1998), vol. IV, pp. 3–51

Varley, Paul H., and Isao Kumakura, *Tea in Japan: Essays on the History of Chanoyu* (Honolulu, HI, 1989)

Vincentelli, Moira, *Women and Ceramics: Gendered Vessels* (Manchester, 2000)

Voskuil, Lynn, 'Robert Fortune, *Camellia sinensis*, and the Nineteenth-century Global Imagination', *Nineteenth-century Contexts*, XXXIV (2012), pp. 5–18

Wakeman, F., 'The Canton Trade and the Opium War', in *Cambridge History of China*, vol. X, part 1, ed. J. Fairbanks (Cambridge, 1978), pp. 163–212

Walvin, James, *Fruits of Empire: Exotic Produce and British Taste, 1660–1800* (London, 1997)

Waugh, Mary, *Smuggling in Devon and Cornwall, 1700–1850* (Newbury, 1991)

——, *Smuggling in Kent and Sussex, 1700–1840* (Newbury, 1985)

Weatherill, Lorna, *Consumer Behaviour and Material Culture in Britain, 1660–1760* (London, 1988)

Wesley, John, *A Letter to a Friend, Concerning Tea*, 2nd edn (Bristol, 1749)

Wickizer, Vernon Dale, *Coffee, Tea and Cocoa: An Economic and Political Analysis* (Stanford, CA, 1951)

Wills, John E., *Pepper, Guns, and Parleys: The Dutch East India Company and China, 1662–1681* (Cambridge, MA, 1974)

Winslow, Cal, 'Sussex Smugglers', in *Albion's Fatal Tree: Crime and Society in Eighteenth-century England*, ed. Douglas Hay et al. (London, 1975), pp. 119–66

Wissett, Robert, *A View of the Rise, Progress and Present State of the Tea Trade in Europe* (London, 1801)

Woods, John, *A Brief History of Tea, with a Glance at the Flowery Land* (Richmond, [1853])

Young, Alfred Fabian, *The Shoemaker and the Tea Party: Memory and the American Revolution* (Boston, MA, 1999)

Zhang, Jinghong, *Puer Tea: Ancient Caravans and Urban Chic* (Seattle, WA, 2014)

Zhuang, Guotu, 'The Impact of the International Tea Trade on the Social Economy of Northwest Fujian in the Eighteenth Century', in *On the Eighteenth Century as a Category of Asian History: Van Leur in Retrospect*, ed. Leonard Blussé and Femme Gaastra (Brookfield, VT, 1998)

——, *Tea, Silver, Opium and War: The International Tea Trade and Western Commercial Expansion into China in 1740–1840* (Xiamen, 1993).

Acknowledgements

This book has been a genuinely collaborative project, and any merits or defects that can be detected in the arguments and facts it presents are jointly owned. Nonetheless, the production of each chapter has been led by an individual writer, and for the purposes of research assessment the following attributions of authorship are declared: Ellis, chapters Two, Four, Seven and Twelve; Coulton, chapters One, Five, Nine and Eleven; Mauger, chapters Three, Six, Eight and Ten.

In the course of this project, we have incurred debts of gratitude to many people for their advice, for patiently answering queries, for offering leads for research and for lending a helping hand: John Barrell, Michèle Barrett, Rebecca Beasley, Jenn Chenkin, Juliet Claxton, Mark Currie, Elizabeth Eger, Jill Gage, Jonathan Goodhand, Charlie Jarvis, Margaret Makepeace, Anthony Ossa-Richardson, Victoria Pickering, Nydia Pineda, Chris Reid, Beverley Stewart, Sam Twining, Tessa Whitehouse, Jennifer Wood and Tory Young. Particular thanks are owing to Ben Dew, Richard Hamblyn and our editor, Ben Hayes, for reading and commenting on the entire first draft: their recommendations have only improved this book. We would like to thank the Mark Fitch Fund and the School of English and Drama at Queen Mary University of London for their generous support of the images in this volume. Richard Coulton and Matthew Mauger would also like to acknowledge the assistance of NYU (London). Papers related to the research have been given at the Society of Dilettanti, the Canton Tea Company at Petersham Nurseries, the Modern Language Association of America, the Geffrye Museum, Birkbeck University of London, the British Society for Eighteenth-century Studies, Queen Mary University of London, and the UK Group of the Foundation of German Business at LSE. Research for this volume was conducted at the British Library, the Bodleian Library, the Wellcome Library, Senate House Library, the National Archives, the London Metropolitan Archives, the Goldsmiths' Company Library, the National Art Library at the Victoria and Albert Museum, the Botany Library and Sloane Herbarium at the Natural History Museum, the Linnaean Society Library, the Royal Society Library, the Huntington Library and the libraries of Queen Mary University of London, University of California Berkeley, University of California Los Angeles, Stanford University and Victoria University Wellington. We thank all the librarians and staff for their assistance and support.

Markman would like to express his particular and personal thanks to his family and friends, most especially Becky, without whom much would slip twixt lip and cup. Richard especially acknowledges the love and patience of Elfrida, Clement, Annis and Chelle, for the first of whom writing this book has taken more than a lifetime, and for the last of whom something similar must seem to have been the case. For Matthew, the forbearance of Ceri (and Shannah, Asher and Elian) for the evenings spent with his co-writers over a 'cup of tea' at the Lord Tredegar in Bow deserves special mention.

Photo Acknowledgements

The author and publishers wish to express their thanks to the below sources for illustrative material and/or permission to reproduce it.

Beinecke Rare Book and Manuscript Library, Yale University, New Haven, CT: p. 74; The Bodleian Library, University of Oxford (John Johnson Collection): pp. 186 (Trade in Prints and Scraps 2 (57)), 190 (Trade in Prints and Scraps 9 (38a)); By permission of the British Library: pp. 28–9 (152.i.5), 99 (443.i.1(1)), 234 (H.1652.m(17)), 239 (8435.eee.4), 243 (7076.aa.51(5); By permission of the British Library (India Office Records) pp. 59 (E/3/92), 64 (E/3/95), 121 (H/763A); By permission of the British Library (Map Collections): p. 92 (c.22.d.30); © The Trustees of the British Museum, London: pp. 69, 150, 159, 220; © The Trustees of the British Museum, London (Banks Collection) pp. 11, 135, 136; collection of Richard Coulton: p. 241; collection of Markman Ellis: photo Factorylad, p. 271; pp. 265, 266; By permission of the Folger Shakespeare Library, Washington, DC: p. 21; Travis Fullerton © Virginia Museum of Fine Arts, Richmond, VA: p. 244; The Worshipful Company of Goldsmiths, London: p. 138; Hong Kong Museum of Art Collection, Hong Kong: p. 216; By permission of The Trustees of the Imperial War Museum, London: p. 260; © The J. Paul Getty Museum, Los Angeles, CA (image courtesy of the Getty's Open Content Program): p. 48; courtesy of The Lewis Walpole Library, Yale University, Farmington, CT: pp. 87, 133, 160, 189; Courtesy of the Library of Congress, Washington, DC, Prints & Photographs Division: p. 207; By permission of the City of London, London Metropolitan Archives: pp. 123, 125, 225, 226; © National Maritime Museum, Greenwich, London: pp. 117, 213; © The Trustees of the Natural History Museum, London: p. 112; © The Trustees of the Natural History Museum, London (Sloane Herbarium): pp. 6, 100, 101; Photography Courtesy Peabody Essex Museum, Salem, MA: p. 217 (lower); Philadelphia Museum of Art, Philadelphia, PA (The Louise and Walter Arensberg Collection): p. 246; © Press Association: p. 13; Rijksmuseum, Amsterdam: pp. 42, 44, 52, 81; © Tate, London: pp. 143, 254; © Victoria and Albert Museum, London: pp. 16, 33, 50, 84, 89, 91, 118, 153, 154, 180, 195, 217 (upper); © Victoria and Albert Museum, London (Pilgrim Trust Collection) p. 255; Wellcome Library, London: pp. 18, 67, 113, 167, 209; Collection of the Winnipeg Art Gallery, Winnipeg (gift of the Everett Family from the Everett Collection, in memory of Patricia Everett): p. 230; Yale Center for British Art, New Haven, CT: p. 142; Yale Center for British Art, New Haven, CT (Paul Mellon Collection): pp. 41, 146.

Index